BETTING ON MACAU

Globalization and Community

Susan E. Clarke, Series Editor
Dennis R. Judd, Founding Editor

(continued on page 375)

BETTING ON MACAU

CASINO CAPITALISM AND CHINA'S CONSUMER REVOLUTION

TIM SIMPSON

Globalization and Community, Volume 35

University of Minnesota Press

Minneapolis

London

A different version of chapter 5 was published as "Macao's Post-Mao Grand Tour: China's Gamble on Urbanization in the Venetian Macao Resort," *Journal of Tourism and Cultural Change* 20, no. 5 (2022): 678–98. A different version of chapter 8 was published as "LIVE Baccarat Calculations: Macau Machine Gaming and the Production of the Post-socialist Subject," *Journal of Cultural Economy* 12, no. 6 (2019): 521–38. Articles are available online at http://www.tandfonline.com/.

Published by the University of Minnesota Press
111 Third Avenue South, Suite 290
Minneapolis, MN 55401–2520
http://www.upress.umn.edu

ISBN 978-1-5179-0030-4 (hc)
ISBN 978-1-5179-0031-1 (pb)

Library of Congress record available at https://lccn.loc.gov/2022052951.

Printed in the United States of America on acid-free paper

The University of Minnesota is an equal-opportunity educator and employer.

UMP BmB 2023

Contents

A Note on Spelling "Macau"

One odd challenge encountered by anyone who writes about this city is the ambiguous spelling of Macau/Macao. Both versions are widely used. A local government directive indicates that the proper spelling of the city is "Macao" in English and "Macau" in Portuguese, except in the case of the "University of Macau," which retains the "u" in both languages. However, as the latter clause in that sentence makes clear, this is primarily a policy of convenience rather than a definitive orthographical rule. In any event, I have chosen to spell Macau with a "u," which is (despite the local policy) arguably the more common form found today in the international English press. However, I have retained the "Macao" spelling (with an "o") in those cases when I am quoting the work of others who chose this alternative form. Ultimately, there is no way to avoid this spelling inconsistency, which, although frustrating, is also a reflection of the endemic historical and cultural ambiguity that makes the city so fascinating.

Abbreviations

CEPA Closer Economic Partnership Agreement
DICJ Gaming Inspection and Coordination Bureau
GBA Greater Bay Area
ICO initial coin offering
IVS Individual Visit Scheme
PAC political action committee
PLA People's Liberation Army
PRC People's Republic of China
PRD Pearl River Delta
SAR special administrative region
SEZ special economic zone
SOE state-owned enterprise

Introduction

ON THE FINAL FRONTIER OF CONSUMER CAPITALISM

> One can behold in capitalism a religion, that is to say, capitalism
> essentially serves to satisfy the same worries, anguish, and disquiet
> formerly answered by so-called religion.
>
> —Walter Benjamin, "Capitalism as Religion"

In *Notes from the Underground,* Fyodor Dostoyevsky's ([1864] 2001) Underground Man railed bitterly from his basement hovel against the rational scientism of modern western civilization and the grandiose utopian schemes of those progressive thinkers who sought to create an unblemished, perfect world. One curious object of his contempt was the Crystal Palace, an enormous glass building designed by horticulturalist Joseph Paxton and constructed in London in 1851 to house the Great Exhibition, the first world's fair. Made of transparent and seemingly weightless materials, the Crystal Palace was a marvel of modern engineering. Visited by more than six million people in its first six months of operation, it was large enough to constitute an encapsulated world in itself. For the Underground Man, the imposing glass structure was a sort of impious cathedral erected to the secular catechism of industrial capitalism.

Dostoyevsky visited the Crystal Palace in 1862, recording his impressions in a travel memoir he published in Russia the following year.[1] Observing the massive crowds of people browsing among the building's vast array of merchandise, offered by 14,000 exhibitors culled from all around the world, Dostoyevsky ([1863] 1997) imagined that he had come face to face with the genuflections and idolatry typical of an ancient orgiastic fertility cult. "It is a kind of biblical scene," he wrote,

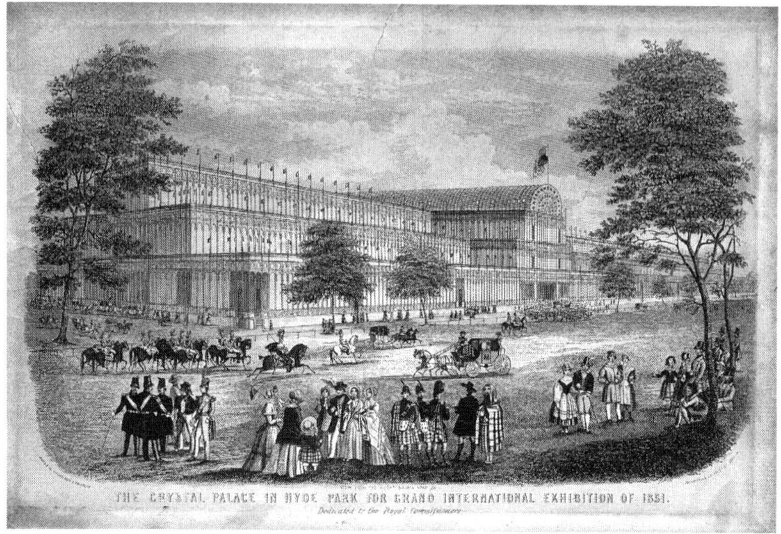

Figure 1. Postcard depicting the Crystal Palace and International Exhibition of 1851, London.

"something about Babylon, a kind of prophecy from the Apocalypse fulfilled before your very eyes" (37).

Of course, the materialistic spectacle that so startled Dostoyevsky has become our own unremarkable creed. Today we know this hedonistic Crystal Palace cult more prosaically as the culture of consumerism. Philosopher Peter Sloterdijk (2013) contends that contemporary capitalism found its paradigmatic expression in the nineteenth century "hothouse" (171) environment of the Crystal Palace. In the confines of this fantastical building, humankind first encountered a "psychedelic" (170) form of capitalism capable of transforming the proletarian public into solitary citizen-consumers. Sloterdijk thus christens the Crystal Palace "the world interior of capital."[2]

The Crystal Palace was the prototype for the innumerable theme parks and mega shopping malls that are now scattered around the planet. As one of the world's first genuine mass tourism events, it also helped set in motion the restive wanderlust that animates our own age. But if the cult of consumer capitalism was conceived in the Crystal Palace, it has reached its architectural apogee today in a massive casino megaresort positioned on the southern coast of the People's Republic of China (PRC), in the five-hundred-year-old former Portuguese territory of Macau.

MACAU'S PALACE PROJECT

In the year 2019, a century and a half after Dostoyevsky's fateful visit to the Crystal Palace, nearly forty million tourists descended upon the tiny city-state of Macau in a remarkable expeditionary spectacle. Most of those tourists traveled from mainland China, and one of every two arrivals visited Macau's Venetian Resort. If Dostoyevsky were alive today, the Venetian would surely elicit his righteous indignation. Conceived and constructed by Sheldon Adelson, the billionaire Las Vegas entrepreneur and benefactor of right-wing regimes in the United States and Israel, the Venetian is one of the world's biggest buildings—and perhaps the largest enclosed themed environment on the planet. Though its walls are not made of glass, the Venetian is the Crystal Palace of our own age as well as the focus of this book.

Although it is easy to dismiss the Venetian at first glance for its derivative faux aesthetics and hubristic excess, what makes the resort so fascinating is the way the building articulates a diverse collection of historical, economic, political, demographic, architectural, and atmospheric elements. These elements have converged in Macau today to transform the city into a global gambling powerhouse and one of the world's wealthiest locales. The Venetian, much like the Crystal Palace before it, is a sort of environmental hothouse, an architectonic biosphere for the cultivation of those tourist visitors.

The Venetian is a key component of what I call casino capitalism. Thinkers from economist John Maynard Keynes ([1936] 2016) to political scientist Susan Strange (1986) have compared capitalism to a casino. However, I use the term "casino capitalism" to refer to the didactic role played by Macau's casino resorts in China's economic reforms, and in the comportment of those nascent Chinese consumers who are so crucial to the future viability of the global economy. In the Venetian Resort, we may observe, in concentrated and intensified form, capital's contemporary entreaties into the post-Mao PRC, the final planetary frontier of consumer capitalism.

Macau is a uniquely compelling stage for this spectacular social theater. Founded in 1557 by Portuguese explorers who were seeking

Figure 2. The Venetian Macao resort, one of the world's largest buildings. *Photograph by Adam Lampton.*

a strategic settlement from which to manage trade with China and Japan, and to accommodate ecclesiastical entreaties into the Middle Kingdom, Macau played a crucial role in the emergence of the global capitalist system in the fifteenth and sixteenth centuries. However, after an initial golden age during which Macau mediated most of the trade between Europe and the Far East, the city faded into historical obscurity in a process that paralleled Portugal's own waning global influence.

Yet Macau quietly endured for nearly half a millennium as an exogenous European enclave on China's southern coast and as the country's longest continuously occupied foreign territory. When Portugal returned the city to the PRC in 1999, two years after Britain's celebrated handover of Hong Kong, Macau was the last remaining European colony in Asia. With its decaying neoclassical colonial buildings, moribund economy, and lethargic ambiance, Macau was a final testament to the faded grandeur of Portugal's once mighty empire.

The city's reunification with a rising China at the turn of the millennium augured the embryonic stirring of a world-historical geopolitical realignment, the scale of which is reminiscent of Europe's five-hundred-year colonial project—and the gradual geographical translocation of the axis of global capitalism from the once-dominant West to East Asia. Yet Macau's designation as a special administrative region (SAR) of the PRC, under the "one country, two systems" regime, somehow only served to formalize the city's endemic alterity. This alterity manifests most clearly in Macau's apostate status as the only site of legal casino gaming in the PRC as well as its unlikely transformation, only a few years later, into the most lucrative locus of gambling the world has ever known.

GLOBAL GATEWAY

I moved to Macau in 2001 to take up a post at a local university. I arrived in the city on the high-speed ferry from Hong Kong, some four centuries after those initial Portuguese seafarers—and only eighteen months after Portugal's abdication of the city to the PRC. At the start of the new millennium, Macau seemed somehow mired in another eon. Geographically positioned just off the beaten path and characterized by an ineffable historical slippage, Macau had eluded the frenetic pace of development that defined nearby Hong Kong, as well as the other neighboring Asian tigers that were busily producing the region's economic miracle. Macau's distinct ambiance was typically described as sleepy, and daily life in the city felt strangely entangled with some wayward dream of a bygone era.

Soon after my arrival, however, several casino industry outsiders set off a series of dramatic changes in the city that rivaled the significance of their Portuguese predecessors. I witnessed the construction and celebrated opening of Adelson's Venetian Resort and the phantasmagoric metamorphosis of Macau's charming colonial-era cityscape, and I experienced firsthand Macau's remarkable socioeconomic transformation. My adventure over the past two decades forms the basis of this book.

To understand Macau's spectacular palace project today, however, we must look backward to the city's formative role in the historical development of global capitalism; backward to the Portuguese "navigations and discoveries" that founded both Macau and the modern world; and backward to the Maoist utopian schemes of the PRC that sought so strenuously to shape that world and its subjects. Today Macau's Venetian Palace project provides a unique window into China's post-Mao reforms and the country's postsocialist transformation into consumer capitalism's final frontier. The two Chinese characters that form the word *Macau* (澳門) literally mean "inlet" and "gate," and medieval Macau was China's original gateway to the global economy. Today, Macau's remarkably remunerative tourist trade has replaced the shiploads of silver, silks, and spices that defined the city's mercantilist origins. Macau's contemporary gateway function is its unique ability to articulate hundreds of millions of Chinese tourists with the billions of dollars of foreign investment capital that flowed into the city after the handover.

We can therefore trace a sort of shadow history of the global economy from the unlikely vantage point of the Venetian Resort. This history extends from the very origins of capitalism in the medieval Mediterranean city-state of Venice to the contemporary construction of Sloterdijk's (2013) consumer "world interior" in Macau. This story is five hundred years in the making, but much of the tale takes place in and around Macau's casinos. One of the plot's key protagonists is the game of baccarat, which attracts so many Chinese tourists to Macau and produces the billions of dollars of annual gaming profits that make the Venetian viable.

MACAU'S CASINO GAMING INDUSTRY

Gambling was legalized in Macau in the mid-nineteenth century in the form of a government-owned monopoly that was farmed out to local associations in exchange for a share of the proceeds. Such gambling syndicates either operated casinos or specialized in individual games, such as fan-tan or the lottery. Macau's early gaming venues were simple affairs that lacked any pretense of glamour or sophistication, populated by common-variety punters who wagered meager stakes at games run by indifferent croupiers, who were often clad simply in slippers and singlets. A Russian journalist based in Manila who spent several years in the 1920s sailing with pirates on the South China Sea offered this typical account of a visit to Macau:

> Described by the tourist agencies as the "Gem of the Orient Earth," and as the Monte Carlo of the Far East, it richly deserves the first name, but there is little justification for the latter. It lacks the tone,

if not the spirit, of the palatial Casino of the French Riviera. As a matter of fact, there is no casino in Macao, but there are twelve dingy opium-reeking dives, the patrons of which wear no formal dress as is the rule at Monte Carlo. On a warm summer day you may rub elbows with half-naked coolies, road-dusty farmers, and fugitive embezzlers as you lay your bets on the gaming tables of Macao. (Lilius [1930] 2011, 75)

In 1934, the Portuguese government granted industry-wide casino monopoly rights for the first time to a single operator. The Tai Heng Company paid a fee of 1.8 million taels of gold for the concession and opened its first casino in the Central Hotel located on Macau's main thoroughfare, Avenida da Almeida Riberio, known colloquially in Chinese as San Malo. The Central Hotel still stands today.

In the decades that followed, Macau generally appeared in the western popular imagination, if it appeared at all, as a vice-laden city of sin and a trope of the exotic Far East, with a picturesque harbor filled with Chinese junks and streets teeming with prostitutes, opium dens, and a general atmosphere of wanton iniquity. Occasional cinematic images of the city reinforced this motif (Lopes 2016; Mao 2016). In *The Lady from Shanghai* (1947), Orson Welles flatly proclaims Macau "the wickedest city in the world." The opening narration of the 1952 Howard Hughes production *Macao* describes the city as a "fugitive's haven" located just beyond the authority of Interpol: "Here millions in gold and diamonds disappear—some across the gambling tables and some mysteriously into the night." That same year, in an episode of the Saturday morning serial *Terry and the Pirates,* a mustachioed Chinese hepcat named Chopstick Joe memorably characterizes Macau as "six square miles of iniquity, where a man can buy or sell anything." These provocative descriptions finally converge a decade later in *Thrilling Cities,* a nonfiction travel memoir written by James Bond creator Ian Fleming. In the book, Fleming narrates a visit to Macau, where he dines with local gold trader Pedro Lobo, the inspiration for the Bond villain Goldfinger, and carouses in the Central Hotel, which he describes as "the largest 'house of ill-fame' in the world" (Fleming [1963] 2013, 23).

Macau's gaming industry underwent a significant transformation when Stanley Ho Hung-sun won the casino concession in 1962 through

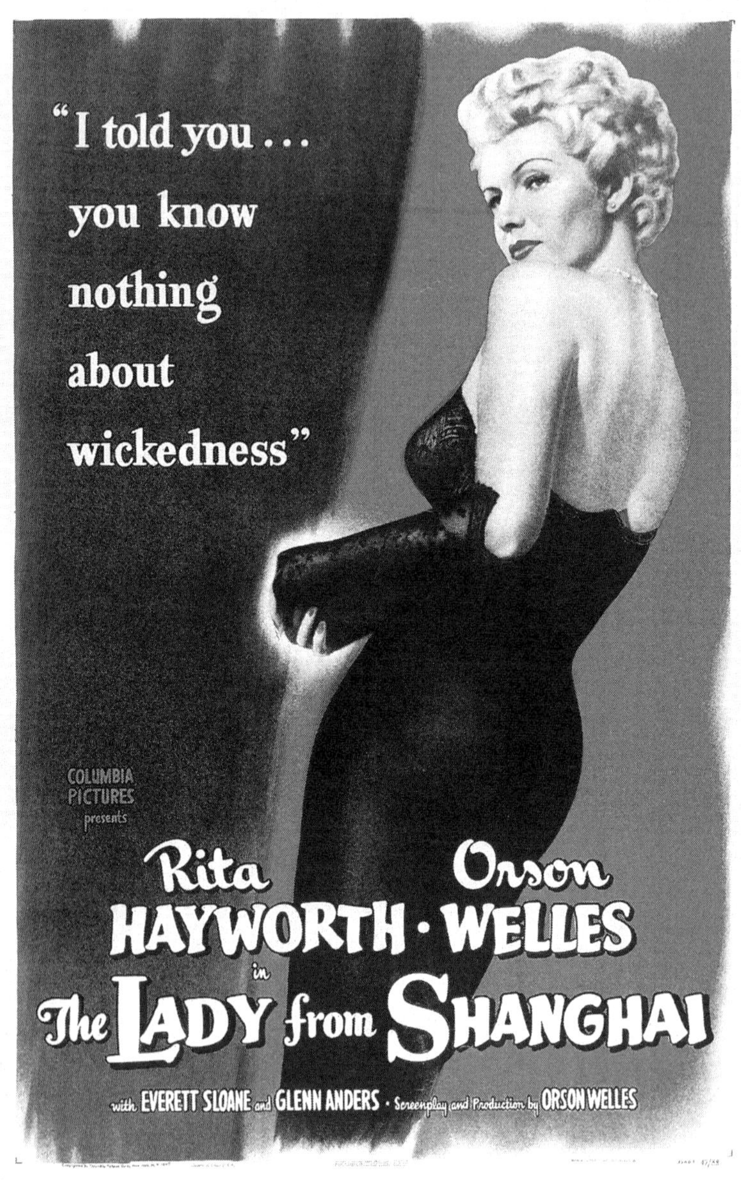

Figure 3. In the 1948 film *The Lady from Shanghai*, Orson Welles proclaims Macau "the wickedest city in the world."

his company Sociedade de Turismo e Diversoes de Macau.[3] Ho controlled the monopoly for forty years, leaving an indelible mark on Macau in the process. Born in Hong Kong in 1921 to a wealthy Eurasian family, Ho's personal background seemingly prepared him perfectly for his role at the helm of the Macau gaming industry. A handsome and multilingual aficionado of ballroom dancing, Ho moved to Macau in 1942 with Japan's wartime invasion of Hong Kong; he made his initial fortune smuggling food and luxury goods into Hong Kong and China during World War II. In addition, Ho's first wife, Clementina Leitão, whom he married in 1946, was from one of Macau's most prominent Portuguese families. Ho would eventually have four wives and father seventeen children; several members of that vast brood play significant roles in Macau's posthandover casino industry.[4]

After gaining the concession, Ho set out to modernize Macau's gaming industry. In late 1962, he opened the Estoril Hotel, which was Macau's first genuine luxury casino resort. He introduced western games such as baccarat and roulette, which eventually displaced the dominant role of fan-tan. Ho operated dog and horse racing venues, and he introduced a short-lived gambling venture around the Latin American game of jai alai. In an effort to upgrade the tourist infrastructure, he also introduced a high-speed hydrofoil to transport tourists from Hong Kong to Macau, which was more efficient than the several lethargic hours required on the existing daily ferry. Finally, in 1970, Ho opened his flagship Lisboa Hotel and Casino, an iconic birdcage-shaped property located on a new parcel of reclaimed land at the end of San Malo, which for several decades would define Macau's modest skyline.

Ho made a dramatic impact on the idiosyncratic operations of Macau's gaming industry in the 1980s, when he began subcontracting private gambling rooms in his casinos to independent agents. Ho's motivation for this arrangement was to address the fact that Chinese Triads, the secret brotherhoods that function as organized crime groups, were purchasing tickets on the new Hong Kong hydrofoil to resell at usurious rates. In an effort to stop this practice, which was interfering with tourist traffic to Macau, Ho counteroffered Triad agents direct access to his casinos via a commission on sales of casino chips to gamblers.

This practice eventually evolved into a VIP contractual system unique to Macau and known locally as the junket trade, which came

Figure 4. Macau gaming tycoon Stanley Ho Hung-sun, 1981. *Courtesy of Getty Images.*

to dominate casino revenues in the city (and which I explore in detail in chapter 6). Junket agents typically recruit high rollers to Macau and advance them credit for gambling. This system operates in a gray area of Macau's gaming law, which prevents casinos from loaning money to gamblers (whereas such casino credit is typical of high-roller gaming finance in Las Vegas), but it does not explicitly prevent private companies from engaging in such loan sharking (Wang and Eadington 2008). Ho exploited this legal ambiguity, as well as the laissez-faire oversight of the city's Portuguese authorities, to establish the junket system.

By the 1990s, Ho operated an entrenched provincial gaming empire frequented by a modest customer base of gamblers primarily from Hong Kong, Taiwan, Japan, Korea, and China, producing annual revenues of around $2 billion. While this is no doubt a significant sum, it was only about half of the amount generated at the time in the second-tier North American jurisdiction of Atlantic City, New Jersey. This revenue made Ho a billionaire and allowed him to dominate a large swath of Macau's small economy through control of not only casinos but also banks, tourism agencies, hotels, apartment buildings, and the city's lone department store. However, in the long shadow cast by gambling giant

Las Vegas, Macau's gaming industry remained a relatively small-time affair.

In the late 1990s, Macau's casino industry suffered a significant blow from the so-called casino wars, a wave of internecine gangland violence that swept through the city and over a three-year period left 122 dead bodies in its wake. The rash of gunfights, kidnappings, bombings, arson attacks, and assassinations of government officials and gambling industry regulators took a palpable toll on the local economy. The violence was attributed to the Triad groups involved in the industry who sought to gain control of the city vice trades before the pending handover to China, and the Portuguese authorities proved powerless to effectively address the violence or punish the perpetrators. The crime wave, in part fomented by a media-savvy Macau gang boss named Wan "Broken Tooth" Kuok-koi, was widely reported in the international press. The author of a notorious 1998 *Wall Street Journal* article inadvertently echoed Chopstick Joe when she called Macau "the most lawless six square miles on earth" (Morrison 1998). The casino wars significantly suppressed the tourist trade, hampering the economy and dampening the morale of residents.

By 1999, Ho's casino business manifested a dilapidated ambience and seedy regional reputation. At the time of the handover, his company's casinos were described by one professional observer as "dismal," with their appearances ranging "from squalid to unexceptional" (Wang and Eadington 2008, 240). "It ain't Vegas" was a typical way other expats described Macau's gaming industry when I first arrived in 2001. Indeed, on my initial visit to the Lisboa, I found the property's main gaming floor located in a cramped and unadorned room in the hotel basement, with low ceilings, threadbare carpets, and well-worn baccarat tables surrounded by dense crowds of chain-smoking Chinese gamblers. It felt like I had somehow stepped back in time. Although the Lisboa's croupiers wore black-tie company uniforms, the overall ambiance remained reminiscent of those early opium den days of road-dusty gamblers and singlet-clad staff. When it opened, the Lisboa Casino had been a revolutionary intervention in Macau's gaming industry. But with its 1970s aesthetic seemingly straight out of a period James Bond film and its circular facade covered with faded yellow Portuguese tiles, by 1999, the Lisboa appeared, much like the baroque colonial buildings in Macau's city center, as a peculiar relic from a bygone era.

Figure 5. Lisboa Casino and Hotel, circa 2021. Opened by Stanley Ho in 1970, the Lisboa modernized Macau's gaming industry, but by the end of Ho's monopoly concession in 2002, it appeared as a peculiar relic from a bygone era. *Photograph by author.*

The Liberalization of Macau's Casino Monopoly and China's New Economy

Sheldon Adelson entered Macau a few years after the 1999 retrocession to the PRC, when the city's nascent postcolonial government administration made a consequential decision to terminate the monopoly arrangement and open the industry to outside investors. The government hoped that foreign competition might stimulate the local economy, professionalize the gambling industry, suppress the outsize influence of organized crime, and even help maintain law and order in the city. Casino owners in Las Vegas, Atlantic City, and Sydney must be free of organized crime contacts abroad or risk losing their casino licenses at home, and the authorities apparently anticipated that the influence of foreign gaming control boards would serve to indirectly regulate the foreign operators in Macau. Adelson was one of several wealthy investors who ultimately won gaming concessions in the city. The select group also included Las Vegas visionary Steve Wynn, who had revitalized the Strip with high-end properties such as the Bellagio,

Treasure Island, and the Mirage; MGM'S Kirk Kerkorian, known in Las Vegas as the father of the megaresort; Australian Publishing and Broadcasting Limited tycoon James Packer; and Hong Kong property magnate Liu Chee Woo. (I provide a detailed account of this process in chapter 4.)

At the time, China was undergoing a process of profound transformation. Macau's return to China and the resulting liberalization of the city's casino monopoly came two decades after paramount leader Deng Xiaoping's bold implementation of capitalist reforms to the country's planned economy—changes he referred to as socialism with Chinese characteristics. The reforms were initially localized in China's new special economic zones (SEZs), which were located along the country's southern coast; two of these zones were intentionally positioned directly adjacent to Hong Kong and Macau in order to benefit from these cities' capitalist economies, as well as the access they provided to networks of overseas Chinese investors. There was a dawning realization outside China that "market-socialism" was more than an incongruous neologism; it was a viable economic system in its own right and a remarkably dynamic form of enterprise.

Many ordinary Chinese citizens living with the country's new experimental market economy were beginning to enjoy disposable incomes and enhanced lifestyles unheard of under Maoist rule. New state policies designed to encourage leisure and consumption activities in order to stimulate economic development prompted a gradual softening of Mao-era constraints on population mobility, creating enhanced opportunities for domestic and cross-border travel. Indeed, individual mobility emerged as one arena of everyday life in which the Chinese central government experimented with relaxation of authoritarian controls and enhancement of personal freedoms, gradually allocating to select Chinese citizens carefully calibrated opportunities for migration and travel while implicitly ascribing greater responsibility to individuals to govern their own behavior. These new state-administered liberties became part of a strategy of "governing at a distance" in an increasingly neoliberal regime that has been described as "socialism from afar" (Ong and Zhang 2008, 3).[5] The aim was to "induce citizens to be self-responsible, self-enterprising, and self-governing subjects."

If the sedentary rural Chinese peasant was the canonical figure of Maoist socialism, then the mobile urban tourist emerged as the personification of China's postsocialist era, embodying the governmental dialectic of circumscribed personal freedom on the one hand and individual self-discipline on the other, which would become the hallmark of this regime.[6] Deeming both Hong Kong and Macau politically safe locales for PRC nationals, the central government had granted both cities "approved destination status" in 1983, although access was highly restricted; Chinese citizens could only travel to these cities as part of a state-sanctioned group tour. However, in July 2003, the PRC introduced an experimental new exit visa called the Individual Visit Scheme (IVS), which allowed Chinese citizens, first from Guangdong province, then later from other select provinces and cities, to travel to the new SARs of Hong Kong and Macau as individual tourists. All of these factors would benefit Macau's posthandover tourism industry, although at the time no one could have predicted what was to come.

In 2004, Adelson opened the Sands Casino, the first foreign-owned casino property in the city—and the first casino anywhere specifically designed to appeal to Chinese gamblers. The contemporary ambiance of the Sands was a stark departure from the aging Lisboa, and a seemingly bottomless reservoir of Chinese tourists excitedly exercising their new freedoms suddenly flooded over the border into Macau, quickly making the Sands the world's most profitable gaming venue. In 2006, Macau's casino revenues reached $7 billion, for the first time surpassing those of Las Vegas, thereby designating Macau as the world's most lucrative casino market. "It ain't Vegas" was suddenly no longer a pejorative dismissal; Macau was now bigger than Las Vegas, and it just kept growing. In 2011, Macau's gaming industry revenues were actually *five times* greater than Las Vegas'. Finally, the city's gross receipts of $45 billion in 2013—which remains the industry record—were seven times greater than Las Vegas and equal to the combined returns of every single casino, in every single gaming jurisdiction, in the entire United States.

When it opened in 2007, the Venetian Resort was Adelson's second casino property in Macau and the city's first Las Vegas–style integrated resort. In the long decade that followed (that is, the eleven years from 2007 to 2017), Macau was visited by more than 300 million tourists, most crossing from mainland China. The city's casinos collectively produced in excess of $313 billion of revenue. The "sleeping giant" of China had clearly awakened, and the sleepy European enclave of Macau was completely transformed in the process. Once a charming and languid colonial backwater, Macau mutated into a bustling metropolis whose cityscape was suddenly replete with iconic glass buildings and massive themed megaresorts, and whose diminutive and outdated infrastructure, along with the patience of the local population, was overwhelmed by tens of millions of tourists.

The billions of dollars generated by those tourists benefits not just the casino owners. The Macau government collects taxes and fees that total 39 percent of casino revenues; these proceeds comprise 80 percent of the annual public budget. (By comparison, the effective gaming tax in Las Vegas is 7.75 percent.) In 2019, Macau had the second-highest per capita GDP in the world, and that year, the International Monetary Fund projected that Macau might soon overtake Qatar to become the world's richest territory.[7] Jobs are abundant for Macau's workers; the city's unemployment rate hovered below 2 percent for a decade. The local life expectancy of eighty-two years is the second longest in the world, just behind Monaco; mainland China's average life expectancy

Figure 6. Sheldon Adelson's visage projected on a screen at the grand opening ceremony of the Venetian Macao resort on August 28, 2007. *Photograph by Adam Lampton.*

is seventy-four years. Local taxes on personal income, residential property, and retail sales range from negligible to nonexistent, and a wealth-sharing scheme introduced in 2008 returns an annual cash payment to residents, a sum that in 2022 amounted to US$1,250 (MOP 10,000) for every person, including children, in the city.

I would venture to suggest that over the past two decades, Macau has changed more rapidly, and more substantially, than perhaps any place on earth. In order to grasp the global implications of this transformation, however, we should keep in mind this useful caveat about the city: it ain't Vegas! Although journalists and academics alike typically describe Macau as the Las Vegas of Asia, Macau is more than an Asian iteration of its North American casino city counterpart.[8] This comparison overlooks Macau's unique role in China's reform era and its ongoing importance to the evolution of global capitalism.

Macau's Casino Megaresorts and China's Urban Revolution

Although it was founded at the start of the twentieth century, the Las Vegas we know today is a unique product of the political economy of postwar suburbanization in the United States. In the years after World War II, prompted by tax incentives and other government initiatives, Americans depopulated the nation's city centers en masse as they flocked to new housing developments in garden-style suburban areas.[9] By 1965, a majority of Americans lived in suburbs rather than cities, and suburbanization was a tremendous boon to the country's economy (Cohen 2003). The move to the suburbs entailed a "radical transformation" of the American lifestyle, "bringing new products from housing to refrigerators and air conditioners, as well as two cars in the driveway and an enormous increase in the consumption of oil" (Harvey 2008, 27). This suburban mass consumption complemented the country's corresponding regime of industrial production. Together, they transformed the United States into the world's largest economy. Historian David G. Schwartz (2003), in his book *Suburban Xanadu: The Casino Resort on the Las Vegas Strip and Beyond,* argues that casino resorts in Las Vegas emerged as a counterpart to this postwar suburbanization and that the design of the resorts modeled the theme parks, highway motels, and shopping malls that served those suburban residents.[10]

However, if the Las Vegas Strip is a leisure reflection of the logic of

American suburbanization, then Macau's casino resorts must be understood as a counterpart to the *urbanization* of China.[11] This massive project of infrastructure development, population displacement, and lifestyle engineering is arguably the most profound urbanization process in global history. The goal of this urban revolution is to transform once-communist China into a colossal consumer society to rival the United States.[12]

China's urban transformation is driven by a macroeconomic project called the National New-Type Urbanization Plan. As I will explain in chapter 3, this project aims to wean the country from the highly remunerative, but ultimately unsustainable, production-for-export regime with which Deng jump started economic reforms in the Shenzhen SEZ. The goal of this plan is to first drive economic development via state-led investment in infrastructure projects, then to sustain that growth by replacing China's current role as the factory for the world with a new economy focused primarily on domestic consumption. This urbanization plan involves the relocation of hundreds of millions of rural Chinese people to cities, which are being constructed on a massive scale to accommodate these new residents.

Today there are more than a hundred cities in China with populations over one million (compared to ten such cities in the United States). The key city responsible for Macau's development is the Greater Bay Area (GBA) megacity, which, if understood as one continuous urban environment, is the largest metropolitan region in the world in terms of both area and population size. This megacity serves as the engine of Macau's casino industry.

The urbanization of China is undoubtedly one of the most significant structural processes in the world today, with important consequences for the global economy. One indicator of the massive pace and scale of this urbanization project is the startling fact that, according to the United States Geological Survey, China consumed more cement during the three years 2011 to 2013 than the United States consumed in the entire twentieth century.[13] Much of this cement was poured to support China's vast infrastructure projects of roadways, train depots, airports, hydroelectric dams, and apartment blocks, an estimated half of which has been constructed since 2000, or roughly since the time of Portugal's return of Macau to the motherland. Therefore, Macau's relatively brief history as a Chinese SAR has coincided with a Chinese urbanization project conducted on a scale far greater than any such project in global history. The goal of this project is to cultivate a massive population of urbane Chinese consumers whose spending habits will drive the country's economic development.

CASINO CAPITALISM: LEARNING TO BE A CONSUMER

China's effort to create a mass consumer society shares much in common with similar processes in other times and places, including not only twentieth-century United States but also eighteenth-century England, nineteenth-century France, and postwar Japan.[14] I situate my analysis of Chinese tourism to Macau, as well as the gambling, shopping, and sightseeing activities of those tourists, within this broad history of consumerism. However, "the consumer as a project took different shape in different traditions" (Trentmann 2016, 9), and this is certainly true of China today. I call this local process of Chinese consumer personification "consumer pedagogy" to highlight the state-directed educational characteristics that are typical of the Chinese case. Indeed, throughout this book, I examine the didactic qualities of the PRC's consumption regime.

Fundamental to my approach is the assumption that humans are not natural consumers who, if only enabled, will enthusiastically embrace consumer behaviors as a central component of their identity, spending the bulk of their discretionary income on purchases of enticing but unnecessary items. Rather, the Chinese consumer subject (much like the preceding socialist subject) is the product of a pedagogical process. Chinese citizens today have the world's highest household savings rates, so it takes a concerted effort to convince those frugal families (whose older generations have vivid memories of severe socialist-era scarcity, deprivation, and economic uncertainty) to redirect those savings to leisure spending.[15] In order to understand China's efforts to encourage consumption as a strategy to drive growth, we must analyze the specific ways in which China's population is mobilized into consumerist attitudes and behaviors.

The case of the United States is instructive. As William Leach (1994) demonstrates, the transformation of the formerly agrarian American nation into a suburban consumer society began in the late nineteenth century. It was based around a widespread "democratization of desire." This process was driven by a new group of cultural "brokers" with diverse stakes in achieving this outcome. These brokers included "investment bankers, corporate lawyers, and credit experts; urban museum curators and art school instructors who taught commercial and industrial 'art' to up-and-coming designers; university professors who trained business leaders; economists who redefined the goals of the industrial order to include greater consumption; advertising agents and travel agents; 'specialists' who created the 'light-and-color' for places like Times Square; and professional model agencies (such as John Powers Incorporated in Manhattan) that brokered female bodies" (10–11). American consumer culture was therefore not the predictable outcome of some natural human inclination. It required complex efforts, by a large and diverse group of individuals and institutions pursuing a wide variety of interests and motivations, to collectively produce what is today a full-blown "consumer's republic," a country of committed citizen-consumers who (incidentally, and directly contrary to the Chinese case) carry the world's highest levels of household debt (Cohen 2006). The implementation of consumer culture in China involves a similar effort, and Macau plays a unique role in this process.

Macau as a Model City

To study the introduction of consumer culture into China today, I focus on the function of Macau's material environments in the process of consumer pedagogy. Drawing on the work of scholars who have analyzed the functional design of commercial arcades, department stores, shopping malls, and theme parks, I analyze the role of Macau's casinos, integrated resorts, retail shops, and gaming machines in the promotion of Chinese consumerism (Benjamin 1969; Benson 1987; Fjellman 1992; Herwig 2006; Miller 1994; Mitrašinović 2006). However, in order to understand the unique forms of consumer pedagogy that are present in Macau, I also draw on indigenous Chinese educational theories. Some of these educational programs derive from Confucian philosophical traditions; others emerged during the socialist era and were influenced by American pragmatist philosopher John Dewey's lectures in China in the 1920s. As sociologist Borge Bakken (2000) demonstrates in his book *The Exemplary Society,* China has a long tradition of the use of educational models—such as model soldiers, workers, factories, or villages—to guide ethical behavior. These exemplary models, which the Maoist government deployed to shape socialist-era China, are particularly important to my conception of Macau as a sort of model city for Chinese consumerism. The fact that Chinese tourists arrive in Macau well versed in such statist efforts at citizen education makes it useful to examine the city's attractions within the context of these Chinese educational techniques.

At this point, it is fair to ask why anyone who is interested in a country as enormous as China should look specifically to tiny Macau to understand China's consumption regime. Macau's resorts are certainly not unique in their pedagogical potential or in their function in the contemporary transformation of the PRC. On the contrary, China's cities today offer a vast array of consumer attractions; the country is home to innumerable retail malls, amusement parks, pedestrianized shopping streets, big-box stores, fast food outlets, and themed housing developments, each of which are no doubt involved in the maintenance of China's consumer economy.

However, China's consumer attractions did not appear overnight upon the implementation of Deng's reforms. Although economic reforms commenced in 1978, they only picked up speed with Deng's 1992 southern tour of the SEZs, which included a visit to Macau's mainland neighbor, Zhuhai. The central government implemented the National New-Type Urbanization Plan in 2014, and China's aggressive urbanization has mirrored Macau's own posthandover transformation. Therefore, the postcolonial development of Macau's gaming industry has paralleled these national reform-era efforts.

It is also important to note that when central government officials initiated economic reforms and sought to mobilize tourism as a key contributor to economic development, they specifically selected Macau and Hong Kong to serve as favored destinations for mainland travelers. In addition, they created new experimental regulations, such as the special IVS travel visa, to enable those citizens to visit these former colonial territories. The Macau SAR is therefore unique in the way in which it has been chosen to serve as a sort of experimental *laboratory of consumption.* Macau serves this function for both China's central government, whose macroeconomic plan aims to utilize the city's unique potentials, and transnational gaming companies, who have spent billions of dollars in Macau in an effort to attract those Chinese tourists.

This laboratory function is enabled by Macau's unique characteristics, including its diminutive size, peripheral location, archipelagic geography, cultural and historical distinction, ambiguous sovereignty, legal exception, population density, and architectural experimentation. Together, these factors render the city a concentrated microcosm of Chinese consumerism and a fecund site of study.

Casino Tourism in Macau

Seasoned casino travelers who visit Macau today will recognize right away that "it ain't Vegas," although they might not be able to immediately put their finger on the reason for this revelation. Anyone familiar with Las Vegas can attest to the city's unmistakable party vibe, characteristic of its "sin city" status and exemplified by the nonstop flow of hedonistic revelers surging down the sidewalks of the Strip. Though Macau's Cotai Strip is named after its Las Vegas counterpart, it does not exhibit quite the same parade of exhibitionism and debauchery, and Macau's affect is palpably distinct from its sister casino city. Don't get me wrong: Macau has its share of sinful attractions, and the city exhibits an endemic seediness that emanates in part from its opprobrious past. We will also see that Macau's gangland history is just as colorful as the mob era in Las Vegas, generating its own minor subgenre of Chinese gangster films, one of which I will discuss in chapter 4. Nevertheless, there is a striking difference in the resort ambiance of both cities, with this difference largely attributable to the distinct role of casino gambling in each locale.

First, Macau tourists gamble, on average, much more heavily than their Las Vegas counterparts. Most tourists visit Las Vegas to attend a convention, see a concert or show, eat at a steakhouse, dance the night away in a club, or simply take in the spectacle of the Strip. These tourists generally proceed to blow some money in a casino mostly as an entertaining afterthought. For this reason, gambling in Las Vegas contributes about 30 percent of total tourist revenues, with the rest spent on restaurants, hotel rooms, resort fees, spas, shows, nightclubs, champagne, limousines, and other holiday attractions (Velotta 2019).

In Macau, these numbers are reversed: an astounding 90 percent of tourist revenue in the city is derived directly from gambling (McCartney 2015; Moura 2019b).[16] The simple fact is that most Chinese tourists visit Macau to gamble, and they tend to conceive of gambling primarily as a means of making money or as an investment in potential economic returns, more than a simple form of entertainment. This is not to suggest that Chinese gamblers in Macau are not enjoying themselves, but the casinos certainly have a different ambiance than the typical Las Vegas party vibe. I would describe that ambiance as workmanlike. For example, whereas a primary part of the attraction of gambling in Las Vegas is the nonstop flow of complimentary cocktails, most gamblers in Macau are too focused on the games to allow alcohol to impede their concentration. They instead enjoy free tea, orange juice, and milk coffee, which enhance their energy and enable extended time at the tables.

Second, the predominant forms of gambling in each city are distinct. Most gamblers in Vegas choose to play the city's ubiquitous slot machines, which in 2018 generated 65 percent of Nevada's gaming revenues (Cano 2019). However, Chinese gamblers in Macau prefer conventional table games, with slot machine play producing only a miniscule 5 percent of annual gaming revenues (Singleton 2018).[17] Third, where those table games are concerned, the most popular such game in Las Vegas today is poker in all its varieties. Macau's most popular table game, by contrast (and by far), is baccarat. Baccarat is the predominant activity in Macau's mass market casinos and is the sole game played in the city's VIP rooms, which have historically generated most of the gambling profits. Taxes derived from baccarat play are also the city's single largest source of public revenue. For these reasons, baccarat is the key to understanding Macau.[18]

Baccarat as Sentimental Education

Several scholars have described poker's popularity as characteristic of America's economy, with the game serving as a playful counterpart to enterprise. For example, in his book about poker, Ole Bjerg (2011) reads each iteration of the game—Draw Poker, Seven-Card Stud, No Limit Texas Hold 'Em—as a parody of the successive eras of American capitalism in which each has been dominant. Edward LiPuma (2017) interprets the contemporary popularity of Texas Hold 'Em as indicative of a "new social imaginary," which he calls "poker nation" and which "reflects and reproduces at the level of entertainment a deeper transformation in the character of capitalism" (257). These insightful approaches inform my understanding of baccarat, but my conception of the game in Macau is distinct from these scholars, who tend to understand poker as a playful reflection of an economic regime that is external to the game. My interest instead is in the productivity of gambling in Macau and its immanent relation to economic behavior.[19]

I have come to understand baccarat as what Clifford Geertz (1972), in his famous study of gambling on the Balinese cockfight, calls deep play.[20] Geertz describes the cockfight as a dramatic model of everyday social relations through which Balinese villagers experience an evocative "vocabulary of sentiment": "the thrill of risk, the despair of loss, the pleasure of triumph" (84). Therefore, gambling on the cockfight ultimately produced a kind of sentimental education in the ethos of the culture. I argue that for Chinese gamblers in Macau, baccarat entails a similar sort of sentimental education in a market ethos that has encroached on China in the reform era.[21] I take my lead from scholars who contend that socialization in the cognitive, immaterial, and affective forms of labor that are common to capitalism today typically occurs outside of the workplace, in everyday activities. Therefore, the specific leisure "sentiments" honed by baccarat may be productively "put to work" in market activities (Virno 2006, 15).[22] That is, baccarat does not merely reflect or represent economic life outside the game, in the manner in which Bjerg (2011) and LiPuma (2017) describe poker. Rather, baccarat play is a formative activity in which those economic dispositions, calculative techniques, and market behaviors are put to work, developed, and refined.[23]

In short, Macau's model city function for Chinese tourists, the pedagogical processes of consumer comportment enacted in the city's resorts, and the sentimental education of the game of baccarat collectively comprise my understanding of casino capitalism. That is, the casino resort in Macau is, among other things, a school for capitalist enterprise.[24] This approach distinguishes my account of casino capitalism from the work of Strange (1986), who popularized the phrase in her widely read book *Casino Capitalism*. Strange uses casino capitalism as a metaphor to describe the highly speculative and risk-intensive forms of financial investment that became increasingly common after 1970, which she argues have transformed the global economy into something resembling a vast casino. However, I take casino capitalism literally, treating it not as an analogy for financial speculation but as a pedagogical process through which post-Mao market subjects are cultivated in casino resort activities. My analysis of Macau's resorts therefore highlights examples of such didactic instruction in the calculative rationalities, consumer behaviors, and ethic of personal responsibility that are indicative of China's consumption regime.

SINO-CAPITALISM: PRODUCTION OF THE POSTSOCIALIST SUBJECT

This discussion of resort "schooling" in the behaviors and sentiments symptomatic of the reform era brings me to the second objective of this project: the effort to use Macau's Venetian Resort to theorize and describe the contemporary comportment of the postsocialist Chinese subject.[25] China's economic reforms and new consumer orientation entail a revolutionary reshaping of not only the country's socialist economy and urban society but also of its citizens. This sort of didactic process is nothing new. I have discussed a similar example of consumer subjectivation in the United States, and China has its own indigenous experiments in citizen behavior modification on which to draw.

With the founding of the PRC in 1949, and in direct contradiction to the consumer economy that was being fomented at the time in the United States, Chinese authorities endeavored to produce a novel ascetic and egalitarian socialist subject for whom consumerism was an antirevolutionary practice and symbol of bourgeois decadence. Socialist officials launched a series of propaganda campaigns in which they deployed poster art, film, radio, and other media to promote a set of model workers and soldiers, whose heroic deeds or modest habits provided productive examples for the citizenry to emulate (Evans and Donald 1999; Lu 2020).

In addition, state planners explicitly fashioned China's cities to shape socialist subjects, creating an urban environment and ambiance markedly different from the industrial cities of the West. The new urban habitats of the socialist PRC were structured by innovative residential and work sites called *danwei,* or "work units." In part inspired by revolutionary Soviet architecture, the work unit was designed to promote a proletarian consciousness. The work unit provided housing, jobs, food, health care, entertainment, and other elements of the so-called iron rice bowl, which was provided by the state and necessary for the reproduction of the workforce. In his definitive analysis of the *danwei* design, geographer David Bray (2005) argues that each work unit functioned as a "spatial machine of subjection" (5), the aim of which was to produce collectivist Chinese comrades whose lifestyles were consistent with the goals of the socialist regime. We will see that the PRC's post-Mao market reforms likewise require a new subject appropriate to the country's new economy. My study of Macau's role in this process involves an analysis of what we may call the city's *subjective economy,* which complements the political economy of urbanization that drives Chinese capitalism today.[26]

The intangible and immaterial qualities of subjectivity render its study problematic. For this reason, I have chosen to follow Bray's lead and to engage with subjectivity indirectly by analyzing a variety of "spatial machines" engineered to engender and refine postsocialist subjects (even though the designers may not have thought of them in those specific terms). An analysis of these devices facilitates study of the process of subjectivation, rather than the phenomenological "personhood" of any particular people. This subjectivation program, along with the concomitant development of citizen-consumers, commenced in China with Deng's introduction of market reforms in 1978, but the tacit logic of this process is especially evident in the exceptional locale of twenty-first-century Macau.

Much like Bray's (2005) analysis of the socialist work unit, my approach to understanding the Venetian Resort is indebted to the formative scholarship of philosopher Michel Foucault and his concept of the apparatus. An apparatus, such as the Chinese work unit or the American suburban home, is a sort of sociospatial machine within which a particular type of person emerges. Whereas the socialist work unit functioned to form egalitarian laborers for the new planned economy, the suburban home was the locus for the new citizen-consumers whose acquisitive lifestyles propelled America's postwar growth. Throughout this book, I analyze the role of a variety of such apparatuses in Macau, of varying sizes and scales. An apparatus may be as large as the GBA megacity, which China has explicitly engineered to engender new types of workers and shoppers necessary to the market-socialist economy, or as small as an electronic baccarat game designed to appeal to Chinese gamblers in Macau. Indeed, I will explain how the megacity, the integrated casino resort, and the baccarat machine function together to cultivate and refine postsocialist citizen-consumers.

I pay particular attention to a category of economic apparatus that the economist Michel Callon, in a contemporary application of Foucault's concept, calls a "market device" (Callon, Millo, and Muniesa 2007). These devices include everything from financial software to shopping carts; they function to coordinate the individual with the specific economic activities that comprise market behavior. Therefore, in chapter 1, I will analyze the Venetian Resort as a unique type of market device that plays an instrumental role in Macau's tourist economy.

A Spatial History of the Integrated Resort

My method for studying the integrated resort in Macau is a spatial history, in which the Venetian Resort is simultaneously both object and subject.[27] That is, the integrated resort is not simply the object of analysis but is also the primary concept through which I understand Macau's gaming boom and the city's role in China's economic reforms. My narrative of the Venetian formation begins in chapter 1 with the Italian city-state of Venice, which not only serves as the inspiration for the Venetian's baroque thematic motifs but also played a significant role in Macau's own trade history (which I will discuss later). I also trace the genesis of the resort to the innovative design of the Crystal Palace, with its unique articulations among architecture, pedagogy, and consumption that are visible in the Venetian today.

Macau's Venetian Resort was modeled on Adelson's original Venetian property, which was inspired by his honeymoon visit to Venice with second wife, Miriam Adelson, and which opened on the Las Vegas Strip in 1999. When Adelson constructed the Venetian property in Macau, he essentially transplanted a Las Vegas–style integrated resort to the city, but this structure was also adapted to the exigencies of the local environment and specifically designed to appeal to Chinese tourists. We will see in chapter 4 that Adelson's Sands Casino served as an initial testing ground for some radical experiments in Chinese casino design that eventually informed the Venetian structure. However, my ultimate goal is to explore how the Venetian Resort functions in China today, much like the work unit functioned in the socialist era, to produce a particular type of Chinese citizen whose cosmopolitan lifestyle and consumer disposition is consistent with state planning of the market-socialist economy of the PRC.

This spatial history of the integrated resort and its function in China's embrace of capitalism today is inspired by Foucault's unique spatial histories of the modern clinic, classroom, factory, and prison, which emerged in the eighteenth and nineteenth centuries alongside the development of industrial society. Foucault demonstrates that these spaces shaped a new kind of autonomous modern subject that was necessary for the growth of the industrial economy. Foucault's most famous such study is his analysis of the panopticon, an innovative penitentiary designed in the eighteenth century by the philosopher Jeremy Bentham. Foucault's spatial account of the panopticon is not a history of prisons per se but rather an effort to mobilize an analysis of the prison design in an indirect inquiry into the ontology of the modern subject.[28] By describing the utilitarian logic of the panopticon's planned operations and extrapolating this logic to the more mundane environments typical of modern life, Foucault derived from his study of the prison apparatus an understanding of the bodily "discipline" and psychological self-control that is inculcated in modern citizens, which everyone eventually learns to internalize and embrace. The panopticon prison therefore provides an exaggerated model of more prosaic social practices that are common in a variety of mundane modern environments. As Foucault (1979) asks at the conclusion of his analysis, "Is it surprising that prisons resemble factories, schools, barracks, hospitals, which all resemble prisons?" (228).

This mode of inquiry linking the design of specific spaces to the production of subjectivity is the model for my own analysis of the relations among the Venetian Resort and China's post-Mao consumers. The Venetian is of course not the only site in the PRC where Chinese consumers congregate; nor is it the country's most important consumer environment. However, because of its exceptional status, exaggerated design, colossal size, and immense popularity with mainland tourists, the Venetian is (much like the panopticon was for Foucault) a fertile locale where the everyday economic attitudes and consumer conduct typical of market-socialism are rendered most transparently. Once we understand the way the Venetian operates as a market device for Chinese tourists, we may grasp the tacit logic of the market-socialist economy that citizens encounter in everyday life. The Venetian makes visible a unique process of consumer subjectivation with Chinese characteristics that is repeated ad infinitum in numerous sites across the country.

THE FINAL FRONTIER: MACAU AND GLOBAL CAPITALISM

China's urban revolution is the catalyst for Macau's remarkable post-colonial metamorphosis. However, the roots of Macau's recent economic miracle actually reach back far before the 1999 handover, to the city's half millennium of history as a gateway between China and the West. Macau's formative role in the birth of capitalism has enabled its resurgence today in China's capitalist reforms. I therefore finally turn to Macau's geohistorical role in global capitalism and the ways this role informs the city's propitious position today on capitalism's final frontier in the PRC. I situate my analysis of Macau within the complementary accounts of the origins and expansion of capitalism offered by French historian Fernand Braudel and Italian sociologist Giovanni Arrighi.[29]

Braudel's (1979) three-volume study, *Civilization and Capitalism, 15th–18th Century,* may be the most substantial account ever produced of the growth of the global economy. Distinguishing specifically capitalist enterprise from other more ordinary forms of market activity, Braudel defines capitalism as an economic system in which entrepreneurs exploit opportunities for enormous profits by linking local markets, often separated by vast distances of time and space, into a type of long-distance trade network that he calls a world-economy. Braudel locates the roots of this capitalist activity in the thirteenth-century Italian city-state of Venice. As I will explain in chapters 1 and 2, the Venetians mobilized both superior maritime technologies and innovative financial practices to profit from trade opportunities around the Mediterranean Sea, and highly skilled Portuguese and Spanish navigators subsequently expanded that trade beyond the region. When those Portuguese explorers founded Macau in 1557, they created the first capitalist world-economy; the role of Venice and the other Italian city-states in this economic system was eventually displaced by a series of other, successively larger locales.

Braudel's definition of capitalism as a type of exchange rather than a mode of production usefully distinguishes his account from that of Max

Weber, who famously identifies the sober Protestant ethic as the over-arching spirit and underlying logic of capitalism's advance. For Weber, it is the individual believer's effort to embrace the Calvinist paradox of predestination by demonstrating his chosen status through the success of his worldly vocation, that enables the explosion of nineteenth-century industry in Britain and the United States. However, Braudel (1979) is insistent on the foundational role played by "Catholic Europe" in the very birth of capitalism: "It was the Portuguese who were the first to reach the East Indies, China, and Japan: these spectacular achievements must be credited to 'lazy' Southern Europe. Nor did the North invent any of the instruments of capitalism: these all came from the South. Even the Bank of Amsterdam was modeled on the Venetian Bank of Rialto. And it was by competing with the state monopolies of the southern countries—Spain and Portugal—that the great merchant companies of the North were formed" (2:569). Braudel's focus on Portuguese maritime trade points to Macau's significance to this story. In addition, however, Braudel argues that every world-economy is anchored by a core city, which manages the essential market activities. His focus on the original centrality of Venice to capitalism's expansion, as well as the successive roles of Genoa, Antwerp, Amsterdam, London, and New York, provides a useful model for my own focus in chapter 3 on not just the city-state of Macau but also the entire GBA megacity region in China's capitalist reformation.

Braudel's pioneering narrative of capitalism inspired the complementary scholarship of Arrighi, who worked for two decades in the Fernand Braudel Center at the State University of New York at Binghamton.[30] In *The Long Twentieth Century,* Arrighi ([1994] 2010) reads Braudel's narrative as a four-act story that has unfolded across the temporal arc of four "long centuries" of development: from the Italian city-states in the fifteenth century, to Holland in the seventeenth century, on to England in the eighteenth century, and finally to the twentieth-century United States. I will explore Arrighi's argument in chapter 6. For the moment, I want to call attention to his insightful observation that successive eras of capitalist growth progress via "an evolutionary pattern towards regimes of increasing size, scope, and complexity" (Arrighi 2004, 532). Arrighi describes how the relative size of the geographical "container" of each capitalist hegemon has steadily increased, from the city-states of Italy, to the united provinces of Holland ("which was more than a city-state but less than a nation state"), to the small island nation of Britain, and finally to the continental United States.

Las Vegas and the Western Frontier

Las Vegas is a product of both the so-called long century of economic growth in the United States and the prodigious size of this continental container of capitalism. Las Vegas was founded in 1904; the city's development mirrored the twentieth-century expansion of the American economy as settlers colonized the western frontier of North America and gradually expanded the country's economic power across the planet.[31] For historian Frederick Jackson Turner (1893) and his famous frontier thesis, the seemingly endless North American frontier enabled not only America's economic growth but also its individualist cultural ethos, Jacksonian democratic sensibilities, and pragmatic state of mind. Freewheeling Las Vegas exemplifies these ideals. In its early years, the gaming industry mobilized this frontier myth to market the city's cowboy iconography and western-themed casino resort attractions to American tourists. This western frontier was crucial to both America's long century of dominance and the economic success of the country's suburban lifestyle.

However, by the end of the twentieth century, the American frontier was exhausted. Indeed, urbanist Mike Davis (1998) precisely dates the denouement of the frontier myth with the 1993 implosion of the Dunes Hotel on the Las Vegas Strip, to clear the way for casino mogul Steve Wynn to build his eponymous resort on the site. As Davis says:

> By obscure coincidence, the demolition of the Dunes followed
> close on the centenary of Frederick Jackson Turner's legendary
> "end of the frontier" address to the World's Columbian Exposition
> in Chicago, where the young prairie historian meditated famously
> on the fate of the American character in a conquered and rap-
> idly urbanizing West. Turner questioned the survival of frontier
> democracy in the emergent epoch of giant cities and trusts . . .
> and wondered what the West would be like a century hence. Steve
> Wynn and the other robber barons of the Strip think they have

> the answer: Las Vegas is the terminus of western history, the end
> of the trail. (54)

The closing of the American frontier poses a problem for the logic of accumulation. With no more larger geographical containers in which capital might develop, Arrighi suggests that the expansion of capitalism today relies predominantly on China and India, which are not larger than the United States in terms of geography but whose populations are four or five times bigger.[32] This population density is the key to growth. After several centuries of relative obscurity, Macau has suddenly emerged once again as a crucial conduit for western capital to reach China's massive population.

If Wynn's implosion of the Dunes Hotel was for Davis (1998) the final act of America's frontier myth, then the more recent construction of Macau's Wynn, Wynn Encore, and Wynn Palace resorts are indicative of capital's encroachment on a new frontier in the PRC. This new frontier of accumulation, located in the density of China's population, is twofold. First, it reaches into the rapid expansion of China's urban fabric as the rural countryside of the PRC transforms into a highly urbanized environment. Second, it stretches deep inside the very subjectivity of the Chinese people as once socialist citizens are aggressively reengineered, by both the Chinese state and transnational capital, into the largest population of consumers in global history. Therefore, understanding Macau's spectacular reemergence on the global stage requires an understanding of the unique design of the GBA megacity, a massive urban environment that Braudel might call the core city of Chinese capitalism. The tiny city-state of Macau is the spatiotemporal nexus where those two frontiers of urbanization and subjectivation converge.

Along with capital's penetration into China's urban spaces and its ontological insinuation into the country's urbane citizens, we can observe a concomitant resurgence of the medieval city-state of Macau as a locus of enterprise (Henders 2001). Arrighi (2004) contends that the "steady increase in geographical size and functional scope of successive regimes of capital accumulation on a world scale" is actually a "double movement, forward and backward at the same time" (534). He notes that each new dominant capitalist regime—that of Holland, then

Britain, the United States, and now China—has revived specific governmental and business structures and strategies from previous eras. This observation helps explain why China's market reforms were introduced not in Beijing or Shanghai but in the Shenzhen SEZ, which has since grown into something like a semiautonomous Chinese city-state (Chen 2017). It also suggests why the central government located other experimental zones, such as Xiamen and Shantou (formerly known as Amoy and Swatow), on the sites of former nineteenth-century British treaty ports. Most importantly, however, it elucidates Macau's unlikely twenty-first-century renaissance after several dormant centuries. In short, China's economic reforms borrow from the lessons of the past and involve this sort of "double movement," both forward and backward. Macau's role in this double movement emanates from its strategic position on the perimeter of the vast urban frontier that drives China's economic development.

China's New Urban Frontier

The year 2006 marked the first time in history that the majority of the world's population lived in cities, and China surpassed its own majority urban population mark in 2011, upending the predominantly rural society that had persisted in the country for several thousand years. "Planetary urbanization" is the "final frontier" of global capitalism (Merrifield 2012, 912). The emergence of an urban planet exemplifies philosopher Henri Lefebvre's famous assertion that capitalism's very survival depends on urbanization and the relentless production of space (Harvey 2008; Lefebvre 1976, 1992, 2003).[33] Today, billions of dollars are invested in not only Macau's casino resorts but also in the infrastructure necessary to support their operations. To enable the construction of the Venetian, for example, the Macau government first had to produce the space on which it sits by undertaking a massive project of land reclamation to create the solid earth of Cotai in the watery estuary between the Macau peninsula and Taipa Island. "Thank you for the land, but I can't find it," Adelson reportedly remarked after first viewing Cotai (Cohen 2021). In turn, Adelson had to transform this reclaimed marshland into actual terra firma substantial enough to support his massive megaresorts.

Therefore, when we view Macau within both the history of global capitalism and the political economy of planetary urbanization, we may better appreciate the city's exceptionalism and the unique function of its new casino megaresorts. It is this geohistorical and geopolitical specificity of Macau's resorts that is my interest in this book. If for Schwartz (2003) "there are few institutions more candidly reflective of American society than the casino resort" in Las Vegas (4), I will explore the manner in which Macau's resorts are reflective of China's contemporary socioeconomic transformation.

To conclude this discussion of the factors that distinguish Macau from Las Vegas, I turn finally to Patricia Ventura's (2012) insightful analysis of the Las Vegas Strip. With reference to Turner's famous frontier thesis, Ventura reads the resort architecture of Las Vegas as exemplary of both the end of the capitalist frontier and the compensatory logic of American neoliberalism in the face of its demise. Ventura argues that the themed resorts that Adelson and Wynn constructed on the Las Vegas Strip, such as the Venetian, Palazzo, Encore, the Mirage, and Bellagio, each reflect the country's neoliberal regime. Much like Davis before her, Ventura argues that the Las Vegas Strip today represents the end of the line for global capitalism: "Capitalism stretched its arms into all parts of the world, and its space for expansion had all but ended. It is the closing of the global frontier that characterizes neoliberal globalization. Without irony, the Strip celebrates capitalism's global saturation by decontextualizing and dehistoricizing the world's historical landmarks for entertainment purposes. Indeed, it offers the verisimilitude of these monuments as compensation for the contemporary loss of historicity" (60). This is an insightful reading of the themed casino resorts of Las Vegas in the context of the economy of the United States, but I take the opposite approach in my own historicized analysis of Adelson's Venetian Resort in Macau. If the built environment of Las Vegas is a material metaphor of American neoliberalism, then Macau's Venetian Resort functions as a spatial machine of postsocialist subjection. While Macau's resorts are only a small component of the PRC's prodigious program of market pedagogy, the city's exceptional elements exhibit the underlying logic of market-socialism most clearly. Therefore, my study of the Venetian Resort apparatus, as well as Macau's myriad casinos, VIP rooms, retail outlets, pawnshops, baccarat tables, and gaming machines, is simultaneously an enquiry into the logic of China's reform-era economy and a genealogy of the postsocialist Chinese subject.

THE STRUCTURE OF THE BOOK

While Las Vegas is clearly an important influence on the city, Macau's contemporary casino boom has a complex lineage that I trace in the first part of this book. But before I do, let me provide an overview of the book's structure. The book has three parts, which correspond to the three topics I previewed in this chapter. Each part analyzes, respectively, Macau's historical role in *global capitalism* as a gateway between China and the West; Macau's pedagogical regime of *casino capitalism* and the city's operation as an experimental laboratory of consumption; and Macau's unique function in *Chinese capitalism* and the engineering of post-Mao subjects for the reform-era economy.

Each part also explores the design of a specific apparatus, which I analyze at descending scales. Part I focuses on the GBA megacity apparatus and its sui generis zone appendages, such as Shenzhen, Hong Kong, and Macau. The GBA is the planet's largest and most populated urban space; this megacity engenders new types of Chinese workers and shoppers who constitute the majority of Macau's tourist visitors.

Part II focuses on the integrated resort apparatus and its component parts, such as the casino, the retail shopping arcade, and the private VIP rooms that cater exclusively to high rollers. The integrated resort functions in reform-era China in a manner homologous to the work unit in socialist China. However, where the work unit produced a collectivist worker for the socialist economy, the integrated resort produces an individualist consumer for the market-socialist regime. These local functions of the resort apparatus are especially evident in the design and operation of what I call the Venetian Palace: an enormous set of four interconnected megaresorts on Macau's Cotai Strip that together form what is perhaps the world's largest enclosure.

Part III focuses on an individual gaming apparatus, an innovative electronic baccarat machine created by a Hong Kong biopharmaceutical company and designed to appeal to Chinese gamblers in Macau. I detail the ways in which this gaming device enables forms of financial calculation that transform the simple game of baccarat into a complex form of capitalist enterprise, turning the individual gambler into what Foucault (2004) might call an "entrepreneur of himself"—a postsocialist subject for China's reform era.

In the final chapter, I return to Dostoyevsky's critique of the Crystal Palace with which I began this introduction, as well as his own addiction to gambling, to reflect on the complementary function of the megacity, the integrated resort, and the baccarat machine in post-Mao China. Here we may finally understand the significance of the Venetian as Sloterdijk's "world interior of capital" and appreciate Macau's pivotal role on the planet's final frontier of consumer capitalism. Five hundred years after Portuguese explorers founded Macau as a crucial port of trade in the first capitalist world-economy, the city has emerged once again in a new world-economy anchored by the PRC. China's economic reforms are a primary catalyst of shifting regimes of global capitalism—a process that Macau illuminates more clearly than any other example. That is, with a microlocal focus on Macau's Venetian Resort, we may comprehend the national, regional, and global scales of this world-historic economic transformation.

Macau Milieux

The Golden Globe

In July 2017, an anonymous tourist from mainland China lost US$75 million playing high-stakes baccarat in an ill-fated gambling binge at Sheldon Adelson's Venetian Macao resort (Lee 2017). Encompassed within that simple card game and its outsize stakes, which brought together a hapless Chinese high roller and one of the world's wealthiest men in a petite principality positioned on the furthest edge of Portugal's erstwhile global empire, is both a remarkable story about the history of capitalism and an allegory concerning the ontology of capital itself. This tale begins with capitalism's birth in the mercantile trade of medieval Venice and culminates in its improbable contemporary renaissance today in post-Mao China.

The $75 million gambling windfall actually set a house record for the Venetian. Appreciative staff asked the departing visitor if there was anything they could do to help assuage the loss, or to simply thank him for his considerable contribution to the company's bottom line. Apparently impressed with the building's baroque theme, the gambler requested a curious memento of his experience: a personal replica of the two-meter-tall golden armillary sphere that sits prominently in the property's main entrance, and which has served since its opening as a picture-perfect backdrop for countless tourist photographs. The company graciously produced a replica of the sphere at a cost of $62,500 (MOP 500,000).

That garish gilded globe is more than a mere keepsake of the gambler's $75 million Macau misadventure. The armillary sphere was a protonavigational device that facilitated Portugal's founding of Macau during the Age of Discovery, and the Venetian globe is therefore a useful point of orientation from which to reflect on the city's foundational role in the emergence of the global capitalist system.

The Venetian's imposing reception hall, with its faux ceiling frescoes, armillary sphere centerpiece, and reflective checkerboard marble floor, is actually not a reproduction of a site in Venice

Figure 7. The golden globe in the lobby of the Venetian Macao resort. *Photograph by Adam Lampton.*

Figure 8. The Venetian globe is a copy of the armillary sphere that Antonio Santucci constructed in 1582 for Spanish king Philip II, which is displayed in the Royal Monastery of San Lorenzo de El Escorial, outside Madrid. *Photograph by Jose Luis Filpo Cabana, and licensed under Creative Commons attribution 3.0.*

but of the royal library in San Lorenzo de El Escorial, outside the Spanish city of Madrid. The library is part of the sixteenth-century palace and monastery complex that served as the residence of Spanish monarch Phillip II, known as the Catholic King, whose forty-year reign at the helm of the house of Habsburg commanded much of Europe and the world.

An armillary sphere is a model of the earth encircled by concentric rings, or armillaries, that represent the planet's celestial environment; it depicts features of planetary orientation such as the ecliptic, meridian, and equator. The specific sphere on which the Venetian version is loosely based was constructed in 1582 in Naples by mathematician and cosmographer Antonio Santucci delle Pomerance. He presented it to Cardinal Ferdinand de Medici, who delivered it to Phillip II in Madrid, where the king kept it in El Escorial together with other gifts he received from around the world (Righini-Bonelli 1967).

Santucci's Ptolemaic sphere was essentially an early mechanical GPS device. The intricate three-dimensional model comprises eighty-two elliptical ligatures that create intersecting points of orientation, such as celestial latitude and longitude, which may be used to precisely map locations on the planet's surface. With a painting of the Almighty at the globe's zenith and a cross affixed to the top of the structure, Santucci's sphere manifests the convergence of Renaissance science and Catholic faith that enabled Iberian seafarers to venture into the vast Atlantic Ocean, to eventually circle the entire earth, and to ultimately create Europe's first global empire.

As an early maritime gateway between Europe and China, Macau was pivotal to that process. In order to understand Macau's new gateway function today, it is necessary once again to locate the precise geohistorical coordinates of the city, much as "Prudent" King Phillip may have done in those reflective moments in the royal library when he contemplated his expansive global empire on the elliptical surface of Santucci's sphere. Such an effort at global positioning is my goal in part one of this book. However, my aim is not a conventional history of Macau. I pursue instead a history of the present, which begins by looking backward from the vantage point of the Venetian Resort to unearth the "complex

course of descent" by which this massive structure has materialized in Macau's metropolitan milieu (Foucault 1977b, 81). So I turn
now to the elective affinities among the medieval genesis of capital
in the city-state of Venice and the enigmatic economic alchemy
of baccarat games in Adelson's Venice-themed Macau casino
megaresort.

1

Venice and the Venetian

A HISTORY OF THE PRESENT

> It might be fun to try to write the history of capitalism within the parameters of a special version of games theory.
>
> —Fernand Braudel, *The Wheels of Commerce*

When it opened, Macau's Venetian Resort was the world's sixth largest building, although mere cerebral recognition of this superlative designation does not adequately evoke the actual experience of traversing the massive edifice. With a total interior area of 980,000 square meters (10,500,000 square feet), the Venetian is nearly twice as big as the Pentagon, and perhaps the largest themed structure on the planet. Much like the island city of Macau itself, surrounded by the South China Sea and attached to the Chinese mainland by a narrow isthmus, the Venetian Resort is a completely self-contained environment. Operating as a sort of semiautonomous city within a city, the Venetian employs nearly 10,000 people and accommodates within its walls a remarkable collection of facilities: 3,000 hotel rooms, 350 retail shops, 100,000 square meters of convention space, a 15,000-seat auditorium, an indoor canal network, and, at the time of its opening, the world's largest casino. It also features restaurants, a clinic, spa, gymnasium, swimming pools, children's playground, private bus fleet, and educational and training facility operated in cooperation with a local university.

Adelson's Venetian property is located on Macau's Cotai Strip, a gambling and shopping enclave made up of a dozen multibillion-dollar megaresorts (plus a private university campus and the Macau garrison of the People's Liberation Army, or PLA). The Cotai Strip sits on the 5.2 square kilometer land reclamation site in what was originally the Seac

Pai Bay of the Pearl River Estuary, which now conjoins the formerly separate islands of Taipa and Coloane. The first time Adelson visited Macau to prepare his bid for a casino concession, the uninhabited Cotai landfill was not even terra firma but rather a remote grassy marshland located near the city's small international airport. At the time, Cotai (whose name was formed, in what might be construed as a gesture to the landfill itself, by combining the first letters of *Coloane* and *Taipa*) was merely the latest of a long series of land reclamation projects undertaken in Macau over the previous several hundred years. The various landfill projects eventually transformed a diminutive appendage of land and archipelago of small islands and rocky outcroppings into a physically contiguous locale. Indeed, more than half of Macau's territory today is composed of such artificial reclaimed land, and the city's total landmass continues to grow apace.

The name Cotai Strip was both coined and trademarked by Adelson, a reference to the more famous Las Vegas Strip, whose outsize neon skyline he envisioned could be recreated on this contrived tabula rasa tract. As a result of the dubious compositional integrity of the landmass at the time of its construction, the Venetian Resort rests atop 1,530 precast concrete pilings driven deep into the landfill in order to provide a foundation substantial enough to support the massive building (Chun Wu Ho Development Holdings Limited, n.d.). The Venetian is the anchor of Adelson's multiresort Cotai complex. This complex includes another of the world's largest buildings, the $4.4 billion Cotai Central resort (which was transformed in 2021 into a London theme at an additional cost of more than $2 billion); the $2.7 billion Parisian Macau property, featuring a half-scale replica of the Eiffel Tower; and the five-star Four Seasons resort. With his $15 billion stake in Macau, which also includes the Sands Macau property located on a different reclaimed landfill in the outer harbor of the Macau peninsula, Adelson is China's largest individual foreign investor (Blaschke 2021b).

The buildings in this resort complex, which are each connected by elevated, enclosed, and air-conditioned pedestrian walkways, collectively comprise what is perhaps the world's largest continuous interior space. This colossal enclosure contains nearly 13,000 hotel rooms and 770 retail shops.[1] The massive footprint of this edifice is all the more remarkable given the fact that Macau is one of the world's smallest territories, with merely 32.9 square kilometers of land (and actually only

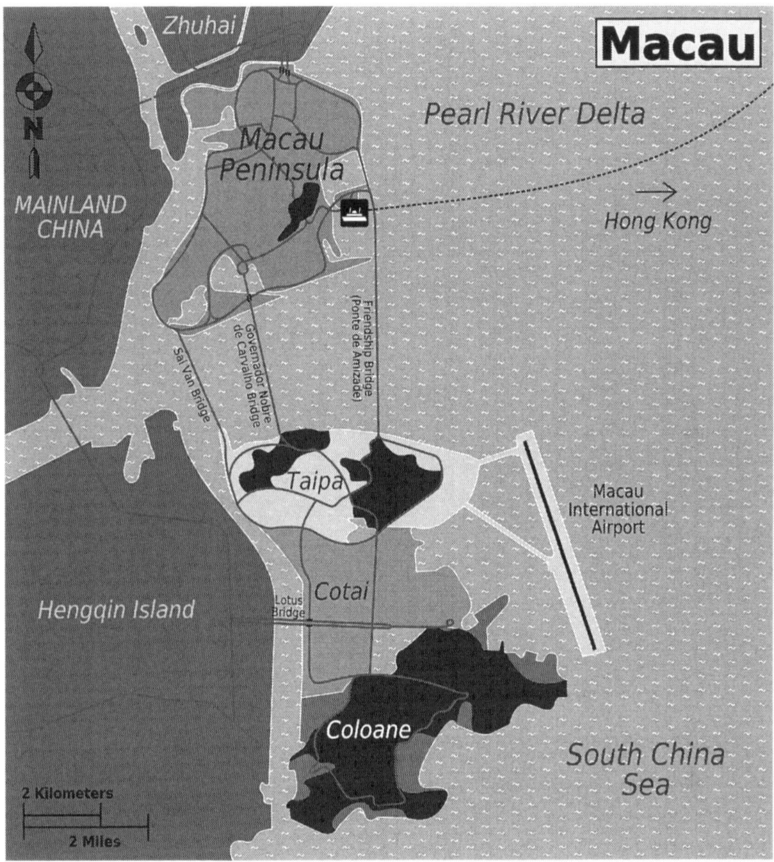

Figure 9. Macau is a tiny territory positioned south of the Chinese city of Zhuhai and east of Zhuhai's Hengqin Island. Macau was formerly composed of a peninsula and two small islands, which have been conjoined by a gradual succession of land reclamation projects. Today, more than half of Macau, including the entire Cotai area, is made up of artificial land. The airport runway to the right of Cotai provides perspective on the city's relatively small size. *Map created by No mas btz, and licensed under Creative Commons 4.0.*

26 square kilometers when the Venetian opened). With a population of approximately 680,000 residents, including 180,000 foreign workers, it is by some measures the world's most densely populated locale, with (as of 2019) 20,400 people per square kilometer (*Macau Daily Times* 2020).

Much like London's Crystal Palace before it, the Venetian Resort is

Figure 10. The Cotai land reclamation site and construction of the Cotai Strip resorts, circa 2006. *Photograph by Adam Lampton.*

a veritable "world interior," comprising both an ingenious feat of architectural engineering and an encapsulated city that offers within its walls every imaginable form of consumer entertainment. However, although the Venetian is a contemporary iteration of its Crystal Palace predecessor, the Venetian's roots reach back far beyond that nineteenth-century structure to the very origins of capitalism in the Mediterranean city-state of Venice. The intriguing historical affinities among Venice and the Venetian Resort, as well as their relevance for understanding Macau's contemporary casino economy, are the focus of this chapter.

VENETIAN FORM VERSUS TOURIST FUNCTION

Constructed as it is by a foreign billionaire on a fabricated landfill, and with an emphatically plagiaristic design, it is almost too easy to describe the Venetian by referencing postmodern semiotic argot inspired by the likes of Roland Barthes, Umberto Eco, and Jean Baudrillard—argot characteristic of the learned accounts of similar leisure theme parks, from Las Vegas to Disneyworld.[2] From this postmodern perspective, the Venetian appears as an ungrounded "free floating signifier," hyperreal "absolute fake," or self-referential simulacrum representative of an era of "late capitalism" in which the logic of simulation has displaced reality itself. The massive size of the Venetian doubtlessly reminds one of Baudrillard's (1994) ruminations on what he called the "most beautiful allegory" (1) of simulation: the Borges fable concerning the cartographers of some forgotten civilization, whose single-minded pursuit of scientific rigor leads them to create a full-scale map of the empire—one identical in size and detail to the territory itself.

It is therefore not surprising that in an early commentary on Macau's posthandover skyline, one Chinese scholar describes the Venetian as a "typical example of a post-modern product in an age of simulation, dramatizing not only a narcissistic display of architectural differences, but also a cultural embrace of imitation, illusion, and invented worlds" (Mao 2006, 69–70). This illusory "cultural embrace" of the absolute fake is seemingly epitomized in the complete "precession of simulacra" achieved by the Chinese tourist I mentioned earlier, who visited Adelson's ersatz Venice in 2017, only to depart $75 million poorer and toting a gaudy reproduction of a counterfeit golden European globe.

However, while this sort of semiotic analytic may illuminate the aesthetics of the themed Venetian form, it tells us nothing about the pragmatic function of the resort for the tens of millions of Chinese tourists who visit each year to gamble, shop, or simply gawk at the spectacle. The Venetian's significance is grounded in the physical materiality of its immense structure rather than in its ephemeral free-floating semiotic excess. Therefore, the postmodern linguistic turn is of negligible use for our purposes. Understanding the Venetian's function in Macau today requires a premodern orientation as well as a geological approach, or material semiotics, that takes the medieval Italian city-state of Venice not as an empty referent for the Venetian's simulated theme but as an instructive historical reference for Macau's role today in China's revolutionary capitalist transition.[3]

Macau was founded in 1557 as a node of exchange in a trade network that was dominated by the Italian city-states of Venice, Genoa, and Florence. As a European trading post established to serve those city-states, located on the distant edge of the Ming emperor's isolationist Middle Kingdom, Macau was the cradle of China's initial encounter with capitalism. Nearly five centuries later, the city's casino resorts serve as an unlikely midwife to the Communist Party's apostate post-Mao economic reforms. However, Venice was the birthplace of capitalism, so it is in Venice that the Venetian Resort's story begins.

We will see that both Venice and Macau share some cosmetic features. These similarities include their archipelagic geography; a reliance on land reclamation projects to compensate for their meager proportions; the development in each city of celebrated casino gambling industries; and the eventual diversification of each city into the business of tourism after its initial trade dominance declined. More importantly, however, the specific forms of business enterprise that emerged in both Venice and Macau prompted the creation in each city of innovative financial instruments—what might be called market devices—such as double-entry bookkeeping ledgers and integrated casino resorts, which have engendered new types of economic agents and engineered novel forms of capitalist enterprise.

In this chapter, I explore the transhistorical articulations among these innovative market devices in Venice and Macau, and their formative role in unique practices of capitalist subjection. Gambling and tourism each serve important functions in this process. Market devices created in both Venice and Macau have played an instrumental role in the creation and evolution of capitalism. Therefore, in what follows, I will recount the birth of capitalism in Venice and the subsequent founding of Macau to serve an emergent European economy that eventually encompassed the entire planet. This will allow me to demonstrate the Venetian Resort's function today in the expansion of consumer capitalism onto its final frontier in post-Mao China. As a coastal city-state with a peculiar legal status and hybrid Eurasian identity, Macau is, much like Mediterranean Venice before it, perfectly positioned today to connect transnational capital with China's vast consumer population.

THE BIRTH OF CAPITALISM IN VENICE

According to Braudel, capitalism first emerged during the thirteenth century in the trading principalities of Northern Italy. As a prominent site of such trade, and despite its unlikely origins and diminutive size, the city-state of Venice was for Braudel the birthplace of capitalist enterprise.[4] Both Braudel's conception of capitalism itself and his account of Venice's role in creating the global economic system provide a useful context for understanding my own approach to Macau in this book.[5]

The city of Venice, founded in AD 400 in a shallow backwater, was constructed across an archipelago of 120 small islands. Much as the Venetian Resort sits on Macau's artificial Cotai landfill, Venice was fabricated on top of an artificial foundation fashioned by driving thousands of wooden stakes into the shallow water. In a fascinating feat of ecological engineering, the stakes were eventually petrified by the salt water and deoxygenated subaqueous environment. The Byzantine Empire granted Venice full independence in 992 in exchange for the city's military support in defeating Charlemagne (Nisen 2012). As a sovereign power, the most serene republic of Venice would become "the world's longest-enduring independent jurisdiction" (Shell 2014, 61).

Positioned in the *lacuna,* or lagoon, at the mouth of the Po and Piave Rivers, and located more or less midway between Northern Europe and Byzantium, Venice was ideally placed to mediate trade between the eastern and western worlds. Vast Venetian fortunes were amassed via the city's domination of the Mediterranean seaborne trade that linked European capitals with Constantinople and the Levant. "Venice developed a commercial empire from nothing by creating land where there had been none," observes literary critic Marc Shell (2014), "and wealth of which no one had ever dreamed"—that is, wealth derived primarily from the extension of credit rather than the production of craft. "Out of the *lacuna* of real estate and unreal money, they made a new republican commercial dominion. Out of nothing comes something," explains Shell (61), in words that could also describe the artificial land base and baccarat tables of Macau's Venetian Resort. This financial exchange in Venice would engender a new type of economic activity that would eventually reach China in 1557 via the Portuguese trading post of Macau.

For Braudel, capitalism involves a distinct mode of economic exchange, which differentiates this capitalist trade from the general economic activity that long predated the emergence of the capitalist system. Braudel's focus on this mode of exchange as a defining characteristic of capitalism is distinct from Marx's focus on the mode of production (such as industrialism). Braudel also argues that innovative forms of financial exchange (which I will describe later) were the key feature of the early form of capitalism that emerged in Venice.[6]

For Braudel, this novel capitalist exchange is merely one component of economic life, and he therefore describes the global economy as a three-tiered hierarchical system. At the base of this economic system is what he calls material life, or the quotidian, self-sufficient economic activity that lies outside the realm of organized exchange. In seeking such material sustenance, individuals may encounter the market economy, the second tier of the system, in its most basic form at a variety of points of contact, such as small stalls and shops, itinerant fairs, and (of course) local markets, which facilitate the basic economic activity necessary for the reproduction of daily life. But the exchange that occurs in these small-scale economic networks, and which is fundamental to the market economy, is primarily aimed at simply making a living rather than accumulating wealth.

The *capitalist* economic system that emerged in Venice constitutes the third tier of this hierarchical economic system. Capitalism involves a unique mode of economic activity beyond base material sustenance, which not only engages with market exchange at a local level but also exploits opportunities for extraordinary profits that may be generated by linking those local markets into a larger world-economy. The development of capitalism in Venice and elsewhere "rests upon a dialectic between a market economy developing almost unaided and spontaneously, and an over-arching [capitalist] economy which seizes these humble activities from above, redirects them and holds them at its mercy," says Braudel (1979, 3:38). The merchants of medieval Venice excelled at this novel overarching mode of capitalist activity.

In this profit-driven economic activity, profit itself eventually emerged as an autonomous category of exchange that could be abstracted from trade and subjected to a variety of legal, financial, and technological innovations, the design and implementation of which aimed to increase exchange value and maximize remuneration. It is this sort of flexible, large-scale exchange activity whose overt goal is accumulation, in and of itself, which rises above normal trade, and which may be properly understood as capitalism. For Braudel (1979), then, capitalism involves a fundamental departure from ordinary trade; it comprises a "superior, sophisticated economy" involving new types of economic agents, new financial activities, and novel business mentalities (2:22). That is, capitalist agents innovate financial strategies, create world-economies, and derive vast profits; these activities ultimately engender more capitalists, who endeavor to expand this system.

Trade in the Middle Ages offered more profitable business opportunities than agriculture or petty manufacturing, and Venice initially lacked the landed resources necessary for agriculture anyway. Therefore, Venetian entrepreneurs mobilized the city's fortunate maritime geography and the formidable naval prowess of the city's famed Arsenal to dominate seaborne trade among markets scattered around the Adriatic and Mediterranean Seas. It was through this mercantile trade that capitalism as an economic system was born. Efforts to expand this trade around the globe prompted Portugal's founding of Macau in 1557. Therefore, Macau emerged in the sixteenth century as an important trading post in a European world-economy that originated in Venice— and that eventually encompassed the entire planet.

Braudel (1979) contends that the maintenance and growth of capitalist activity depends on the formation of such a world-economy, which he distinguishes from the more general global economic system. The global economy is simply the sum total of all economic activity on the planet. However, a world-economy is a subset of this global activity that "only concerns a fragment of the world, an economically autonomous section of the planet able to provide for most of its own needs, a section to which its internal links and exchanges give a certain organic unity" (3:22). More than one such world-economy may exist at any particular historical moment, but each is defined by a dominant city that organizes and profits from economic activity. "A world-economy always has an urban centre of gravity, a city, as the logistic heart of its activity," Braudel says. "News, merchandise, capital, credit, people, instructions, correspondence all flow into and out of the city" (3:27). This core city is the anchor of capitalist enterprise, both managing its central operations and accumulating the vast wealth that it generates.

During the height of an empire whose dominance stretched from approximately 1380 to 1500, Venice was the core city in the first capitalist world-economy. When Venice eventually declined in global significance, other cities emerged to replace it, and "hegemony then passed successively to Antwerp (1500–1560), Genoa (1560–1600), Amsterdam (1600–1800), London (1800–1929), and finally to New York" (Howard 1985, 471).[7] Braudel's analysis ends with the global economic dominance of the United States in the twentieth century. However, with China's recent emergence as a manufacturing powerhouse and the second-largest economy on the planet, it is possible (if Braudel's account is accurate) that a Chinese city may eventually command a new dominant East Asian world-economy. I will explore this idea in chapter 3 in a discussion of China's GBA metropolis (which is a sprawling megacity that encompasses Macau) and its central role in a Sinocentric global economic system.

Finance and Gambling in Venice

Seeking to account for the causes of capitalism's emergence, Braudel (1979) observes that "a major element in capitalist development was risk-taking and speculation" (2:578). In fact, risk and speculation are the defining characteristics of not only capitalism but also gambling; it is therefore not surprising that each of these complementary activities emerged in Venice. That is, Venice was the birthplace of both capitalist exchange and the Ridotto, Europe's first state-sanctioned casino, which opened in 1638 in the city's San Moise Palace. Entrepreneurs, tourists, and aristocrats alike could mingle at the Ridotto's gaming tables in a leisure activity that was a sort of playful financial counterpart to commerce and that involved a new repertoire of games that were based on the economic logic of capitalist speculation. With the mathematical odds of these gambling games organized according to calculations of risk and return, the potential monetary windfall that could be derived from this new form of entertainment also illustrated the paradox evident in Venetian finance itself: "out of nothing comes something."

"The opening of the Ridotto presented a historic union between mercantile gamblers, who ran games for profit, and government authorities, who sought to legitimize the gamblers for purposes of public order and revenue enhancement" (Schwartz 2013, 10). The Ridotto thus established an early model of the use of gambling revenues to support state finance, which would later influence the casino cities of Las Vegas and Macau. It is therefore possible to begin at Venice's Ridotto and draw a straight line that culminates in the billions of dollars of annual revenues produced at Macau's Venetian Resort.

Much like the games in the Ridotto, the potential profitability of Venetian maritime trade was also measured against its inherent risks and potential returns; it was largely through the realm of finance that Venice was able to elevate ordinary maritime exchange into a capitalist world-economy.[8] During the city's economic heyday, Venice relied on a variety of financial innovations to extract profits from maritime trade. Among other things, these innovations enabled merchants to raise the substantial amounts of capital necessary to fund maritime voyages. In addition, these novel financial instruments also enabled new techniques to protect against the unique risks that were endemic to such long-distance seaborne trade, in situations where securing collateral for investment loans was problematic given that "the capital literally sailed out of sight" when the voyage commenced (Puga and Trefler 2014, 12).

Maritime trade involved individual trips of months on end, during which a ship's crew might encounter not only capricious markets or inconstant goods but also unpredictable weather delays, debilitating illness, devastating shipwrecks, or pirate attacks. The legal and financial innovations that enabled the Venetians to profit from this trade have been of great interest to economic historians. Chief among these was a form of limited partnership called the *colleganza,* the precursor to the joint stock company, in which a sedentary investor and a traveling merchant collectively pool the initial capital and risk, then divide the subsequent proceeds according to a prearranged agreement. The *colleganza* was one important Venetian financial device, but the complete list of such financial innovations created in Venice by the fourteenth century is remarkable: "Limited liability business forms; thick markets for debt (especially bills of exchange); secondary markets for a wide variety of debt, equity, and mortgage instruments; bankruptcy laws that distinguished illiquidity from insolvency; double-entry accounting methods; business education (including the use of algebra for currency conversions); deposit banking; and a reliable medium of exchange (the Venetian ducat)" (Puga and Trefler 2014, 768). Perhaps the best known of these financial innovations for the layperson, and the one that will be most useful in understanding the specific role that the Venetian Resort plays today in Macau's casino market, is the practice of double-entry bookkeeping. This form of business accounting came to be known as bookkeeping *alla vinizinia,* or Venetian style. Although such bookkeeping practices actually first emerged elsewhere, double-entry bookkeeping was perfected and codified by merchants in the Italian city-states in the thirteenth or fourteenth centuries; it was popularized in a didactic treatise that Franciscan monk Luca Pacioli published in Venice in 1494. This treatise served as a sort of early accounting textbook, providing an extended set of practical examples that illustrated how businessmen could deploy the double-entry bookkeeping method to manage their financial affairs (Gleeson-White 2013).[9]

The Accounting Ledger and the Integrated Resort

As a financial device, the double-entry accounting ledger played an integral role in the development of capitalism. A brief analysis of the Venetian business ledger will enable us to better comprehend the innovative role that Macau's Venetian Resort plays today in China's own heterodox form of capitalist enterprise. Although they offer distinct arguments, Max Weber, Werner Sombart, and Joseph Schumpeter have each suggested that the device of double-entry bookkeeping served a crucial practical function in enhancing a calculative ethos and rational economic demeanor. Recording each individual financial transaction twice, once as debit and then again as credit, allowed the merchant to monitor the exact amount of capital in his accounts, to evaluate past decisions, and to plan strategically for future transactions.

In addition, however, Schumpeter implies that the accounting ledger itself proffered a sort of discursive performativity, or nonhuman agency, that facilitated capitalist enterprise. As the bookkeeper records transactions, these kinesthetic and cognitive accounting practices organically function to shape and intensify the capacity for calculation that is necessary for a capitalist mindset. As "a product of the evolution of economic rationality, the cost–profit calculus in turn reacts upon that rationality; by crystalizing and defining it numerically, it powerfully propels the logic of enterprise," Schumpeter says. That is, the tedious and meticulous practice of bookkeeping gradually refines in the bookkeeper a calculating mentality endemic to the capitalist subject. Sombart went so far as to claim that the practice of bookkeeping was inseparable from the existence of capitalism itself: "The very concept of capital is derived from this way of looking at things," he argues; "one can say that capital, as a category, did not exist before double-entry bookkeeping" (Schumpeter and Sombart quoted in Carruthers and Espeland 1991, 33).

In addition to the accounting ledger's use as a technical device for calculating capital accounts and enhancing economic rationality, the discursive materiality of such accounting books exhibited a normative rhetorical function, with important moral overtones that were crucial to the development of capitalism. The self-contained ledger, with columns of recorded transactions, depicted commerce as an activity whose inherent fairness and legitimacy was demonstrated by the observable equilibrium among debit and credit accounts.[10] This rhetorical function of the ledger implicitly defended budding Venetian capitalists from accusations by a skeptical clergy, steeped in Scholastic philosophy, that these businessmen were profiting from simple usury, or the practice of deriving interest on loans, which was forbidden by the church. The accumulation of interest, or "money born from money," seemingly usurped God's solitary responsibility for procreation. In addition, profit derived from interest enigmatically served to monetize time itself, and time was considered the sacred provenance of God, not man. Finally, much like gambling, finance paradoxically created profit without human labor; it lacked any productive contribution to social life. Each of these characteristics of capitalism provoked religious condemnation, ultimately forcing the Christian creditor contemplating his eternal salvation to face the unenviable choice between "your money or your life."[11]

In this sensitive religious context, accounting provided useful tools to mask or redefine these usurious practices.[12] The ledger's presentation of debit and credit accounts therefore did not simply benefit the businessperson. Bookkeeping was also aimed at "an audience that distrusted the merchant-banker as an offspring of the god of theft, Mercurius; a man who for generations had been rebuked both publicly from the pulpit and privately in the confessional booth, as a purveyor of unearned gain and community parasite" (Aho 1985, 42). In this way, the accounting ledger functioned as a mute secular justification of usury.

In short, without overemphasizing the importance of double-entry bookkeeping, we can at least note that the Venetian accounting ledger constituted an innovative financial device that played a small role in the development of capitalism. The ledger enabled the subjection, normalization, and justification of a calculating economic subject; it also enabled a mode of financial exchange on which the emergent capitalist regime depended. The ledger was an early example of what academics

Figure 11. The entrance to the construction site for the Studio City resort, circa 2007. The Venetian hotel building and faux St. Marks Campanile are visible in the background. *Photograph by Adam Lampton.*

today in the field called the social studies of finance call a market device, an apparatus through which individuals engage in economic activity in order to construct a specific type of capitalist market (Callon, Millo, and Muniesa 2007).

This admittedly long detour to describe the Venetian accounting ledger usefully returns us, half a millennium hence, to the contemporary function of the Venetian Resort in Macau. If we approach the Venetian from the standpoint of the social studies of finance rather than postmodern semiotics, we might conceive of the integrated resort as a similar such market device. Much like the role of the accounting ledger in the creation of capitalism in medieval Venice, this contemporary Venetian Resort device plays a complex role in Macau's gaming market and indirectly in China's reform economy.

As I will explain in chapter 5, the integrated casino resort is an architectural innovation that actually originated in Las Vegas, but it was adapted in Macau to address the specific exigencies of the local gaming market. The implementation of the integrated resort device in part resolved a specific dilemma in Macau's casino industry. At the time of the city's 1999 handover to China, Macau was plagued by the violence and social disorder of the city's casino wars, which was largely attributed to the quasi-legal loan-sharking activities and organized crime affiliations of local junket agents operating out of the VIP rooms in the Lisboa casino. The lucrative business of moneylending was a combustible locus of brutal competition in the city's casino economy, with often deadly outcomes. I will discuss this violent crime wave in detail in chapter 4, but for now, I want to suggest that the commodious design and compelling atmospherics of Macau's new international integrated resorts placed the city's casino gambling activities (including junket usury) within a modern architectural environment that manifested an overarching ambiance of safety and social order.

The integrated resort therefore provided gambling in Macau with an agreeable ambiance and connotation, much like the double-entry ledger had accomplished in the sensitive religious context of Venice. In addition, the foreign-owned casino resorts coated Macau's junket industry with a veneer of professional legitimation that allowed the junket mode of finance to continue to function unencumbered after Macau's reunification with China and to provide the majority of the city's vast casino revenues. In this way, the Venetian Resort's design involves more than mere aesthetics. The resort mimics, in a practical manner, the rhetorical function of Venice's double-entry accounting ledger, with its implicit justification of both secular business enterprise and sacrilegious usury.

However, in addition to this legitimation of gambling industry finance, I will seek to demonstrate throughout this book that Macau's integrated casino resorts provide an inadvertent yet essential function for Chinese tourists. The articulation of the design of the resorts with the state-directed mobility of those tourists, as well as the gambling and shopping activities in which they participate, function to produce and refine in those tourists both a calculating economic mentality and a neoliberal ethic of competitive self-sufficiency. Each of these is a stark departure from the collectivist assumptions of China's socialist governance. This calculating mentality and the corresponding ethic of individual responsibility are conducive to China's reform regime.

The "calculating economic mentality" to which I refer is characteristic of the emergent post-Mao economic subject that I will explore throughout this book. This novel subject takes shape in a neoliberal social context in which life is increasingly conceived as a competitive arena, and in which the individual is exhorted to turn his or her life into an entrepreneurial project designed to maximize self-interest for the benefit of China's economy. Foucault (2004) famously calls this contemporary subject an entrepreneur of the self. In the PRC, this neoliberal ethic has subsumed the social contract of state socialism, where it was the responsibility of the state to provide for the population, and the members of that population collectively shared an understanding that their role was to contribute to the common good rather than seek individual benefit. In reform-era China, however, "the adoption of such neoliberal imperatives thus penetrates to the core of what it means to be (and to behave) Chinese today" (Ong and Zhang 2008, 3).

The Venetian Resort is therefore more than a remunerative casino or enticing repository for millions of Chinese tourists, although it is certainly both of these things. The Venetian is an innovative architectural apparatus, a spatial machine that was transplanted into Macau from abroad by the new foreign casino concessionaires, then adapted and calibrated to appeal to Chinese tourists. The Macau resort materializes the complex logic of a calculating subject operating in a neoliberal socioeconomic regime. Much as Venice's Ridotto and Venetian bookkeeping practices were foundational elements of capitalist subjection, Macau's Venetian Resort engenders new economic subjects on a new frontier of global capitalism in China.

The Socialist New Man and the Postsocialist Quality Consumer

While it admittedly may seem strange to suggest that the integrated resort building is implicated in a process of tourist subjection, we must understand this function not only within Braudel's grand narrative of the historical development of capitalism but also within the more circumscribed context of Chinese socialism. When Chinese revolutionaries formed the PRC in 1949, they set out to enculturate a socialist New Man, an ascetic, self-sacrificing, collectivist worker amenable to authoritarian rule and dedicated to achieving the utopian aims of communism (Cheng 2008). These efforts of socialist subjectification emanated from Mao's belief that humans are malleable creatures that may be molded to achieve a particular outcome. They were part of an intensive pedagogical program personally directed by Mao, the national teacher. In didactic texts such as "On Practice," Mao (1937) formulated his belief that practical participation in social environments and productive activities was the only reliable mechanism for gaining and retaining useful knowledge. This belief guided the process of socialist subjectification in China.

To produce this New Man of socialism, Chinese planners drew on a variety of influences including indigenous Confucian traditions, Soviet ideology, and experimental practices of American pragmatist philosophy that Mao and his comrades learned from John Dewey's lectures in China (Wang 2008). Officials set out to mold this socialist New Man using a wide variety of initiatives, and Chinese authorities developed a number of different pedagogical strategies to shape this new socialist subject. In rectification campaigns, personal self-criticisms were invoked for the purpose of individual thought reform. With model emulation initiatives, the party promoted exemplary soldiers, workers, factories, and villages, whose moral commitment and practical contribution to state socialism provided citizens with specific behaviors appropriate for imitation (Landsberger 2001). Finally, with the design and construction of unique architectural innovations like the *danwei*, or work unit, urban Chinese citizens lived and labored together in a collective and egalitarian environment in which communist ideals were made manifest in the practical activities of daily life (Bray 2005).

The *danwei* combined the factory workplace, accommodation for workers and their families, and all of the attributes of social support and community life into a self-contained spatial machine designed to produce collectivist workers appropriate to the socialist regime (Bray 2005). The work unit ultimately inculcated a mode of everyday experience that would reproduce in those communities the tenets of Chinese communist ideology. Therefore, it is within this tradition of socialist design that I approach the postsocialist function of the Venetian Resort, as well as Macau's many other oversize casino properties.

Today, China's reform-era government similarly aims to create a distinct Chinese subject who is appropriate to the new market-socialist regime. I contend that the integrated resort is one of a number of such devices that play a functional role in this process. Reversing a Maoist pronatal emphasis on building population *quantity,* the focus of the central government today is the enhancement of individual citizen *quality* (*suzhi*). The goal is to produce a population of increasingly educated, refined, and self-enterprising citizens who are prepared to compete in a global marketplace and to contribute to the country's economic development (Sigley 2009).

Quality is a crucial word in this governance regime. In this Chinese context, *quality* delineates "the *physical and quantifiable features of the body*" itself, which is conceived as a "material substance that can be physically shaped and administered" to a desired end; it also refers to conduct that may be "measured in terms of ethical, moral, and cultural value" (Sigley 2009, 547). That is, *quality* is understood as an individual collection of physical, intellectual, and ethical characteristics, which may be molded and enhanced to conform to the goals of the state. Most importantly, however, the central government's attention to identifying individual *suzhi* characteristics aims to valorize those subjects who achieve a high level of autonomy in social life. It is this autonomous and self-reliant Chinese citizen whom the government aims to recognize and reinforce. In chapter 5, I explore the role of the Venetian Resort in comporting such quality tourists.

This mode of reform-era governance, which seeks to delineate, measure, modify, and enhance the life force or vitality of the population and to shape it to desired ends, is an example of what Foucault (2004) calls biopolitics. Biopolitics denotes the merging of a political program with the very biological essence of the population (that is, the essence which is identified by the *-zhi* in *suzhi*). It also illustrates the manner in which life's very vitality becomes an object of governmental focus under capitalism. This biopolitical aspect of Chinese governance is clearly described by Harvard University anthropologist Susan Greenhalgh, who deploys the concept in her studies of China's one-child policy (Greenhalgh 2008, 2010; Greenhalgh and Winckler 2005). Greenhalgh's (2010) account of Chinese biopolitics is instructive for my own analysis of tourists in Macau:

> I argue that since the outset of the reform period, the People's Republic has witnessed the emergence of a new mode of governing its people, one that works through modern science and technology, focuses on the biological body at aggregate and individual levels, and aims to both speed and optimize China's transformation into a global power. Population politics—a domain I call biopolitics or vital politics—has been central to the globalizing agenda of the

reform regime. By helping to transform China's rural masses into modern workers and citizens . . . and by boosting China's economic development and comprehensive national power, the biogovernance of the population has been vitally important to the rise of global China. (xi)

Greenhalgh notes that the development of this biogovernance project in China encompasses not merely technocratic central government initiatives but also a "widening range of state, quasi-state, and non-state political actors" (9). We may therefore include Adelson in this governance regime. In addition, the fact that the Venetian integrated resort is located in the Macau SAR, rather than on the mainland, is consistent with a complementary Chinese governmental strategy, which uses designated locales, such as economic zones, to experiment with new forms of governance.[13] Macau's integrated resorts thus participate today in this biogovernance of the Chinese population in a manner consistent with China's reform-era government strategies. This is what I mean when I say that the Venetian Resort plays a functional role in China's economic reforms and that it operates today on a new frontier of global capitalism in the PRC. The biopolitical significance of the Venetian Resort in the production of quality citizens is highlighted if we consider the importance of tourist mobility to China's economic reforms—a role that is clarified if we return one last time to the instructive example of Venice.

THE GRAND TOUR AND PEDAGOGICAL TRAVEL

After Venice's vast fortunes and military dominance began to decline in the sixteenth century, the city reinvented itself as a tourist attraction. Venice emerged as arguably the most prominent destination on what became known in the seventeenth and eighteenth centuries as the European grand tour. The grand tour was a sort of gap-year pedagogical endeavor for British and French youth in which extended visits to Southern European cities, which had been the veritable birthplace of western civilization, provided practical instruction in aesthetics, civility, politics, and culture. "Italy for many decades served indeed as a sort of substitute university" for European travelers. "There, green youths of good family could soak up skills in art, rhetoric, poetry, music, and general good behavior, while studying (under the eye of their tutor) the visible ruins of that classical world so beloved by their countrymen" (Davis and Marvin 2004, 31). The Venetian Resort shares this "substitute university" function with Venice.

Interestingly, London's Crystal Palace also served as a similar sort of educational environment for tourists. I began this book with an account of the Crystal Palace's role in the creation of consumer society, but it also had a complementary educational function. The original Crystal Palace structure, which was located in Hyde Park, catered primarily to aristocrats and members of the middle class, but when the building was relocated in 1854 to the London suburb of Sydenham, it was marketed mainly to working-class visitors, who were accommodated by a reduced admissions fee (Shears 2017). In addition to informing visitors about industry and manufacturing innovations, the reconstructed Crystal Palace structure had didactic design features that aimed to civilize them. Touring the Crystal Palace substituted for otherwise inaccessible international travel, "as visitors walked through architectural courts that took them on a trip around the world and through the ages" (Young 2015, 177).

For example, the various Italian, Greek, Pompeiian, Assyrian, Byzantine, Alhambra, and Egyptian exhibits featured in the building's Fine Arts Courts, as well as the paleontological models displayed on the surrounding grounds, were explicitly designed to provide a Victorian "visual education." According to a participating geologist, the intent was "teaching directly through the eyes" (Hawkins 1854, 444).[14] Organizers hoped that these exhibits would serve to silently civilize the crowds of proletarian citizens. To that end, designers drew on the scholarship of Swiss educator Johan Heinrich Pestalozzi to present a sensual pedagogy that aimed to uplift the morality of visitors. Commitment to a belief in the calming effect of the gradated polychromatic color scheme of the exhibits in the Fine Arts Courts was a key feature of the Crystal Palace civilizing program (Zafutto 2013).

Within the historical context of both Venice and the Crystal Palace, we may understand Chinese tourism to Macau and Hong Kong today as comprising a similar sort of civilizing grand tour. Alongside its economic benefits, the Chinese government sees tourism as "an inexpensive substitute for education," according to anthropologist Pal Nyiri (2009, 154). Tourism is therefore a civilizing practice that helps create

Figure 12. Postcard depicting visual education in the Crystal Palace Roman Court, Syndenham, 1854. Organizers hoped such exhibits would civilize the crowds of proletarian visitors.

the quality citizens desired by the regime. In Chinese tourism, "mobility serves a function of *embourgeoisement*" (157), which is similar to the original goals of both the European grand tour and the educational mission of the Crystal Palace. For China's central government, tourism is an arena for "learning proper forms of consumption, experiencing modern infrastructure, and learning modern forms of entrepreneurship" (Nyiri 2010, 124).

Today, the central government views the country's most prosperous cities, such as Beijing, Shanghai, and Guangzhou, as a "comprehensive university of society" *(shehui zonghe daxue)*, where millions of rural migrants may develop their *suzhi*, with the added benefit that this informal schooling poses no cost to the state (Yan 2008).[15] If China's interior cities may be mobilized as educational sites for the rural population, then cities located across the border may serve this purpose for those citizens with the wherewithal to travel outside the country. With their "approved destination status," both Macau and Hong Kong were deemed early on to be appropriate destinations for this goal. Therefore, these postcolonial cities also serve as a Chinese "comprehensive university of society."

Just as the ancient structures of Venice, such as the Piazza San Marco, Rialto Bridge, and the Doge's Palace, were fundamental components of the educational process of the grand tour, contemporary structures such as Hong Kong's luxury shopping malls and Macau's integrated casino resorts play a pedagogical role for Chinese tourists. This appeal to the educational function of the built environment is based on the assumption that learning is not merely cognitive but also corporeal; it demonstrates the ways in which, as geographer Colin McFarlane (2011) says in his book *Learning the City,* "learning emerges through practical engagement with the world" (15). In the case of Macau, the integrated resorts (much like the Italian, Assyrian, and Egyptian exhibits in the Crystal Palace) make up a "spatial grammar of urban learning" indicative of the central government's civilizing mission and urban consumption regime (1).[16]

What is important to my argument about the Venetian Resort and its role in China's promotion of urban consumption is not the structure's thematic motifs but its inherent urban quality. As I explore in chapter 5, the Venetian has a variety of urban elements, including accommodations and eateries, parks and playgrounds, medical and educational facilities, retail environments and transportation networks, and even an air-conditioned and scented microclimate, complete with atmospheric lighting and a faux cloud-flecked blue sky above the retail promenade. These features render the Venetian Resort into, if not exactly Venice, certainly something like an interiorized city with its own indigenous metropolitan features. My aim is not to make a value judgment about the integrated resort as a cultural attraction but rather to analyze the practical functions the resort serves for those tourist visitors.[17]

While the association among civilizing educational practices and Chinese tourism to the Venetian mimics the motives for the European grand tour to Venice, as well as the Crystal Palace tours taken by members of Britain's working class, the strategic use of mobility as an educational tool also has indigenous roots in Chinese socialism. Chinese tourism today mirrors the Maoist practice during the Cultural Revolution of sending young urbanites to the countryside for practical reeducation. This earlier form of state-driven socialist mobility was intended to undermine the potential opposition to Maoist policies among the urban elite by isolating individuals who posed an implicit threat and displacing them to a rural environment. Once they were safely relocated to the countryside, the practical work activities of those urban youth and their intimate association with a bucolic peasant community might forge those young citizens into socialist revolutionaries. In a similar fashion, Chinese tourism today increasingly provides urban residents of the PRC with opportunities for cross-border travel, in which modern infrastructure, material culture and attractions, and fraternization with foreigners or other Chinese tourists may function to enhance individual levels of quality so that these individuals can contribute to China's macroeconomic goals (Nyiri 2009). "Tourism is an arena in which the production of cultural discourse penetrates everyday consumption, one in which Chinese subjects self-consciously consume complex representations of culture and respond to them in quotidian activities," contends Nyiri (2006). "As such, it is a key sphere in which the reinvention of the Chinese subject takes place" (97). It is in this "reinvention" of the tourist and the cultivation of the postreform Chinese subject that both the Venetian Resort and the city-state of Macau play a functional role.

If Venice was a key site of the European grand tour, whose purpose was to instruct Northern European youth in codes of civility and practical education, then Macau's Venetian, Parisian, Wynn Palace, Studio City, Galaxy, and City of Dreams resorts are sites that take on a specific relevance in a state-driven Chinese grand tour that aims to enculturate "civilized" Chinese consumers.[18] Where the original grand tour itinerary included specific Southern European locales chosen because they imparted to participants the formative elements of European culture, today, hundreds of millions of Chinese citizens visit the southern coastal cities of Hong Kong and Macau, where European capitalism first took root in the Middle Kingdom. Indeed, in 2005, many of Macau's colonial-era buildings were provided the official international imprimatur of designation as a UNESCO World Heritage site, thus recognizing Macau as a unique locale of Sino-Lusitanic communication, collaboration, and cohabitation.

However, while the European grand tour provided Venice with an opportunity to maintain its cultural relevance by trading on the city's storied past long after its capitalist power had faded, Macau's attempt to capitalize off its own colonial cityscape and casino gaming industry as attractions for mainland tourists has permitted the city to take on a new economic relevance. The significance of Macau's new relevance for the Chinese economy mimics or even surpasses its original mercantile function.

MARKET-SOCIALISM AND CASINO CAPITALISM IN MACAU

In chapter 2, I will recount the events that precipitated the founding of Macau within premodern Mediterranean trade networks, and I will describe the city's formative role in China's initial encounter with capitalism. However, in order to situate my analysis within Braudel's account of the historical development of capitalism, I will conclude this discussion by noting that tourism as a mode of (re)education and the integrated resort as a spatial machine of subjection each exemplifies my literal approach to understanding the logic of China's market-socialist economy. I conceive of market-socialism as more than Deng Xiaoping's clever equivocation. That is, market-socialism is not simply a contradictory postcommunist catchphrase intended to legitimate China's capitalist reforms and counter domestic leftist critique by coyly labeling those market innovations as nothing more than "socialism with Chinese characteristics." Rather, market-socialism is a hybrid socioeconomic system that merges specific elements of state socialism with the capitalist market. This heterodox combination of contradictory components is especially evident in contemporary Macau, which is itself a unique combination of European and Chinese traditions.

Braudel (1979) argues that capitalism emerged from the groundwork of European feudalism and developed by taking advantage of the lower stages of the ordinary market economy and the "simplest forms of trade" that constituted the material life of the ancien régime (2:22). I similarly understand market-socialism as an emergent form of market activity that likewise depends on the lower stages (or, more accurately, the prior forms) of Chinese socialism—that is, the socialist spaces, mentalities, policies, and traditions on which it is constructed.[19] As such, market-socialism involves the literal assemblage, or piecing together of, socialist governmental innovations such as the work unit, which are latent in either China's social environment or in the collective memory of the population, and an overarching capitalist world-economy that seizes hold of these elements from above and assembles them into forms of market activity. For example, pedagogical tourism practices and the Venetian Resort device each involve a governmental innovation of Maoism (the rustication of urban youth and the subjectification of the work unit, respectively), which is combined with a market function in order to create a novel hybrid entity for China's market economy. Indeed, it is through such state-directed tourism that individual Chinese citizens encounter transnational capital in Macau's integrated resorts. We may therefore understand these casino resorts as marketplaces, within which those tourists interact with global capitalism in specific activities of gambling and shopping.

Incidentally, the Venetian Resort resembles the city of Venice in this way as well. As Braudel (1979) observes, "The economic climate of Venice was a very special one. The intense trading activity of the city was split up into a multitude of small transactions" (3:132). A similar diversity of economic transactions manifests in the extensive variety of VIP rooms, baccarat tables, and electronic gaming devices in the Venetian Resort, in which thousands of individual, adjacent, and simultaneous market transactions operate twenty-four hours a day, seven days a week. This activity makes the casino megaresort in Macau a mega-marketplace of capitalist activity.

If Venice was the birthplace of both mercantile capitalism and the commercial casino, then Macau today is a site of a literal casino capitalism where postsocialist Chinese tourists practice the specific kinesthetic behaviors and calculating mentalities appropriate to the new regime. Much as the widespread use of double-entry bookkeeping in Venice contributed to both refining a capitalist mentality and rationalizing new forms of financial exchange, the integrated resort in Macau shapes the Chinese economic subject in a manner that is palatable to antecedent socialist experience. The integrated resort adopts the form, if not the content or ideology, of the work unit (an argument I explore in chapter 5).

I therefore approach casino capitalism in a manner distinct from its typical use in popular commentary today. Casino capitalism is commonly presented as an analogy for the global proliferation of risk-intensive financial instruments, whose operations render the global economy into a sort of colossal casino, where predatory mortgages and retirement pensions are gambled away in precarious trades of derivative securities (Strange 1986). However, I conceptualize casino capitalism by collectively treating Macau's actual casinos, VIP rooms, and electronic gaming machines, as well as the integrated resort environment itself, as a site of what I call materialist pedagogy where postsocialist Chinese tourists receive didactic training in calculative and consumption activities that are crucial to market-socialism. Given that China's population of 1.4 billion citizens today comprises the largest single market in world history, refining the consumption behaviors of Chinese citizens is crucial to not only market-socialism but also the global economy.

Macau is therefore not simply a leisure locale where Chinese tourists enjoy a compensatory respite from the labor that occurs on the mainland. Rather, tourists in Macau practice "the labour of leisure" (Rojek 2009), or the valorization of otherwise idle time and activities that occur outside of the formal production process in order to engage in a specific set of market activities that enhance the levels of individual quality crucial to China's economic development.[20] The material practices of casino capitalism in Macau deploy the leisure activities of gambling and shopping for the benefit of China's market-socialist regime. As the first foreign territory established in China, Macau was the country's original exceptional enclave and capitalist marketplace. As such, I will argue in chapter 3 that Macau inspired the enclave logic of China's reform process in the country's GBA metropolitan region. Nearly five hundred years after its founding, Macau has emerged once again as a crucial site for realizing those reforms through a biopolitical process of materialist pedagogy enacted in the city's integrated casino resorts.

Macau's role in China's encounter with global capitalism today resembles its original role several centuries ago as a Portuguese port for managing Europe's trade with China. In chapter 2, I turn to the Portuguese founding of Macau in 1557 to facilitate enterprise in a Mediterranean seaborne trade network. I analyze the manner in which the new city integrated the Middle Kingdom of the isolationist Ming dynasty into an expansive European world-economy organized by long-distance mercantile trade networks enabled by the audacious navigational exploits of Portuguese explorers.

2

Terrestrial Globalization

PORTUGAL AND MACAU

> The pragmatic heart of the Modern Age was located in the new science of risk-taking. The globe is the monitor on which the field of generalized investment activities can be viewed. At the same time, it is already the gambling table at which the adventurer-investors place their bets.
>
> —Peter Sloterdijk, *In the World Interior of Capital*

Portugal's sixteenth-century navigations and discoveries inaugurated the historical era that Sloterdijk (2013) calls "terrestrial globalization," defined by the circumnavigation of the globe and the concomitant expansion of European colonialism (9). By linking Lisbon with distant locales such as Goa, Nagasaki, and Macau, Portugal's global voyages created the embryonic contours of the contemporary world system and animated the modern imaginary. For Sloterdijk, terrestrial globalization is but one phase of the more general history of spheric thought, the process through which humans came to understand the earth as a self-contained and knowable globe. Globalization itself originated with ancient philosophers who conceived of the earth as the center of a vast cosmos that could only be observed from the inside. Terrestrial globalization is the modern process by which this initial relation to the globe was inverted; the planet became knowable from the outside as "an eccentric orb whose roundness we could verify ourselves by external viewing" (6). That transformation of humankind's relation to the earth was enabled by the external perspective of the planet that was afforded by such globular devices as Santucci's armillary sphere.

In his unique philosophical account of globalization, and with the gradual enclosure of the earth within the geoeconomic environs he calls the "world interior of capital," Sloterdijk (2013) identifies two specific dates that respectively mark the origin and demise of the terrestrial era. First, on August 3, 1492, Christopher Columbus departed Spain under the auspices of Ferdinand and Isabella. Seeking a new route to the Indies but inadvertently discovering a New World, Columbus unleashed an era of tremendous global expansion that was dominated by Europe's insatiable appetite for colonial conquest.[1]

Nearly five hundred years later, on July 22, 1944, in the wake of Europe's implosion into the most devastating conflict humanity had ever endured, leaders from across the globe gathered at a conference in Bretton Woods, New Hampshire, whose goal was to buttress the faltering global economy. There they debated, drafted, and signed the document known as the Bretton Woods Agreement. With this eponymous international monetary plan, capital would finally enclose the entire earth, Old and New World alike, within an expansive economic "interior" whose apogee was the ethereal sign of the United States dollar. The dollar would serve as the gold-backed global reserve currency and stabilizing mode of exchange in the planet's postwar economic system.

We will see that Macau's own history directly parallels this process. If Portugal's eventual decolonization after the country's 1974 Carnation Revolution marked the final abdication of Europe's five-hundred-year colonial project that so profoundly shaped the modern world, then Macau's return to China in December 1999 was its denouement. The trajectory of terrestrial globalization encompasses the entire duration of Portugal's lengthy presence in Macau, whereas the demise of this terrestrial era in our own day has coincided with China's revolutionary reemergence on the global stage to helm a capitalist economy that was created by the Portuguese.

PORTUGUESE MARITIME EXPLORATION

The effort to circumnavigate the globe was born from the tension that emerged among capitalism's relentless tendency toward expansion and the inherent limitations imposed on European trade by the circumscribed physical boundaries of the Mediterranean Sea. If profits were to be accumulated by linking far-flung maritime markets into global trade networks, then entrepreneurs were naturally driven to expand the reach of those networks. However, this expansion required enhanced maritime equipment and a nuanced set of navigational skills appropriate for the open sea. Because the Mediterranean Sea is a relatively small and self-contained environment, Venetian pilots could easily navigate this area by keeping close to the shoreline, where visible landmarks served as points of orientation. However, this mode of navigation was not possible in bodies of water as large as the Atlantic or Indian Oceans. Therefore, it became increasingly clear that the key to business expansion lay in improvements in the seafaring technologies and navigational acumen that might enable long-distance journeys. The Portuguese excelled at this particular activity. "Portugal was the detonator of an explosion which reverberated round the world," observes Braudel (1979, 3:138). "This was her finest hour." In order to realize their expansive economic ambitions, Portuguese inventors developed not only new sailing vessels and navigational techniques but also novel ways of converting esoteric scientific knowledge into practical use. These efforts ultimately created a new global economy in which Macau played a crucial role.

One outcome of Portugal's maritime efforts was incremental improvements in ship and sail design. One pivotal innovation was the caravel, which possessed greater endurance and durability than existing ships, and whose lateen (or triangular) sails were better "able to convert winds from many directions into forward motion" (Law 2012, 112)—a technological advancement that would power Portugal's global exploration. The caravel operated solely by wind power, so unlike Venetian vessels, required no oarsmen. This reduced the number of bodies necessary to operate the ship, which also increased the caravel's carrying capacity for supplies and cargo, ultimately enabling longer and more lucrative journeys.

As Portuguese sailors began to explore the seas south of the Mediterranean in search of opportunities for trade, the first significant natural obstacle they encountered was Cape Bojador, or the Cape of Fear, "a terrifying promontory of projecting reefs" near the Canary Islands (Gipouloux 2011, 113). Given the cape's location off the coast of the Sahara, there were limited opportunities for landed respite from the dangers of the sea, leaving the ship's pilot to fend for himself in the hostile waters. Seafarer Gil Eanes proved in 1434 that it was possible to navigate beyond the dangerous cape by traveling along the African coast; however, navigators found it difficult to make the return trip to Portugal through the same rugged seas as a result of the violent adverse currents and winds (Gipouloux 2011). Portuguese sailors eventually discovered that rather than attempt the return journey northward up the African coast, they could instead sail in a counterintuitive easterly direction, directly away from the coast and toward the Azores, then take a circular return route to Lisbon, a route that they called the *volta.* But because this route took the ship out on the high seas and far from coastal landmarks, it required the pilot's ability to accurately determine his location via astronomical indicators. Such navigational challenges necessitated a reliable system by which to approximate the global position of the ship. This practical challenge prompted the Portuguese maritime ingenuity that would eventually allow their caravels to navigate vast ocean spaces.

In 1484, Portugal's king, John II, convened a four-person scientific commission, perhaps the first of its kind, whose mission was to determine a way to translate existing scholarly knowledge about astronomy, which was accessible only to an educated elite, into a practical set of instructions for astronomical orientation that could be learned and applied by unschooled sailors.[2] One outcome of this process was the development of the planispheric astrolabe, a navigational device that was a simplified version of existing scientific instruments for studying the cosmos (Waters 1976). We may think of the mariner's astrolabe as a sort of flat, disc-shaped projection of an armillary sphere, without the extraneous and cumbersome physical model of the celestial environment. The mariner's practical version of the astrolabe was also stripped of some of its more esoteric academic functions; it was accompanied by a set of instructions, the Regimento do Astrolabio et do Quadrante, which was prepared by the commission. These instructions allowed mariners to use the device to approximate the altitude of a celestial object, such as the sun, and to apply that information to determine the ship's latitude. The commission also provided sailors with a Portuguese translation of Sacrobosco's *Sphaera Mundi,* an introductory text from 1250 concerning the earth's spherical nature (Law 1984, 248).

Ultimately, the "heterogeneous engineering" of this network of diverse components—that is, natural forces such as currents and winds, new forms of codified cosmological knowledge, and material devices

Figure 13. The planispheric astrolabe enabled unschooled pilots to navigate ships on the high seas by reference to celestial objects. This innovation played a crucial role in Portuguese maritime exploration in the fifteenth and sixteenth centuries. On display in the Louvre Museum. *Photograph by Marie-Lan Nguyen, and licensed under Creative Commons attribution 3.0.*

such as lateen sails and navigational tools like the astrolabe—resulted in a revelation in oceanic orientation as well as the production of a new type of Portuguese seafaring subject. This novel Portuguese "astronomical navigator" (Law 2012, 120) was able for the first time in global history to confidently explore the earth's vast "waterworld."[3]

Entrepreneurial Christian Capitalism

In addition to these scientific innovations, however, Sloterdijk (2013) contends that the five-hundred-year-long process of terrestrial globalization, as well as the corresponding expansion of capitalist exchange, was also driven by the Iberian explorers' Christian-capitalist faith in globalization itself. That is, globalization required their Catholic commitment to the very conception of the world as an observable, mappable, and ultimately knowable globe. The willingness of these visionary "globonauts" (81) to depart from the safety of home, and to plunge headfirst into the expansive "pure outside" (109) of the ocean, was rooted in a pious conviction in the inevitability of their eventual return. Sloterdijk likens this impressive feat of oceanic exploration to a form of ecstatic religious "transcendence to the horizontal plane" (79), which contrasts with the vertical ascension to the extraterrestrial heavens idealized in ancient cosmology.

This European global expansion was propelled by a peculiar propensity for risk and the overwhelming "urge to generate profits in order to repay debts from investment loans" that funded the voyages (Sloterdijk 2013, 50), such as the Venetian *colleganza,* Geonese *commenda,* or Florentine *societas* (Braudel 1979). In this way, maritime trade created the modern figure of the entrepreneur (or "debtor-producer"), who would be so important to the expansion of capitalism, by enabling the "positivation of debt" itself (Sloterdijk 2013, 46). Just as Venetian markets had normalized financial modes of exchange and the double-entry bookkeeping ledger had helped to legitimate the profits earned from interest-bearing loans, maritime trade transformed the incursion of debt, which in the medieval mind was evidence of an individual moral deficiency, into a positive incentivizing force of entrepreneurial motivation. The circular process of debt-financed departure and remunerative return, which promised to enrich the seafarers and their benefactors alike, naturalized the orbicular monetary logic of the business cycle and "return on investment."[4] In this way, the circular routes that characterized the Portuguese ocean voyages created the very logic of modern enterprise.

The Portuguese navigations eventually produced the first global empire. When Bartholomew Diaz rounded the Cape of Good Hope in Africa in 1487, he opened Europe's gateway to the Indian Ocean and the extensive array of trading posts positioned along the continent's coastline. After seizing important eastern ports in Hormuz (1507), Goa (1510), and Malacca (1511), Portuguese explorers landed on the coast of China. In 1557, on behalf of the Portuguese crown, they reached an agreement with the Ming emperor to create a port and trading post in the small Chinese locale that became the city of Macau (Gipouloux 2011; Clayton 2009). Macau initially served as a conduit for Catholic missions into China. However, the tiny European enclave eventually mediated the vast majority of the isolationist Ming dynasty's extensive trade with both Europe and Japan, the latter of which was otherwise forbidden by imperial edict. In this way, Macau became a crucial port in the first global capitalist economy.

"SORT-OF" SOVEREIGNTY

Two features of Macau made it unique among the other ports in Portugal's trade network. First, when assembling their global trading system, Portuguese explorers typically took over existing trading sites through violence or threat of force. However, Macau was distinct in that it was the only Asian city that the Portuguese actually created (Gipouloux 2011).

Second, although it remained a Portuguese territory for nearly half a millennium, when it was founded, Macau was not technically a colony. When the Portuguese first settled in Macau, China did not formally yield power to the Europeans, and there was no explicit designation of the specific size or boundaries of the territory (Breitung 2007). Portugal initially paid an annual rent of 600 taels of silver to the Chinese emperor in order to occupy the territory. However, no existing historical records document the specific Macau agreement forged between China and Portugal, and the territory never clearly belonged exclusively to one or the other empire. Macau instead existed as a unique hybrid Sino-Lusitanic locale, with the sort of respective dual allegiances to different masters that was typical of many medieval European cities (Alsayyad and Roy 2006; Henders 2001).

Anthropologist Cathryn Clayton (2009) describes Macau's indefinite geopolitical status as the city's "sort-of" sovereignty. "The details surrounding the earliest Portuguese settlement in Macau are lost, or, more likely, were never recorded," notes Clayton. "To many historians, the haziness of this origin story is the origin of Macau's sovereignty problem. To others, this haziness was the condition of possibility for the very existence of Macau" (41). I concur with the latter claim. Indeed, Macau's innate ambiguity would arguably prove to be the city's greatest asset. This duplicity still pays dividends today.

The Macau Formula and the Enclave City

Macau historian Kai-cheong Fok (1999) suggests that China's approach to Macau's governance constituted an experimental "Macau formula" for managing foreigners in Chinese territory. This formula aimed to accommodate the potential benefits afforded by the lucrative maritime trade without sacrificing the security of China's dynastic rule. Ultimately, as Fok says, "the formula permitted trade with Westerners in Chinese territory, but Westerners were to have trade and no more" (38). While this policy was never codified, Fok contends that the formula's successful intervention in Macau led to its later implementation in Canton, eventually inspiring China's expansive coastal landscape of European trade concessions. Fortunately, this Macau arrangement satisfied Portugal's economic goals as well, enabling the substantial benefits that both empires could reap from the tiny territory.

In 1586, the viceroy of Portuguese India granted Macau the formal status of a city, and, recognizing its unique identity, he presumptuously christened Macau the singular "City of the Name of God in China." The bestowal of city status on the territory had the benefit of granting Macau's European residents a relatively high amount of autonomy in self-governance with regard to their relationship to the Portuguese crown (Clayton 2009, 42). In accordance with medieval Portuguese traditions, the residents organized a municipal council, or Senado, to which they could elect members to govern the city's affairs (Wu 2002, 44).

Incidentally, at the time of the formation of the council, Macau was technically under Spanish rule rather than Portuguese authority. In

1580, Spain's king, Phillip II, had taken advantage of a Portuguese royal succession crisis to assert dominion over Portugal and to unify all of Iberia under the house of Habsburg (Clayton 2009). Though Macau's Portuguese residents duly recognized Phillip II as their king, they defied his expectations to hoist the Spanish flag in the city. Therefore, when Portugal ultimately regained its independence from Spain in 1640, in appreciation of the city's allegiance, the Portuguese king added to Macau's name the additional honorific title: "There Is None More Loyal." Thus, Macau's municipal council became known as the Leal Senado (loyal senate), and both the senate building and its honorary nomenclature endure in Macau today.

Macau's designation of city status was important to its autonomy, but the city's unique design emanated from its dual sovereignty and complementary Portuguese and Chinese influences.[5] In developing Macau, the Portuguese followed settlement patterns that were typical of their own indigenous cultural traditions. These traditions included strategic use of islands and peninsulas to facilitate sea trade, the use of shelter bays for ship maintenance, and a preference for occupying hilly areas for defense against possible incursion. However, the Chinese villagers who settled in the area followed their own local feng shui traditions. The Chinese sought out flat areas, which were close to water and buttressed by hills in the rear; they avoided physical impediments in the environment that they believed might disturb the flow of chi. Interestingly, both the Portuguese and Chinese favored walled compounds, but for different reasons. The Portuguese built walls primarily to defend from outside attack, while the Chinese did so to promote and enforce a cosmological Chinese social order within the self-contained community. The convergence of these distinct but complementary traditions formed Macau's unique design.[6]

One consequence of these contradictory Portuguese and Chinese traditions was that although the two communities lived side by side and there was some intermarriage among the residents, each community largely kept to itself. As a group, the Portuguese made little attempt to blend in with the Chinese, and vice versa. In fact, in keeping with the desires of both communities, a wall was constructed across the middle of the Macau peninsula to divide the territory into two separate enclaves. On the seaward side was the Christian city, made up of the Portuguese who were subjects of the country's king. On the inland side was the Chinese territory, whose residents were subjects of the emperor. "For centuries there were, in theory, two cities: the Portuguese citadel and the Chinese bazaar, on either side of the city walls," explains anthropologist João Pina-Cabral (2002, 1). "You were either a Catholic subject of the King of Portugal or a subject of the Emperor, respectively—the two things were not compatible" (3). Since its origins, Macau has been composed of distinct enclaves organized by disparate cultural traditions and subject to different modes of governmental authority. We will see later that Macau's unique enclave design played a formative role in China's reform era.

The Jesuits and the Japan Trade

Macau's early prosperity derived from its role as the node through which Portuguese traders connected China with an emergent capitalist economy. Macau was the lone gateway mediating the Middle Kingdom with Europe, but the city also facilitated trade between China and Japan, which was managed by the Portuguese. Given that direct trade between the two Asian empires was forbidden by China's emperor, the Portuguese traders in Macau were uniquely positioned to capitalize off Japan's desire for gold and Chinese silks, as well as China's need for the copper and silver produced in Japanese mines.

For a thirty-year period in the second half of the sixteenth century, at the height of Macau's trade empire, the Portuguese constructed and piloted vessels that were at the time the largest ships in the world (Boxer 1968). The Portuguese East India carrack was known among awestruck observers as "The Great Ship from Amacon," with some of these ships reaching 1,600 tons (Boxer 1968, 12). As these immense vessels sailed the trade routes between Goa, Macau, and Nagasaki, they carried the planet's most valuable cargo. Depending on the specific leg of the journey, the primary freight of fine silks and silver and gold bullion, which was transported on the carracks, might also include Japanese swords and lacquer cabinets, Portuguese wine, Flemish clocks, Indian cotton and calico fabrics, Siamese shark skins and deer hides, and aromatic woods culled from markets in Malacca and Batavia. This cargo sometimes included more fantastical fare, such as caged hawks, peacocks, antelopes, pedigreed Arabian horses, and Bengal tigers (Boxer 1968).[7]

However, as vital as this trade was to the formation of global capitalism, and as much wealth as it produced for Macau merchants, Portuguese sailors, and their European investors, Macau's golden age was relatively brief. Macau's trade dominance was initially curtailed after Japan closed trade at Nagasaki in 1614 and expelled the foreigners. It was definitively concluded when the Dutch seized Malacca in 1641 and blockaded the Strait of Malacca, thereby terminating Macau's crucial link to Goa (Gipouloux 2011). "With the crippling of Portuguese access to trade routes and markets, Macau's economy collapsed and its population declined, and its culture and society became increasingly insular" (Porter 1993, 8).

Aside from this early trade function, Macau also played an important role as an evangelical ingress linking European clergy to China and Japan. Italian Jesuit Matteo Ricci arrived in Macau in 1582 to further the expansionary efforts of ecclesiastical Christianity; he planned to study Chinese language and customs in Macau in preparation for proselytizing in China. A number of other Jesuit scholars followed, studying Chinese at Macau's Colegio de São Paulo, the first western university in East Asia, before venturing into the Middle Kingdom. One key to the success of the Jesuit missions was Ricci's initial decision to adopt an accommodative style (Mungello 1999). Rather than introducing Catholicism as a foreign doctrine in competition with indigenous Chinese beliefs, Ricci explained the tenets of the faith through existing Chinese precepts and practices. In doing so, he created a syncretic gospel, a European tao. This hybrid dogma reflected the dualistic enclave design of Macau itself.

Ricci's activities in China were diverse; in addition to religious instruction, he impressed the emperor's court with his scientific knowledge, taught Euclidean geometry to Chinese scholars, practiced cartography and astronomy, and translated important European scientific works into the Chinese language (Boxer 1991; Zhu 2008). The Ming and Qing emperors allowed the Jesuits to reside in the empire; their presence fostered intercultural interchanges with reverberations for the scientific knowledge and aesthetic practices of both Europe and China. The Jesuits remained in China until the Catholic Church's Chinese Rites controversy, which pitted Dominicans and Franciscans against the Jesuits in a debate that stemmed from Ricci's original

Figure 14. Images of Portuguese caravels, with both lateen and square sails, constructed with *calçada portuguesa* pavement stones around Macau's Largo de Senado. *Photographs by Gonçalo Lobo Pinheiro.*

accommodative approach and that revolved around the status of Chinese rituals such as ancestor worship. Were these rituals secular practices that could be acceptable within the tenets of Catholic faith, or were they religious rites that contradicted Christianity? The fallout from this theological controversy ultimately led the Kangxi emperor to expel the Jesuits in 1721.

Colonial Macau and the Origins of Casino Gambling

Macau's fateful venture into commercial gambling was prompted by the economic ascendance of nearby Hong Kong. When China ceded Hong Kong to Great Britain in 1843 after the signing of the Treaty of Nanking at the end of the first Opium War, the declaration of Hong Kong's free port status led the city to displace Macau as the region's primary trade anchorage. Hong Kong's much deeper harbor was able to accommodate larger and more sophisticated ships that could not navigate Macau's small channel. In the face of this competition, local authorities determined that Macau's ability to compete with Hong Kong would require Portugal's assertion of sovereignty over the territory, much like the British had done in Hong Kong.

In 1846, João Maria Ferreira do Amaral was dispatched from Portugal to serve as Macau's governor. He immediately sought to reverse the city's economic decline by unilaterally declaring Macau a Portuguese colony. In order to enforce Portuguese authority in the territory, Amaral imposed a series of new taxes on residents, ceased annual rent payments to China, and occupied the nearby island of Taipa, which was not Portuguese territory (Daniel 2018). None of these actions endeared him to the Chinese, and while supervising construction of a new road near the border gates that separated the city from China, Amaral added the unfortunate insult of destroying some Chinese tombs in the area. The immediate consequence of these actions was Governor Amaral's shocking assassination and decapitation by a small group of Chinese villagers whom he encountered while riding his horse outside the city gates. Three days later, in an effort to defend the Christian enclave against Chinese incursion, Colonel Vicente Nicolau de Mesquita led Macau's Portuguese military contingent in a surprise attack on a Chinese fort near the city gates, prompting the Chinese to retreat. Mesquita's attack was a significant moment in Portugal's assertion of sovereignty in the city, the first time in the city's history that Macau "managed to impose by force its independence from the Chinese State" (Pina-Cabral 2002, 63).

In 1887, the Qing emperor signed the ironically named Portuguese Treaty of Friendship and Commerce, which formally declared Macau to be a Portuguese colony and also granted "the perpetual occupation and government of Macau and its dependencies by Portugal, as any Portuguese possession" (quoted in Clayton 2009, 47). Emboldened by this new authority, the Portuguese authorities undertook a series of actions, the aim of which was to mitigate Macau's declining trade business by legalizing a variety of vices and marginal economic activities, including gambling, opium production, prostitution, and the "coolie" trade.

Probably the most explicit assertion of Portuguese colonial power in this era was the legalization of indentured servitude. Between 1851 and 1874, nearly 215,000 Chinese were shipped from Macau to labor overseas, primarily in Cuba and Peru, although several hundred each also went to Guiana, Surinam, and Costa Rica (Asome 2014). This lucrative trade was prompted by Britain's own abolishment of slavery in the 1830s, which meant that the practice was forbidden in Hong Kong, and it opened a new market for Macau. While some of these workers no doubt shipped off voluntarily to pursue what they thought were genuine opportunities, brokers in Macau entrapped some Chinese into servitude by extending loans for gambling and then collecting repayment in flesh, while a number of others were kidnapped or coerced into debilitating long-term contracts.

A SHADOW HISTORY OF THE TWENTIETH CENTURY

When this terrible human trade was eventually ended, Macau became a full-blown colonial backwater, neither politically nor commercially significant (Porter 1993, 9). In fact, however, Macau's increasing isolation from the global economy created new economic opportunities, sparking a variety of unlikely events in the city that collectively read like a fascinating shadow history of the twentieth century. Sun Yat-sen operated a modest physician's practice and pharmacy in a shop house on the Rua das Estalagens (incidentally, located just a short distance from my apartment), while he planned China's Nationalist revolution from his Moorish-inspired Macau mansion near the city's Lou Lim Ieoc Garden. A couple of decades later, in 1935, a small group of Vietnamese communists secretly held their fateful first party congress in a nondescript Macau hotel that still stands today.

Portugal's declaration of neutrality during World War II meant that Macau was not officially occupied by Japan (although the city was nevertheless inundated with Japanese agents), and it therefore served as an attractive haven for spies, refugees, and drifters from across the globe. Crafty smugglers, such as future casino magnate Stanley Ho, took advantage of the city's strategic location and noncommittal political allegiances to move wartime goods through Macau and into Hong Kong and China. Even after China's 1949 socialist revolution, Macau served as a clandestine site for business and trade conducted by the Communist Party, for whom the city was a convenient and inconspicuous outlet for activities that were illegal, or at least clearly counterrevolutionary, on the mainland. As a result of the economic blockade of China by western powers in the 1950s, Macau served as a site of transport for significant amounts of steel, gasoline, and other materials needed by the communist regime (Pina-Cabral 2002).

During the Korean War, Macau was a conduit for weapons smuggling into China in an effort to circumvent United Nations mandates (Dicks 1984). After the armistice, Macau became a quasi-official gateway for North Korea's diplomatic and financial concerns, with a local trading company serving as the de facto consulate of the Democratic People's Republic of Korea. In 1995, Stanley Ho even opened a casino in Pyongyang (Linter 2007). Incidentally, Kim Jong Nam, the older half-brother of North Korea's leader, Kim Jong Un, lived for many years with his second wife and two children in self-imposed exile in Macau, where he gambled in the city's casinos, often dined in his favorite Michelin-starred Italian restaurant, and occasionally even spoke out against the country's hereditary regime (Carvalho 2017). Kim survived at least one assassination attempt in Macau before he was killed by North Korean agents in early 2017 while waiting at the Kuala Lumpur airport to board a return flight to Macau. In a moment of political intrigue reminiscent of cinematic Cold War espionage, two unwitting young nightclub hostesses smeared Kim's face with an experimental weaponized nerve agent in what they apparently thought was a prank for a reality television show.

The Postwar Return of "Sort-of" Sovereignty

In the wake of World War II, Portugal reversed its claims to Macau sovereignty and began to assert that Macau was not technically a colony, a move hearkening back to the city's original ambiguous "sort-of" sovereignty. This attempt to again define Portugal's relationship to China vis-à-vis Macau was motivated by the changing connotations of the word "colony" in the mid-twentieth century. When the United Nations was established in 1945, U.N. member states with colonial territories were expected to relinquish those possessions and work toward their establishment as independent and self-governing entities (Clayton 2009, 49). Portugal's prime minister, Antonio Salazar, who ruled over the twentieth century's longest-enduring authoritarian regime, desired to retain the country's overseas possessions and therefore resisted U.N. pressure to relinquish Macau.[8] In 1951, Portugal eliminated the phrase "colonial empire" from the country's constitution, redefining Macau and other foreign possessions as "overseas provinces" that were to be considered components of a far-flung "plural-continental," but nevertheless "unified and indivisible," Portuguese state (Clayton 2009, 49).

This new characterization of the colonial relationship between Portugal and Macau persisted until an unexpected Maoist uprising erupted in Macau in 1966, when the Cultural Revolution suddenly spilled over from China in what became known as the 12-3 Incident (short for December 3). Though the revolutionary activities were short-lived, they engendered significant long-term consequences for the city, with China exploiting the opportunity to assert influence over Macau affairs. The burst of Maoist activity in Macau was precipitated by Portuguese government delays in approving a new wing for a Communist Party primary school on the island of Taipa. When the school board illegally commenced construction, the colonial government dispatched the police to halt the workers, and several people were injured in the ensuing melee.

Ten days later, a new Portuguese governor coincidentally arrived in the city. His office was soon besieged by local youth wearing Mao badges and clutching Mao's Little Red Book. On December 3, 1966, two days of rioting erupted in Macau, punctuated by gunfire that resulted in at least six dead and hundreds injured (Lam and Clayton 2016). This event set in motion the de facto abdication of the Portuguese administration of the city in deed if not in law, putting Macau on the path to eventual decolonization.[9] From that day forward, the Portuguese ruled Macau without confidence and made decisions only with the tacit approval of Beijing. A western diplomatic field report observed three years later that Macau "today seems at times like a remote-control Chinese theocracy presided over by the brightly lithographed icons of a beatific Mao Tse-tung, the new Messiah of the Masses" (Hanna 1969a, 1).

The ensuing events also led to the banishment of the Chinese Nationalist Party from Macau. Ironically, although Sun Yat-sen had planned the Nationalist revolution while living in Macau, on January 3, 1967, the Portuguese administration banned the flying of the Nationalist flag in the city.[10] Many Portuguese left the city in the wake of the insecurity, including the army commander and the police commandant who had ordered the original action against the school board project (Dicks 1984, 120). The only institution seemingly unscathed by the Maoist riots was the Catholic Church, whose local bishop, Dr. Paulo Jose Tavares, banned the idolatrous deification of Mao and the study of Maoist doctrines in church-supported classrooms (Hanna 1969b, 13).

After Portugal's 1974 Carnation Revolution, which overthrew the post-Salazar dictatorship of Marcelo Caetano, the Portuguese government began the formal process of decolonization. It made two separate attempts over the next several years to return Macau to the PRC, only to have China refuse both offers (Clayton 2009, 50). Eventually, in 1979, the two countries established formal diplomatic relations, reaching a secret agreement to characterize Macau as a "Chinese territory under Portuguese administration." This compromise created an entirely new legal entity, meaning that Macau was now not a colony—but it was also not a sovereign state. Thus, under this agreement, Macau returned to something resembling its original "sort-of" status (Clayton 2009, 51).

East Meets West

In the final decade of Portuguese rule, the outgoing authorities pedestrianized the city center area immediately in front of the Leal Senado building, creating a public commons called the Largo de Senado. They covered it with *calçada portuguesa,* the decorative pavement stones ubiquitous throughout the urban centers of Lisbon, São Paulo, and Rio de Janeiro. Today, the stones provide a charming attraction for tourist foot traffic in Macau (Simpson 2018; Zandonai and Amaro 2018). The project was part of a larger effort to give material and symbolic shape to a particular interpretation of Portugal's legacy in the city before the handover to China by producing a narrative that presented the history of Macau not as a story of European colonial conquest but as a mutual process of friendly intercultural cohabitation and exchange. In this narrative, the city is understood as a happy amalgamation of East and West; the aim is to demonstrate that the Portuguese presence in China had the salutary benefit of creating a unique hybrid "Macanese" culture that exists nowhere else. Today, this parable of friendly intercultural relations is heavily promoted in the city's heritage and tourism industries.

Interestingly, the *calçada* stones literally paved over a latent Chinese counternarrative to this official story. During the 12-3 Incident, zealous protestors toppled one particularly visible symbol of Portuguese colonial authority: a bronze statue that had stood for many years across the street from the Leal Senado building. It depicted Colonel Mesquita, the Portuguese military officer who had led the 1846 attack on the Chinese fort after the assassination of Governor Amaral.[11] After the statue was upended, the Portuguese government installed a decorative fountain on the statue site. Years later, the *calceteiros* laid the pavement stones that constructed the Largo de Senado, and Portuguese authorities began an extensive heritage project to preserve the city's colonial-era architecture in preparation for Macau's successful bid in 2005 for UNESCO World Heritage status. The government ultimately installed a large armillary sphere on top of the fountain in front of the Leal Senado building, on the former site of Mesquita's bronze statue. Today the armillary sphere in Senado Square, much like the golden globe in the Venetian Resort lobby, serves as a reminder of the crucial role such celestial and terrestrial globes played in the Portuguese voyages that created both Macau and the modern world.

The demise of the era of terrestrial globalization is symbolized for Sloterdijk by a variety of concurrent twentieth-century phenomena, including Portugal's decolonization after 1974 and NASA's famous 1972 "blue marble" photograph of the earth from the Apollo 17 spacecraft as it journeyed to the moon.[12] However, Sloterdijk (2013) precisely dates the consummation of the process in 1944, "with the establishment of the gold-based monetary system by Bretton Woods" (12), which finally integrated the disparate elements of the global economy within a world

Figure 15. During the 1990s, Macau's outgoing Portuguese administration erected an armillary sphere in the Largo de Senado. The sphere sits on the former site of a statue of Portuguese Lieutenant Colonel Vicente Nicolau de Mesquita, which was toppled in 1966 by anticolonial protestors. The Senado building in the background was built in 1784. *Photograph by author.*

interior of capital. Agreements signed at the postwar Bretton Woods conference established the International Monetary Fund, fixed an international exchange rate based on the gold-backed U.S. dollar, and tightly regulated the sale of gold on the world market, with a price set at $35 per ounce.

Interestingly, Portugal's neutrality in World War II meant that the country did not sign the Bretton Woods Agreement. Therefore, Macau's ambiguous geopolitical status as an "overseas province" of Portugal, combined with its advantageous maritime location, allowed the city-state to exploit its position outside the global system, as well as to enjoy a brief and belated economic renaissance as the unlikely hub for an illicit global gold trade. The city's "sort-of" sovereignty meant that greedy gold traders in Macau could evade the global price controls imposed by the Bretton Woods Agreement.

On July 16, 1948, the *Miss Macau,* a small seaplane transporting gold cargo between Hong Kong and Macau, became an historical footnote as the site of the world's first recorded air hijacking (Linter 2003). When the plane crashed, killing all but one of the twenty-seven passengers and crew on board, the lone survivor admitted that he had commandeered the plane after learning about the gold payload. From 1949 to 1973, gold totaling 934 tons was legally imported into Macau and never seen again.[13] Presumably the gold was smuggled overseas into Hong Kong for resale, although no official records document this process. "If all that bullion had stayed in Macau," muses Pina-Cabral (2002, 6), "the city would now be paved in gold." Those fantastical golden riches would be a glittering harbinger of the billions of dollars Macau would eventually reap from the city's baccarat tables.

United States president Richard Nixon's abandonment of the Bretton Woods Agreement in 1971 with the unilateral "Nixon shock" termination of the gold standard upended the global economy, destroyed the stabilizing Bretton Woods system, and eliminated the idiosyncratic advantage that had enabled Macau's illicit gold trade, which ended in 1974. The demise of the city's aberrant status, which had fortuitously positioned Macau outside the Bretton Woods system, finally served to integrate the city-state within the global economy. The Nixon shock therefore repositioned one of the planet's last remaining extrinsic peripheries within the overarching symbolic confines of Sloterdijk's (2013) capitalist "world interior." That is, the entire five-hundred-year trajectory of terrestrial globalization essentially began and ended in Macau. Today, that era of earthly exploration has been replaced by a contemporaneous world of virtual globalization, with every planetary nook and cranny immediately discoverable with a simple smartphone; an ambient global market stretches from Amazon to WeChat, Alibaba to Zappos.

The extinction of the gold standard also marked the unceremonious end of the postwar economic system known as embedded liberalism. The aim of this system, which originated at that fateful meeting of economists in Bretton Woods, was to ensure planetary peace and global security by protecting against the devastating economic crises, such as the Great Depression, which contributed to the crippling global conflicts of the twentieth century. This Fordist-Keynesian system, which embedded free-market trade within a planned and regulated macroeconomic framework, involved an implicit bargain among states, corporations, and labor unions to manage the industrial regime. The Fordist bargain ensured high rates of employment as well as individual incomes and welfare benefits sufficient to ensure that western workers could afford to consume the products of their own labor. The steady accumulation derived from these complementary systems of mass production and mass consumption provided a remarkable period of sustained economic growth in the West in the latter half of the twentieth century, making the United States the world's wealthiest country. The gold standard functioned in this global economy to ensure a system of fixed exchange rates that facilitated free trade and guaranteed the stable markets necessary for mass production (Hardt 2005).

This system began to break apart in the late 1960s and early 1970s amid a variety of systemic crises that included war in Indochina, global social unrest unleashed in May 1968, and OPEC's embargo of oil shipments to the West during the 1973 Arab–Israeli war. But chief among these debilitating factors was the increasing failure of Fordist production to return acceptable rates of profit (Harvey 1991). In response, the conservative American and British administrations of Ronald Reagan and Margaret Thatcher implemented a new "disembedded" or "neoliberal" economic system to replace the policies that had supported Keynesian embedded liberalism. Among other outcomes, this encroaching neoliberal regime undermined collective bargaining at home and created an international division of labor by steadily shifting production overseas to the developing world in search of cheaper workers. This nascent international labor force included tens of millions of communist workers in China's coastal SEZs, which Deng established in 1979 to kick-start the country's economic reforms. In fact, in his book *A Brief History of Neoliberalism,* David Harvey (2007) inaugurates Reagan, Thatcher, and Deng as the secular trinity of the neoliberal era. If so, then Macau's 1999 retrocession to the PRC marked the return of China's wayward prodigal son to serve this new economic regime.

Cyclical Regimes of Capitalism

Throughout the half millennium that defined the modern world, Macau leveraged its fortuitous locale and ambiguous geopolitical status for economic advantage. Indeed, the city's relatively recent reunification with the motherland is no exception; Macau's legal status today as the only site of casino gaming in China has provided a massive local economic windfall. However, in order to comprehend the global significance of Macau's casino riches, we must locate the city within the grand narrative sweep of Braudel's history of capitalism.

Braudel's (1979) unique conception of capitalism revolves around his construct of a world-economy, which he distinguishes from the broader global economy, and which he describes as an "economically autonomous section of the planet able to provide for most of its own needs," with internal links which produce "a certain organic unity" among participating states (3:22). In an effort to demonstrate the viability of this construct, Braudel points to historical evidence derived from synchronized price movements of consumer goods across large geographical areas and over long temporal rhythms.[14] He contends that consistent prices for the same goods, which cohere across a circumscribed space and time in a set of far-flung locales, is evidence of a unified world-economy in which those prices are stabilized in different individual markets.[15]

The information culled from analysis of these economic rhythms allows Braudel to demonstrate the trade networks that created the capitalist world-economy and therefore to track the emergence and decline of successive dominant capitalist regimes over the past five hundred years. Starting in the sixteenth century with the Italian city-states of Venice and Genoa, economic hegemony passed to the united provinces of Holland, then to Great Britain and its global empire, and finally to the United States.[16] According to Braudel, each world-economy is anchored by a core city that consolidates its enterprise, and during the American-dominated twentieth century, that city was New York.

In his analysis of the hundred-year (or "secular") economic cycles that he argues define the development of global capitalism, Braudel pinpoints 1974 as the peak of the New York–dominated cycle of this world-economy, which is to say the apex of the temporal trajectory that defines the United States' role as the world's dominant economic power.[17] I should note that the date of 1974 immediately follows both Portugal's Carnation Revolution that prompted Macau's return to the PRC and Nixon's apostate abolition of the gold standard; that date also marks the emergence of a deep global economic malaise that economists dubbed "stagflation." By highlighting this historical moment, within the context of his argument that each world-economy is anchored by a core city, Braudel (1979) implies a pending geographical displacement of the urban "center of gravity" (or spatiotemporal locus) of global capitalism (3:27).[18]

Although Braudel (1979) discusses China's historical role in an Asian world-economy (and in fact calls the Far East between the fifteenth and eighteenth centuries "the greatest of all world-economies" [3:484]), he understandably does not anticipate (in work published in 1979) China's pending post-Mao emergence as a global capitalist power. And although Braudel clearly implies the approaching decline of American hegemony, he offers no suggestion of what might come next.[19] However, Arrighi (2009a), a Braudel acolyte, extends his analysis to predict the imminent emergence of the reform-era PRC as the planet's new dominant economic power.

Even without engaging in such prognostication, however, there is little doubt that as the world's second-largest economy, in possession of the largest population of consumers in global history, China's contemporary market-socialist regime is of fundamental importance to the sustainability of capitalism. It is therefore possible today to identify a new core city, or urban center of gravity, which organizes this new heterodox Chinese economy that merges Marxist central planning with the free market. In chapter 3, I will analyze the GBA megacity as an innovative regional metropolis with idiosyncratic Chinese characteristics, then explore the role of this new core city in both China's market-socialist economy and Macau's sudden recent resurgence on the global stage.

I suggest that as the first, and longest enduring, European site in China, Macau actually inspired the unique design of this Chinese megacity, as well as China's incongruous "one country, two systems" regime. This influence hearkens back all the way to Portugal's founding of Macau in 1557. As we have seen in this chapter, although Macau is certainly a Chinese territory through and through, it is also endemically Portuguese. Without Portugal's maritime innovations, without the Portuguese Christian-capitalist project of entrepreneurial navigations, and without the country's medieval European logics of sovereignty and city planning, there would be no Macau—at least not in its present form. Macau is a peculiar product of disjunctive Sino-Lusitanic urban engineering, and this unique amalgamation of both cultural traditions (for good or bad) is crucial to the city's identity. The ultimate unification of these disparate halves of the bicameral city-state in the last days of 1999, in a quixotic eleventh-hour Judgment of Solomon, has enabled sleepy Macau to rise once again as a crucial geoeconomic gateway between China and the West.

3

Greater Bay Area

CORE CITY OF SINO-CAPITALISM

> A world-economy always has an urban centre of gravity,
> a city, as the logistic heart of its activity.
>
> —Fernand Braudel, *The Perspective of the World*

The Macau Tower is the city's tallest structure and most visible land-mark. Resembling Seattle's Space Needle, and an almost identical copy of Auckland's Sky Tower, the edifice was designed by New Zealand architect Gordon Moller, and the project was conceived and financed by Macau casino tycoon Stanley Ho at a cost of US$130 million. The tower was one component of a US$1.4 billion land reclamation project that completely transformed Macau's charming Praia Grande neigh-borhood, enclosing the seaside locale within 130 hectares of additional area, including two artificial lakes that are perfect for hosting annual dragon boat festival races and a popular international fireworks com-petition. The reclamation project increased the total area of the Macau peninsula by 20 percent. The horizontal expansion of urban land was complemented by the striking vertical elevation of the tower.

Construction of the tower began in 1998, just one year before Portu-gal's return of Macau to the PRC and three years before the termination of Ho's forty-year monopoly casino concession. The decision to end the monopoly arrangement and to liberalize the gambling industry even-tually paved the way for the opening of the Venetian Resort, as well as a dozen other casino megaprojects that began to appear in Macau a few years later, each of which was also constructed on reclaimed and ersatz earth. The tower was therefore a lofty harbinger of the dramatic

Figure 16. The Macau Tower, "the tenth-tallest tower of its kind," located on the Nam Van land reclamation site that increased the size of the Macau peninsula by 20 percent. *Photograph by Diego Delso, licensed under Creative Commons attribution 4.0, CC-BY-SA.*

changes to Macau's cityscape that would be unleashed by the dismantling of Ho's casino monopoly.

On the date of its inauguration, the Macau Tower, standing 338 meters tall, earned global recognition as the "tenth-tallest tower of its kind"—admittedly a mediocre distinction. The qualification "of its kind," according to the technical definition offered by the Council on Tall Buildings and Urban Habitat, denotes a self-supporting, noninhabitable structure, taller than it is wide, and regularly accessible by visitors. Subsequent global developments in this curious engineering genre, including three recent towers in mainland China, have since demoted the Macau Tower to number eighteen on the list. However, what the Macau Tower lacks in sheer verticality is compensated, as is the case of all of Macau's architectural superlatives, by the fact that it stands in one of the world's smallest territories, which is composed today of merely 32.9 square kilometers. This tiny size is all the more surprising given that more than half of the city sits on the sort of artificial reclaimed land on which the tower was constructed (Daniel 2018).

Today the tower stands at the axis of Macau's imbrication in two complementary geospatial processes that bookend capitalism's birth in medieval Venice and its unorthodox metamorphosis today in post-Mao China. The first is the process of terrestrial globalization that I explore in chapter 2: the era of European colonial expansion that founded Macau, and in which the city played a seminal role as the primary site of trade between Europe and the Ming dynasty. The terrestrial era essentially ended with Macau's retrocession to the PRC in 1999. However, this final act of European colonial politics officially conjoined the city with a second world–historical spatial transformation: the contemporary urbanization of China. The fundamental importance of China's urbanization for the very sustainability of capitalism today perhaps rivals in global significance the half millennium of European expansion that immediately preceded it.

This Chinese urbanization project commenced in 1978 with Deng Xiaopeng's introduction of the country's economic reforms, but it has increased dramatically in the intervening years. As recently as 1980, only about 25 percent of China's of 980 million citizens lived in cities. However, by 2011, for the first time in history, more than half of the country's population—which by then had reached 1.3 billion—was urban (Li 2019). By 2019, China's urban population comprised nearly 60 percent of the country, and this number continues to increase. Of course, there have always been prominent Chinese cities, but the rapid urbanization of the country today has upended the predominantly rural culture that defined China for several thousand years. This reversal of rural preeminence is not mere happenstance. Over the past decade, the central government has moved more than two hundred million rural peasants to cities, and China's National New-Type Urbanization Plan, which was introduced in 2014, details the government's goal to urbanize 250 million additional rural residents by 2026.[1] State investment in urban infrastructure projects to accommodate these new residents, as well as the concentration of these new workers in urban areas, has contributed to dramatic increases in the country's industrialization level and GDP.

However, under a market economy, the city is not simply a container for living and working. The capitalist city is a stimulating environment, whose affective attractions implicitly promote the metropolitan qualities that sociologist Louis Wirth (1938) has called "urbanism as a way of life"—the density, heterogeneity, anonymity, creativity, and increased individualism that shapes a distinct urban personality. Incidentally, these characteristics of urbanism were intentionally eliminated from China's cities during the Mao era in an effort to create a collectivist society of communist workers whose egalitarian lifestyles were opposed to the capitalist cities of the West. However, today, the central government hopes that China's new urbanites, who at present have some of the world's highest household savings rates, will purchase automobiles and furnish homes; shop in malls and supermarkets; dine in fine restaurants and fast food outlets; visit cinemas and amusement parks; and capitulate to the latest beauty and fashion trends. Authorities believe that these residential and lifestyle purchases of hundreds of millions of new city dwellers will markedly increase domestic consumption levels and stimulate economic development, thus weaning China off the unsustainable manufacturing regime that defined the initial reform period. And with a current population of 1.4 billion, as goes China, so goes the world. China's rapid urbanization promises to sustain capitalist growth, but it also contributes to a new planetary condition with profound consequences for the global climate, the sustainability of the earth's natural resources, and the future of humanity.

Macau sits today at the spatiotemporal intersection of the termination of terrestrial globalization, the European expansion that created the modern world, and the dynamics of Chinese urbanization that will define the planet's future. Macau's cityscape provides a three-dimensional testament to the terrestrial era; the far-flung consequences of Portugal's global voyages are materialized in the neoclassical heritage buildings and baroque Catholic cathedrals located in the city center. However, the significance of China's massive urban transformation only becomes evident from atop the Macau Tower. The tower's observation deck is the ideal vantage point from which to comprehend Macau's sudden reemergence, five hundred years after it was founded, on the frontier of another decisive moment in the development of global capitalism.

THE *ILINX* OF CHINESE URBANIZATION

The Macau Tower attracts more than one million visitors each year, but it is not the first stop on the typical tourist's itinerary. An exception is a handful of travelers whose primary motivation for visiting Macau is the opportunity to leap from the World's Highest Bungee Jump, located at the tower's apex. This Guinness World Record attraction offers daredevil visitors the exhilarating vertiginous experience that surrealist sociologist Roger Caillois ([1958] 2001) calls *ilinx.* The word *ilinx* denotes the playful altered perception, or "voluptuous panic," produced when individuals subject themselves to an abrupt "spasm, seizure, or shock which destroys reality with a sovereign brusqueness" (23). *Ilinx* is one element of the typology of play that Caillois explores in his famous book *Man, Play, and Games,* and which includes the playful activities of *agon, alea,* and *mimesis* (competition, chance, and mimicry).

In coining the expression *ilinx,* which is the Greek word for "whirlpool," Caillois creates a term to identify the objective of a child who playfully twirls in circles to induce a happy state of dizzy intoxication. *Ilinx* thus perfectly captures the childish desire of the tourist who travels to Macau in order to propel himself from the planet's eighteenth tallest tower (of its kind). The intrepid traveler who ascends the tower in search of the sheer psychophysiological disorientation that emanates from the controlled risk of the 233-meter plunge perhaps finds his aleatory counterpart in the Chinese high roller (and there is apparently no shortage of them) who seeks the "voluptuous panic" of an all-in bet at the baccarat table.

If descending the tower attached at the ankles to a bungee is an exercise in purposeful disorientation, then the sixty-second ascension in the tower's high-speed elevator has the inverse effect. The tower's fifty-eighth-floor observation deck provides the visitor with an unexpected spatial orientation and its own awe-inspiring experience of *ilinx.* Although Macau's European colonial past is clearly visible on the ground below, from the top of the tower, it is actually possible to see the planet's urban future.

From the tower's observation deck, the initial impression of Macau that was formed below—a small, self-contained city separated from both Hong Kong and China by natural sea barriers, immigration checkpoints, and palpable geopolitical boundaries—suddenly melts away. That ground-level impression is replaced by the breathtaking vision of a massive urban expanse of remarkable density, color, and texture, which stretches out in every direction as far as the eye can see. Viewed from the tower's vantage, the heritage buildings and resort attractions

Figure 17. The view from the Macau Tower of the GBA megacity, which stretches out in every direction as far as the eye can see. The channel on the far left separates the Macau peninsula, on the right side of the channel, from the mainland Chinese city of Zhuhai, which is on the left side. *Photograph by Adam Lampton.*

of Macau's tiny cityscape merge seamlessly into the Pearl River Delta region, which the United Nations has designated as the world's largest urban area. This Chinese megacity, which sociologist Manuel Castells ([1966] 2000) describes as "the most representative urban face of the twenty-first century" (439), covers 50,000 square kilometers and has a population of upward of 120 million people.

Where the city does not yet exist, it is under construction; skeletons of half-built towers of a variety of shapes and sizes protrude from the earthen terrain below. One barge after another plies the narrow sea channel at the base of the tower, loaded with sand and gravel cargo that will become the bedrock of new land reclamation projects set to alter the contours of the coast.[2] Indeed, visitors to the tower in 2022 may observe no fewer than seven concurrent reclamation projects underway in Macau alone, which, when completed, will increase the size of the city by an additional 12 percent and accommodate 350,000 people. One project is the manmade island in Macau's outer harbor, which serves as the termination point for the newly constructed Hong Kong–Zhuhai–

Macau bridge, a $15 billion, 55-kilometer behemoth that, when it opened in 2018, was deemed the world's longest water-spanning bridge.

The Pearl River Delta (PRD) region is the epicenter of China's market reforms; it constitutes what Braudel might call the core city of Chinese capitalism and the "logistic heart" of the country's postsocialist enterprise. If Braudel (1979) is correct that "a world-economy always has an urban center of gravity," then to comprehend the economic logic of China's market-socialist regime, we must understand the unique Chinese characteristics of this massive new megacity (3:27). This PRD megacity is therefore a window into the future of global capitalism.

As I explain in chapter 1, capitalism first emerged in the unique urban environments of Venice, Florence, and Genoa. Their small size, advantageous geography, and anomalous autonomy distinguished these medieval Italian city-states from their larger territorial counterparts, enabling the enterprise by which their nascent capitalist entrepreneurs connected distant markets into a European world-economy. Today, China's market-socialist economy is similarly born from the distinct (although altogether different) design of the PRD megacity. The dramatic development of Macau's gambling industry today is a product of Macau's specific role in this Chinese metropolis.

Macau is therefore not simply an external vantage point from which to observe this massive new urban system. Rather, it serves as an integral component in its operation. I contend that the tiny Portuguese enclave was the very inspiration for the spatial logic of China's reform economy; as a new SAR of the PRC, Macau's endemic "sort-of" sovereignty enables the city's contemporary function in the development of the country's innovative market-socialist regime. In this chapter, I describe the unique structural logic of the PRD megacity and explore its core city function in an ascendant East Asian world-economy.

However, as I will suggest here, then explore throughout the remainder of this book, the key to China's new political economy is the development of a concomitant *subjective economy* in which Macau plays an important role. China's economic reforms began with Deng's creation of the SEZs along China's southern coast. These new zones were designed as laboratories of production where China would tentatively embrace transnational investment, cooperate with foreign companies, and simply study capitalism itself. The adjacent Hong Kong and Macau SARs function today as complementary laboratories of consumption to which Chinese tourists travel to gamble or shop, and in which new quality Chinese citizens are cultivated. The Venetian Resort plays an important role in this process.[3]

THE PRD BECOMES THE GBA

The PRD is the low-lying geographical expanse that surrounds the Pearl River Estuary, where China's massive Pearl River, the country's third-largest river system, flows from three tributaries on the mainland and empties into the South China Sea. This region today encompasses Guangdong province as well as the adjacent cities of Hong Kong and Macau. Guangdong itself includes the immense city of Guangzhou (formerly known as Canton), one of China's most populated places, as well as Shenzhen, Dongguan, Foshan, Zhongshan, Jiangmen, Zhuhai, Huizhou, and Zhaoqing. Along with Shanghai's Yangtze River Delta and Beijing's Silicon Valley–style Zhongguan Cun, the PRD is one of the three spatial engines that drive China's economic transformation (Arrighi 2009a; Ng and Tang 1999).

Canton was the heart of China's early engagement with capitalist Europe in the nineteenth century. Today the Chinese government hopes to recapture this economic function by linking each of the region's locales into an integrated innovation hub that they have named the Greater Bay Area. The central government has chosen to rebrand the Pearl River Delta as the Greater Bay Area because authorities believe this growing metropolis may surpass, in both global economic significance and popular culture resonance, its Silicon Valley Bay–area namesake on the California coast (as well as the Hudson Bay area of New York and the Tokyo Bay area in Japan).[4] China's GBA is currently the factory to the world; it produces the bulk of the planet's "electronics, household appliances, telecommunications and computer equipment, toys, timepieces, lighting apparatus, garments, footwear, plastic products, and ceramics" (Bie, de Jong, and Derudder 2015, 104). However, the central government projects that by 2035, China's GBA will be the vibrant urban center of a new Sinocentric global economy that may eclipse both Japan and the United States.

This expansive GBA megacity is also a crucial contributor to Macau's contemporary development because most of the city's tourists

Figure 18. The megacity under construction, looking south from the Macau Tower toward Hengqin Island (above, June 2015; below, June 2020). *Photograph from 2015 by Adam Lampton; photograph from 2020 by author.*

travel from this region.[5] Again, this is not mere happenstance. The central government has selected these tourists for enhanced opportunities for cross-border travel to Hong Kong and Macau with a unique exit visa called the Individual Visit Scheme (IVS). As I explain in chapter 1, these Chinese citizens are mobilized today in a program of capitalist "reeducation," which mirrors (in inverted fashion) the rustication of youth during the Cultural Revolution, and which involves their participation in a contemporary grand tour of the casino resorts and retail attractions of Hong Kong and Macau. In order to understand how these postcolonial cities came to serve this function, however, it is first necessary to clarify their distinct role in the overall design of this new bay-area metropolis.

Although the GBA is the world's largest and fastest-growing urban area, it is not a conventional metropolis with a characteristic organic development or consistent composition. Rather, the GBA is a completely contrived "city" composed of a variety of distinct locales that have been assembled into a dynamic whole. These elements include economic zones, administrative regions, "coastal open cities," factory towns, urban villages, reclaimed islands, and leisure and residential theme parks, each of which is designed to fulfill a specific function in the region's economic activities and its articulations with global capitalism.[6] The unique urban design of the GBA region is characterized by a peculiar condition of "exacerbated difference" (Chung et al. 2001, 704) that makes it a sui generis environment.

The City of Exacerbated Difference

In 2001, Dutch architect Rem Koolhaas, along with a group of postgraduate students enrolled in the Harvard Design School, produced a seven-hundred-page document of the development of the PRD entitled *Great Leap Forward,* in which they famously refer to what is now the GBA as the "city of exacerbated difference." Whereas a "traditional city strives for a condition of balance, harmony, and a degree of homogeneity," they argue, this new Chinese megacity "is based on the greatest possible difference between its parts—complementary or competitive" (Chung et al. 2001, 704). This characteristic of "exacerbated difference" is crucial to not only the design of the GBA region but also to the economic system of market-socialism itself, which combines the contradictory systems of communism and capitalism. Macau's specific function in the GBA becomes clear only within the context of the exacerbated difference that defines both this megacity and China's post-Mao economy.

Koolhaas's (2000) team suggests (and I agree) that Macau and the other European concessions actually inspired the exacerbated difference of the GBA's design. Speaking of Macau and Hong Kong, they contend that "the land concessions in the PRD established the idea of a different China—a China of enclaves" (83). It is this enclave morphology, defined by distinct foreign territories within a larger Chinese environment, which has taken form in the GBA today.[7] In addition, however, we may recall from chapter 2 that Macau was not merely a Portuguese enclave in China; Macau itself actually had an internal enclave design, with distinct Christian and Chinese components. We might conceive of Macau's original design as an early example of the exacerbated difference that appears in the GBA today.[8] That is, with its conjoined Christian and Chinese areas, separated by a dividing wall and under the respective authorities of the Portuguese crown and Ming emperor, Macau was the singular Catholic "City of the Name of God in China," and as such was the original expression of the exacerbated difference that defines the GBA metropolis today. Therefore, Macau was the urban prototype for the unique spatial logic of China's economic reforms.

How can we understand the combination of internal exacerbated differences and overwhelming massive dimensions that characterize China's GBA metropolis today? Contemporary urban scholarship arguably lacks the vocabulary necessary to describe this unique urban region, much less explain Macau's particular function within it. The problem is that urban scholarship is constrained by a "methodological cityness," or an implicit epistemological assumption that the global urban landscape still comprises distinct, self-contained cities (Angelo and Wachsmuth 2014). However, Harvard University urbanist Neil Brenner (2014) argues that in order to grasp the expansive and amorphous urban space typical of the planet today (and which certainly characterizes the GBA), we must move beyond an approach that takes "the city" as the primary unit of analysis, instead embracing "a new vision of urban theory *without an outside*" (15).[9] That is, the key to understanding capitalism today is not the autonomous cities that once dominated the global economy, such as New York, London, Amsterdam, or Venice, but rather the open-ended process of urbanization itself. Just as Caillois ([1958] 2001) appealed to ancient Greek for the word *ilinx* in order to describe a particular type of play, we must reach beyond the conceptual nomenclature of contemporary urbanism if we are to adequately capture the organizational logic of China's GBA metropolis and its formative role in the country's market-socialist economy.

Urban scholars have actually challenged this "methodological cityness" by coining two widely used terms, "megalopolis" and "megacity," to characterize such expansive urban spaces. However, although both terms are certainly relevant for describing China's GBA, they carry conceptual baggage that limits their applicability to this particular Chinese case. We will see that the megalopolis is the urban product of the distinctly post-Fordist economy that emerged in the United States after 1970, whereas the megacity is a postcolonial phenomenon that was produced by the termination of terrestrial globalization at the same time. However, although the GBA encapsulates both of these postcolonial and post-Fordist conditions, China's core city is a uniquely postsocialist urban space, a sort of megacity with Chinese characteristics.

For this reason, China's GBA metropolis is not really a conventional city at all. Instead, it is exemplary of what Lewis Mumford (1967), writing in a different context, calls a megamachine. A megamachine is a complex apparatus that incorporates individual human bodies as components in its operation. Mumford's megamachine concept helps clarify the GBA's role in a subjective economy central to China's reform era. In addition, thinking of this massive city as an urban megamachine allows me to demonstrate Macau's function as a laboratory of consumption, one in which subjectivity itself becomes the object of experimental policies and in which a new Chinese consumer is cultivated and refined. So I turn now to an analysis of the megalopolis, the megacity, and the Chinese megamachine.

THE MEGALOPOLIS AND THE MEGACITY

In 1961, Jean Gottman declared the arrival, along the Boston-to-Washington corridor of the eastern seaboard of the United States, of a new urban form he called the megalopolis (Gottman 1964).[10] "We must abandon the idea of the city as a tightly settled and organized unit, in which people, activities, and riches are crowded into a very small area clearly separated from its nonurban surroundings," (5) he asserted, in words that might well describe the view of China today from atop the Macau Tower. Instead, Gottman envisioned an urban future of contiguous populated settlements with indistinct boundaries morphing into massive, ill-defined agglomerations to create an entire urban world in which (to paraphrase Castells) there are ironically no longer any actual cities.

However, Gottman's megalopolis is a specific product of the postindustrial restructuring of the United States.[11] As the North American economy shifted, after 1970, from the rigidities of Fordist-heavy industry to more "flexible" forms of enterprise, such as finance and information, industrial production was displaced from first-world city centers, such as Cleveland and Detroit, to an international division of labor. This shift carried with it a corresponding centrifugal explosion of the North American metropolis into expansive new liminal "edge cities" characterized by corporate parks, big-box stores, repetitive suburban housing estates, and an abundance of office and retail floor space (Garreau 1992). The work and lifestyle activities typical of America's postindustrial service economy are carried out primarily in the low-rise office parks, shopping malls, and suburban homes of these interurban areas.

Gottman's post-Fordist megalopolis is distinct from the alternative archetypal mass urban form known as the megacity. Janice Perlman (1976) coined the term "megacity" in 1976 to describe the transformation of such places as São Paulo, Caracas, and Mumbai, which resulted from the collapse of the global colonial order. If the post-Fordist American megalopolis was formed by the centrifugal explosion of people away from city centers into "edge city" settlements, then the postcolonial megacity of the developing world was created by the inverse movement. When European powers withdrew from their colonial possessions and these former colonies embraced their independence, a centripetal implosion of people was prompted as rural villagers swarmed into urban centers in search of work (McGrath and Shane 2012). Much of this rural population would be displaced to massive urban slum communities, where they would contribute to the crises of density, housing, crime, and public health that would plague third-world development. Therefore, although both terms identify expansive urban settlements, Gottman's postindustrial megalopolis is distinct from Perlman's postcolonial megacity. However, as useful as these terms may be, neither exactly describes the characteristics of China's GBA metropolis, which is a unique urban space with its own indigenous Chinese characteristics.

Castells ([1996] 2000) has made the most detailed and persuasive attempt to apply the megacity concept to the reform-era PRC. He suggests that the emerging Chinese megacity foreshadows the coming shape of the global economy. In his three-volume treatise, *The Rise of the Network Society,* Castells looks directly to China's GBA region to suggest that it is the megacity, rather than Gottman's megalopolis, which is the "new spatial form" of an emergent global economic regime, organized by immaterial flows of information and finance. Castells argues that new digital information technologies have introduced a novel "space of flows," which has upended traditional urban development (434). Castells presciently predicted, in work originally published in 1996, that China's GBA region would be the prototype of the new urban world.

Looking over the same urban expanse visible from the Macau Tower, Castells ([1966] 2000) memorialized this emergent megacity, whose ill-defined contours were only just taking shape, with an awkward yet apt sobriquet: "the Hong Kong–Shenzhen–Canton–Pearl River Delta–Macau–Zhuhai metropolitan regional system" (436). Although this unwieldy name has evaded common usage, it accurately denotes the "spatial discontinuity," or exacerbated difference, which defines the GBA, and the manner in which this odd "city" is assembled by piecing together formerly distinct locales (439).[12] Castells was the first scholar to capture the innovation, excitement, and sheer economic force at the heart of GBA development. However, as useful as his early account of this urban region may be, the benefit of hindsight reveals several limitations of his description of this new megacity, which detract from an understanding of the way the GBA functions today as the core city of Chinese capitalism. The problem is not necessarily with the general applicability of Castells's theoretical model. Rather, it reflects the peculiarity of the Chinese case. The GBA metropolis simply spills over the categorical boundaries of the megalopolis/megacity taxonomy.[13] Therefore, I will briefly address several limitations of Castells's approach to the GBA in an effort to arrive at an account of the unique characteristics of this core city of Sino-capitalism, which will allow us to understand the specific roles of both the GBA and Macau in the economy of the PRC.

THE CHINESE CHARACTERISTICS OF THE GBA METROPOLIS: MEGALOPOLIS OR MEGACITY?

First, Castells ([1966] 2000) differentiates the Chinese megacity from Gottman's North American megalopolis, and while his basic point is accurate, he overlooks some important structural similarities among these spaces. Castells claims that megalopolitan "edge cities" have little descriptive value for understanding the GBA because the edge city is "very specific to the American experience," and exemplifies America's twentieth century expansion into the country's undeveloped frontier (431).[14] However, he fails to notice the extent to which China's GBA developed not according to new electronic flows of information but instead around an expanding physical network of roads, highways, and other infrastructure that was actually modeled on the American case. Thomas Campanella (2008) argues that as futuristic as the GBA may appear, the "corridor urbanization" (44) of the GBA actually replicates the railroad-driven development of nineteenth-century North America. In addition, several of the region's most significant infrastructure projects, including the Guangzhou–Shenzhen Expressway and the Hong Kong–Zhuhai–Macau Bridge, were conceived by Hong Kong developer Gordon Wu of Hopewell Industries and were self-conscious attempts to mimic specific American megalopolitan developments.[15]

However, if the GBA is simultaneously both like and unlike the post-Fordist American megalopolis, then the same is also true of its resemblance to the megacity concept that Castells uses to describe this region of China. While the GBA is certainly a megacity in the literal sense of a massive urban space, as a technical concept, "megacity" has a specific meaning. "Megacity" denotes the spontaneous, unplanned nature of postcolonial urbanization as rural residents across the globe rapidly decamped to city centers in the wake of European decolonization. Therefore, the technical meaning of "megacity" renders this concept inaccurate for describing the unique case of China.

Unplanned or Planned?

To be sure, China shares some characteristics of the Latin American megacities that prompted Perlman (1976) to coin the term. There is a social implosion in China today as vast floating populations of peasants move to cities in search of temporary migrant work. In fact, contemporary rural-to-urban migration in China constitutes the largest movement of people in human history (Buck and Walker 2007). However, while the Latin American urbanization that Perlman observed was defined by a groundswell of unintentional and unplanned social changes, China's contemporary urbanization is actually the product of careful top-down macroeconomic planning. Therefore, China's contemporary rural-to-urban migration is not like the spontaneous population implosion experienced elsewhere in the developing world; rather, China's internal migration involves the central government's intentional mobilization of the rural population for specific economic ends.[16] In fact, this state planning intends to guard against what Chinese authorities have described as the potential "Latin Americanization" of the country's cities; China is unique in its surprising lack of the kind of urban slum communities that are so common in the developing world (Wallace 2014). Thus, although the GBA shares some characteristics of the third-world megacity (as well as the American megalopolis), China's urbanization process carries specific Chinese characteristics that are exemplified by its planned logic.

Of course, China's enormous size and complexity make it impossible for the central government to completely regulate development from above; there is no way for authorities to plan every detail of the lives of a billion people. Informal, unanticipated, and opportunistic enterprises do indeed emerge. However, what is perhaps even more distinctive about China is the extent to which such informal phenomena, if not specifically planned per se, are part of an overall mode of planning. According to political scientist Sebastian Heilmann (2008), Chinese state planning generally proceeds through a process of "transformative experimentation" (3) in which local officials are given wide latitude to allow opportunistic developments. This distinct Chinese mode of planning, which he calls "guerilla policy" to reference its origins in Mao's revolutionary guerilla warfare tactics, inverts conventional forms of governmental policy making.[17] In both the Maoist and reform eras, the PRC has experimented with new policies and programs by using this "practice-based epistemology" that proceeds through pilot testing and experimentation (8).[18] "The rationale behind guerilla policy-making is precisely to *embrace uncertainty* in order to benefit from it," Heilmann says (22). In short, the second way that China's bay area urbanization is distinct from its counterparts around the world is the extent to which it is planned rather than unplanned.

Novel Urban Future or Persistence of the Past?

However, perhaps the most serious limitation of Castells's account of the GBA megacity emanates from the future-oriented temporality of his theoretical orientation. Castells sees the GBA as a spatial product of the Information Age poised at the forefront of innovative technologies that promote economic globalization, which he contends create a radical new "space of flows."[19] However, this approach leads him to overlook the way the key spatial dimensions that define the region's unique morphology are not novel developments produced by digital electronics but instead existing geosocial forms that are latent in the physical environment and that have reemerged in the present day.

Careful attention to Sloterdijk's (2013) philosophical approach to globalization, which I recount in chapter 2, reminds us that China's GBA megacity marks not only the emergence of a new era of virtual globalization and a novel space of information flows, but also the concomitant demise of the preceding era of terrestrial globalization. Terrestrial globalization was enabled by earlier technologies, such as the armillary sphere, mariner's astrolabe, and lateen sail, which were no less radical in their own time than the electronic circuits that power the Information Age. In chapter 2, we see how these navigational technologies led to Europe's encounter with China during the terrestrial era and produced unique spatial forms, such as the European concessions on China's southern coast. Today China has mobilized these earlier European spaces to introduce the country's new reform-era economy. This is why China's first SEZs were located on the former British treaty ports of Amoy and Swatow; why the colonial cities of Macau and Hong Kong were transformed into Chinese SARs; and why the logic of Macau's original enclave design is reproduced across the entire GBA. These antiquated European spaces form the contemporary bedrock of market-socialism in the PRC.

It would be foolish to deny Castells's basic point that the GBA plays a formative role in the Information Age. In fact, the iPhone, perhaps the era's most iconic innovation, is assembled in Foxconn factories located in the region. The production of the iPhone depends on China's cheap labor force, as well as on the region's connections to foreign business acumen, global capital, and international supply chains, which are enabled by the "disjunctive" urban form that Castells so well describes. However, the key spatial logic of the GBA does not derive from the model of information or the morphology of the electronic circuit, as Castells contends, but from the sedimented processes of terrestrial globalization that adhere in the regional geography.[20] The open coastal cities, economic zones, and administrative regions comprising the structure of the GBA are either inspired by, or are literal replications of, the concessions created during China's earlier engagement with capitalism. The Ming emperor's Macau formula for managing foreigners became the template for these new economic spaces that were latent in the physical landscape of the GBA. As such, I understand the GBA as comprising a recombination of spatial forms created in earlier times. We will see that these recombinant forms include not only European colonies and treaty ports but also elements of the Maoist built environment, such as the socialist work unit.[21] The persistent influence of such existing colonial and communist spaces, not Castells's electronic circuits, informs the structure of this new metropolis. These Chinese characteristics make the GBA a unique urban form that conforms to the logic of market-socialism.

Political Economy or Subjective Economy?

This brings me to my final point about Castells's ([1966] 2000) conception of the GBA metropolis. Regardless of his appeal to information technology as the basis of a new social formation, organized by "a circuit of electronic exchanges" (442), Castells ultimately understands the "space of flows" in terms of a conventional political economy, defined by a new relation between mobile and cosmopolitan elites on the one hand, and immobile and disorganized workers on the other. However, as we can see in chapter 1, the overarching goal of the Chinese state today is to enhance the quality of the population and to create self-governing cosmopolitan citizens poised to compete in the global marketplace. Therefore, the function of the GBA is not simply to dispossess the labor force in a production regime that operates for the benefit of a class of elites. It must also create a new type of Chinese subject. This new citizen is prepared to contribute to market-socialism as both flexible producer and discerning consumer.

In order to understand the design of the GBA metropolis, we therefore must look beyond the concerns of political economy, instead analyzing China's subjective economy and its role in the country's new economic regime. This is what is truly novel about this new Chinese city. It is for this reason that I now turn to Mumford's megamachine to describe this massive metropolis.

LEWIS MUMFORD AND THE GBA MEGAMACHINE

Mumford, an urban historian and public intellectual, published prodigious amounts of popular architecture criticism and books on urban planning. He is perhaps best known for his 1961 book *The City in History,* which traces the historical development of urban forms. However, Mumford's ([1967] 1971) discourse on what he calls the megamachine is a component of his two-volume *Myth of the Machine,* an exploration of humanity's historical relations to tools and technology, or "man's total equipment for life," which he calls "biotechnics" (308).

With the megamachine, Mumford conceives not of a city per se but of a machinelike social mechanism that incorporates regimented human subjects as its component parts. The prototype megamachine was the archaic human effort that constructed Egypt's pyramids with nothing more than the primitive technologies of the lever and inclined plane. In this so-called social machine, "human beings themselves are constituent pieces of a machine they compose among themselves and with other things (animals, tools) under the control and direction of a higher authority" (Deleuze and Guattari 1987, 456–57). This Egyptian megamachine necessitated the production of new subjectivities, including workers conditioned to obediently execute each task as well as members of a priesthood and secular bureaucracy that organized knowledge and carried out instructions.[22] However, the megamachine was not simply a primitive Egyptian apparatus. Mumford observes a contemporary megamachine operating in the postwar United States military-industrial complex, enabled by that era's so-called organization man and symbolized by the Pentagon.

My appeal to the megamachine, rather than the megacity, to describe the integration of the GBA metropolis with the post-Mao subjects of market-socialism highlights Macau's distinctive function in this new core city of Chinese capitalism. My approach is indebted to the scholarship of Félix Guattari and his use of the megamachine concept to explain the role of cities in producing urban subjects.[23] Much like the Egyptian construction of the pyramids or America's military-industrial complex, the GBA metropolis may be understood as a social machine designed to produce subjectivity. Guattari calls subjectivity the key commodity of contemporary capitalism. He argues that capitalism perpetuates itself by continually producing new subjectivities, with novel identities and desires and in search of new consumer experiences. For Guattari (2015), it is the physical "enunciations" (114) of the city, such as architecture and infrastructure, that form specifically urban consumer subjects.[24] Understood in this way, then, the GBA is a massive machinic apparatus assembled from a variety of disjunctive spatial components, the function of which is to produce not only the smartphones, Nike shoes, ceramic ashtrays, and plush toys that fuel China's economic growth but also the new citizens necessary for the market-socialist regime. These megamachine operations contribute to a subjective economy in China that produces new quality postsocialist consumers to rival Mao's socialist New Man.

Although I earlier critiqued Castells's ([1966] 2000) account of the GBA metropolis, I should note his apt observation of one important factor in this development. "In some cases," he says of the information megacity, "the most unlikely sites become central nodes because of historical specificity that ends up centering a given network around a particular locality" (444).[25] This is indeed exactly what happened with Macau's 1999 retrocession to the PRC. Macau played a crucial role in the origins of capitalism five hundred years before, only to fade into historical obscurity with Hong Kong's economic ascendance, the waning of Portugal's global influence, and the Maoist revolution on the mainland. However, with Deng's implementation of China's economic reforms in 1978 and the emergence of the GBA as an engine of Chinese capitalism, Macau is once again poised at the spatiotemporal nexus of a new era of global capitalism. The city now serves as a geoeconomic gateway between state socialism and the global market. Therefore, I finally turn to the complementary relationship among China's new SEZs and postcolonial SARs in the subjective economy of this GBA metropolis. This will allow me to illustrate both the recombinant spatial forms that construct market-socialism and the production of subjects who are crucial to this new economic regime.

SEZs as Laboratories of Production

The first phase of Deng's economic reforms involved the development of a production-for-export regime, which took shape in the new SEZs along China's southern coast. In 1979, a part of Bao'an county near Hong Kong was declared the Shenzhen economic zone, and several months later, three more SEZs were created: Zhuhai (directly adjacent to Macau), and Xiamen and Shantou (formerly known as Amoy and Swatow). Hainan Island was later declared an SEZ.

These new zones were established as what I call laboratories of capitalist production, where the central government would facilitate joint manufacturing projects funded by foreign capital. This investment came largely from the diasporic Chinese populations of Hong Kong, Taiwan, and Southeast Asia, and the new factories established in these zones employed China's vast supply of cheap labor who traveled from the countryside. The governmental logic of the SEZs is reminiscent of what I identify in chapter 2 as the Ming emperor's Macau formula. Foreign companies were relegated to the new coastal zones so that China could benefit from participation in new manufacturing projects, but those foreigners would have "trade but no more" (Fok 1999, 38). The intention was to segregate the capitalist activity in the zones, away from China's hinterland, in order to protect the country's autonomy. If this economic experiment was ultimately unsuccessful, it could simply be terminated, and most of China's population would never know that it had existed.

Chinese authorities established the economic zones as experimental classrooms, "social and economic laboratories where foreign technologies and managerial skills could be observed" (Harvey 2007, 130). Deng was forthright in his hope that the SEZs would constitute a "learning laboratory" for studying manufacturing technology, labor management techniques, and a private real estate market (Chung et al. 2001, 121). The Shenzhen zone became China's primary locale in which to experiment with these economic and governmental innovations, and Shenzhen eventually grew beyond the original confines of the zone and into one of the country's most prominent cities.[26] In the tradition of China's "transformative experimentation," provincial officials across the country were instructed to "learn from Shenzhen" as a model of economic development (O'Donnell, Wong, and Bach 2017). Therefore, just as provincial authorities were urged to mimic the experimental Shenzhen model, Shenzhen's own unique spatial form was learned from the example of China's former foreign concessions.[27]

The reforms that were tested in the new SEZs, and which merged the communist Chinese state and transnational capital into the hybrid economic form of market-socialism, required a new type of postsocialist Chinese laborer distinct from the socialist counterpart (the *gongren*), and who embodies the hybrid logic of this new form of capitalism. China's socialist workers, as well as the postsocialist laborers that followed, were the product of unique architectonic structures, or spatial machines, that were designed to accommodate both the job site and worker residence. The socialist worker was formed in the *danwei,* or work unit, a collectivist locus of social life that combined both the workplace and worker residence in one self-contained location; it also provided childcare, medical care, education, and other elements of community support. The *danwei* provided residents with not only jobs but also cradle-to-grave security, the iron rice bowl of Chinese socialism. However, just as the socialist *gongren* was forged in the spatial machine of the work unit, the postsocialist workers in the new experimental economic zones are also products of a specific spatial mode of subjectification. The initial labor force of the SEZs consisted primarily of young rural women who relocated temporarily to these zones to live and work in a new type of dormitory-factory. These new factory and residence spaces resemble the *danwei* form but lack the requisite socialist content.

In *Made in China,* her ethnographic account of these young female factory workers, anthropologist Pun Ngai (2005) describes how the Chinese state cooperates with transnational capital in the SEZs to fashion the "new social body" of this gendered laborer (4). This novel Chinese subject, which was produced in the SEZ "dormitory labor regime," is distinct from the socialist worker created in the *danwei.* While the *danwei* exemplified the state's lifelong commitment to laborers, the dormitory-factory in the SEZ is merely a temporary home for transient workers, funded by transnational capital rather than the state. While the *danwei* provided a cradle-to-grave social contract, thereby ensuring reproduction of the labor force to serve the socialist economy, the postsocialist employees living in the dormitory-factories of the new economic zones have no such security. These young women ultimately enjoy no social contract beyond the exploitative terms of the state, patriarchy, and wage labor.

Ngai demonstrates the microphysical process by which the bodies of these women are disciplined in dormitory life and conditioned for factory work. Ultimately, in her account, what is "made in China" is not simply the industrial products that are manufactured in the GBA's factories but also is this new postsocialist subject. We may understand these worker bodies as components of a biopolitical social machine that manufactures new subjects necessary for the reform economy. This process ultimately illustrates the unique reuse and recombination of prior spatial forms in postsocialist China, including the colonial-era land concessions that inspired the governmental logic of the economic zones and the socialist work unit that is the formal template for the postsocialist dormitory-factory. In short, this recombinant process exemplifies the subjective economy of the GBA megamachine, a new type of megacity with distinctly Chinese characteristics.

SARs as Laboratories of Consumption

If budding Chinese entrepreneurs initially learned the lessons of capital by studying in the learning laboratories of Zhuhai and Shenzhen, and if new postsocialist workers are created in the dormitory-factories in the new economic zones, then the consumer acumen of these citizens is cultivated today in the shopping malls and casino resorts of the Hong Kong and Macau SARs. Both Macau and Hong Kong serve as didactic laboratories for Chinese consumerism, and in these cities, the consumer behaviors promoted by the central government are pursued in a condensed and intensified form. The Macau and Hong Kong SARs are spaces of consumption that mirror the spaces of production just across the border in the SEZs.

While China's SEZs were crucial to the initial phase of market reforms, the SARs function in a complementary second phase of this process. This second phase of reforms addresses limitations of the SEZ production regime. I describe these limitations in detail in chapter 4, but in short, the central government gradually grasped the unsustainability of an economy based on producing goods primarily for export because it relies too heavily on foreign consumers, whose purchases of Chinese products may be affected by a variety of factors outside China's control, such as fluctuating exchange rates, global pandemics, and social unrest. Rather than rely solely on foreign consumers to finance Chinese industry, authorities determined that the country must develop its own mature domestic consumer market. Indeed, a similar arrangement of complementary systems of mass production and mass consumption powered the twentieth-century postwar economy of the United States, and Chinese authorities intend to mimic this American model. The development of this domestic consumer economy is one specific goal of China's National New-Type Urbanization Plan.

Both Hong Kong and Macau possess distinct characteristics that enable their roles in this economic program. Hong Kong's early economic advantage was its status as a free port, and the city has long been a dynamic marketplace that is often rated the world's freest economy. Hong Kong is a sort of consumer laboratory for Chinese tourists, a whopping forty-four million of whom visited the city in 2017. Hong Kong even has an indigenous architectural form, the podium shopping mall, with a consumer function that rivals Macau's casino resorts. These high-rise malls, typically located on top of Hong Kong's underground train stations, are a by-product of the city's unique colonial land management system (Lai 2016). In his account of Hong Kong's shopping mall "dreamworlds" of consumption, architect Stefan Al (2016) counts several hundred such malls in the SAR—perhaps the densest and tallest collection of shopping malls in the world. These Hong Kong malls make the city a shopping paradise and are a key attraction for Chinese tourists.

Entire retail districts have emerged near the Hong Kong–Shenzhen border, which cater exclusively to mainland shoppers, many of whom make day trips to take advantage of the city's favorable retail environment (Buckley 2015; Yeung and Yee 2012). Retail shops in the tourist areas of both Hong Kong and Macau are geared toward mainland customers; they primarily proffer such products as cosmetics, gold and diamond jewelry, and designer fashion goods. Favorable taxation regimes in the SARs mean these products are significantly cheaper than they are on the mainland, and these exclusive items have the added benefit of enhancing the quality of those individuals who purchase them (Cartier 2013b).

Figure 19. Chinese tourists in the Largo de Senado pack a suitcase with diapers and other mundane consumer items purchased at nearby shops. These items are slightly cheaper in Macau than mainland China, and their compositional integrity and brand veracity are guaranteed by Macau's regulated consumer environment. *Photograph by Adam Lampton.*

In addition, however, tourist-oriented shops in both Hong Kong and Macau also stock such mundane products as infant formula, diapers, shampoo, toothpaste, and liquid soap, which are slightly cheaper than they are on the mainland, and whose compositional integrity and brand veracity are assured by their purchase in the relatively well-regulated environments of these cities. (In contrast, mainland China is notorious for pirated goods and loose controls on brand and intellectual property.) It is common to see Chinese tourists on the sidewalks of Macau stuffing small suitcases with these quotidian items, or visiting tourist attractions while toting unwieldy prepackaged plastic bags packed with promotional goods ("buy four bottles of shampoo and get one free"), purchased at pharmacies or cosmetics chains such as Watson's, Mannings, or Sasa. Such scenes demonstrate the ways in which Hong Kong and Macau function as laboratories of consumption and cultivate those calculating consumers whom China desires for its reform regime. The PRC's productivist mainland economic zones and consumerist postcolonial administrative regions thus play complementary roles in the subjective economy of the GBA.

THE VIEW FROM THE TOWER

This discussion of the unique Chinese characteristics of the GBA metropolis, the unorthodox core city of China's new market economy, finally returns us to the Macau Tower, where we began this chapter. The Macau Tower is an ideal vantage point from which to observe the spatial logic of China's reform regime. From the top of the tower, it is possible to envision the operations of the massive urban megamachine that organizes the country's subjective economy below. We have seen that Macau inspired the exacerbated differences and enclave design characteristic of the GBA region, and a variety of latent geospatial forms from China's protocapitalist and socialist eras have reappeared to play distinct roles in the country's new economy.

China's SEZs, with their novel dormitory-factories, were designed to discipline the workers necessary for the joint manufacturing enterprises with foreign companies with which Deng initiated economic reforms, and which ultimately turned China into the factory for the world. Likewise, the SARs of Hong Kong and Macau play their own unique roles in the current phase of reforms, the goal of which is to cultivate quality consumers to contribute to China's domestic consumption economy. Today Macau is positioned at the nexus of the dual urbanization and subjectivation processes that define the reform era.

If the pyramids and the Pentagon were Mumford's transhistorical architectonic archetypes of the megamachine, and if China's GBA megacity is a contemporary example of its operation, then the Venetian Resort is the model spatial machine in Macau's consumer palace project as well as the city's indigenous regime of casino capitalism. Therefore, I next turn to an exploration of the events that enabled Adelson's entry into Macau's gaming market and the eventual opening of the Venetian Resort. By exploring the design and operations of the Venetian, we will be able to understand Macau's role today as an experimental laboratory of consumption for China's new economic regime.

PART II

Casino Capitalism

The Crystal Tower

As we saw in Part 1 of the book, Portugal's administration of Macau encompasses the entire five-hundred-year epoch of terrestrial globalization as well as Europe's shaping of the global system with the Age of Discovery and concomitant era of colonial geopolitics. Perhaps the most iconic reminder of that Portuguese presence in Macau today is the majestic Ruins of St. Paul's, which is (aside from the Venetian Resort) the city's most popular tourist site.

The baroque structure of St. Paul's cathedral was destroyed in 1835 by a fire that started when some soldiers quartered in the building accidentally knocked over a lantern. The cathedral was never rebuilt. All that remains today of the Colegio de São Paulo complex and its magnificent cathedral, which was once the Jesuit gateway to China, is the sacred stone frontispiece. That imposing

Figure 20. Tourists pose in front of the Ruins of St. Paul's cathedral. *Photograph by Adam Lampton.*

monolith was fashioned after an altar retable and inscribed with an elaborate ecclesiastical catechism, a "sermon in stone" (Porter 2009, 67).

The retable is the sacred structure positioned behind the altar in a cathedral. It typically houses the Holy Eucharist. St. Paul's may be the only architectural structure in China that bears this unique form. The entire retable-shaped facade manifests a coded iconographic message dedicated to the theme of the Assumption of Mary to the Heavens; her immaculate body, which once bore Christ, is likened to the tabernacle retable where the consecrated host is stored. Thus, St. Paul's is a monument to the miracle of transubstantiation, the ritual transmutation of earthly bread and wine into the body and blood of Christ.

However, St. Paul's stone symbolism also features unmistakable eastern motifs. This hybrid design was in keeping with Matteo Ricci's accommodative missionary practices that sought to present Christian doctrine as consistent with local theology. The design was also likely influenced by the fact that the craftsmen who created the stonework were Japanese Christians who converted during the Jesuit entreaties into Japan and who were expelled from their country in 1587, when shogun Hideyoshi banned the practice of Christianity (Pina-Cabral 2002). Therefore, orthodox canonical figures on the facade, such as Mary and the infant Jesus, are accompanied by unorthodox motifs of a more local origin. In one such heterodox image, the Virgin Mary steps vehemently on a seven-headed hydra. Accompanying Chinese characters read, "Holy Mother tramples the heads of the dragon." The base of the structure is likewise guarded by six stone Chinese lions.

The ruin stands adjacent to the remains of the Fortaleza do Monte, or Monte Fort. In keeping with traditional Portuguese settlement patterns, both buildings were erected on one of the highest points on the peninsula, manifesting a *monte sacro,* or sacred mountain, for the cathedral and providing an ideal defensive position for the European settlers. Indeed, in 1622, Macau faced a well-planned attack by a seaborne contingent of six hundred Dutch soldiers and sailors, who sought to take the fledgling township in order to gain control of the regional trade network.[1] The attackers, who drilled intensively for a week in preparation, were organized into three detachments, each equipped with six barrels of gunpowder, six hundred pounds of small shot ammunition, and a surgeon, as well as scaling ladders and sandbags with which to mount the assault.

As day broke on June 24, the feast day of St. John the Baptist, the stealthy Dutch contingent lit a barrel of gunpowder to create a cover of drifting smoke (incidentally one of the earliest known tactical uses of smoke screen in battle) and launched the landing force on the city. In a preemptive volley against the attack, Italian Jesuit mathematician Padre Jeronimo Rho fired a single cannon shot from the half-finished fort on Monte Hill so accurate (or lucky) that it struck a barrel of Dutch gunpowder. The barrel exploded in the bosom of one enemy formation, causing numerous human casualties as well as the loss of most of the gunpowder supply, ultimately prompting the remaining invaders to retreat.

If a cannon were fired from the remains of Monte Fort today, the volley would likely strike the Grand Lisboa resort, Stanley Ho's iconic posthandover contribution to the cityscape, which was completed in 2008 and which stands directly opposite the Monte Hill on a parcel of reclaimed land, adjacent to the original Lisboa Casino. The Grand Lisboa is a conspicuous point of orientation that is readily visible from any location in the central city. This glittering golden glass tower, whose own unconventional silhouette was supposedly inspired by the bountiful headdress of a Las Vegas showgirl, appears today like some sort of surrealist "profane illumination" rising above a sea of small apartment buildings in the city center.[2] The design has earned the Grand Lisboa its ignominious inclusion on various compilations of the world's ugliest skyscrapers, and the structure is rendered all the more disquieting by the incorporation, on the oblong base of the tower, of the world's largest integrated LED screen. The resulting Grand Lisboa light show is a precocious contemporary catechism, alternately illuminating impious images of gigantic rolling dice, a hand of playing cards, and even a solitary blinking eyeball.

The unsettling juxtaposition of the sacramental Ruins of St. Paul's and the irreverent Grand Lisboa neatly encapsulates,

Figure 21. If a cannon were fired from Monte Fort today, the volley would strike the Grand Lisboa Casino and Hotel, which sits on reclaimed land in the central city. *Photographs by Adam Lampton.*

in one Walter Benjamin–style dialectical image, Macau's five-hundred-year metamorphosis from Portuguese trading port to postcolonial Chinese tourist mecca. No simple cannon shot today, however accurate, could quell the annual advance on the city of tens of millions of eager visitors, most of whom come from the GBA megacity of the PRC. I turn now to the physical transformation of Macau's cityscape at the turn of the millennium to accommodate those new post-Mao tourists, and the inauguration of the city's own Crystal Palace project and heterodox casino capitalism regime.

4

Macau SAR

LABORATORY OF CONSUMPTION

> In contemporary capitalism, subjectivity is
> the product of a global mass industry.
>
> —Maurizio Lazzarato, *Signs and Machines*

On an otherwise ordinary afternoon on November 26, 1996, Lieutenant Colonel Manuel Antonio Apolinario, vice director of the Macau government's Gaming Inspection and Coordination Bureau (DICJ), was shot two times at close range by a motorcycle gunman while sitting behind the wheel of his car on the busy street outside his office. One bullet passed through both his cheeks; the other struck his neck, barely missing his spine. Although he was gravely injured, he survived the ambush. Apolinario was a former army commando and veteran of the guerilla warfare tactics common to the entrenched nationalist insurgencies waged in Portugal's African colonies, but he did not expect to encounter such an attack on the relatively sleepy streets of Portuguese-controlled Macau (Fraser 1997).

There had been earlier intimations of an emerging security problem in the city, such as the explosion of two homemade bombs outside of the new Grandview Hotel on Taipa Island in January of the same year. But the audacious attack on a government gaming official in broad daylight would later be remembered as the symbolic first shot levied in a shocking three-year campaign of violence in Macau, which claimed 122 lives and which came to be known as the casino wars.[1] "Macau, City of Fear: The Peace is Finished," announced a prophetic front-page headline in the Portuguese daily newspaper *Macau-Hoje* the day after the Apolinario shooting. The casino wars would indeed have a tremendous impact on life in the city in the final years of Portuguese rule (Letter from Macau 1997).

Authorities determined from the spent shell casings that the gunman's pistol was issued by China's People's Liberation Army, an indication that he had been recruited for the job from across the border. But they assumed that the shot caller behind the crime was most likely a member of one of Macau's several local Triads, the Chinese criminal brotherhoods, or organized crime syndicates, involved in the city's casino junket trade. It was lost on no one that among the main duties of the DICJ is to license, monitor, investigate, and (if need be) penalize the activities of junket promoters. In fact, just a few days before the shooting, Apolinario had proposed an elevation of government control over the management of the city's VIP rooms.

Apolinario actually returned to his DICJ duties several months later (albeit with additional protection provided by around-the-clock bodyguards and a government-issued bulletproof car), but while he was convalescing in Portugal, the city underwent a significant transformation. The shooting sparked a subsequent series of violent events that would stretch for several years, including bombings, shootouts among rival gangs, arson attacks on cars and motorcycles, kidnappings for ransom, gruesome chopping assaults by gang members armed with meat cleavers, and the targeted assassinations of police officers, government officials, and gaming industry regulators.

One customs officer was shot in his car while his young daughter sat in the back seat on a morning ride to school. The third-ranking official at the DICJ was shot and killed while he was walking outside the headquarters of the judiciary police. Three prison guards who had been purposefully recruited from Portugal to impose some professionalism in the operation of Macau's Triad-filled Coloane prison were ambushed by a gunman while having drinks at an outdoor café on a Friday evening, and two of them were killed. And on and on the victims mounted.

Although the particular motives of each individual act were difficult to ascertain, authorities presumed the crime wave generally emanated from efforts among rival Triad factions to claim their share of proceeds from illicit enterprises as the city prepared for the transfer to Chinese control. These lucrative activities included loan sharking, extortion, prostitution, smuggling, and trafficking drugs and counterfeit cigarettes. However, what elevated this violent activity above the normal nitty-gritty of gangland turf wars was the almost cinematic quality of these events, which, in contrast to the normally inconspicuous nature of Triad activities befitting a secret brotherhood, seemed specifically calculated to achieve maximum visibility.

A Molotov cocktail was matter-of-factly hurled onto the manicured grounds of the governor's mansion. Hit men holding pistols in both hands calmly executed rivals as they dined in crowded restaurants. And riderless motorcycles with flaming tissues stuffed into open gas tanks careened down empty streets to explode dramatically into glass shop windows. These media-friendly events invited international attention, concern, and condemnation; contributed negatively to both the city's tourism industry and the citizenry's morale; and prompted increasingly loud calls for PRC authorities to step into the Portuguese territory and exercise control over the mayhem.

Much of the violence was attributed to an internecine conflict within the city's 14K Triad. Senior gang member Ng "Street Market" Wai, a Filipino Chinese who earned his nickname from his early days running a protection racket in the Mongkok market in Hong Kong, engaged in a power struggle with former protégé Wan "Broken Tooth" Kuok-Koi, a charismatic upstart who would become Macau's most notorious gangster.[2] With a bona fide strongman reputation in Macau's Triad community, Ng had actually worked closely with Stanley Ho to establish Macau's unique VIP trade, and when Ho was recruited by Philippines president Ferdinand Marcos to develop a casino gaming industry in that country, Ng's personal relationship with Marcos enabled him to help carry out the assignment. Because Ng had played such an important formative role in regional gaming, Broken Tooth's challenge to his authority took on added significance.

Broken Tooth was a poor kid from the Macau slums who had earned respect by rising from the bottom rung of the gang hierarchy to achieve a leadership role. For his part, the flamboyant Broken Tooth contributed significantly to the theatrical ambiance of Macau's Triad activity, openly boasting of his gangland prowess in interviews he conducted with the Asian editions of *Time* and *Newsweek.* He ultimately even produced the Hong Kong film *Casino,* a thinly veiled autobiographical account of his rise to power in the Macau underworld. This B movie, inspired in part by the 1996 Martin Scorsese film of the same name about the role of organized crime in Las Vegas, featured handsome

Hong Kong leading man Simon Yam in the starring role (identified in the film as "Broken Tooth Giant"). Because the Macau government understandably refused to grant permission for the project, the film was shot illegally in the streets of the city, including a fight scene staged just outside the police headquarters.

Casino's gangland motif walked a thin line of realism on several fronts. In addition to Broken Tooth's dual role as financier and central character, lead actor Yam's brother was a senior member of the Hong Kong police force; he had even served as the head of the city's organized crime and Triad bureau. The film also featured enough fistfights, stabbings, gunplay, and brutal beatdowns by pipe-wielding thugs to match the events unfolding in the city. Indeed, the opening scene of the film depicts an actual episode from the conflict between Ng and Wan, a spectacular drive-by shooting initiated by Broken Tooth's henchman in the porte cochere of Taipa's New Century Hotel, whose casino was controlled by Ng. This cinematic blurring of fact and fiction resulted in a gritty and compelling urban noir, which unsurprisingly depicts "Giant" in a positive light as a violent but principled gang leader. In the film's conclusion, a journalist character describes the gang leader as a kind of "hero," a common man simply using his wits to survive within the confines of a corrupt system.

Throughout Macau's actual crime wave, Triad members appeared to act with virtual impunity. In the face of their brazen attacks, Portuguese authorities were unable to effectively address the violence, punish the perpetrators, or maintain any semblance of law and order in the city. For example, of the 122 gang-related murders that occurred from 1996 to 1999, none were solved.[3] The absurdity of the situation reached its nadir when the city's undersecretary for security, Brigadier General Manuel Monge, remarked during a press conference that tourists need not be afraid to visit the city because "our triad gunmen are excellent marksman" who "would not miss their targets and hit innocent bystanders" (Linter 2007, 23). Incidentally, only a short time later, General Monge's personal chauffer was shot and killed one morning as he left his home.

The casino wars culminated in yet another event that seemed made for the movies. On May 5, 1998, the personal minivan of Antonio Marques Baptista, the chief of Macau's judiciary police, exploded in his driveway while he was walking his dog nearby. Baptista (whose

Figure 22. Wan "Broken Tooth" Kuok-Koi (center) is arrested on May 1, 1998, by Macau police chief Antonio Marques Baptista, aka Rambo (right). *Courtesy of Reuters.*

nickname was Rambo) was not injured in the blast, and several hours later, he and his men burst into a private dining room in the Lisboa Hotel to arrest Broken Tooth, where they found him watching an interview of himself on a Hong Kong television station. To protest the arrest, members of the 14K Triad descended on Macau, and in a two-hour period, they set fifty cars and motorcycles alight. Two days after Broken Tooth's arrest, the film *Casino* debuted at a Hong Kong theater, although it was banned in Macau.

Court proceedings against Broken Tooth commenced on April 22, 1999—although not to adjudicate the car bombing, for which there was no physical evidence of his involvement. Instead, he faced charges for an older allegation of criminal intimidation of a croupier that carried a maximum sentence of five years. However, after many delays, combined with the forgetful testimony of a number of witnesses, Broken Tooth was ultimately acquitted of the charge (even though the act in question had been recorded by the casino's surveillance cameras).

A second trial focused on the more serious allegation of Broken Tooth's membership in a Triad organization, which is a crime in Hong Kong and Macau. This one-month trial was also marked by a variety of complications, including the presiding judge's sudden resignation and return to Portugal, and the resignation of the primary defense attorney as well as a string of his unenthusiastic replacements. Near the end of the testimony, the members of the three-judge tribunal that presided over the court proceedings retired to their chambers to view *Casino,* which they concluded was indeed an accurate autobiographical portrayal of Broken Tooth's Triad activities. After two weeks of deliberation, on November 23, 1999, Broken Tooth was found guilty, with his own film comprising part of the evidence used to convict him. The court sentenced him to fifteen years, to be served in a special high-security wing of the Coloane prison that had been constructed especially to hold him. The court also demanded state seizure of his sizable assets and jailed his brother and a number of other gang affiliates.

The casino wars constituted the unceremonious final act of Portugal's governance of Macau and ostensibly set the stage for China's sovereign takeover of the city. On December 20, 1999, one month after Broken Tooth's incarceration, the Portuguese flag was lowered in a solemn ceremony after nearly 450 years of administration, and Macau formally became a Chinese territory. This world-historical event marked the end of Europe's five-hundred-year colonial project and the termination of the era that Sloterdijk (2013) refers to as "terrestrial globalization." In addition to asserting governmental authority over Macau, the PRC seized the opportunity provided by the social unrest to march a contingent of five hundred PLA soldiers into the city only twelve hours after the handover ceremony—an act in direct contradiction to the agreement that had been forged between Portugal and China. Given the recent breakdown in public order, Macau's populace for the most part positively received not only the city's retrocession to the PRC but also the intervention of the PLA, hoping that the administrative changes would produce a more stable environment. This was in stark contrast to the ambivalence expressed by Hong Kong residents about the former British colony's return to China two years earlier, as well as the uneasy embrace of the "motherland" in that city that still persists today.

FROM CASINO WARS TO CASINO CAPITALISM

In her ethnographic study of the complex cultural identity of Macau residents at the time of the handover, Clayton (2009) claims that the casino wars problematized the legitimacy of the city's "sort-of" sovereignty. The consistent representation of Macau throughout its history, as an illicit enclave operating outside the normal international order, which was exacerbated on the global stage by the lurid media accounts of the Triad violence, and which culminated in Broken Tooth's film, was a "way of representing Macau as a kind of 'matter out of place,'" says Clayton (2009, 98). Macau's exceptional status was ultimately presented not as Portugal's salutary contribution to Occidental–Oriental relations but as a potent problem that could only be corrected by the city's integration into the international system under the calm hand of China's central government.

However, in seeking to understand Macau's role in the PRC today, my own interest is not in the question of representation, or how the world came to view Macau as a failed state whose deficiencies were attributable to its ambiguous sovereignty. I am interested in the city's pragmatic function in China's economic reforms. That is, I want to explore how the PRC mobilized Macau's semisovereign status, and even its once-taboo casino industry, for its own governmental purposes. From this perspective, the PRC's posthandover designation of the enclave as a special administrative region was not so much a normalization of Macau as a conventional actor in a Westphalian international order as it was a formalization and protraction of the city-state's ambiguous status. The perpetuation of this "sort-of" status, even after the city's retrocession to China, would allow Macau to play a useful role in the very market-socialist regime that the city had itself inspired. The casino wars became the impetus not merely for Macau's belated inscription into the Westphalian system but for the reincorporation of the Chinese motherland into a capitalist world-economy.

Macau's retrocession to the PRC provided the final component of the regional GBA metropolis necessary for its function as the core city of China's reform economy. As a leisure locale conveniently located on the periphery of the mainland, with a legal casino industry, a distinct cultural ambiance, and the official imprimatur of the central government's "approved destination status," Macau would become a primary terminus for Chinese tourists and a spatial instrument for enhancing their quality and human capital. In short, Macau's specific function in the GBA today is defined by the emergence in the city of a distinct regime of casino capitalism.

By using the term "casino capitalism," I do not intend its popular use today to describe a risk-intensive and capricious global economy that emerged in the post-1970 era of neoliberal deregulation and unfettered financialization. Rather, my use of "casino capitalism" in the context of Macau delineates the pedagogical and biopolitical role played by Macau's casinos, gambling machines, and megaresort environments in cultivating Chinese economic subjects. As I note in chapter 3, both the Mao and post-Mao regimes have relied on experimental modes of practice to generate policy innovations that, if successful, may be formally adopted at a national scale. According to Heilmann (2008), in this process of "transformative experimentation," local officials are often granted broad discretion to test new methods of problem solving with which to confront specific governmental challenges. These "model experiments" (11), which are undertaken in self-contained "experimental points" (7) such as an economic zone or administrative region, may generate practical solutions that can then be adopted elsewhere, in a method known in China as "proceeding from point to surface" (7).

We might understand Macau today as a site of such experimental policy formation, an urban laboratory in which several distinct but complementary interests have converged in a process that aims to comport postsocialist subjects. Local authorities in Macau's new posthandover administration were granted wide latitude by the central government to revitalize the gaming industry by introducing new policies to liberalize and regulate the city's gaming monopoly. Those foreign casino companies that won the right to operate in the city contributed a massive influx of capital and industry acumen to develop the city's casinos in order to attract a new clientele of Chinese tourists. The Macau SAR ultimately became a petri dish of policy formation in which the central government experimented with new freedoms of population mobility as a strategy to counteract unanticipated threats to the new economic regime, which emerged in the forms of both a regional financial crisis and an infectious disease epidemic. At the same time, the local Macau government experimented with industry liberalization measures that authorities hoped would make the city safe in the wake of the casino wars.

In short, the five-hundred-year old city of Macau would undergo an unlikely transformation into an innovative urban milieu in which to comport a new kind of Chinese tourist for the simultaneous benefit of Macau, the central government, and transnational capital.[4] Key to this process was the construction of Adelson's Sands Casino, which was the first foreign gaming property in the city and an architectonic stepping-stone to Macau's remarkable transformation.

LABORATORIES OF CONSUMPTION

In chapter 3, I discuss the enclave urbanism of the GBA and the way that Chinese authorities created the SEZs to serve as laboratories of capitalist production, where the country could learn from foreign companies about management, labor, and manufacturing so it could experiment with a market economy. The first SEZs were intentionally positioned along China's southern coast—as far as possible from Beijing and from the country's predominantly rural heartland, but close to the colonial enclaves of Hong Kong and Macau and the access these cities provided to the overseas Chinese populations in Taiwan and Southeast Asia who might be persuaded to invest in these enterprises. The SEZs were the locus of the production-for-export regime with which China launched its economic reforms; if capitalist enterprise was successful in these experimental zones, then the resulting knowledge could applied "from point to surface" to other mainland locales. After their return to the PRC, Hong Kong and Macau were designated as SARs and deployed to function in a similar manner: as experimental sites of economic reform. If Deng promoted the SEZs as laboratories of capitalist production, then we might conceive of the SARs as complementary laboratories of consumption where China experiments with a domestic consumption regime.

To be clear, I do not mean to claim that at the outset of the reform movement in 1978, the central government developed a plan to create a consumer economy and to mobilize Hong Kong and Macau for this purpose. Rather, as we will see, what transpired was a tentative process of experimentation in which policy innovations were introduced in Macau and Hong Kong in reaction to unexpected events, such as the crisis of public order created by Macau's casino wars. It was through this process of "transformative experimentation" that the SARs emerged as laboratories of consumption crucial to China's reforms.[5] In addition, a new type of postsocialist Chinese tourist began to take shape in Macau's urban milieu. Macau's reincarnation as a laboratory for such experiments began with the revision of Stanley Ho's forty-year casino monopoly, an arrangement that had enabled Triad infiltration of the industry via VIP room operations, and that therefore bore a significant share of the blame for the casino wars.

RESTRUCTURING MACAU'S MONOPOLY CONCESSION

Under the terms of the 1999 retrocession and Macau's mini constitution, and much like the British return of Hong Kong in 1997, Macau's economic, administrative, and legal frameworks will remain autonomous from mainland China for fifty years before the city is fully integrated into the PRC. After the handover, and under a general policy guideline of "Macau people ruling Macau," the new government administration was to be headed by a locally born Chinese chief executive officer, a position that replaced the Portugal-appointed governor. Macau's first chief executive was Edmund Ho, son of Tai Fung bank founder Ho Yin, the influential local businessman who benefited from the city's Bretton Wood–era gold trade and who had played a decisive role in resolving the Maoist 12-3 Incident in 1966.

China's central government indicated that it had no objection to the continuation of the casino gaming sector in the SAR (which was of course Macau's only viable economic advantage), as long as no mainland Chinese company controlled the gaming concession. In an effort to stimulate the economy, the new Ho administration decided to terminate the existing monopoly arrangement and open the industry to (limited) competition. Government officials believed that the involvement of foreign operators might strengthen the legitimacy of Macau's postcolonial administration by professionalizing the gaming industry, increasing government tax revenues, and even helping maintain law and order (Lo 2005). Because gaming operators in North America or Australia are bound to abide by the legal regulations of those home jurisdictions even when operating casinos abroad, the expectation was that those foreign restrictions might function to regulate local activities (Cormier and Faiss 1986). Foreign gaming companies would presumably seek to ensure that their casino operations in Macau adhered to an international legal standard so as not to threaten their other casino ventures; their caution might therefore curb the Triad influence in Macau's gaming industry.

The Macau government announced a plan to replace the monopoly arrangement with three new casino concessions and launched a public tender to solicit applications, employing international accounting firm Arthur Anderson to rank bids on the basis of applicants' gaming industry experience. In order to submit a bid, applicants had to commit to investing a minimum of US$500 million (HK$4 billion) in Macau. The tender commission received twenty-one bids. Although several Las Vegas companies participated in the process, there was relatively subdued enthusiasm for Macau's prospects among established North American companies. The well-publicized casino wars, as well as some lingering confusion about the legal terms of the handover agreement, had prompted concerns about Macau's security and regulatory environment. For example, Las Vegas–based Harrah's Entertainment, one of the world's largest gaming companies, declined to submit a Macau bid.

The Las Vegas companies that did participate included Adelson's Las Vegas Sands, Wynn Resorts, MGM Mirage, Mandalay Bay, and Park Place Entertainment. Failed Atlantic City gaming magnate Donald Trump submitted a joint bid with a local Macau partner.[6] The interest of Las Vegas Sands was piqued by a discovery made by several company executives when they conducted scouting research in Macau in 2001. They found that the average daily revenue of each of Stanley Ho's mass market tables in the Lisboa Casino was an astounding US$45,000—an amount that compared quite favorably to the average take of $2,500 per table on the Las Vegas Strip (Cohen 2017b). Harnessing this potential profit would surely justify the investment, if not the accompanying risk. In addition, Adelson had been contacted by Hong Kong businessman Richard Suen, who claimed his personal relationships in China would facilitate the ability of Las Vegas Sands to mount a successful bid, and he assured Adelson that the concession would be immensely lucrative. Suen would later sue Adelson in a Las Vegas court for allegedly reneging on his agreement to compensate Suen in the event of a successful bid (Armental 2019).

Although Adelson was convinced of Macau's potential, he launched his original bid in a joint venture with Taiwan's China Development Industrial Bank; the partnership only served to underscore Adelson's inexperience in regional politics. The bank's chairman was the chief finance officer of the Kuomintang Party, which had been banned from Macau since the 1966 eruption of Maoist unrest in the city during the 12-3 Incident (Cohen 2014; Dicks 1984). Given the fraught relations among the mainland and Taiwan, as well as political sensitivities emanating from the inclusion of several Taiwanese generals on the bank's board of directors, the partnership had almost no hope of securing a license.

However, Chief Executive Ho and the gaming tender committee members were apparently enamored of Adelson's bold vision to build a massive Venetian Resort on Macau's new Cotai land reclamation site, a 5.2 square kilometer land parcel awaiting development near the city's newly constructed airport. Adelson claimed that Cotai could eventually house a Las Vegas–style strip of properties rivaling the world's primary gaming destinations. This prospect prompted Macau officials' desire for Adelson to launch a competitive bid.

While those officials contend that the decision to award concessions was made at the local SAR level, according to some accounts, Adelson's bid may have been buttressed by support from elements of China's central government. If Adelson had miscalculated his original partnership with Taiwan, he did make useful contacts in the PRC that were apparently facilitated by Suen. In early July 2001, Adelson met with China's vice premier, Qian Qichen, at the Purple Light Pavilion at Zhongnanhai, headquarters of the Communist Party and the state council, and Qian apparently invited Adelson to bid for the Macau concession.[7] That same weekend, Adelson also met the mayor of Beijing, who sought Adelson's assistance with another matter. The PRC was in the process of launching a formal bid to host the 2008 Olympic Games in Beijing, and the mayor allegedly asked for Adelson's help to dissuade conservative members of the U.S. Congress from submitting a planned bill to officially oppose Beijing's Olympic bid. Adelson reportedly stepped out of the room to phone House of Representatives majority whip Tom DeLay, who took the call while he was attending a Fourth of July cookout. DeLay was Adelson's political ally (as well as a beneficiary of his financial support); he was also cosponsor of the bill in question. The bill was never brought to the floor of the House for vote. Whether or not Adelson's overtures caused the desired outcome, his efforts appeared to curry favor with China.

Whatever the motivation, Macau officials privately suggested that Adelson consider mounting a joint concession application with Hong Kong's Galaxy Entertainment, a newly formed company controlled by Hong Kong property tycoon Liu Che Woo, who had experience operating hotels but no experience in casino gaming. Neither company was a strong individual candidate, but together they possessed a wealth of complementary experience. Galaxy Entertainment had the additional advantage of being Chinese owned without carrying the prohibitive baggage of the Kuomintang. Galaxy and Las Vegas Sands proceeded with the joint bid. The tender committee then merged the Arthur Anderson ranking report with their own internal list of criteria, which awarded additional points for the scope of each company's proposed project. On February 8, 2002, the gaming tender commission announced the three winners of the concessions: Wynn Resorts, Stanley Ho's reformed SJM, and the Galaxy Entertainment–Las Vegas Sands partnership.

Under the original terms of the partnership, the role of Las Vegas Sands was merely to manage the casino for a fee, with an option to purchase equity later. However, as he became increasingly convinced of Macau's revenue potential, Adelson agitated for a more significant presence. As a result, the partnership quickly became antagonistic; problems emanated from competing company views about budgets, conflicting corporate cultures, and additional concerns on the part of Las Vegas Sands that Galaxy's plan to emphasize VIP junkets would not pass the scrutiny of Las Vegas gaming officials. With the partnership at an insurmountable impasse, and with skepticism about the viability of launching a new public tender, the government proposed that the companies divide the joint venture into two separate entities: one concession and one so-called subconcession, each of which would share the same license but would otherwise operate completely independently.[8]

While that decision resolved the immediate problem, it created a different set of complications. Macau's two other concessionaires protested what they perceived to be a favorable arrangement that had been extended to Galaxy Entertainment, and government officials had to become reconciled to the fact that they had little choice but to allow the other concessionaires to also award subconcessions of their respective licenses. In this way the three original planned concessions were doubled into six entities, creating a much different market environment than originally intended.

The financial benefit to the concessionaires was significant. Wynn profited US$900 million simply by selling his subconcession to Melco-PBL, a partnership between Lawrence Ho (Stanley Ho's son) and Australian gaming and publishing tycoon Kerry Packer. Stanley Ho sold his own subconcession for US$200 million to MGM China Holdings Ltd., a company jointly owned by MGM Resorts International and Ho's daughter, Pansy Ho. That is, the ostensible effort to dismantle Ho's monopoly ultimately led to members of his immediate family controlling, either fully or partially, three of Macau's six new gaming concessions.[9] This process resulted in the final composition of Macau's posthandover gaming oligarchy: Sands China Ltd.; Wynn Macau; Galaxy Entertainment; MGM China; PBL/Melco; and SJM. However, to understand the role of these companies in Macau's development, we must account for an unexpected event that altered China's emerging market economy in a way that substantially benefited Macau's tourism market.

THE ASIAN FINANCIAL CRISIS AND DOMESTIC CONSUMPTION IN CHINA

The 1997 Asian financial crisis, which started in Thailand but quickly swept across the continent, raised concerns within China about the country's nascent market economy. While China's financial system was relatively unaffected by the immediate fallout of the crisis, the country's reform strategy was indirectly threatened by its regional effects. One consequence of the crisis was the devaluation of many Asian currencies, which constrained the capacity of neighboring countries (particularly Japan, South Korea, and Thailand) to purchase Chinese exports. This was one motivating factor for the central government's decision to revise the country's economic plan and to promote enhanced domestic consumption in order to decrease China's reliance on foreign consumers.

In order to achieve this goal, the government set out to position tourism as a key growth area of the economy, hoping to mobilize the Chinese population in domestic tourism practices that would lead to enhanced levels of consumption. This new tourist promotion inverted decades of socialist rhetoric that had pejoratively characterized tourism as bourgeois decadence. Authorities revised state policies that had discouraged or even prevented population mobility. In 2000, the central government formalized the overt practice of leisure by creating three annual public holidays, known as Golden Weeks, to encourage domestic and cross-border tourism (Nyiri 2006). To do so, authorities drew on the Maoist practice of using large-scale ideological campaigns, such as the Great Leap Forward or the Down to the Countryside Movement, to mobilize the population and produce the country's socialist New Man. They also borrowed from China's ancient tradition of literati travel as a mode of aesthetic education when they launched an extensive information campaign designed to inform citizens of the moral value of travel and the specific behaviors deemed proper to modern tourism (Nyiri 2006, 2010). This new state-sanctioned leisure time was not meant to simply be a respite from labor; it was specifically designed to serve as another productive component of economic life.

Promoting what they deem a "scientific view of consumption," Chinese authorities conceive of a productive integration of tourism practices, consumption habits, and individual tourist quality, thereby differentiating such consumption from general hedonism or wasteful excess (Nyiri 2010, 78). As I describe in chapter 1, alongside tourism's economic benefits, the Chinese government sees tourism as "an inexpensive substitute for education" (Nyiri 2009, 154), a pedagogical or civilizing practice that produces "quality" Chinese citizens who are desired by the regime (157). The central government's decision to deploy tourism as a means of individual and economic development has roots in sixteenth-century China, when travel was an important component of elite aesthetic education. This premodern Chinese literati travel was predicated on the existence of predetermined "scenic spots," or specific sites of beautiful natural scenery, which had been identified and inscribed by scholars in earlier times; represented in poetry, painting, and woodblock prints; and codified into a general tourist itinerary that served an educational and civilizing purpose.

In fomenting the new reform-era tourism regime, the Chinese state drew on this premodern tradition, actively promoting a new set of scenic spots for contemporary tourists to visit. These sites primarily reflected the government's interest in enhancing nationalism and patriotism, and promoting modernization and development (Nyiri 2006). Therefore, the itinerary of new scenic spots included patriotic education sites such as Mao's mausoleum, as well as landmarks important to the new market economy such as the Hainan SEZ, which became one of China's primary tourist attractions. Books, magazines, and travel guides promoted the sites and specified the appropriate activities through which they should be understood and appreciated. In addition, the Chinese government developed and promoted new themed environments, which also came to serve as popular scenic spots. These included Shenzhen's "Splendid China," with miniature reproductions of famous Chinese and global landmarks, and China folk culture villages, featuring performances from costumed ethnic minorities who live on site (not unlike the ethnological exhibitions in the turn-of-the-century world's fairs).

In addition, the market economy contributed to this repertoire by producing a wide variety of new themed environments that would also serve as popular tourist destinations. During the 1990s, as many as 2,500 new theme parks opened in China; these sites became components of a "new cultural grammar" to be mastered by budding tourists (Nyiri 2006, 12; Campanella 2008). As Nyiri (2006) says of the transhistorical relations among premodern travel by intellectuals to "scenic spots," and new forms of tourism for the masses, "The desire to travel could once again be the desire to validate one's knowledge of canonical representations, and this was now true for a much larger part of Chinese society, one which was poorly versed in the literati tradition beyond its superficial signs and had no code of travel behavior at its disposal" (12). Visiting themed environments became a "proto-tourist activity" for many Chinese (15)—an opportunity to essentially *learn how to be a tourist.* The need to learn basic tourist behavior is of course not unique to China. As anthropologist Orvar Löfgren (1999) explains in his social history of the modern European holiday, "vacationing has served as a laboratory for trying out new lifestyles or forms of consumption," and the Chinese tourism industry similarly became a laboratory for experimenting with new forms of mobility, subjectivity, and consumption.

As I outline in chapter 1, the nineteenth-century European grand tour was a formative travel activity that provided civil and aesthetic education to Northern European youth. We may understand China's promotion of tourism to a new set of scenic spots as comprising a similar state-driven Chinese grand tour, whose pedagogical aim is to create civilized and quality consumers. The goal is to promote a form of domestic consumption whose economic benefits will supplant the country's initial reliance on the SEZs and the export-oriented production regime that had made China the world's factory. This Chinese grand tour would eventually incorporate the country's newest special zones: the former colonial cities of Hong Kong and Macau. However, these cities could only become Chinese tourist destinations if they were made accessible for cross-border travel by those Chinese tourists.

THE EPIDEMIC AND THE IVS

The specific emergence of Macau and Hong Kong as popular tourist sites and laboratories of consumption was in large part the product of the PRC's reaction to another regional crisis, one that threatened the very tourism industry that China was working so hard to develop. The severe acute respiratory syndrome outbreak in southern China during spring 2002—three years after Macau's handover, and only a couple of months after the government announced the results of the gaming tender—constituted a profound public health emergency that posed another obstacle to China's macroeconomic planning.

While the scale of the epidemic on the mainland was obscured by the central government, the effect on Hong Kong and Macau was immediately evident. With the syndrome's spread, the World Health Organization released what was at the time the most strict travel advisory in the institution's history. It specifically cautioned against traveling to Hong Kong, which devastated the city's economy. Between March and June 2002, nearly four thousand Hong Kong businesses closed, and the city's tourism industry suffered. At the height of the crisis in April and May, hotel occupancy dropped by 20 percent, and in April alone, the average daily number of passengers on Hong Kong's flagship Cathay Pacific airlines decreased by nearly 90 percent (Baehr 2008). However, the epidemic did not simply reduce the number of tourists in Hong Kong. The origin of the epidemic was traced to a specific group of tourists who had visited Hong Kong and resided on the same floor of a particular hotel, inadvertently spreading the disease to seven other global sites when they departed the city (Ng 2008).[10] Therefore, given the epidemic's locus in Hong Kong and its global dissemination via leisure travel, it directly undermined the logic of China's new tourism economy.

But the epidemic had more than economic ramifications. I lived through it and spent significant time in both Macau and Hong Kong during the period, so beyond these economic ramifications, I can attest to its consequences in personal terms. Although they were novel to me, these experiences will now seem common to anyone who has endured Covid-19. The daily psychological trauma of living in a palpably toxic environment, characterized by a mysterious but potentially fatal illness, profoundly transformed quotidian life in both cities. Surgical face masks were de rigueur, contributing to a dystopian atmosphere; handwashing hygiene stations were installed throughout the cities; visitors underwent mandatory temperature checks at building entrances; and security measures meant that civil servants like me were banned from unauthorized travel. Each SAR constructed secure facilities in which to quarantine those at risk of infection, with the number of citizens restricted to this Kafkaesque confinement mounting daily. An innocent cough on a public bus would prompt a reaction from other passengers. In addition, the syndrome both demonstrated the precarious permeability of the newly defined political border separating the SARs from the mainland while reinterpreting the border itself as a biopolitical technology of contagion, belying the central government's pronouncement that the SARs and the mainland were part of "one country."

In July 2003 and the immediate wake of the crisis, Hong Kong citizens staged the largest demonstration in the city's history. They emphasized their dissatisfaction with the handling of the epidemic and subsequent decline of local real estate values, but they also protested the central government's plans to introduce new security measures to the city (Bradsher 2003). Less than a month later, and with great fanfare, the PRC announced a new Closer Economic Partnership Agreement (CEPA) with Hong Kong and Macau that aimed to stimulate their respective postepidemic economies (Kong 2003).

One specific component of CEPA was the launching of the Individual Visit Scheme, a revolution in personal liberty in the PRC that allows select tourists from particular mainland cities and provinces to travel to Hong Kong and Macau on individual visas without having to join a government-sanctioned group tour. This experimental scheme initially applied only to residents of eight cities of Guangdong province, Beijing, and Shanghai, but when the IVS proved successful, the central government gradually expanded its reach and adjusted its scope. Today, the IVS applies to residents of forty-nine Chinese cities. The policy controls the number of trips these Chinese citizens may make to Macau and Hong Kong in a given year, the length of time they must wait between trips, and the maximum duration of their visits.

The IVS prompted an explosion of Chinese tourism in Macau, with the number of general tourist arrivals steadily climbing: eleven million in 2002, twenty-one million in 2009, thirty-one million in 2014, and forty million in 2019. These visitors enabled Macau's dramatic posthandover transformation. However, this transformation must be understood within the context of the specific responses of the newly integrated Chinese state, launched at several different scales, to address the three crises I have discussed in this chapter. First, a crisis of public order was created by the casino wars, which exacerbated the SAR's security problem and threatened to undermine the city's suitability for international investment. Second, the Asian financial crisis of public finance challenged the viability of China's production-for-export regime, prompting a compensatory shift to consumption-led development. Third, the crisis of public health mounted by the advance of the severe acute respiratory syndrome epidemic threatened to undermine the very tourism industry that the country had mobilized to enhance consumption (Simpson 2018). These new experimental policies were tested in the SARs and contributed to Macau's unique urban milieu, creating the "conditions of possibility" within which the city could become the world's most lucrative site of casino gaming.

"THE MOST UNIQUE DESIGN OF A CASINO EVER"

One material point of the convergence of these crises and their respective policy responses was the Sands Casino, an entirely novel Macau environment that opened in 2004, whose outsize dimensions and innovative design contrasted dramatically with the city's prehandover casino properties. The success of this new casino would revolutionize the local gaming industry, particularly in terms of the mass market sector, as well as convincing global financial institutions that Macau was a viable site of investment. The Sands would also serve as a stepping-stone to the eventual introduction of the integrated resort into Macau's gaming industry, a spatial machine whose innovation and development in

Las Vegas is largely attributed to projects by Kirk Kerkorian of MGM, and Wynn and Adelson (Cohen 2016).[11]

Macau's early twentieth-century gaming environments were notorious for a lack of enticing facilities or innovative design, down to their unprofessional and casually dressed croupiers. Even after Stanley Ho's 1961 intervention in the industry with his introduction of the Lisboa Casino and Hotel in 1970, Macau's mass market gaming rooms remained relatively threadbare, unornamented, and unremarkable, and the VIP rooms reportedly did not fare much better.[12] In casino design parlance, such functional gambling structures are consistent with the once-influential approach of casino design consultant Bill Friedman (2000), who published a weighty 620-page manifesto entitled *Designing Casinos to Dominate the Competition,* in which he offers thirteen principles to guide successful design. Friedman advises that casino owners limit decorative frills so as not to distract players from the principal activity of gambling. His design axioms are based on the presumption that most gamblers prefer to hunker down in secluded alcoves where they can wager away from prying eyes. Friedman's principles therefore include such recommendations as "Standard Decor beats Interior Casino Themes," "A Compact and Congested Gambling Equipment Layout beats a Vacant and Spacious Floor Layout," and "Low Ceilings beat High Ceilings."

The Sands Casino in Macau was designed by Paul Steelman, who is arguably the world's most accomplished casino architect, and whose firm is responsible for a significant number of casino resort projects in Las Vegas and around the world.[13] While the austere and unadorned design of the extant Lisboa casino reflected many of Friedman's design principles (and probably more importantly Ho's reluctance to invest in property upgrades), Steelman took an entirely different approach with the Sands. But to ascribe the Sands' design to a simple contrast with Friedman's philosophy is to miss the radical singularity of Steelman's vision for Macau.

Wynn and Adelson had already reinvented the Las Vegas casino resort in the 1980s and 1990s with luxury properties on the Strip. The involvement of their respective companies in Macau promised to introduce Las Vegas–style resorts to the city. Even so, the Sands Casino was something different. Steelman (2001a; personal interview) refers to his work on the Sands as constituting "the most unique design of a casino ever." Not only was it markedly distinct from anything that existed in Macau at the time, but it was also a radical departure from a number of prevailing global trends in casino design. In preparing the initial foreign casino for the Macau market, Adelson and Steelman hoped to demonstrate that they were not simply importing a Las Vegas model into the city (even if the planned Venetian Resort was a replication of Adelson's Vegas property). Rather, they were introducing an indigenous design innovation that was appropriate to Macau—one specifically adapted to Chinese gamblers.

Adelson was anxious to open the Sands quickly so he could get a foot in the door in Macau while he was building the Venetian, whose substantial size and complexity necessitated a lengthy construction process. Steelman was given only the long Labor Day weekend to complete the Sands design.[14] The small land parcel near the ferry terminal in Macau's outer harbor, which had been granted to Adelson for this initial project, would not accommodate the expansive footprint typical of American casino resorts. Steelman thus made the counterintuitive decision to design a multitiered environment, placing the casino on the building's second floor rather than adjacent to the lobby. Therefore, in contrast to a typical Las Vegas property, which aims to immediately impress visitors as soon as they step into the building, with the Sands design, Steelman says, "We put the 'wow' in the casino, not the lobby" (personal interview).

The property was designed according to Chinese geomancy, or feng shui, principles, which Steelman claims was a first for global casino design, although it has since become more common, given the increasing importance of Chinese gamblers to the industry. Ho's 1970 Lisboa property also reportedly has a feng shui design: an advantageous orientation toward Taipa Island, with a birdcage shape that would ostensibly trap gamblers and their money inside the building. However, the common-variety mass market casino inside the Lisboa property has no such design elements. The feng shui elements in the Sands include ensuring three ways to get into and out of the building; having one entrance that faces the water in order to mobilize its energy, or chi; and using rounded shapes rather than pointed edges. These feng shui considerations are evident in the undulating curved segments that define the Sands' interior. After the basic construction was completed, the company had a feng shui master from Hong Kong review the building and made final corrections on the basis of his recommendations.

Other insights that informed the Sands' unique design were the product of preparatory fieldwork that Steelman had conducted in Macau. While observing Chinese gamblers in the city, Steelman noted that their play was generally not a tandem activity, one undertaken in conjunction with other pursuits. In Las Vegas, most visitors gamble while also participating in other activities, such as shopping, dining, or attending a convention, but Steelman observed that most visitors to Macau were there solely to gamble. This observation drove Steelman's design. Rather than planning for conventional restaurants in the Sands, Steelman opted for a noodle bar on the edge of the gaming floor, which gamblers could visit for quick bite before returning to the tables.

Steelman also observed that gambling in Macau often took the form of a head-to-head competition (which he called a gladiator contest) between the gambler and the casino. In addition, other patrons often behaved as if they were members of a team collectively competing against the house. They would gather around a table to observe the action, animatedly cheering on the outcomes, even "back betting" on the wagers of other gamblers who were riding a hot streak. This behavior distinguished the Macau style of gambling from its Las Vegas counterpart. Therefore, Steelman decided to design the Sands Casino in the style of a stadium, the structure of which would facilitate such practices.

The result was a massive casino space with distinct proportions. With a total size of 21,300 square meters (175,000 square feet), at the time it was built, the Sands was the largest casino in the world. (This superlative designation was overtaken several years later by Adelson's Venetian Resort.) However, the most striking feature of the Sands is the main gaming floor's seventy-foot ceiling, which dramatically increases the volume of space in the building. This is not only a direct contradiction to Friedman's principle "Low Ceilings beat High Ceilings" but also a stark contrast with prevailing casino design trends. This particular design element provoked the most surprise among industry insiders, and Adelson himself had to be convinced of its suitability before he agreed to proceed with the plan.

The stadium-style design of the Sands renders the main gaming floor

Figure 23. Interior of the Sands Casino, "the most unique design of a casino ever." The seventy-foot ceiling towers above the gaming floor, while a curtain on the left covers the expansive windows that create the "day-lit" casino environment. Rounded edges throughout are exemplary feng shui elements. The stadium-style design allows for maximum visibility. *Photograph by Adam Lampton.*

visible from the open galleries of the floors that circle above it. This not only promotes the idea of gambling as a spectator sport but also suggests a subtle logic of transparency and panopticism that was important in a gaming environment that had been tainted by the pervasive threat of Triad violence. To that end, Steelman also designed the Sands' brightly illuminated gaming floor for maximum visibility. The Sands was Steelman's first "day-lit" (Steelman 2001a; personal interview) casino, with an expansive window extending across the eastern wall of the building, which opens the Sands to the outside environment. This design element flies in the face of the stereotypical assumption that a casino should be a cloistered environment segregating gamblers from the outside world.

Taken together, Steelman's innovations produced perhaps the world's first casino to be designed specifically for Chinese gamblers and adapted to the specific exigencies of its local environment. One Macau junket executive who had worked for several decades in casinos in Las Vegas, Reno, and Atlantic City observed the success of the experiment:

As an outsider I can say the Sands Macau was probably the most perfectly designed casino I have ever seen. It was a home run in every aspect. It was laid out perfectly, with the customer lines, with the toilets just next to the escalator so that they can find them immediately when they are looking for them; the bar is situated perfectly, the layout of the tables, the ceiling height, and the lighting. Out of jealously, some people said it is the "box of baccarat," but that is what it was intended to be. The intention was not to build an integrated resort, but it was the first step for the company to enter the Macau market and to change the rules of the game, and they were changed dramatically. (quoted in Simpson, Chung, and Tieben 2009)

Given my attempt in this book to explore a spatial history of Macau, it may be useful to briefly address these design innovations within the context of Foucault's (1979) scholarship on architecture and its relation to subjectivation. The Sands belongs to a genre of modern architecture that is not only built to be seen from the outside, like a palace, but is also designed (in a manner consistent with Foucault's comments about nineteenth-century clinics, classrooms, and prisons) "to render visible those who are inside it" (172). This visibility is enabled not only by the copious space, high ceilings, and stadium-style terracing but also by the proprietary structures Steelman designed (and patented) to float above the tables and hold lights and surveillance equipment, because the high ceilings are not conducive to this purpose.

The difference between the Sands Casino and Ho's Lisboa property is not merely a difference in interior casino design. It also includes the distinct governmental regimes in Macau that are materialized in the built environment. By choosing the Lisboa name and using yellow Portuguese tiles to decorate the exterior of the building, Ho symbolically kowtowed to the Portuguese colonial administration in the city. The Lisboa's labyrinthine interior and hidden VIP rooms were a spatial manifestation of the dubious legal and moral complexion of the junket industry. The entire edifice, with its unornamented casino and lack of cosmetic upgrades, was an expression of Ho's monopoly control of the industry. Combined with Ho's popular designations as the godfather or king of Asian gambling, the Lisboa exemplified the function of classical architecture: when "the art of building responded firstly to the need to make power, divinity and might manifest" (Foucault 1986, 9).

In contrast, the ways in which the Sands came to serve on the one hand as a conduit for circulations of Chinese tourists and on the other hand as a convergence of strategic governmental reactions to emergent crises of public health, finance, and social order, exemplify Foucault's concept of architecture as techne. The Sands demonstrates how modern architecture surpasses purely symbolic aspirations and "begins to concern itself closely with problems of population, health and urbanism" (Foucault 1986, 9). The Sands may be understood as not merely a benign tourist destination but also as "an architecture that would operate to transform individuals: to act on those it shelters, to provide a hold on their conduct, to carry the effects of power right to them, to make it possible to know them, to alter them" (Foucault 1979, 172). In short, the Sands served to attract new Chinese tourists, whose travel to the "scenic spot" of Macau was enabled by new central government policies and whose movements need not be deterred by the threat of Triad violence. But the Sands also functioned to shape the expectations and behaviors of those tourists, and (as we will see later) to ultimately position them in a market economy.

THE WORLD'S MOST PROFITABLE CASINO

On May 18, 2004, in the morning, before the Sands' official opening, a sizable crowd gathered on the street outside the property. A rumor (which some claimed was started by Adelson) spread through the crowd that the first guests inside would each receive a free MOP 500 gaming chip. Excited patrons, many of whom had taken advantage of China's new visa policy to make their first visit outside of the mainland, began to climb over the property's steel barricades, surging against the glass doors at the entrance.

The crowd was so boisterous that Sands security agents became increasingly concerned that people might be inadvertently crushed in the ensuing melee. Given that the movement of the doors, which were designed to swing outward, was impeded by the masses of people pressed against them, the security team ultimately decided that it was necessary to literally break sixteen glass doors off their hinges to accommodate the overwhelming physical ingress of the crowds. The indelible image this created of a massive group of tourists smashing down the doors of the resort in their eagerness to get to work at the gaming tables resonated strongly with the city's new concessionaires and gaming industry observers. Approximately forty thousand people visited the Sands on the opening day, triple the venue's actual capacity (Cohen 2014). A new gaming regime had clearly arrived in Macau, but now, in this posthandover environment, the threat of Triad violence was replaced by the more benign peril of being trampled underfoot by overeager tourists.

Those tourists apparently arrived with deep pockets; initial returns on the Sands investment surprised everyone. The Sands quickly became the most lucrative casino in the world. Profits generated by his first Macau venture not only allowed Adelson to recoup his entire initial $240 million investment in only ten months of operation but also caused him to leap up twelve spaces on the Forbes 400 chart, becoming the third wealthiest individual in the United States in 2006. *Forbes* estimated that over the preceding two years Adelson earned almost US$1 million per hour from his investments (Cohen 2014).[15] Within two years, the Sands' annual revenue had nearly doubled. Though the Sands was originally intended to be a temporary building (Adelson planned to close it when the Venetian opened in Cotai), it was so profitable that Adelson decided to leave it open and later added a hotel tower.

Figure 24. Tourists break through barriers at the Sands Casino grand opening on May 18, 2004. Forty thousand people visited the property on opening day, triple the actual capacity of the building. *Courtesy of Getty Images.*

These profits did more than benefit Adelson's bottom line. The shocking scale of Macau's early revenues energized global financial markets in a manner that was directly traceable to the Sands. The casino's success legitimated Macau as a site of international investment and gave capital markets the confidence to support other Macau projects. As Steelman (personal interview) says, "That one little building set in motion a set of wheels that were impossible to stop through the financial markets, because all of a sudden the returns on investment were unheard of in our industry."

CASINO CAPITALISM REDUX

At the beginning of this chapter, I contended that Macau's retrocession to China after the casino wars resulted in the emergence of a regime of casino capitalism in Macau. Now I will conclude this discussion by clarifying my use of the term "casino capitalism." London School of Economics professor Susan Strange (1986) used the term "casino capitalism" to characterize the increasingly volatile post-1970 global economic regime. "The Western financial system is rapidly coming to resemble nothing so much as a vast casino," she proclaimed, evocatively describing financial trading offices staffed not by cautious bankers clad in pinstriped suits but by reckless "chain smoking young men" busily making electronic financial trades. "They are just like the gamblers in casinos watching the clicking spin of a silver ball on a roulette wheel and putting their chips on red or black, odd numbers or even ones," she observed (1). But the crucial difference between ordinary gambling and this global financial casino is the manner in which we are all involuntary participants in the latter financial games, with mortgages, pension plans, and life insurance policies increasingly converted into derivative tradeable securities. "This cannot but have grave consequences," Strange (1986, 2) prophesied. Indeed, the global financial crisis of 2007, which brought even Adelson's Las Vegas Sands company to the brink of bankruptcy, was a realization of her fears (Benston 2008).

Strange dates the origin of casino capitalism to 1973's Nixon shock, when the United States abandoned the gold standard and the Bretton Woods Agreement, which had stabilized international monetary markets; incidentally, this decision also ended Macau's lucrative gold trade in the city's final years, as well as its position outside the international order. It is certainly tempting to characterize Macau's booming posthandover economy, which started with the remarkable revenues generated from gambling at the Sands, as a manifestation of unregulated markets and a general neoliberal restructuring of global capitalism into a giant casino, but that is actually not my intention here. My invocation of casino capitalism is focused not on the casino as an analogy or representation of financial markets but as a pedagogical site of economic subjectivation.[16]

The Sands was the initial step in a process that would transform much of Macau's cityscape in both a phantasmagoric and functional manner. Consistent with the didactic dimension of Macau's resorts, which I will explore in detail in the chapters that follow, we may conceive of the Sands in much the same way as Foucault (1979) described the design of the nineteenth-century school building under a disciplinary regime: as "a mechanism for training, a pedagogical machine" (172). The transformative policy experimentation of the Chinese government to address crises of public order, public finance, and public health, combined with Steelman's architectural innovation, helped transform Macau into a laboratory of consumption, a productive component of the GBA metropolis that would complement China's market reforms. The Sands was a precursor to the integrated resorts that would soon follow. It is this pedagogical capacity of Macau's gaming environments to serve a process of economic subjectivation that I describe as casino capitalism. This system of casino capitalism would be fully realized in Adelson's Venetian Resort and Macau's palace project, which I turn to next.

5

Integrated Resort

WORK UNIT FOR CONSUMER COMRADES

> The point, it seems to me, is that architecture begins at the end
> of the eighteenth century to become involved in problems of
> population, health and the urban question. Previously, the art of
> building corresponded to the need to make power, divinity and might
> manifest. The palace and the church were the great architectural
> forms along with the stronghold. Architecture manifested might,
> the Sovereign, God. Then, late in the eighteenth century,
> new problems emerge: it becomes a question of using
> the disposition of space for economico-political ends.
>
> —Michel Foucault, *The Archaeology of Knowledge*

"Unleash Consumption," urges the bold headline of a July 2006 editorial in the *China Daily,* succinctly capturing the macroeconomic logic of the county's reform era. The editorial in the widely circulated Communist Party newspaper notes that "in recent years, China has attached paramount importance to stimulating domestic demand to balance its investment- and export- driven economy." However, lamenting the country's overreliance on state-sponsored public investment in infrastructure projects at the expense of increased personal spending by citizens, the editorial emphasizes the importance of an enhanced social safety net to ease uncertainty about the future in order to facilitate individual financial planning. It recounts a series of laudatory central government policies, including subsidizing rural education costs and raising the minimum wage, whose ultimate goal is to help "people save more money and encourage them to spend it as consumers."

The unambiguous message of this Communist Party missive is that China's new economy requires a new type of Chinese consumer, whose heightened confidence about the future will overcome his reluctance in the present to part with his hard-earned savings and purchase Chinese products. However, the desire for this new Chinese consumer extends far beyond the country's borders. In contemporaneous remarks on trade relations with China, United States president George W. Bush invoked an identical concern about Chinese consumer confidence and a similar vision of a spendthrift Sino-shopper. During a September 2007 trip to China to meet with President Hu Jintao, Bush commented on the crucial importance of Chinese consumption to the global economy.

"We certainly hope that China changes from a saving society to a consuming society," Bush (2007) said, reflecting the same sentiment as the editors of the *China Daily.* For Bush, it was vital that China's citizens "feel comfortable coming into the marketplace, the global marketplace, so that our producers can see the benefits directly with trade with China." Bush clearly recognized that China's new consumers are a crucial factor in the sustainability of global capitalism.

The *China Daily* editorial projects the image of a rational consumer that is consistent with the central government's "scientific view of consumption" and that understands consumer spending as more than simple hedonism or wasteful excess (Nyiri 2010, 78). This calculating economic actor who navigates the social world making cost–benefit analyses, balancing future security against present-day gratification, is the epitome of the *homo economicus* idealized in neoclassical economic theory. However, although consumer decisions may certainly contain a calculating quality, consumerism is not simply an ideology to be embraced in cognitive fashion, then unleashed in a flurry of purchases. Rather, consumption is an embodied activity that takes a particular material and spatial form in the contemporary Chinese city.

THE SPATIAL LOGIC OF CONSUMPTION

"Although we have begun to understand the postsocialist transition," geographer Fulong Wu (2003) said of PRC economic reforms, "its spatial restructuring is crudely understood" (1334). Throughout this book, my spatial history of Macau has aimed to understand this geospatial restructuring of both the GBA metropolis and the city-state of Macau and to demonstrate Macau's material function in market-socialism. Macau plays an operative role in the central government's revision of the country's macroeconomic policy, from an initial reliance on export-driven production that exploited China's vast reserves of cheap labor to initiate market reforms, to a recent drive to enhance the quality of those workers so that their local purchases might contribute to more sustainable growth.

Each of these respective economic policies has a corresponding spatial logic. Production for export is enabled by the SEZs along China's southern coast that serve as laboratories of capitalist production. The SEZs manage itinerant rural workers who live and work for a time in combined dormitory-factories, a spatial innovation that has made the GBA the world's factory for the production of toys, cosmetics, and small electronics (Pun 2005).

With the recent introduction of the National New-Type Urbanization Plan, the central government aims to replace this export-production regime with a consumption-led economy. This drive to urbanize China's population is based on the assumption that citizen purchases to support a new urban lifestyle hold the key to the country's economic development. I argue that Hong Kong and Macau have been mobilized to serve as laboratories of consumption in which to experiment with new economic subjects to serve this regime. Tourism to these cities, which is enabled by government policies such as the IVS, enhances citizen quality so that these leisure practices may contribute to economic growth.

In this chapter, I explore the functional role of Macau's integrated casino resorts in this national urbanization plan. Macau's resorts may be understood as spatial machines that produce a new urbane Chinese consumer. "In projects of political subjectification or governmental self-formation, appropriate bodily comportments and forms of subjectivity are to be fostered through the positive, catalytic qualities of spaces, places, and environments," contends geographer Margo Huxley (2007, 195), and this is certainly true of the tourists who visit Macau's resorts. We will see that the integrated resort in Macau functions as an apparatus of economization, a market device that articulates Chinese tourists with a model program of urban consumption practices.

By analyzing the unique design of the resort device, we may uncover the underlying logics of market-socialism and contemplate the countenance of the new Chinese consumer.

THE LABOR OF LEISURE: THE WORK UNIT AND THE INTEGRATED RESORT

I closed the last chapter with an analysis of architect Paul Steelman's innovative design of the Sands Casino. The Sands was the first foreign gaming property to open in Macau after the 1999 handover of the city to China, and it was specifically designed to appeal to Chinese gamblers. The Sands helped normalize casino tourism in the city after the adverse effects of the violent casino wars; it also served as a stepping-stone to the subsequent introduction of the integrated casino resort.

The integrated resort is a comprehensive gaming and entertainment complex that typically combines a casino with a hotel, retail promenade, and other attractions, such as convention halls, performance venues, swimming pools and exercise facilities, restaurants and a food court, and family-oriented amusements. The integrated resort originated in Las Vegas in ambitious projects initiated by MGM, Wynn, and Adelson over the last several decades. When these companies were awarded casino concessions in Macau, the expectation was that they would introduce such Las Vegas–style resorts to the city. Sure enough, Macau's Venetian and Wynn resorts are reproductions of existing Las Vegas properties, and the Parisian, Cotai Central, Wynn Palace, MGM Grand, and MGM Cotai properties extend this trend.

Scholarly accounts of these Las Vegas resorts tend to conceive of them as examples of "postmodern architectural experimentation" (Waltrep 2002, 137) and to explore how these environments provide a leisure respite for tourists, an "elsewhere for escape" from the workaday world (Shields 2013, 112). To understand the local function of Macau's new integrated resorts, however, we must look beyond their postmodern signification and seek instead to understand them as postsocialist spaces that play a specific role in the economy of the PRC. The Macau integrated resort is a local spatial form that is designed, much like the Sands Casino, to appeal to Chinese tourists; this design differentiates the Macau resort from its Las Vegas counterpart. If the Macau resort buildings themselves do not appear markedly different from Las Vegas resorts, their specific uses are distinct, and the postsocialist characteristics of Macau's resorts reflect the urbanization and spatial restructuring of the PRC. We will see that Chinese tourism to Macau is no simple escape from the travails of work life. Rather, Chinese tourists in Macau's resorts engage in a labor of leisure that is necessary for the reproduction of the market-socialist regime (Lonsway 2009; Rojek 2009).

To understand the function of Macau's resorts in Chinese tourism, it is helpful to contrast these postsocialist structures with the *danwei,* or work unit, that played an innovative role in Maoist China. The *danwei* was a collectivist form of urban life under state socialism's planned economy that organized the everyday life space and activities of people employed in the same organization, providing such services as housing, food, childcare, medical care, and education in a delineated environment. The *danwei* had a complex function in the socialist city. The *danwei* was the site for the organization of collective consumption. It delivered the iron rice bowl of welfare benefits provided to workers; it equipped residents with a supportive social network and public "face," or social identity; and it formed the "key basic unit of urban life" under socialism (Bray 2005, 36). In short, *danwei* "were the building blocks not just for an ambitiously industrializing economy, but indeed for constructing a utopian new form of collectivized urban life" (5). If the socialist Chinese worker *(gongren)* was forged in these work units, which produced a collectivist proletarian subject and ensured the reproduction of labor power, then a postsocialist consumer is forged today in the country's numerous shopping malls, theme parks, and branded retail spaces, which function to ensure the reproduction of leisure power necessary for the new consumption-led economy (Bosker 2013; Jewell 2015; Ren 2011).

The integrated casino resort in Macau is an exemplary "ideal type" Chinese consumption environment through which we may clearly envision this complex process of post-Mao consumer subjectivation. Macau's resort regime is not entirely consistent with the underlying rationale of the *China Daily*'s proposal to "unleash consumption" in an effort to motivate consumer spending. The newspaper calls for a Keynesian-style social safety net to inspire consumer confidence, thus implying that a state-sponsored system of "embedded liberalism" should replace Maoist cradle-to-grave security. But Macau's integrated resort apparatus presents a disembedded or neoliberal response to this problematic that is consonant with actually existing market-socialism. As self-contained urban enclosures, Macau's resorts offer all the social elements once provided by the Maoist work unit: accommodation, food, health care, childcare, education facilities, transportation, and entertainment. In this context, however, the Chinese state has retreated from the organization of collective consumption and the provision of the Maoist iron rice bowl; it is the tourist's own responsibility to pursue these services in a commodity logic.

Rather than providing a comprehensive social safety net, the post-socialist state extends new freedoms of mobility to select citizens. Those citizens in turn mobilize tourism practices to maximize personal quality; they do so through particular consumption behaviors that are designed to enhance remunerative personal characteristics while minimizing their demands on the Chinese state. Within the context of the central government's efforts to mold citizen-consumers, we will see that Macau's integrated resorts comprise a materialist pedagogy that conforms to this neoliberal consumption regime.

CHINA'S NEW URBAN ECONOMY

As I outline in chapter 3, the PRC is rapidly urbanizing hundreds of millions of rural peasants. Chinese leaders hope that the housing, lifestyle, and purchasing habits of those newly urbane, quality citizens will sustain the country's economic growth. They hope that this new urban workforce will contribute to a knowledge and service economy that will gradually replace China's industrial base. Prioritizing Chinese cities as a strategy of development involves not only a stark reversal of Mao-era policies but also a reinvention of the socialist city itself. The socialist city in China was defined not by a stimulating and heterogeneous urban lifestyle but by the monotonous spatial dispersal of monolithic state-owned enterprises (SOEs) and their respective *danwei,* which served as the city's functional and unornamented building blocks (Wu 2009). Distinctions among rural and urban residents were formalized through household registration (*hukou*) that tied citizens to their place of birth; domestic migration from countryside to city was discouraged or even prohibited by the central government.

Daily life for citizens in the socialist city was centered in the respective work unit, which reduced the need or opportunity for people to move around the city. This constrained mobility, tied to a general lack of formalized leisure time, meant that citizens engaged in relatively little use of public spaces outside of the *danwei.* Therefore, Chinese cities under socialism lacked the quality of urbanism that defined the modern European metropolis (Wu 2009), explored in the tradition of western urban sociology typified by the work of such scholars as Georg Simmel, Louis Wirth, Walter Benjamin, Siegfried Kracauer, and Richard Sennett.

However, today, the Chinese state facilitates population mobility in an effort to engineer urban growth. Rural residents are urbanized to create Chinese citizens in the classical sense of the word: urbane and cosmopolitan individuals with refined tastes and capabilities (Jacka 2009). This transformation of the population involves concomitant institutional and infrastructural development. New superlative architectural attractions—many of which are financed by transnational capital and designed by global "starchitects"—have replaced the SOEs in China's contemporary urban fabric (Ren 2011).[1] These ubiquitous Chinese shopping environments collectively comport consumer bodies and shape bourgeois moral mindsets appropriate to this economic regime.

In this chapter, I will explore Macau's unique contribution to China's consumer landscape, and the city's pedagogical role in promoting an urban lifestyle conducive to consumption or "urbanism as a way of life" (Wirth 1938). Urbanism is an affective characteristic of Macau's integrated resorts; it is consistent with the accumulation strategy that drives China's economic transition (Wu 2009). The particular form of urbanism that is enacted in Macau's massive megaresorts reflects the state–consumer nexus of Chinese market-socialism.

Macau as a Model City

My analysis of Macau's integrated resorts is informed by scholarly attention to China's use of normative models—such as model soldiers, model workers, model factories, and model villages—to guide ethical behavior. Bakken (2000) refers to China as *The Exemplary Society* in order to emphasize the productive role of such pedagogical models in Chinese social life. "It is one of the fundamental assumptions in the Chinese theory of learning that people are innately capable of learning from models," he says (8). China's exemplary society "can be described as a society where 'human quality' based on the exemplary norm and its exemplary behaviour is regarded as a force for realizing a modern society of perfect order" (1). This Chinese exemplarity constitutes a "moral science" (1), the pedagogical aim of which is to shape behavior according to normative guidelines that are embodied within the exemplary models that are promoted by the state and that citizens are urged to emulate. As encapsulated, interiorized, and miniature model cities, Macau's integrated resorts play a role in the production and maintenance of a normative mode of urbanism as a way of life consistent with the goals of China's National New-Type Urbanization Plan and the country's economic reform regime. Macau's resorts have unique Chinese characteristics that combine both capitalist and communist components; this design is consistent with China's program of model pedagogy. According to Bakken (2000), even contemporary Chinese educational models employ some traditional elements; within the context of model innovations, this recombinant "re-emergence of tradition" (4) is evident in both Macau's resorts and the system of market-socialism itself. That is, although Macau's integrated resorts are model urban environments that serve a pedagogical function for the new economic regime, antecedent elements of the socialist built environment, such as the work unit, provide a "normative core of tradition" (4) that is latent in the contemporary resort form. This recombinant form produces a uniquely Chinese spatial environment, distinguishing the function of Macau's resorts from their counterparts in Las Vegas.

Macau's built environment comprises a didactic *materialist pedagogy* for Chinese tourists, who visit Macau already steeped in the practice of learning from models. However, to fully appreciate this model function, it is helpful to conceive of learning as more than simply a cognitive process of knowledge acquisition, and to understand it instead as what Colin McFarlane (2011) calls "a distributed assemblage of people, materiality, and space that is often neither formal nor simply individual" (3). Indeed, in his book about urban learning, McFarlane sounds not unlike Mao in his insistence that "learning emerges through practical engagement with the world" (15). This "practical engagement" with the resort environment is my focus. If London's Crystal Palace functioned as a sort of greenhouse to cultivate citizen-consumers for the emergent industrial society of the nineteenth century, then Macau's integrated resorts provide a massive immersive environment for learning the logics of China's urban consumption regime.

To understand the contemporary function of Macau's integrated resort device, it is useful to briefly recount Bray's genealogy of the *danwei* design; specific features of this Chinese spatial form are important for understanding the function of Macau's resorts. According to Bray (2005), the *danwei*'s design had a variety of influences, including ancient Chinese walled cities, traditional courtyard homes, and nationalist organizations, as well as radical Soviet planning practices that influenced socialist-era Chinese architects. The most prominent physical feature of the *danwei* was its enclosed form. The *danwei* was separated from the larger urban environment by a high wall, with access to the *danwei* compound mediated by a gate; together, these wall and gate features created "a discrete spatial realm" for daily life (Bray 2005, 145). This design recalls the important role played by walls in Chinese urban and residential design: both ancient Chinese cities and traditional Confucian courtyard homes deployed walls to mark off territory and "to produce and regulate particular kinds of subjects" (35). This practice reappeared in the *danwei*.

China's socialist cities were centers of production, and the cityscape was structured by the spatial distribution of *danwei*. Each *danwei* belonged to an individual SOE, which was responsible for its financing, and in which the residents of the work unit were employed. The effect of this production regime on the urban fabric was the "'strips and chunks' (*tiao-kuai*) administrative structure" of Chinese cities, which separated the more or less autonomous *danwei*—with its factory, residential area, and supporting infrastructure—from the administration of the city within which it was located (Bray 2005, 143). "Each state-owned *danwei* thus became an island or small kingdom within the city, with almost complete control over its own spatial realm and with a source of funding independent of city authorities," notes Bray. This independence was reinforced by the high wall that surrounded the *danwei* compound, which marked off the discrete and autonomous space.

The modern Chinese city was therefore organized as a patchwork of self-contained work units, each of which produced proletarian and political subjects appropriate to advancing the goals of state socialism. We will see a similar design and autonomous governance function reflected in Macau's integrated casino resorts and their place in the city's general urban fabric. Bray (2005) suggests that "detailed study of spatial formations can provide new insights into the nature of political and social relationships in China" (1), and it is in the spirit of this claim that I take up my study of the unique design of Macau's resorts.

THE INTEGRATED RESORT AS POSTSOCIALIST SPACE

The iconic structure of Macau's casino industry liberalization is the city's massive Venetian Resort. The Venetian was Adelson's second Macau property after the Sands, and it is one of the largest buildings on the planet. When it was constructed, the Venetian contained the world's largest casino. In addition, the property boasts three thousand hotel rooms; three hundred shops; a fifteen-thousand-seat auditorium; Asia's largest medical tourism facility; an employee training center; and a transportation network, which includes an underground parking garage, three indoor canals, and a fleet of buses for tourists and staff.

When it opened, the Venetian was the world's sixth largest building in terms of total area. However, the company described the resort as the world's second largest inhabitable building, with the word "inhabitable" used in order to distinguish it from other megastructures, like the Dutch flower auction facility and the Beijing and Dubai airport terminals, that dominated several of the top spots on lists of the world's largest buildings. This nomenclature might be dismissed as a simple marketing ploy intended to artificially inflate the resort's superlative status. However, the fact that the structure is indeed "inhabitable" points to the resort's formal similarity with the *danwei.* The Venetian is more than a massive consumer space; like the *danwei,* it is a semi-autonomous and self-administered urban enclosure, which includes within its walls the provision of many of the basic services necessary to urban life. Therefore, to understand the function of the Venetian for Chinese tourists, we must first understand the formal characteristics of this unique urban enclosure.

An influential tradition of semiotic criticism, popularized by Jean Baudrillard (1994) and Umberto Eco (1986), typically characterizes casino resorts such as the Venetian as postmodern architectural amusements. The existing theoretical lexicon culled from the work of these scholars is defined by such analytical concepts as implosion, simulation, and hyperreality. These concepts identify representational characteristics of the built form that, if taken to their logical conclusion in this particular mode of critique, may collectively function to create an architectonic simulacrum, a self-referential or even meaningless structure with an overabundance of signifying elements but a lack of grounding referents. Put simply, the Venetian's formal characteristics simulate the city of Venice, but the superficial structure ultimately fails to achieve its ostensible object.

In contrast to this type of analysis, I argue in chapter 1 that the Renaissance city-state of Venice is not an empty *referent* for the Venetian Resort but rather a morphological and historical *reference* for understanding the Venetian's role in contemporary Chinese capitalism. Attention to both Venice's physical design as a city-state constructed on a unique land reclamation site and its role as the birthplace of capitalism and genesis of market devices such as the double-entry bookkeeping ledger is instructive for understanding Macau's contemporary function. I extend that discussion now by exploring the integrated resort in Macau as a specifically postsocialist space. As such, and in contradistinction to the conceptual assumptions of postmodern semiotics (implosion, simulation, hyperreality), Macau's resorts may be understood as highly differentiated and enclosed environments with characteristic features of urbanism acclimated to China's contemporary consumption regime. Viewed from this perspective, the integrated resort is not a meaningless simulacrum but an apparatus of subjectivation, a spatial machine that produces postsocialist consumer subjects.

The Integrated Resort as a Differentiated Space

The integrated casino resort provides diverse components of leisure experience in one self-contained structure. This feature of the integrated resort is often described as exemplary of postmodern implosion or dedifferentiation—that is, the collapsing together of formerly separated social spheres or activities (Ritzer and Stillman 2001). In an integrated resort such as the Venetian, for example, gambling, shopping, entertainment, dining, education, and medical care are imploded together within a single dedifferentiated structure.

This is certainly an accurate description of Macau's integrated resorts, but the focus on dedifferentiation within a single property overlooks the way in which the resorts serve collectively as a highly differentiated postsocialist space; it also overlooks the disjunctive manner in which the Macau city-state is itself differentiated within the GBA megacity. Macau's sui generis history and contemporary exacerbated difference distinguish it from the rest of the regional metropolis; this distinction is important to the city's function. Each integrated resort is in turn a discrete, enclosed, and interiorized urban space funded by transnational capital and marked off from the surrounding city by walls that create a distinct spatial logic. This characteristic is further exaggerated by the fact that the integrated resorts are constructed on land reclamation sites that are themselves enclave formations within the city. This morphology is consistent with the enclave logic that originated with Portugal's founding of Macau; indeed, it has persisted throughout the city's history.[2] In addition, this design characteristic of the integrated resort shares much in common with the SOE-financed *danwei;* such homologies with the work unit in the socialist city illustrate the function of the integrated resort in the postsocialist city.

The Integrated Resort as a Spatial Fix

At first glance, the Venetian Resort might also seem to be the epitome of a postmodern logic of simulation. As a copy of the eponymous Venetian property in Las Vegas, which is itself a romanticized reproduction of the city of Venice, the Venetian Resort seems a perfect example of a simulation that confounds modernist distinctions between surface and depth, original and copy, real and imaginary. However, while this critical approach certainly identifies representational characteristics of the themed architectural form, it tells us little about the pragmatic functions of the built environment.

To understand the function of Macau's integrated resorts for Chinese tourists, we must look beyond the simulated characteristics of the resort—such as its ornamental facade and free-floating historical or geographical motifs—and focus instead on the materiality of the environment and the articulation of the design with the antecedent spaces of the socialist Chinese city. To focus on the material use value of Macau's tourist environments is to suggest that there is actually something meaningful about Chinese tourism to these sites.[3] Obviously no one spends billions of dollars to construct a meaningless building. To dismiss the Venetian, which is visited by millions of people every year, as a semiotic artifice is to overlook its actual significance.

From a materialist perspective, the integrated resort is a physical manifestation of what Harvey (2005) calls a "spatial fix" for capital. The benefit of Harvey's political economy for understanding Macau's resorts is the way it enables us to move beyond an analysis of representation in order to understand the function of the integrated resort in the development of capitalism in the region. In his attempt to understand the steady growth and expansion of cities around the world, Harvey notes that capitalism periodically encounters crises of overaccumulations of labor and capital, which may sit side by side without a way of bringing them together in an economically productive manner. This sort of problem may be resolved "by geographical expansion and geographical restructuring" (Harvey 2012), in which capital is relocated from the "primary circuit" of industrial production, invested instead in the "secondary circuit" of the production of space, and "fixed" in new urban development projects. This production of new urban spaces provides an alternative avenue for profit, and this process propels urban growth.

Harvey (2005) points out that as transnational capital is "fixed" in a new space, like a land reclamation site or resort in Macau, it is also temporally deferred; "surplus capital gets displaced into long-term projects that take many years to return their value to circulation through the productive activity they support" (88). Even allowing for the lucrative Macau gaming revenues that let Adelson recoup his $240 million Sands investment in only ten months, the $2.4 billion Venetian construction costs, as well as ongoing maintenance and operating expenses, means actual profits from this investment are a long-term prospect. But in the meantime, this "spatio-temporal fix" may also include investments in the "tertiary circuit" of capital, such as the training of the local labor force. Such tertiary activities are evident in new degree programs in gaming management and hospitality that emerged in several Macau universities soon after the Venetian opened. Another example is the staff training facility inside the Venetian property, which the company jointly operates with the University of Macau.

Over time, regional economies such as the GBA emerge; Harvey (2005) says they may "achieve a certain degree of structured coherence to production, exchange, and consumption, at least for a time." This "structured coherence," notes Harvey, "typically encompasses attitudes, cultural values, beliefs, and even religious and political affiliations among both capitalists and those whom they employ" (102). In this way, Macau's resorts naturalize both the combination of consumerism, citizen quality, and individual responsibility that are characteristic of market-socialism and the distinct urban way of life promoted by the central government.

The Integrated Resort as an Urban Environment

It is also easy to use postmodern jargon to describe the Venetian as a hyperreal environment. The seemingly hyperreal characteristics of the Venetian are exemplified by comments I have heard from several tourists who have traveled to Venice and who contrast that city unfavorably with the resort. Such tourists note that the Venetian is cleaner and has a more pleasant odor than Venice; that the Venetian feels comparatively safer than Italy in general, the result of a visible security regime and a relative lack of pickpocketing and other such petty crime; and that the comfortable air-conditioned environment distinguishes the Venetian from Venice's (and Macau's) hot and humid summer climate.

Of course, these observations may be accurate, but the Venetian is only hyperreal if we conceive it as a failed simulation of the real Venice. However, if we simply take the Venetian at face value, we may conclude that it is an authentic urban space in its own right. That is, the Venetian is a massive heterogeneous environment with a diverse variety of functional elements. It has a substantial infrastructure to facilitate movements of water, electricity, gas, garbage, and sewage; it houses thousands of workers who undertake a wide variety of responsibilities, including cleaning, cooking, retail sales, personnel management, security, construction, training, and entertainment; and it is visited by seventy-five thousand tourists each day (Cohen 2017a). In this sense, the banal Venetian characteristics are typical of any tourist city; even its privatized concessionaire governance is similar to the so-called privately owned public spaces that are increasingly ubiquitous features of many cities in the West (Kayden 2000; Mitrašinović 2006). From this perspective, the Venetian's perfumed odor, personal safety, and thermal homogenization are less hyperreal and imperfect (or too perfect)

Figure 25. Tourists in St. Mark's Square at the Venetian Resort. *Photograph by Adam Lampton.*

representations of Venice, as they are elements of the structure's own indigenous microclimate.

My point here is descriptive, not prescriptive. I do not mean to claim that the Venetian is an ideal space, that it compares favorably to the city of Venice, or that is has some inherent cultural, aesthetic, or architectural value. Rather, my point is that these normative claims may detract from our understanding of the Venetian's specific function for Chinese tourists.

Certainly there are serious political consequences to the privatization of the social sphere and the increasing public influence of individuals such as Adelson, who both derives enormous wealth from Chinese tourists and inadvertently shapes their lifestyles in an effort to benefit his bottom line—an issue I will return to later. However, to understand the way the Venetian functions in market-socialism, it is not useful to merely point to how it differs from Venice. Instead, it is helpful to highlight the didactic nature of its urban characteristics.

For my purposes, what is important about the design and ornamentation of the resort is not its hyperreality but rather the specific urban quality of the environment (regardless of what particular city might be referenced by the theme). Urbanism as a way of life is defined by a particular set of characteristics that include heterogeneity, density, anonymity, segmented roles, and heightened mobility as well as interpersonal contact with others that is superficial, impersonal, and transitory. Wirth believed that these city qualities shape a distinct urban personality, and I will focus now on the function of these qualities in shaping the metropolitan mien of Chinese tourists. Weber contends that urbanism was the breeding ground of capitalism; these distinct urban features are also important to the development of Chinese market-socialism (Wu 2009, 419).

I should note that each of these urban qualities was absent in the *danwei* lifestyle of communist China that I described earlier. The design of the *danwei* encouraged communal use of facilities and promoted deep and long-term engagement with a limited number of residents. In the *danwei,* even the boss was expected to participate in the "mass line" by sharing living space and community life with other workers. Thus, the highly differentiated integrated resort is a self-contained enclave city within a city that adopts the form of the *danwei* but combines it with an urbanist content.

Wirth identified "segmented roles" as a characteristic feature of urbanism; these segmented roles are a feature of Macau's interior resort urbanism. For example, Macau's casino resorts differentiate among different types of gamblers, identifying mass market players, several grades of premium mass market players, and VIP gamblers. Each type is granted different amenities and services, and each is relegated to a different area of the property. These areas include, respectively, public spaces on the casino gaming floor; restricted and semipublic spaces that require membership cards to access; and completely private spaces accessible only to those VIP gamblers who travel to Macau as customers of the junkets. In this way, the heterogeneous tourist population is stratified, segmented, and spatially distributed, much like the population of any urban environment. These characteristics enhance the urban quality of the resorts.

Incidentally, architect Paul Steelman (designer of Macau's Sands Casino) explains that this spatial distribution of different player groups is one way in which Macau's integrated resorts are distinct from their Las Vegas counterparts.[4] "In Las Vegas we will make one very large room and then maybe a smaller baccarat room or something of this nature," he says. "What Macau and Las Vegas Sands [operations in Macau] brought about was the era of the stratified casino where the casino was designed in five or six market segments. That has changed the IRs [integrated resorts] significantly, it has changed the buildings significantly, it has changed profitability significantly and it has changed the diversified set of operators that use any particular facility" (quoted in Cohen 2018, 15). From Steelman's explanation, it is clear that Las Vegas casinos are not designed to reflect and reproduce such segmented roles in the manner common in Macau. This segmented and stratified design deploys characteristics culled from the urban environment and reproduces them inside the integrated resort. Of course, this stratification is also a stark departure from the egalitarian logic of the socialist *danwei* design.[5]

The Commodity Logic of Collective Consumption

Transnational capital's organization of collective consumption within the integrated resort also distinguishes it from its SOE-managed *danwei* counterpart. Everyday products, facilities, and services that were once the provision of the socialist iron rice bowl and were administered by one's peers in quotidian *danwei* life are delivered today by anonymous service workers in Macau's integrated resorts and are available only for purchase. Browsing in the retail environment of the Venetian, for example, turns up not only typical consumer products such as clothing, cosmetics, and jewelry, but also shops that offer everyday necessities such as baby formula and Chinese medicine. A Watson's Baby store in the Galaxy Resort, which is adjacent to the Venetian, exclusively offers products for prepregnancy and infant care, such as diapers, baby food, bottles, and children's toothbrushes. While a baby-oriented store may seem like an odd attraction in a casino resort, it exemplifies the way that the Macau integrated resort is equipped with the essential elements of a quotidian consumer lifestyle.

The same logic is true of childcare facilities. In the *danwei,* members of the immediate community provided resident childcare services as part of the implicit social contract of communism. In contrast, the Venetian features a Qube Kid's Play Zone staffed by anonymous on-site attendants. Parents and children may socialize in play activities with other families, or one parent may stay with the child while the partner gambles or shops elsewhere in the resort. However, these childcare services are only available for an hourly fee, and the provisions of such care are also segmented and stratified, with "Qube Clube" members able to access additional facilities for extended times at a significantly higher rate. Even the socks required for playground activities must be purchased on site. (Incidentally, the Qube play facility in the Cotai Central property is even designed like a mini city, with facades of a police station, café, and other urban building types on the perimeter of the play area, inadvertently reflecting the underlying logic of China's urbanization regime.)

Just as *danwei* childcare was designed to ensure socialist reproduction of labor power by meeting all daily domestic needs so that parents could devote themselves to other labor tasks, the Qube play facility ensures reproduction of leisure power by providing care for children so that parents may consume elsewhere, all while naturalizing a neoliberal commodity logic. That is, the overall lesson materialized in Macau's resort environment is that childcare, housing, education, health, food, and entertainment are available—much like the SOE provided in the *danwei*—but individual tourists are responsible for purchasing these provisions at a market-determined price.

The commodified logic linking consumption and reproduction is perfectly captured by the Venetian's 2017 "Shop Your Way to a Hotel Stay" promotion. Signs displayed throughout the environment, in a manner not unlike the didactic poster propaganda of the Chinese state, depicted a photograph of a fashionable Chinese woman surrounded by shopping bags and gift boxes stuffed with purchases, with instructions that anyone who made retail purchases in excess of US$2,500 (MOP 20,000) would be provided complimentary hotel accommodation. Such promotions ensure that carefully calculated consumption activities enable reproduction of consumers in an inverted logic of *danwei* reproduction of the labor force.

Cultivating the Quality Chinese Consumer

The underlying logic of the integrated resort consumption regime is that in contrast to *danwei* workers, who generally produced some specific industrial product (or service such as education), the object of work in the postsocialist Macau resort is the Chinese consumer subject himself. Given China's use of tourism to promote consumer spending, the overriding goal of the tourist under this regime is to enhance the individual quality specific to an urbane consumer.[6] To that end, the retail and service offerings in the resort are primarily focused on the refinement of the tourist body: cosmetics, jewelry, and fashion; spas, health clubs, foot massage, hair care, and cosmetic surgery; and various other means of toning, refining, and perfecting individual appearance. The resort activities participate in the literal practice of comporting consumer bodies and fashioning quality subjects. Even the promotion of the Qube play facility highlights didactic enhancement of children's quality. As the resort website explains: "Qube is designed to offer more than just great fun. It's also a tool for personal development and to boost children's ability and confidence."

Figure 26. The comportment of the quality Chinese consumer. *Photograph by Adam Lampton.*

Of particular significance in these efforts is the Venetian's Malo Clinic. The largest medical tourism facility in Asia, and the only such regional facility located in a casino environment, the clinic includes six operating rooms, fifty-eight spa rooms, state-of-the-art wet and hydro facilities, and a self-described world-class hair salon. It employs fifty international physicians and a hundred spa therapists. The clinic offers a variety of medical services, including dermatology; cosmetic surgery, such as eyelid lifts and breast augmentation; and traditional Chinese medicine.[7]

However, central to such services is the clinic's innovative and proprietary cosmetic dental surgery, pioneered by the Portuguese oral surgeon who created the Malo Clinic concept (Matos 2018). The clinic offers a wide range of dental services as part of its dedication to "the art of creating smiles," but the particular focus is the physical repair or reproduction of malformed, damaged, or missing teeth, which is realized by the clinic's specialization in orthodontics, prosthodontics, and implantology. It should be noted that given the poor oral hygiene typical of the socialist era, such visible dental ailments are relatively common among China's older generation, making treatment at the Venetian's Malo Clinic a crucial component of a project of enhancing remunerative forms of quality necessary for participation in a service-oriented market economy.

Therefore, when we move beyond the representational elements of the Venetian and focus on its spatial function, we may understand the integrated resort not as a self-referential simulacrum but as an apparatus of subjectivation that functions in a market-socialist regime. That is, the Venetian is not a sign but a machine. Foucault (1977a) describes his concept of the apparatus in a manner that helpfully highlights the Venetian function: "What I'm trying to pick out with this term is first a thoroughly heterogeneous ensemble consisting of discourses, institutions, architectural forms, regulatory decisions, laws, administrative measures, scientific statements, philosophical, moral and philanthropic propositions—in short, the said as much as the unsaid. Such are the elements of the apparatus. The apparatus itself is the system of relations that can be established among these elements" (195). The Venetian Resort is the locus of the "thoroughly heterogeneous ensemble" that articulates together the set of factors we have explored thus far. These factors include Macau's legal gaming regime; the concessionaire and subconcessionaire arrangements; transnational investment capital; China's CEPA with Macau; the special visa scheme that facilitates tourist travel to Macau; the new state-directed moral economy of Chinese tourism; the regulation of Golden Week holidays in the PRC; Macau's hospitality-oriented university programs; and Steelman's casino designs. The "system of relations" among these elements enables the Macau integrated resort to function (much like the work unit functioned under socialism) as an apparatus of subjectivation of an urbane consumer appropriate to the postsocialist regime.

To put a finer point on the function of the resort, we may characterize this type of apparatus, within the context of market-socialism, as exemplary of Callon's market device—that is, a sociotechnical apparatus that affords or enables market behavior.[8] Economic sociologists have analyzed such market devices as accounting ledgers, stock tickers, shopping carts, electronic trading screens, and consumer score cards to study the ways such technical and intellectual devices configure the calculative capacities of individuals.[9] To conceive of the integrated resort as a market device demonstrates the resort's function in the subjective economy of casino capitalism and its role in producing a quality Chinese consumer. This dynamic consumer is an object of careful study in Macau's gaming industry.

> The co-chairman of Macau casino operator MGM China Holdings Ltd., Pansy Ho, has said Chinese visitors to the city are becoming more discerning. "We're already beginning to see that the customers walking through our doors are more demanding. They now know how to differentiate," Ms. Ho said on Bloomberg TV. "They will now ask you how many restaurants there are in your facility, and if there are Western restaurants they want to know whether the food is French or Italian," she said. "They have become more selective. They actually would say: 'I have choices. I have to determine where to go, where to spend my money and how best to spend my time.' It's all evolving." (Newsdesk 2014a)

The discerning Chinese consumer, poised to pursue an urban lifestyle that will drive China's economic development, is the realization of the subject hailed by both President Bush and the Communist Party editors of *China Daily* at the outset of the chapter. However, it is important to note again that these consumption activities are not the product of an enhanced social safety net. Rather, the visitor to the Venetian Resort confronts a materialist pedagogy of neoliberal "responsibilization" in which the state administers new freedoms of mobility to citizens while transnational capital constructs the environments through which they circulate. However, it is people's individual responsibility to enhance remunerative quality and enable care for themselves without making additional demands on the state. "To govern in this sense," says Foucault (1994) of the practices of governmentality, "is to structure the possible field of action of others" (138). Indeed, the integrated resort provides a pedagogical field of operation. Ultimately Macau's resorts complement other elements of an emergent urban landscape of consumption in China that includes shopping malls, gated communities, housing estates, consumer clubs, community organizations, pedestrian shopping streets, and theme parks (Wu 2005), all of which collectively promote urbanism as a way of life.

CHINA'S GAMBLE ON URBANIZATION

The qualities of urbanism exemplified in the design and provisions of the Venetian Resort apparatus facilitate an urbane lifestyle, encourage consumption behaviors, and produce quality subjects. However, as a macroeconomic strategy, urbanization itself is a high stakes gamble that carries significant risks for the Chinese state. Cities that are characterized by the heterogeneity and aleatory encounters that derive from the qualities of urbanism tend to aggregate populations in ways that equip citizens physically and psychically for antiauthoritarian or counterstate activities.[10]

In an analysis of the surprising longevity of the Chinese Communist Party in a global context in which the authoritarian communist states of Eastern Europe have all fallen, Jeremy Wallace (2014) notes the practical problems posed by urbanization to the survival of China's regime: "The danger that large cities, especially capitals, pose to regimes is an old story. Cities bring together masses of people, improve communication links among them, and increase the ability of private grievances to accumulate and circulate. Cities are particularly prone to disruptions via barricades, transforming key nodes in the transportation network into strongholds for resistors" (3). Wallace contends that a key factor in the Chinese Communist Party's endurance has been its strategic management of urbanization and its use of fiscal and migration policies to contain farmers in the countryside and prevent their movement to cities. As for urban residents, the *danwei* functioned as a sort of self-contained village within a city; it facilitated citizen surveillance while isolating discrete urban communities from one another. This prevented assembly and guarded against mobilization of the population for popular uprisings. Therefore, China's gamble on the city as the locus of economic reforms constitutes the inherent contradiction of the country's macroeconomic strategy. The more urbanized the population and the more citizens adopt urbanism as a way of life, the more likely those citizens are to organize, assemble, petition, and protest against the interests of state authorities.

However, by replicating the enclosed *danwei* form, Macau's own Venetian Resort city provides an interesting hedge on the government's risky wager on urbanization. The Venetian's encapsulated and privatized environment exemplifies capital's own covert contribution to authoritarian governance; it provides an architectonic resolution to the contradiction underlying China's economic strategy. So I turn, finally, to the political significance and normative moral function of Macau's increasingly privatized urban commons.

The Venetian Palace

Adelson's properties on the Cotai Strip actually comprise four resorts: Venetian, Plaza, Cotai Central, and Parisian. The massive scale of this resort complex is a key condition of its model function.[11] When they opened, the Venetian and Cotai Central resorts were, respectively (and in the tiny context of Macau, remarkably), the sixth and seventh largest buildings in the world. The eventual construction of an elevated and enclosed walkway that connects the conjoined Venetian and Plaza properties with the $4.4 billion Cotai Central property across the street, as well as another enclosed passageway that appends these structures to the adjacent $2.5 billion Parisian resort, created a seamless amalgamated and interiorized neourban experience in Macau. This structure now comprises more than 2.3 million square meters of space.

The Venetian Palace constitutes what is perhaps the world's largest enclosure. This encapsulated city includes 12,360 hotel rooms, nearly

150,000 square meters of convention space, 81,000 square meters of casino space, and more than 194,000 square meters of retail area with 770 shops. The vast scale of this enclosed urbanity is all the more remarkable given the tiny size of Macau's total landmass. When considered as a proportion of the overall territory of Macau, surely the Venetian Palace has no equal elsewhere in the world. If one totals the interior floor area of all of these hotel rooms, shops, casinos, restaurants, promenades, spas, auditoriums, offices, convention centers, meeting rooms, training facilities, and so on, over the myriad levels and floors of these buildings, this interior space is equal to nearly 15 percent of the entire surface of the three islands that comprise the territory of Macau (Simpson 2014). This expansive quantity of floor area is remarkable in itself. However, this does not begin to account for the vast volume of space inside these buildings.

Once inside, tourists can comfortably amble for hours. They may move among the baroque Venetian landmarks; the five-star ambiance of the Plaza, with its Four Seasons Hotel and assortment of luxury retail shops; across the Parisian's simulated Versailles attractions and glass-covered shopping arcades; and to the new Londoner motifs of the Cotai Central property. While a generalized homogeneity across these various spaces makes the experience seamless, each property is a distinct narrative fragment, with different themed ornamentation, ambient noise, mood lighting, perfumed air, atmospherics, and attractions. The stimulation is constant. The properties' diversity approximates that of an actual city (although one that stretches across several continents and historical eras in a manner indicative of the space-time compression that marks the Information Age). Along the way, visitors encounter not only other tourists who are gambling, shopping, or sightseeing around various statuary, fountains, and atrium gardens, but also an enormous variety of retail sales personnel, food and beverage workers, hosts, security guards, sex workers, croupiers, entertainers, and cleaning and maintenance staff, who comprise a stratified and diverse urban population.

Having documented the magnitude of Adelson's Venetian Palace, we are now prepared to address the function of this encapsulated environment in China's normative program of moral education. Taken together, the diverse elements of the Venetian Palace illustrate the elusive object of one theoretical discipline of Chinese exemplary education science known as "cultural systems engineering" (Bakken 2000, 59), which aims to enhance individual quality through a process of "environmental moulding" (*huanjing taoye*) (158). Such methods of molding are conceived as forms of unconscious education through which an individual may "be imperceptibly influenced by what one constantly sees and hears" in the physical environment (156).

According to Chinese educational theorists, this engineered cultural system may include such diverse components as art and literature, landscaping and architecture, dress and cosmetology, museums and exhibition halls, green space and foliage, and tourism practices (Bakken 2000, 59). The "imperceptible" environmental influence that emanates from the collective articulation of such sites and bodily practices involves "a method of education in aesthetics which supposedly exerts a favourable influence on people's character and appeals to feelings and values" (157). In the case of the Venetian Palace, the cultural system that shapes the subject is exemplified in the myriad retail shops with displays of clothing, jewelry, and cosmetics; the Malo Clinic's eyelid lifts, breast augmentation, and dental reconstruction; full-scale reproductions of classical art, sculpture, and architecture; indoor gardens, simulated rock formations, waterfalls, and picturesque canals; homogenized thermal space and environmental atmospherics; and the copious meeting areas and urban promenades. As such, the interiorized city constitutes a model environment whose imperceptible influence explicitly promotes and inculcates a form of normative moral education concerning the proper uses of urban space.

The practical political relevance of this model city for China's urbanization strategy is illuminated when it is set against the example of the neighboring SAR of Hong Kong. With a breathtaking skyline, world-class public transportation, one of the world's freest markets, and a vibrant economy, the central government originally promoted Hong Kong as an exemplary Chinese urban environment. However, although both Hong Kong and Macau are beneficiaries of the IVS travel visa and are popular sites for cross-border tourism, travel to Hong Kong resulted in contentious relations among Hong Kong citizens and mainland tourists, with negative encounters documented extensively in local media. It became increasingly clear that these interpersonal relations reflected a more general antagonism between Hong Kong and the central government, and Hong Kong eventually emerged as a site of oppositional intrastate political activity, ultimately prompting the central government to introduce a new security law in the city in June 2020.

This opposition was manifested in the 2014 Umbrella Movement, when tens of thousands of Hong Kong citizens joined a student-led protest and occupied several barricaded streets in the central city to agitate for universal suffrage and sovereign autonomy. This demonstration was followed by the city's surprising wave of civil unrest in 2019, including entrenched conflicts between police and protesters that started in the city streets and then spilled over into subway stations, government buildings, shopping malls, the international airport, university campuses, a cross-harbor traffic tunnel, and even the underground sewer system. This particular activity of Hong Kong citizens drew on a different disposition, or latent potential, of metropolitan public space; it referenced an alternative European urban history (from the nineteenth-century Paris Commune to the barricades of May 1968)—a stark departure from the benign urbanism of Macao's interior city spaces. Indeed, protest activities in Hong Kong exemplified the inherent risk that urbanization of the population poses for China's central government.

As a highly urbanized environment and the most densely populated territory in the world, even without the forty million annual tourist arrivals, Macau might seem prone to such public demonstrations, but they are surprisingly rare. While there are historical explanations for both the relative political apathy of Macau's citizens and the city's congenial relations with the mainland (Lo 2007), I would suggest that the rapid progressive encapsulation and privatization of Macau's urban commons informs the behavior of both tourists and locals alike.

The enclosed forms of encounter in the Venetian Palace create an urbanism that illustrates Hardt and Negri's (2000) famous contention that contemporary conditions of global capitalism have produced a social environment in which "there is no more outside." For these thinkers, the spatial division between inside and outside was a "foundational characteristic" of modern political philosophy that informed theories of sovereignty, liberalism, and war. Hardt and Negri contend that capitalism has progressively undermined this division, thriving rather on integration, commerce, and interchange. Today we live under what these scholars call the "real subsumption" of society to capital, which precludes any vantage point "outside" the capital relation (186). This condition is embodied in the encapsulated and interiorized space of the Venetian Palace.

"There Is No More Outside"

Hardt and Negri cite Guy Debord's (2011) classic analysis of the "society of spectacle" as illustrative of this contemporary condition. In fact, the twenty-first-century convergence in Macau of the last global emissary of international socialism and the last European colony in Asia, manifested in the architectural amalgamation of the socialist work unit and the Las Vegas–style resort, epitomizes what Debord calls the integrated spectacle. The integrated spectacle of the Venetian Palace seamlessly links together the diffuse spectacle of democratic free-market capitalism and the concentrated spectacle of the authoritarian centrally planned economy. "The spectacle is at once unified and diffuse in such a way that it is impossible to distinguish any inside from outside—the natural from the social, the private from the public," claim Hardt and Negri (2000, 188). By permitting transnational capital to conceive, construct, develop, and manage such a significant component of Macau's urban space, the PRC has essentially outsourced its own authoritarian command into a privatized "total landscape" (Mitrašinović 2006).

Debord's (2011) spectacle is often misunderstood to be manifested merely in a fascination with visual stimuli, calling to mind the members of a captive audience collectively mesmerized by a radiant cinema screen. However, Debord understands the spectacle not as a regime of images but as a "technology of separation," the "inevitable consequence of capitalism's 'restructuring of society without community'" (Crary 2001, 74).[12] As such, the normative enclosure of Macau's urban commons inside the resort walls of the Venetian Palace demonstrates the fact that "spectacle is not an optics of power but an architecture" (74–75).

Indeed, this is where the contrast between the community-building Chinese *danwei* and the privatized integrated resort becomes most instructive. The Venetian complex is both an apparatus of subjection of citizen-consumers and an exemplary model city of benign urbanism for Chinese tourists and Macau locals alike. Taken together, we can understand the various tourist activities in the resort as a form of what Chinese educational theorists call "over learning" (*guodu xuexi*),

Figure 27. "There is no more outside." The interior of the Venetian Resort, one of the world's largest buildings. *Photograph by Adam Lampton.*

a practice that "inculcates" knowledge and commits the lesson to embodied "memory and consolidation" through imitative-repetitive behaviors (Bakken 2000, 146).

Repetition with a Difference

Of course, an integrated casino resort is clearly not a *danwei.* It differs so greatly from that socialist formation, with its innovative community-building and proletarian functions, that this exercise in spatial history that reads the resort through the work unit may strike some readers as peculiar. My point is that while the integrated resort is a generic transnational apparatus with local applications in many casino jurisdictions around the world, within the context of the PRC, this resort apparatus is a recombinant structure. The integrated resort in Macau adopts the *danwei* form without the corresponding content. It replaces the productivist strips-and-chunks morphology of the socialist city with an interiorized metropolitan habitat befitting the aims of China's National New-Type Urbanization Plan. The deployment of the antecedent *danwei* form in the integrated resort environment is illustrative of what Bakken (2000) identifies as "repetition with a difference" in China's model pedagogy (4). The work unit form is the basic component in the assembly of a market device appropriate to the logic of China's market-socialist regime.

Viewing Macau's integrated casino resorts from the "oblique angle" of the socialist *danwei* is to analyze "the situated constellations of socialist rule, neoliberal logic, and self-governing practices that shape varied situations emerging across the nation" (Ong and Zhang 2008, 5). This analysis of Chinese tourism in Macau is therefore an exploration of the spatial logics of postsocialism. Macau's privatized integrated resorts function as spatial machines for the production of quality postsocialist consumers. These consumers in turn learn to practice urbanism as a way of life in a manner conducive to the absolutist socioeconomic aims of the central government.

6

VIP Room

JUNKETS AND GEOPOLITICS

> Perhaps the greatest single omission from mainstream theories of
> consumption is geopolitics. Economists tend to focus on individuals
> seeking to maximize pleasure and minimize pain. Sociologists,
> meanwhile, see consumption as a sign of emulation and distinction
> among groups. Other writers look at mentalities, such as the romantic
> imagination, with its dream-like disposition for future pleasure, or
> at practices, such as cooking or home improvement. Global power
> is conspicuous by its absence from these approaches.
>
> —Frank Trentmann, *Empire of Things*

In May 2013, Sheldon Adelson was granted honorary citizenship to the
city of Jerusalem. The recognition was no surprise because Adelson is
well known for his Israel activities. He owns a conservative broadsheet
that is the country's largest-circulation newspaper; he is close to former
prime minister Benjamin Netanyahu; and he has donated $200 million
to hospitals, universities, and museums across Israel (Rudoren 2013).
Adelson is also intensely involved in politics in the United States. His
donations of more than $200 million in the 2012 and 2016 U.S. presi-
dential elections were in support of candidates such as Newt Gingrich
and Donald Trump, whose policies he was confident would enhance
his wealth and advance his Israel agenda. The importance of Macau
casino revenues to Adelson's political largesse was underscored by the
fact that he brought along to the citizenship ceremony entertainment
in the form of three Italian gondoliers from his Venetian Macau resort.
In keeping with the Venetian theme of Adelson's property, the perform-
ers were clad in period-appropriate long brocade jackets and tricorn

hats as they serenaded the audience with renditions of "O Sole Mio" and "That's Amore."

Adelson's Jerusalem ceremony highlights several factors important to understanding the posthandover transformation of Macau that I chart in this book. The first factor is the importance of city-states, such as Venice and Macau, to both capitalism's European origins and its current Chinese incarnation. At first glance, the presence of Adelson's simulated Venetian Resort in Macau's UNESCO World Heritage–certified Portuguese cityscape may seem as incongruous as landlocked Italian gondoliers performing at an Israeli citizenship ceremony. However, just as Venice and Macau were key nodes in a sixteenth-century world-economy that linked Europe and China, today, Macau (as well as the Venetian) plays an important role in the current "rotation of the centre of gravity of the global economy back to East Asia where it was in premodern and early modern times" (Arrighi and Silver 2001, 274).

According to Arrighi ([1994] 2010), the contemporary East Asian economy is dominated by a "capitalist archipelago" (380) that stretches from the city-states of Hong Kong and Singapore to Taiwan, Japan, and South Korea, its collective function mirroring the medieval Italian city-states where capitalism first developed. François Gipouloux (2011) goes so far as to declare this Asian maritime region (encompassing the Sea of Japan, the Yellow Sea, the South China Sea, the Sulu Sea, and the Celebes Sea) an "Asian Mediterranean," which replicates the transnational flows of goods, people, and money among the city-states located on the Mediterranean Sea in the premodern era.[1]

The second noteworthy factor highlighted in the Israeli ceremony is Adelson's transnational allegiances. As a U.S. citizen who got rich in Las Vegas before doubling down on casino investments in Macau and Singapore while simultaneously receiving honorary Jerusalem citizenship for his Zionist philanthropic agenda, Adelson is a fully credentialed member of the "transnational capitalist class" (Sklair 2000). As such, he personifies a particular type of "footloose" business enterprise that, in the words of Arrighi (2003), "occupies places but is not defined by the places it occupies" (143). Adelson operates opportunistically within a "space of flows" that both produces his massive wealth and facilitates his political agenda.

Finally, the Jerusalem ceremony was also notable for who was not present. The ceremony implicitly linked the casino revenues that Adelson derived from the Venetian Macau resort with his Israel philanthropy, but it omitted the most important factor in the equation. Most of Adelson's Venetian profits are actually derived from high-stakes baccarat games played in private rooms inside the resort. These VIP rooms are managed by local junket operators, the sometimes shadowy financiers of high-stakes gaming in the city. True to their opaque origins, and conspicuous by their absence in Jerusalem, these junket agents are the key to Macau's gaming revenues, and the focus of this chapter.

However, to understand the way in which such junket financiers function in Macau's casino industry and Adelson's philanthropy, we must look beyond the birth of capitalism in medieval Venice, which I discuss in chapter 1, and to its cultivation in the neighboring city-state of Genoa, which both Braudel and Arrighi argue played a distinct but equally important role in the development of global capitalism.[2] The economic power of Genoese merchant bankers in the sixteenth century was enhanced by their strategic partnerships with Iberian monarchs who were seeking to expand their global empires, such as Prince Henry the Navigator of Portugal, Queen Isabella of Castile, and King Phillip II of Spain, and with ordinary Portuguese and Spanish privateers from whom the Genoese bought protection for their maritime trade. We will see that Adelson, Wynn, and the other concessionaires in Macau benefit today by purchasing a not dissimilar sort of protection from the local junket operators, whose primary function is to hedge against the risk incurred in granting credit to the high-stakes gamblers who produce the majority of Macau's casino revenues.

MACAU'S LEHMAN MOMENT

The vast scope and heteroclite characteristics of those junket operations was dramatically revealed on May 2014, almost exactly a year after Adelson's Jerusalem ceremony. Media reports disclosed that a Macau junket agent who worked with the Kimren Group (and who had been surreptitiously raising money from investors to finance junket loans for high-stakes gambling with promises of guaranteed monthly profits of 2.5 percent) had disappeared from the city—along with an astounding US$1.3 billion in funds. Although even a pilfered sum this substantial did not threaten to undermine the overall profitability of the industry, it was certainly sizable enough to shock industry insiders and rivet local attention. As concerned investors cautiously pulled back their remaining funds, the junket industry faced an emerging liquidity problem that some commentators called Macau's Lehman moment.

This analogy referenced the blow to global investor confidence provoked by the 2008 bankruptcy of Lehman Brothers. This bankruptcy, which was prompted by a liquidity crisis created by the company's overexposure to subprime mortgages, played a major role in the subsequent global economic crisis that many saw as the inevitable realization of Susan Strange's (1986) prophetic warnings about the dangers of casino capitalism. The Lehmann Brothers analogy was indeed pertinent. Macau junkets are essentially shadow banks that receive cash from investors, which they in turn loan to gamblers; profits are then returned to the investors in the form of monthly dividends (Lo and Kwok 2017; O'Keeffe 2014b).[3]

Junket investor sentiment took another hit in September 2009, when a cage worker for the Dore Entertainment junket stole US$64.5 million from the company's VIP room at the Wynn Resort (Master 2015). Just a few months later, another junket employee made off with $13 million from a VIP room at SJM's L'Arc casino across the street from the Wynn (Carvalho 2016). The Kimren Group junket thief was eventually captured by a bounty hunter in Cambodia twenty-eight months after he disappeared with the funds; he was transported to Ha Long Bay, Vietnam, for safekeeping while industry representatives considered their next move. The thief acknowledged his guilt and expressed deep regret for his actions; he even announced that he was prepared to pay back the wronged investors. This fortunate turn of events was one of a number of factors that restored confidence in Macau's VIP sector and caused a significant rebound in the faltering industry (Cohen 2016).

Around the same time, Adelson's financial support of Trump's successful presidential campaign paid off when Trump announced his controversial decision to relocate the American embassy in Israel from Tel Aviv to Jerusalem, Adelson's new honorary home. Less than a year later, Trump presented Adelson's wife, Miriam Adelson, with the Presidential Medal of Freedom, the country's highest civilian award. If the Adelson's contributions of $133 million to Trump and other Republican candidates in the 2016 election cycle played any role in the decision to bestow this honor, then she owed it, at least in part, to Macau's junket trade.

INFORMAL NETWORKS AND REAL CAPITALISM

Taken together, these anecdotes about billionaire financiers united by Macau's VIP gaming industry enlighten both Braudel's (1979) account of the five-hundred-year development of capitalism, which has guided my analysis of Macau, and Strange's (1980) use of the term "casino capitalism" to characterize the post-1970 global economy and to describe the transformation of the global economy, starting in the 1970s, into a vast casino of risky trades in which global financiers gamble with securities derived from the mortgages and pension funds of unwitting investors. For Strange, the qualifier "casino" connotes a distorted or degenerate form of capitalist enterprise.

What I hope to demonstrate in this chapter is that Macau's junket trade is not a degenerate form of capitalism, such as we might find in the unfortunate efforts of those Lehman Brothers traders whose careless greed almost destroyed the global economy. Rather, Macau's junket trade is consistent with what Braudel calls "real capitalism" (1:24). It is a direct descendent of that seminal capitalist enterprise, which was enabled by the innovative ways in which Venetian merchants, Genoese financiers, and Portuguese navigators linked dispersed marketplaces such as Antwerp, Goa, Nagasaki, and Macau into a world-economy. As we will see, however, this junket activity in Macau contains Chinese characteristics that certainly make it distinct, but not degenerate.

One of these indigenous attributes is a type of informal business network that has operated for a millennium within the region's Sino-centric tribute-trade system. These networks operate today through a logic of conceded informality (Schoon 2014) that is key to not only Macau's gaming economy but also China's postreform policy implementation.[4] As such, understanding market-socialism requires attending to the manner in which it revives and repurposes antecedent historical and cultural elements. As Arrighi (2004) emphasizes, the onset of each new era of capitalism entails a "double movement, both forward and backward at the same time" (534) as features that characterized a previous era emerge again in a new form. This forward-and-backward logic is exemplified in Macau's junket industry.

As I discuss in chapter 3, Deng Xiaoping opened China to the global economy in 1978 when he introduced market reforms by creating a series of SEZs along China's southern coast. The SEZs were established as laboratories of capitalism where China could experiment with a market economy, attract foreign direct investment, and study western production and management techniques (Chung et al. 2001; Harvey 2007). The first two SEZs, Shenzhen and Zhuhai, were located adjacent to the erstwhile European city-states of Hong Kong and Macau. These former colonial concessions, as well as the Macau formula through which they were established, provided the original inspiration for the SEZs and for the broader enclave-oriented mode of capitalist production that developed in China's GBA metropolis, which I call the core city of Chinese capitalism. Thus, the unique form of the GBA metropolis derives in part from the premodern enclave morphology of the region and is a local manifestation of a more generalized "medieval modernity" of multiple sovereignties and fragmented urban governance (Alsayyad and Roy 2006).

In his study of China's reform economy, Arrighi (2003) contends that a significant contributing factor to its success is the overseas Chinese diaspora in Southeast Asia, whose members have invested capital and business acumen in ventures in the SEZs that have turned China into the factory for the world. Arrighi contends that the operations of these Chinese investors mirror those of the Genoese financiers of Portuguese maritime trade five hundred years before:

> First, like the networks of commercial and financial intermediation
> controlled by the sixteenth-century Genoese diaspora, the business
> networks controlled by the Chinese diaspora occupy places (Hong
> Kong, Taiwan, Singapore, as well as the most important commercial
> centers of Southeast Asian countries and mainland China) but are
> not defined by the places they occupy. What defines the networks is
> the space-of-flows (the commercial and financial transactions) that
> connect the places where individual members or sub-groups of the
> diaspora conduct their business. (136)

We may understand the junket financiers who operate in Macau's VIP gambling industry as members of this diasporic group.[5]

According to Arrighi (2003), these investors from the overseas Chinese community rely on a type of informal business network that has dominated trade in the region for a millennium. Because of the relatively small amount of western foreign direct investment in East Asia compared to other regions of the world, businesses in East Asia never developed the sort of "vertical integration of economic activities across different political jurisdictions" typical of American corporate capitalism (135).[6] For this reason, "the crossborder organization of business enterprise in the region relied heavily on informal networks among juridically independent units, rather than vertical integration within a single multi-unit enterprise" (135). That is, local middlemen have served a crucial role. As a result, the overseas Chinese, who are able to exploit these informal networks, have been more successful than business entities from Japan, the United States, or Europe in capitalizing off China's economic growth. Arrighi (2009a) says that the overseas Chinese "could bypass most regulations, thanks to familiarity with local customs, habits, and language, to the manipulation of kinship and community ties—which they strengthened through generous donations to local institutions—and to the preferential treatment that they received from CCP [Chinese Communist Party] officials" (352).

Therefore, these Chinese financiers function as "matchmakers" linking foreign companies and Chinese workers (Arrighi 2009a, 351). Arrighi contends that the central government's cooperation with the capital provided by this overseas Chinese diaspora today "closely resembles the relation of political exchange that 16th century Spain and Portugal entertained with the Genoese capitalist diaspora" (359). We can observe a similar logic in the operation of Macau's junket trade, with mutually beneficial informal relationships forged among the casino concessionaires and local junket privateers. These Chinese characteristics are a distinctive characteristic of Macau's junket industry.

MACAU'S VIP GAMING TRADE

Macau casino monopoly holder Stanley Ho created Macau's unique VIP gambling system with his fateful decision in the 1980s to subcontract private gambling rooms in his casinos to independent agents. With this arrangement, Ho hoped to resolve an obstacle to casino tourism created when Chinese Triad agents began buying blocks of tickets on the ferry service (owned by Ho) connecting Hong Kong and Macau, then reselling those tickets for profit. In an effort to stop this practice, which was interfering with tourist traffic to Macau, Ho instead offered Triad agents a commission on sales of casino chips to gamblers. This practice eventually evolved into Macau's junket trade.

Wang and Eadington (2008) suggest that Ho was possibly inspired by Deng's introduction of the socialist-market "contractual system" (245) in the SEZs, whereby socialist SOEs experimented with subcontracted privatized management in joint venture initiatives with foreign companies. It could also be that Ho was simply replicating the logic of his own casino concession, essentially granting informal subconcessions of his gaming license. Either way, the junket system may be understood as a product of the conceded informality of the GBA. Such conceded informality is exemplified both by the central government's pragmatic bottom-up or practice-based approach to policy implementation that permits local authorities in the SEZs to field test policy innovations and by the Portuguese administration's laissez-faire oversight of the casino monopoly in prehandover Macau that allowed Ho to innovate unique gaming practices such as junket financing.[7]

The junket arrangement existed in a legal lacuna. Although as the casino concessionaire Ho was prevented by law from loaning money to gamblers, no such restrictions applied to the junket middlemen because their role in the industry was never codified in regulations (Siu 2007). These agents therefore operate today as quasi-institutional loan sharks who bring high rollers to Macau, host their gambling and leisure activities, and advance credit for high-stakes gaming.

The junkets are crucial to the industry because the PRC (as well as Taiwan and South Korea) tightly restricts the cross-border movement of currency. Chinese nationals can transport only RMB 20,000 (US$2,873) over the border, and they may make ATM withdrawals of only RMB 10,000 per day while abroad. Therefore, Chinese gamblers wishing to wager large stakes in Macau need access to cash loans in the territory. The typical junket gambler wages anywhere from US$125 to $300,000 per hand of baccarat, and gambling (and losing) such amounts easily exceeds the legally available cash (Lam and Eadington 2009). But it is not only VIP gamblers who need access to cash in Macau. Even on the city's mass gaming floors, the average minimum bet on baccarat table games is US$270 per hand, which means all but the luckiest tourists need access to local funds to finance their activities. (Incidentally, the average minimum bet in Las Vegas is US$20 per hand [Riley 2014].)

Gambling debts are not legally enforceable in the PRC. This makes it impossible for people who advance gaming credit to Chinese gamblers in Macau to pursue legal recourse for bad loans in China. In addition, Macau's gaming law does not allow the casino concessionaires to write off bad debts. Therefore, Macau moneylenders must be confident of their ability to extract repayment of debts through extralegal means. For this reason, some junket financiers allegedly maintain ties to Chinese Triads, who did not retreat from the city in the wake of the casino wars. These relationships provide the "protection" for credit that Macau casino operators need to facilitate the lucrative high-stakes gaming in the territory. These groups have their own informal networks of associates on the mainland, which they use to move money through gray or black markets and to pressure gamblers to repay debts.

Vertical Differentiation of Macau's Casinos

Most global gaming jurisdictions have junkets, but Macau's junket system is unique.[8] In many ways, the system is a reflection of the quirky political, social, and cultural milieu of Macau itself. Not only is junket financing a product of the particular constraints posed by China's restrictions on cross-border currency movements, but the relationships among the junkets and the casino concessionaires with whom they cooperate in Macau is also distinct.

In Las Vegas, the casino VIP rooms are simply one subcomponent of the larger gaming company. All employees of those VIP rooms are employees of that parent company, which bears the profits or losses incurred in the rooms. In short, the VIP rooms in these North American casinos may be understood as units of what Arrighi (Arrighi and Silver 2001) calls the "vertically-integrated and bureaucratically-managed" (262) western corporate structure that characterizes the North American gaming industry. By contrast, the Stanley Ho–inspired VIP rooms in Macau's casinos are distinct operations that are largely separated from the oversight of the concessionaire; they are managed by the individual junket company that controls the room. Therefore, Macau's VIP rooms are *vertically differentiated* in a manner that contrasts with their vertically integrated Las Vegas counterparts, where large corporations own individual casino resort properties as well as the VIP rooms therein.

The junket company is granted control of the Macau VIP room on the basis of an agreement to purchase a minimum quantity of chips from the concessionaire each month. The junket operator gets a commission on the chip purchase that constitutes the operator's revenue from the arrangement, while the wins or losses that VIP gamblers incur with those chips are borne by the concessionaire. Under Ho's monopoly, the commission was generally 0.7 percent of the chip value, although the amount increased after industry liberalization. In 2007, one junket consolidator, which pooled several different agents, negotiated an exclusive deal with Melco-PBL for a 1.35 percent commission. Fear among concessionaires that this rate was not sustainable prompted the government to formally cap the commission rate at 1.2 percent.

While the concessionaire provides the croupiers and security personnel in Macau's VIP rooms, all the other workers in the room are employed by the junket company. These junket personnel include the so-called chip rollers, who are typically attractive young Chinese women clad in matching outfits who sell (or "roll") the junket chips to gamblers; the "cage" personnel, who handle the money within the room; and management personnel, who oversee operations. In addition, the junket company that has the agreement with the casino concessionaire to manage the VIP room may also subcontract gaming tables in the room to other subsidiary junket agents, whose responsibility in turn is to use their own networks to get more gamblers into the room. Therefore, multiple entities may cooperate to conduct gambling business in the same VIP room—entities beyond the oversight of the concessionaire. Taken together, these characteristics are a manifestation of the vertical differentiation of the business.

Even the casino architecture in Macau reinforces the autonomous operations of Macau's junkets. While a Las Vegas casino typically has one VIP room with numerous gaming tables, most Macau casinos have multiple, self-contained VIP rooms that are each managed by a different junket operator. The *vertical differentiation* of Macau's VIP business is clear to anyone riding the elevator of the Galaxy Star World resort. While the Star World's main casino for mass market customers is located on the first floor, Sun City VIP Club is on the fifth floor, Meg Star International VIP Club on the tenth, Tak Chun VIP Club on the eleventh, and Guangdong VIP Club on the twelfth. Therefore, vertical ascension of the building reinforces the impression that the Galaxy

Figure 28. Vertical differentiation of casino management in the Star World resort, pictured on the elevator panel. The property's mass market casino is on the first floor, while the independently managed Suncity VIP Club, Meg-Star International VIP Club, Tak Chun VIP Club, and Guangdong VIP Club are each located, respectively, on the fifth, tenth, eleventh, and twelfth floors (circa September 2021). *Photograph by author.*

property is actually subdivided among a variety of distinct gaming companies, each accorded its own particular space in the building.

Dead Chips and Gaming Credit

The junket company issues the high-stakes player in a VIP room a gambling loan in the form of what are called dead chips. Once purchased (or, more precisely, borrowed), these chips can only be wagered; they cannot be exchanged for cash. However, the gambler's winnings are returned in regular chips that are convertible into cash or may be exchanged again for more dead chips.

The VIP gambler may receive a discounted price on the face value of the dead chips he borrows; this serves as incentive for the gambler to conduct business with a particular junket rather than a competitor, as well as incentive for the borrowing of a larger quantity of chips in order to capitalize off the volume of the discount. In this way, junket agents share part of their commission with the gambler in order to secure his business. This practice also serves to ingratiate players in friendly relationships with agents. These affective associations help ensure the subsequent repayment of debts.

The relative autonomy of VIP room management, as well as the confidentiality of activities that occur therein, enables activities that may exist beyond the oversight of both the concessionaire and the government. For example, surreptitious wagers may be made in amounts that exceed the face value of the chips. That is, the junket agent and the gambler may privately agree to multiply the value of the chips by, say, a factor of 10, such that a bet that involves HK$10,000 of chips is actually a wager of HK$100,000. Or they may agree that the bets will be accounted in U.S. dollars rather than the Hong Kong dollar face value of the chips (given the exchange rate, the latter arrangement would constitute a multiplier of 8). The multiplier is essentially a parallel bet; the wager made on the face value of the chips is a bet placed with the casino concessionaire, while the additional wager that exceeds the chip's face value is made with the junket agent.

Under such an arrangement, the immediate winnings and losses would be collected in the face value of the chips, and the gambler and the junket would settle the additional multipliers later. Such an agreement would conceal the actual revenues from both the concessionaire who owns the casino license and the local government authorities who collect taxes on casino revenues. Although it is impossible to know the extent of such arrangements, a 2007 journalistic investigative report alleged that the practice that year may have cost Macau casino concessionaires a combined total of US$2.5 billion in lost revenue (Gough 2007). However, although the existence of multiplier bets is common knowledge, the actual size of such estimates is disputed by junkets and government officials alike. (Incidentally, the Kimren Group executive who absconded with the billion-dollar windfall was, by some accounts, raising funds to finance multipliers.)

The dead chip is an innovative financial device unique to Macau's gaming industry.[9] The function of dead chips in the city's economy is in some ways reminiscent of the function of double-entry accounting ledger in sixteenth-century Venice, which I discuss in chapter 1. We may recall that the parallel debit and credit columns in the accounting ledger allowed the merchant to accurately monitor abstract money flows while also making commerce appear fair and equitable, thus rendering usury profits palatable to a skeptical clergy. The double-entry accounting ledger helped to produce capitalists and to enable capitalism. The dead chip likewise enables a distinct form of capitalism—casino capitalism—in Macau.

On the surface, the dead chip appears deceptively simple; it looks identical to the ordinary gaming chip used in casinos around the world. The conventional casino chip is merely a convenient proxy for cash. At the start of a typical gambling session, the gambler exchanges an amount of cash for the equivalent in chips, and when the play is completed, whatever chips remain are exchanged again for cash. The chip's color-coded monetary value and uniform, stackable shape allows the croupier to count and collect wagers, wins, and losses more efficiently while reducing both potential mistakes in calculation and the opportunistic theft of funds.

However, the dead chip is not a surrogate for cash. Rather, it is a repository of debt—that is, of a specific type of gambling loan that is legal in Macau (or, more accurately, not illegal), but that is not lawful across the border, where both the gaming credit and the gambler's assets are actually located. In addition, the dead chip's multiplier function covertly enables two simultaneous bets with different stakes, in different currencies, and even against a different house (the casino, which owns the gaming concession, and the junket, which does not). Finally, the dead chip is also a material mnemonic of the informal fiscal and affective relationship that binds creditor and debtor—a relationship that becomes closer with each subsequent roll of additional chips. Therefore, despite the inert connotations of its name, the dead chip is actually a form of "vibrant matter" (Bennett 2010) that affords a variety of financial activities involving multiple participants and coexisting in distinct spatiotemporal locales.

In addition to the dead chip credit that moves through the junket trade to finance VIP gaming, there are other innovative and informal means by which gamblers may transfer money to finance both VIP and mass market gaming. For example, pawnshops are located in the immediate vicinity of every casino in Macau, and they are clustered in the city center, near a number of popular gaming venues. Macau pawnshops serve the traditional function of allowing a gambler short on cash to present a watch or other small item of value as collateral for a short-term loan. If the gambler fails to pay back the loan within an agreed-on period, the pawned item becomes the shop's property and can be resold. Although Chinese law limits the amount of cash that gamblers may transport across the border, nothing prevents individuals from buying gold or expensive jewelry in China and selling it for cash in Macau, or using it as collateral for a local loan.

Additionally, however, Macau pawnshops (and certain other retail establishments) facilitate cross-border currency movements via UnionPay debit/credit cards, a financial product of China's central bank. A Chinese tourist may use the UnionPay card to purchase an expensive item in Macau, then immediately return that item to the shop for a cash refund. The shop retains a percentage of the purchase price as its fee, and the customer leaves with the remainder of the money; Macau banks charge the merchant a fee of 1 to 2 percent per transaction. In this way, what is essentially a cash withdrawal appears as a purchase of goods, with no paper trail of the actual transaction. Chinese tourists in Macau may use this technique to make cash withdrawals in amounts exceeding what is allowed by Chinese law. The Macau Monetary Authority estimates that in 2012, approximately RMB 50 billion was moved from China to Macau via UnionPay cards, and about 90 percent of the transactions were "highly concentrated in jewelry, ornament and luxury watch sales" (Pomfret 2014).

In addition, some enterprising moneylenders have smuggled into Macau portable UnionPay card machines that are registered on the mainland and connected to mainland computer servers. Macau-based transactions made on these machines appear to have taken place on the mainland. This provides an illicit means to mask cash withdrawals in the city (Pomfret 2014). In short, VIP room dead chips, pawnshops, and credit card machines each function to facilitate cash liquidity for gambling.

Informal Networks in the Junket Trade

When they opened their businesses in Macau, Adelson and Wynn initially refused to work with local junkets because they had concerns that these associations might have a negative effect on their American gaming licenses. These foreign concessionaires planned instead to recruit their own VIP gamblers and to operate their VIP rooms in a manner consistent with junket operations in Las Vegas. Wynn even pressured the Macau government to revise the gaming law to permit concessionaires to advance credit directly to gamblers, ostensibly allowing the junket middlemen to be cut out (SCMP Reporter 2003). As a result, the government promulgated Casino Credit Law 5/2004, which permits these direct casino loans (Lam and Eadington 2009).

Regardless of their plans, however, the American operators soon discovered, as Portuguese explorers had half a millennium before, that they had to operate within the existing system that preceded their presence in the region; otherwise, they would not be able to compete with Stanley Ho's entrenched relationships.[10] The Americans needed the local expertise of junket operators with access to networks of high rollers, as well as knowledge about mainland wealth necessary to recruit new gamblers. That is, the junkets were positioned to play the matchmaker role between the concessionaires and Chinese high rollers. The junkets also possess the extrajudicial means to collect debts outside the reach of the legal system—the "protection" necessary to hedge against the risk of bad credit that might jeopardize their investments in the city.

The difficulty the American operators confronted in Macau was adjusting to what one industry journalist calls the "relative informality" of the relationship between junkets, agents, and gamblers (Newsdesk 2010, 30). This relative informality is an expression of those regional "informal business networks" identified by Arrighi. The Macau junket business is held together by informal oral agreements among associates who have developed a degree of mutual trust. This arrangement—an expression of the Chinese cultural logics of *guanxi*—contrasts with the relative formality of western business practices, which are characterized by concomitant responsibilities to shareholders and regulators (Wang and Zabielskis 2010). In fact, the junkets were effectively unregulated until March 2007, when the Macau government introduced junket operator regulations. However, by some accounts, the regulations merely formalized the existing structure of informal agreements rather than introducing measures and controls consistent with international business standards (Siu 2007).

THE MACAU BARGAIN

To understand the function of Macau's junket industry within China's reform economy, it is useful to return again to the comparisons that Arrighi and Gipouloux draw between medieval Mediterranean city-states and the contemporary "Asian Mediterranean." Arrighi and Silver (2001) describe the city-states of Singapore and Hong Kong, as well as the capitalist "islands" of Taiwan, Japan, and South Korea, as the "cash-boxes" of the post-1970 global economy, explaining that these locales "owe their fortunes to a strict specialization in the pursuit of wealth rather than the pursuit of power." They contend, "Not since the elimination of the Dutch Republic from the high politics of Europe have cash-boxes of this kind exercised as much influence on the politics of the modern world as they do now" (275).

Of course, these remunerative islands of the East Asian "capitalist archipelago" function in a region that is dominated by the much larger country of China, the world's largest "state container" of capitalism, to use Arrighi's language. Operating in this environment, the overseas Chinese financiers, like the Genoese before them, "are an interstitial formation that thrives on the limits and contradictions of very large territorial organizations" (Arrighi 2003, 136). The city-states of Hong Kong and Singapore likewise thrive on the "limits and contradictions" of the region.[11] For example, Hong Kong's centrality as a banking and finance hub is made possible by the global confidence in its financial institutions inspired by the British colonial roots of the city's legal system, combined with its geographical, political, linguistic, and cultural access to China. As such, Arrighi ([1994] 2010) argues that the city-states of contemporary East Asia mimic the specific functions of their premodern Mediterranean counterparts: "Finally, the two smallest but by no means least important 'islands,' Singapore and Hong Kong, are city-states combining ultramodern technologies and architectures with a political capitalism reminiscent of the Renaissance city-states—the commercial-industrial entrepot functions exercised by Singapore making it resemble Venice, and the commercial-financial entrepot functions exercised by Hong Kong making it resemble Genoa" (79). It is understandable that Arrighi, writing in the late twentieth century, did not anticipate Macau's unlikely postcolonial economic ascendance. However, as a gambling–financial entrepôt that productively articulates annual flows of tens of millions of Chinese tourists and billions of dollars of liquid capital, yet lacks Hong Kong's current contentious civil politics, Macau may be the city-state par excellence for the market-socialist regime.[12]

By generating tens of billions of dollars of annual revenue, Macau certainly serves as a cashbox for the global economy; it is the epitome of a locale that owes its "fortunes to a strict specialization in the pursuit of wealth rather than the pursuit of power" (Arrighi and Silver, 2001). However, we have seen that in Macau's casino industry, "cashbox" is not merely a figurative expression used to describe the city's gaming revenues but is a literal description of Macau's internal casino gaming operations. The "cashbox" function denotes the vertically differentiated VIP rooms themselves, within which the VIP credit trade is organized, as well as the city's numerous pawnshops and the credit card machines they use to process transactions. Together, this triumvirate collection of cashboxes in Macau facilitate annual cross-border movements of billions of dollars of Chinese currency. However, the monetary innovation that powers Macau's cashbox function is the dead chip that makes VIP gambling possible.

The revenues generated by the junket system constitute by far the single most significant factor in Macau's economy. In 2013, the most profitable year to date for the city's casinos, there were 235 licensed junkets in Macau, and casino revenues totaled US$45 billion (Chan and Chan 2013); approximately 60 percent of that revenue was derived from the junket business. As I noted previously, the Macau government receives about 39 percent of gaming revenue in the form of annual concession fees, direct taxes, and required contributions to social welfare and culture funds (Pessanha 2008)—an amount dwarfing the maximum 6.75 percent gaming tax in Las Vegas. These funds provide 80 percent of the Macau government's annual public budget (Li and Sheng 2018).

Remittances to the Macau government from gaming taxes ultimately fund a generous welfare regime for locals in the city, creating close to full employment, providing an annual cash handout to citizens, and generating what soon may be the highest per capita GDP in the world. This conceded collusion among the state, an oligarchy of casino concessionaires, and local junkets, which benefits the overall welfare of the local population, may be understood as a Macau bargain. In the short term, and on the tiny scale of the city-state, it perhaps rivals the Fordist-Keynesian bargain that characterized the twentieth-century United States economy.

However, Adelson's role in this arrangement hearkens back to the origins of capitalism itself. I began this chapter by pointing out the relationship among Adelson's transnational allegiances and his business operations that capitalize off the space of flows, and thereby drew a comparison among Adelson, Genoese merchant bankers, and Macau's junket financiers. However, what distinguishes Adelson is the way he deploys his profits to pursue a more or less classic model of global power and political influence. Although Adelson is not a national leader with expansionary territorial ambitions, he consorts with elected officials and seeks to exert his power at the highest levels of government in the United States and Israel—not only to facilitate his business operations and shield his fortune from income taxes but also to advance the territorial interests of the state of Israel. Therefore, the credit protection that Adelson purchases from the junkets serves not only his personal financial interests but also his global political ambitions. This is where we may draw a direct parallel among Adelson's junket operations in Macau and the earlier Genoese–Iberian capitalist regime.

Arrighi ([1994] 2010) observes that the Genoese–Iberian era of global capitalism was organized by a "dichotomous agency" composed of the Iberian "aristocratic territorialist component," which specialized in providing protection and pursuing power, and the bourgeois Genoese capitalists, who specialized in selling commodities and seeking profits (123). The collective success of this partnership was forged in the complementary nature of these two distinct sets of motivations. The desire of Iberian monarchs for global power and territorial conquest, which was in part motivated by their Catholic religious fanaticism, created trade opportunities for the Genoese; the profits that the Genoese derived from this arrangement helped buttress the effectiveness of the Iberian territorial apparatus.[13]

The religious component of the Spanish and Portuguese maritime discoveries was a crucial factor in this arrangement; from the standpoint of the strictly profit-oriented goals of the Genoese, the prospect of opening their own global trade routes involved incalculable risks that were, in Arrighi's (2010) words, "beyond the horizon of rational capitalist enterprise" (125). It was the conflation of Catholicism and capitalism, or what Sloterdijk (2013) calls the Iberian "entrepreneurial religiosity" (47), that justified the risks necessary to make their African, Asian, and American discoveries possible. We may understand the opportunistic partnership among Macau's casino concessionaires and the junkets as a contemporary example of this sort of "dichotomous agency," but in Macau, this agency has distinct local characteristics. Through the use of regional informal networks of a type that has persisted in the region since the premodern era, the junkets provide local protection while Adelson pursues global political power. To return again to Arrighi's formulation about the historical development of global capitalism, each step forward by a new regime is simultaneously a step backward.

STATE RESPONSES TO CASINO CAPITALISM IN MACAU

As we have seen, concessionaires, junket operators, and other investors in Macau's casino industry often operate in the gray zones of both Chinese and U.S. law, capitalizing off Macau's semiautonomous status and geospatial novelty. As such, the junket trade is exemplary of those activities that for Braudel constitute real capitalism. Remember that Braudel conceives of capitalism not as simple market activity but as the extraordinary forms of commerce that occupy the opaque zone above the conventional market. The marketplace tends toward market freedom, genuine competition, fair exchange, and ordinary revenues. Long-distance capitalism, on the other hand, gravitates toward monopoly control and extraordinary profits.

Securing those exceptional profits requires the support of the state. However, Braudel notes that the state's relation to capitalism is dynamic and contradictory, alternating between being both the guarantor of the monopoly advantage of capitalists and the regulator of their activities. This dynamic relationship has persisted throughout the five-hundred-year history of global capitalism. "The state undoubtedly encouraged capitalism and came to its rescue," observes Braudel (1979); yet "the state also discouraged capitalism which was capable of harming the interests of the state" (2:554).

This same ambivalence is characteristic of the relations among Macau's gaming industry and Chinese authorities. On the one hand, China's central government guarantees Macau's favorable monopoly on legal casino gambling in the PRC and (with the IVS) provides both the bulk of the customers and capital to fund it. The Macau government likewise guarantees the limited competition enjoyed by an oligarchy of gaming concessionaires, as well as the monopoly currency of dead chips that is a requirement for participation in the junket trade.[14] At the same time, however, the central government is clearly concerned about the casino industry and the consequences of cross-border casino finance for the mainland economy. The greater the profits of the junket trade, the greater the concerns.

Similarly, the money flowing from China into Macau, and then into the United States through the finances of individuals such as Adelson, has drawn the attention of American authorities, with calls at the highest levels of government to monitor or regulate these funds. In some cases, the Macau VIP rooms themselves have become a sort of proxy theater for indirect skirmishes between these two state regimes. I thus now turn to these state responses to capitalism.

Adelson's Macau earnings first gained attention in the United States when, in the wake of the 2010 *Citizens United* ruling that changed campaign finance laws by eliminating limits on donations to political action committees (PACs), he pledged to spend US$100 million in the 2012 presidential election in an effort to unseat Barack Obama. When Adelson donated $10 million to a super PAC supporting Mitt Romney's presidential campaign, Romney's Republican rival, John McCain, raised concerns about "foreign money" influencing the presidential election. McCain remarked, "Much of Mr. Adelson's casino profits that go to him come from his casino in Macau, which says that obviously, maybe in a roundabout way foreign money is coming into an American political campaign" (Sink 2012).

However, attention to the source of Adelson's profits obscures the more serious question about the political consequences of the scale of his largesse. Sloterdijk (2013) claims that China's particular form of authoritarian state capitalism today flies in the face of neoliberal assumptions that conflate freedom and the free market; instead, it "proves the separability of capitalism and democracy on a grand scale" (166). However, in the pay-for-play political system of the United States, it appears that unrestricted megadonors such as Adelson, in their own way, have proved the same thing.[15] As Braudel emphasizes, real capitalism exemplifies not the free market but the antimarket.

Perhaps the most significant challenge to junket operators emerged in 2012, when the Chinese president, Xi Jinping, launched a crackdown on official corruption that would develop into one of the largest such anticorruption campaigns in modern Chinese history. In 2013 alone, the central government punished 182,000 officials for corruption (Yuen 2014). While foreigners are not privy to the complex nuances of Chinese domestic politics that motivated the corruption crackdown, one clear objective of the campaign was an effort to stem the country's rampant capital flight, and these moves had a significant effect on Macau's economy.[16] "At its height in 2013, $1 trillion left mainland China via Macau's VIP tables," notes one industry journalist. "Those outflows helped curb inflation during China's peak boom years. Now, in a less explosive economy shifting from investment- to consumption-driven growth, there's an increasing incentive to keep that money at home" (Cohen 2016). The efforts to control outflows of capital also intersected with concerns that some government officials or state enterprise executives might be gambling in Macau with public funds.[17] Chinese officials began to strongly urge the Macau government to diversify the local economy away from the overreliance on VIP gambling. (I explore these efforts in chapter 7.)

The corruption campaign arrived in Macau's casino industry in December 2014, when, in a meeting held at the monetary authority of Macau, local officials reached an agreement with the central government to grant China's economic crimes investigation bureau real-time access to all transactions in Macau involving China's UnionPay card (Fraser 2014; Macau Monetary Affairs Bureau 2014). The central government's ability to monitor UnionPay transactions in Macau meant that a primary tool for gray-market money transfers to fund gambling by mainland tourists was visible to the scrutiny of mainland authorities.[18] Only two days after the government announced the new policy, President Xi made a state visit to Macau to participate in events commemorating the fifteenth anniversary of the city's return to China and to swear in Macau's chief executive for his second five-year term. Xi couched his official remarks in Macau in the sort of vague language typical of Chinese officials, and although he made no specific mention of Macau's casinos, the central government's concern about Macau's reliance on VIP revenue was clear: "It is important for Macau to adopt a global, nationwide, future-oriented and long-term perspective, formulate appropriate plans and blueprints for its development and promote sound economic and social development. Focus on building a global tourism and leisure center . . . promote the Macanese economy's appropriate diversification and sustainable development. This is of great importance for the interests of the people of Macau" (Jim 2014). The consequences of these new measures on VIP revenues were significant. In 2015, Macau's GDP plunged 25 percent—a decline so sudden and significant that as a percentage of total GDP, it was perhaps second that year only to Yemen's economic woes during the throes of the debilitating coup d'etat that led to that country's civil war (Cohen 2016). In February 2015, a month in which the Chinese New Year holiday normally produces exceptional casino profits, gambling revenues fell 49 percent compared to February of the previous year, setting a new record for year-on-year declines. Industry analysts attributed much of the loss to the constraints that the corruption crackdown imposed on illicit outflows of money from China, though the disorder of Hong Kong's Umbrella Movement (discussed in chapter 5) and the Macau government's implementation of citywide smoking prohibitions (discussed in chapter 7) also contributed to the downturn.[19]

In fact, in a conference call with investors at the end of October 2014, a month that had seen a 20 percent decline in gaming revenues compared to October of the previous year, Wynn referred to the confluence of these three factors—the corruption crackdown, Umbrella Movement, and smoking regulations—as a "perfect storm" that had descended on Macau. "I am confused at the moment," he said, taking stock of the financial climate of the industry. "I don't know if it is a squall or if we are in a rainy season, or how long it will last" (Newsdesk 2014b).

Finally, Macau's interstitial position mediating Adelson's investments in China and relationship with Trump on the one hand, and China's national interests on the other, was solidified in 2019, around the time of the twentieth anniversary of the SAR, when the central government proposed Macau as a potential meeting place for a summit between Xi and Trump to negotiate the ongoing United States–China trade war, although the event did not materialize (Hamlin 2019).[20] I thus finally turn to a broader consideration of the role of Macau's casino capitalism in the relationship between the United States and China.

ONE STEP FORWARD, ONE STEP BACK

The mid-twentieth-century mass production and consumption economy of the United States achieved a sustained rate of growth and profit unmatched in the five-hundred-year history of global capitalism. China's National New-Type Urbanization Plan aims to replicate the American model. However, Fordism's increasing failure to return acceptable profits in western economies starting in the 1970s has provoked a variety of macroeconomic responses that can be collectively understood within the rubric of neoliberalism, a departure from the Keynesian policies of embedded liberalism that dominated the twentieth-century American regime (Harvey 2005, 2007). The crisis of Fordism also prompted an explosion of strategies of financialization that sought to recover profits no longer available from production. Strange (1986) suggests that this financialization heralds a new economy of casino capitalism.

However, from the perspective of Braudel's *longue durée,* financialization is not a unique characteristic of the contemporary era but rather a recurring component of each successive regime of capitalism: from the Italian city-states to Holland, Britain, and now the United States. When either conventional trade or production begins to fail in its capacity to return substantial profits, each regime turns to financialization as a compensatory strategy of accumulation. Braudel, drawing on his understanding of the cyclical temporality of capitalism, poetically refers to financialization as a sign of the "autumn," or maturity, of each regime. Arrighi (2010) interprets this remark to indicate the imminent demise of what he calls a "hegemonic cycle" of capitalism.[21] "If past tendencies are any guide to the present and future," contends Arrighi, "we could expect that the financial expansion would temporarily restore the fortunes of the leading capitalist agency of the epoch, the United States, but would eventually result in a change of leadership in the center of capital accumulation on a world scale" (371). Therefore, for Arrighi, the current era of financialization is a signal crisis, indicating the coming replacement of the dominant role of the United States by a new regime of capitalism in China.

It is possible that Arrighi's prognostication about a coming Chinese long century may prove correct. However, what is useful for my own study of Macau's gaming industry is not Arrighi's predictions about the future but rather his orientation to the past. Attention to the history of the GBA region, as well as the way this history informs understanding of Macau's role in market-socialism, provides a useful counterpoint to contemporary theories about neoliberal urban government and a clearer understanding of Macau's particular style of casino capitalism. This is evident if we return once again to the role of Adelson and the other concessionaires in Macau's gaming industry. With his expenditures of approximately US$15 billion to construct resort properties in Macau, Adelson is China's single largest foreign investor, and he exemplifies the undeniable financial success of the Macau government's decision to liberalize Ho's casino monopoly.

In the language of post-Fordism, the concession agreement that allows Adelson and the other casino operators to work so profitably with the local junkets may be understood as a public–private partnership. Harvey (1989) argues that such partnerships are typical of the post-1970 neoliberal restructuring of the economy as metropolitan governments in the West have transitioned away from the managerial provision of services for the local population that typified urban governance in the 1960s and toward the entrepreneurial attraction of private investment. From this perspective, Macau's concession agreement exemplifies what Harvey calls a "consumerist style of urbanization" (9), which serves to enable Macau's competition with other regional cities to attract Chinese tourist dollars.

In the language of poststructuralism, the same concession arrangement becomes what Ong (2006) calls a "state-transnational network" (88), and the Macau SAR designation itself is a "zoning technology" (7) in an innovative East Asian (that is, nonwestern) program of "neoliberalism as exception." In this account, Macau's casino concession arrangement is an "optimizing" (3) market calculation that pragmatically sets aside the country's ideological concerns in order to articulate the PRC with global capital.

Indeed, each of these arguments is relevant to understanding Macau today. However, from the standpoint of postsocialism, and within the geohistorical context of the GBA region that I analyze in Part I, we may also understand the concession agreement as a contemporary iteration of the sixteenth-century Macau formula. With this formula, the Ming emperor confined European capitalist activity to the coastal colonial concessions so that China could benefit from trade without compromising the country's territorial sovereignty and cultural integrity; under this arrangement, "Westerners were to have trade and no more" (Fok 1999, 38). This geopolitical logic, whereby the central and Macau governments cooperate with a variety of "footloose" (Arrighi 2003, 134) nonstate actors, such as high-profile Las Vegas billionaires and opaque Chinese financiers, is less post-Fordist or postmodern than premodern, a manifestation of a resurgent medievalism reminiscent of the Genoese–Iberian long century of capitalist hegemony.[22]

This use of a geriatric Chinese governmental strategy in Macau's contemporary gaming industry replicates the ways in which (as I discuss in earlier chapters) Deng used the extant model of the European colonial concessions to inspire the country's new experimental economic zones; China's contemporary pedagogical tourism project is modeled on the Cultural Revolution–era rustication and reeducation of urban youth; and Macau's integrated resorts replicate the form (but not the content) of the socialist *danwei*. In each case, we may observe the unique spatial logic of China's economic reforms and the central role that Macau has played as both subject and object of market-socialism. That is, the Portuguese city-state of Macau inspired several of the experimental strategies that are the pillars of China's reform economy, and in turn, the postretrocession Macau SAR is a prime beneficiary of these same innovations. Each of those recombinant governmental programs recovers antecedent elements of China's protocapitalist or socialist history and assembles them into contemporary market devices to create market-socialism. This process exemplifies the sort of "double movement, forward and backward at the same time," which Arrighi (2004, 534) contends is typical of each successive capitalist regime, but it does so with recurrent Chinese characteristics that persevere from the past.

Here is where I draw my distinction from other scholars of East Asian capitalism. Castells sees in the GBA a futuristic megacity, whose disjunctive and dynamic components function in the manner of digital circuits that direct information through computer networks. Ong (2006) similarly observes a novel state-transnational network structure underlying the "exceptional" neoliberal political rationalities in East Asia. However, I prefer to highlight the ways in which China's market-socialist economy relies on those same low-tech informal human networks that have persisted in the region since the premodern era; it also relies on the sedimented spatial forms that are the local by-product of terrestrial globalization. Even as Adelson mobilizes his Macau cashbox casino profits and new American campaign finance laws to advance his political interests, he is playing a centuries-old game reminiscent of those Genoese bankers who steered global finance while their Portuguese and Spanish partners assumed the risks of navigating global trade routes. As Arrighi (2003) notes, in words that seem prescient when one considers Castells's network society, Ong's zoning technologies, or Adelson's hyperreal Venetian Resort, "the most piquant irony" of the recent explosion of capitalism in East Asia "is how premodern 'postmodernity' looks in what has become the most dynamic region of the capitalist world system" (138).

Finally, attention to Macau's junket trade allows us to also reconsider Strange's (1986) conception of casino capitalism. Just as we have learned from Braudel and Arrighi that post-1970 financialization is less a novel event than it is a recurring characteristic of each cycle of capitalism, the VIP industry that drives Macau's economy is not a degenerate form of market activity that requires a pejorative qualifying adjective like "casino" to set it apart from some more ideal form of accumulation. Rather, Macau's VIP junket business is consistent with Braudel's real capitalism, rendered in a form as pure as the Portuguese long-distance trade in which the city was founded five hundred years before.[23]

The key figure in this trade is the Macau junket agent, who productively assembles the individual Chinese high roller, the concessionaire's gaming license and casino resort, and the credit for gambling that is materialized in the innovative instrument of dead chips. We may understand the junket agent as a direct descendent of the Portuguese privateer, who cooperated with Genoese or Belgian financiers to pursue the vast profits of the Far East frontier enabled by long-distance seafaring, arbitrage, and trade. Today these junket financiers operate as indispensable intermediaries, strategically positioned between the state and the market in China;[24] between China's market-socialist economy and transnational capital; and perhaps (if Arrighi's predictions are correct) even between two competing superpowers that meet today on the perimeter of capitalism's new twenty-first-century frontier.

Baccarat and Biopolitics

The Velvet Rope

The entrance of the Hermès store in Macau's Wynn resort is flanked by a plush red velvet rope affixed to gold stanchions. On those days when the shop is overwhelmed by customers, the rope is positioned to indicate the appropriate place for interested shoppers to queue while they wait for their turn to enter the premises.

Such velvet palisades are a common feature at several of Macau's most exclusive fashion outlets, each of which is located in the lavish retail arcades found inside the city's five-star casino resorts. During especially busy travel seasons such as the Chinese New Year holiday, when up to one hundred thousand tourists may pour into the resort property daily, Chinese shoppers often stand idle in lines at the doors of these establishments in anticipation of their opportunity to purchase high-priced designer merchandise. But even during more subdued seasons, when tourist numbers decrease and the arcades are noticeably less busy, the velvet ropes remain at the threshold of each boutique, serving as a tacit reminder of implicit expectations concerning the orderly comportment of Chinese consumers.

These adumbrated assumptions about the demeanor of prospective Chinese shoppers contrast with the sensationalistic accounts widely publicized in the international media in recent years that highlight the disorderly and indecorous behaviors that Chinese tourists sometimes exhibit in their travels abroad. The PRC deputy prime minister, Wang Yang, became so concerned about the cringeworthy behavior of such intemperate Chinese travelers that in 2013, the central government released a sixty-four-page guidebook on "civilized travel" detailing state expectations for appropriate tourist conduct. Chinese travelers are asked to refrain from such unbecoming activities as spitting, squatting on toilet seats, or carving their names onto the surfaces of historic monuments, but prominent on the list of prohibited behaviors are more proactive instructions that citizens should queue systematically for tourist attractions and refrain from the temptation to cut in line.

Figure 29. The velvet rope in front of a luxury retail store in the Wynn resort. *Photograph by Adam Lampton.*

The problem of queue-jumping came to a head in 2018, when upmarket French brand Balenciaga faced a social media backlash from Chinese tourists, who posted upward of two million online comments in reaction to an incident of assault against a Chinese tourist by French personnel working in one of the company's Paris stores. The Chinese victim of the Balenciaga staff's aggression garnered sympathy because he was allegedly defending his mother in a scuffle with fellow tourists that started when another shopper jumped the queue of those waiting to enter the shop (Thomas 2018).

As an everyday social phenomenon, the banal queue seems to be the great equalizer of mass society, requiring people from all walks to life to assemble one after the other and wait their turn. However, unlike the ubiquitous and utilitarian ribbons of retractable Tensabarrier fabric webbing stretched taut between nondescript steel posts to mark the mazelike queuing pathways so common in social life today (Sharr 2015), Macau's genteel velvet ropes do not function to remind China's *renmin*—the numerous members of the country's once-egalitarian masses—of their common humanity. Rather, Macau's velvet rope queue is proffered to only a select population of elite tourists who play a resonant role in the country's reform era.

The ability to adhere to international norms of queuing behavior and to comply with expectations of general tourist demeanor is one element of the corporeal characteristic of quality (*suzhi*) that the PRC central government explicitly aims to enhance in the Chinese people in an effort to maximize the country's economic development. More than serving as a momentary pause in an architecture otherwise designed to facilitate mobility, Macau's velvet queue apparatus marks an aperture where select tourist bodies are temporarily immobilized and aggregated in a state of suggestive repose. Each microphysical act of proper bodily comportment is tactile testament to those otherwise intangible aspects of courtly cultivation that have been accrued by the individual.

The tourist body standing patiently behind the velvet rope is the very locus of quality, here conceived not as a natural characteristic of the individual but as a supplement to the bare life of the subject, which may be accumulated only through proactive efforts to acquire human capital. For its part, the velvet rope hanging demurely outside the luxury retail store implies the very subject who will form up in its presence. The rope does not dictate or command specific forms of behavior; instead, it gently suggests the place and position at which anticipatory shoppers should stand, all the while presupposing that each shopper comprehends and will conform to the expected etiquette. That is, the velvet rope implies that a certain class of tourist will wait patiently in an orderly queue in anticipation of their turn to purchase an expensive designer item—an item whose exclusivity will itself impose further distinction, or quality, on the owner.

Velvet has played a formative role in the historical development of capitalism, softening the tactile surfaces of the domestic interior and distinguishing the plush bourgeois boudoir from the simple working-class hovel. Within the cultural landscape of nineteenth-century Paris, for example, "velvet gowns and linings functioned not simply as protection from modernity, but also as facilitators of a new consumerist paradigm of suspended gratification" (Hartzell 2009, 52). Today, Macau's velvet retail ropes serve a similar function. The velvet rope cordons off refined bodies replete with accumulated quality (and poised to acquire more with every discriminating purchase), separating them from the disordered, ambling tour-group hordes whose members inadvertently display their corresponding lack of such quality as they move conspicuously en masse through the retail promenade.

This new discriminating consumer subject, the focus of China's National New-Type Urbanization Plan, is the opposite of the stereotypically uncouth Chinese tourist whose boorish behavior is the object of derision in the international press. We might call this quality Chinese shopper an urbane consumer. The convergence of cosmopolitanism and shopping savvy in this subject creates the ideal-type citizen cadre who will contribute to the new China.

7

Porcelain Ashtrays

TAMING THE VOLATILITY OF BACCARAT

> Taking a drag from a cigarette is inhaling a multitude of trajectories.
> To inhale is to breathe a very particular socio-historical trajectory; is
> to invest in a very particular economy; is to indulge in a very particular
> chemical reaction; is to construct a very particular aesthetic. . . .
> A cigarette is an object that, through its capacities to collect or coalesce
> trajectories, is imbued with a special significance. Without the cigarette
> these networks would have no space to interact, no common ground
> and would occur to us as if operating through disparate directions.
>
> —Andrew Daly and Chris L. Smith, "Architecture, Cigarettes, and the *Dispositif*"

On January 3, 2019, just two days after Macau authorities implemented the final phase of comprehensive citywide smoking regulations, a public security police officer got into a physical altercation with three male Chinese tourists who defied his instructions to refrain from smoking in a designated nonsmoking area immediately outside the doors of the Galaxy Resort's Diamond Lobby. An amateur video widely shared on social media captured approximately two minutes of the frenzied encounter. Much of the video account focuses on one of the men, clad in an alabaster hooded sweatshirt prominently embossed with the name of French luxury brand Balenciaga, who repeatedly provokes and charges the officer against the protestations of an unidentified woman and several members of the Galaxy security staff attempting to restrain his outbursts. The beleaguered officer, apparently unable to subdue the three agitated men with the police baton he wields in his left hand, suddenly unholsters his service pistol and fires a loud warning shot into the air, to the visible and audible surprise of onlookers.

Other officers eventually arrived to arrest the three men, who were fined, briefly jailed, and then forced to leave the city. In the wake of the incident, some pundits expressed surprise at the officer's decision to fire his weapon in a crowded area to address the fallout from a simple smoking infraction. However, the police officer's desperate pistol shot resonated with the explosive volatility of the admixture of Chinese tourists, cigarette smoking, and casino gambling in Macau.

Men from mainland China are among the world's heaviest smokers, and anecdotal evidence from Macau (as well as international medical research) would suggest that smoking is especially popular with that subset of the group who are dedicated gamblers.[1] For this reason, for the many years leading up to Macau's implementation of tobacco regulations, cigarette smoking in casinos was a ubiquitous activity among Chinese gamblers in the city.

When I arrived in Macau in 2001, I was surprised to discover that almost no smoking prohibitions existed in the city. Although my university had actually just implemented some modest smoking controls, indoor smoking was permitted in government offices, casinos, hotels, nightclubs, saunas, bars, restaurants, cafés, and even the city's first Starbucks, which opened in 2002. This open policy persisted until January 1, 2012, when the local government implemented the smoking prevention and control law. However, this initial program of tobacco regulations exempted many locales, including casinos, as a result of industry concerns that smoking restrictions would negatively affect gaming revenues.

Indeed, the cigarette serves in Macau's casinos as both an instrument of social bonding among Chinese men and a potent psychochemical elixir for regulating the specific forms of stress inherent in the risk-taking activities that are typical of high-stakes gambling.[2] Therefore, any intervention in smoking practices was likely to reverberate through the industry. Nevertheless, in October 2014, the government extended smoking prohibitions onto the city's once untouchable casino floors, and at the start of 2019, the restrictions were finally applied to the sacrosanct VIP rooms, whose highly lucrative operations were the subject of chapter 6. The implementation of these smoking policies, even in the face of significant resistance from gaming industry leaders, was largely motivated by the concerns of local croupiers, the frontline casino workers who had begun to complain loudly about their smoke-filled and unhealthy workplace environments.[3]

VITAL POLITICS

Such governmental efforts to productively guide citizen behavior in order to enhance the health, vitality, and security of the population are exemplary of what Foucault would call a biopolitical strategy of governance. "Biopolitical governance, or *biogovernance,* is aimed at the management of the vital characteristics of human populations, and exercised in the name of optimizing individual and collective life, health, and welfare," says Greenhalgh (2009, 208). Here, in the final part of this book, I explore the convergence of China's vital politics with Macau's gaming industry and analyze attempts in the city's casinos to mold and refine the behavior of Chinese gamblers.

China's contemporary regime of biogovernance roughly coincides with the country's economic reforms. "Around 1980," says Greenhalgh (2010), "China's party-state began to construct an elaborate social-systems apparatus designed to 'engineer' the nation's rise by transforming China's backward masses into a scientifically normalized, modern society fitting of a global power" (37). Greenhalgh's analysis of China's one-child policy demonstrates that the central government's efforts to first constrain the *quantity* of the country's population, then to enhance its *quality,* were motivated by the belief that "humans are shaped by a broad array of genetic, environmental, and educational factors, most of which can be nurtured so that human potential can be molded to meet the nation's needs" (58). In this context, Macau's smoking regulations may be understood as a component of the more general program of biogovernance of Chinese tourists in the city's resorts. Some tourists visit the Venetian Resort's Malo Clinic for skin treatments, dental work, or cosmetic surgery that will enhance the quality of their physical attributes (as I discuss in chapter 5). However, Macau's regime of smoking restrictions reaches beyond such physical qualities, into the very biochemical composition of those tourists, in an effort to modulate their subjectivity to meet the goals of the state.

Anthropologist Ann Anagnost (2004), in her account of China's ongoing efforts to create and refine quality citizens, argues that in this biopolitical realm of governance in China, "human life becomes a new frontier for capital accumulation" (189). In these final chapters, we will see that this "new frontier" of economic value, which reaches deep into the protean subjectivity of Macau's post-Mao Chinese tourists, is not only a concern of China's central government but also the object of an intensive program of biopolitical experimentation in the global gaming industry. The aim of this experiment is to engineer a new kind of mass market Chinese gambling subject in Macau. The hope is that the habits of this new Chinese gambler will diversify the industry away from its predominant reliance on VIP high rollers, whose unique gambling activities pose some specific quandaries for both the Chinese government and the casino companies. The crux of these concerns is the problem of volatility.

THE ASHTRAY AS VIBRANT MATTER

Macau's smoking prohibitions have no doubt created a healthier casino workplace environment. Today smoking is permitted only in designated rooms inside the casinos, and gaming tables and gambling machines must be located at least three meters away from the automated sliding doors that separate smoking activities from general casino play.[4] However, before the full implementation of the smoking ban, stories shared among casino workers indicated that the imminent danger posed by smoking in VIP rooms did not emanate only from the clouds of secondhand smoke wafting through the rooms. A less immediately conspicuous, but perhaps even more compelling, concern was the ashtrays sitting on the baccarat tables where the city's most popular casino game is played. Positioned within easy reach of a hapless high-stakes Chinese gambler at the moment his losing cards are revealed, the ashtray might suddenly transmogrify into a perilous armament.

When an agitated gambler instinctively grasped an ashtray in his immediate vicinity and indiscriminately launched it in a physical expression of his sudden financial misfortune, there was no way to predict where the hurled object might land. In at least one exceptional account, an ashtray struck a chandelier hanging over a baccarat table, prompting glass shards to shower down. More typically, however, the errant ashtray would inadvertently hit a card dealer or a random member of the security staff who happened to be standing in its path on the other side of the room.[5]

The ashtray is therefore more than a simple inanimate object. The ashtray on a VIP room baccarat table may be understood as a kind of "vibrant matter" that manifests a certain disposition, or "thing power," which is actuated when it finds itself in the hands of an unlucky gambler (Bennett 2010). The casino ashtray assembles Foucault's "heterogeneous ensemble" of aesthetic, addictive, anatomical, and affective vectors that are embodied in the baccarat gambler in Macau, but that only become perceptible as they coalesce around this otherwise banal object.

As such, the ashtray provides a unique analytic aperture into the VIP baccarat trade—as well as into the ongoing efforts among government and industry alike to tame the *volatility* of Macau's entire baccarat-based economy. These efforts to recalibrate Macau's gaming economy revolve around attempts to convince Chinese tourists to gamble on electronic gaming machines rather than the table game of baccarat that such gamblers prefer. The underlying motivations of this preferential promotion of machine gambling is an attempt to resolve the various political and socioeconomic obstacles created by the central government's anticorruption campaign, which I outline in chapter 6, as well as to manage an additional set of constraints emanating from within the industry itself, which I explain here. Although Macau's casino concessionaires would not describe the benefits of machine gambling in exactly these terms, their efforts to convince Chinese tourists to gamble on machines rather than baccarat tables is consistent with the biogovernance regime of the central government. These particular governmental strategies aim to foster "the emergence of more calculating, self-governing, 'market-socialist' subjects," says Greenhalgh (2010, 51). The ashtray therefore provides a potent point of entry into an analysis of this biogovernance regime.

To understand the role of ashtrays in Macau's baccarat games, we must begin with the gaming rooms themselves. For the most profitable Macau junket companies, whose annual turnover at the high-stakes tables may reach into the hundreds of millions, if not billions, of dollars, the city's casino concessionaires spare no expense in designing the private VIP gaming rooms in their resorts. Therefore, in the most extravagant VIP rooms, whose construction and decor may cost upward of $30 million, before the implementation of the smoking ban, it was not unusual to find the finest-quality ashtrays.[6]

Among the most ordinary and cost-effective ashtrays are those made of melamine, a hard plastic that gained infamy in the PRC during a massive 2008 public health crisis, with the disquieting discovery that it was an incongruous ingredient in a deadly concoction of bogus infant formula that tragically killed six babies and hospitalized more than fifty thousand others (Branigan 2008). The fallout from this food safety scandal still drives the desire among Chinese tourists to purchase milk powder in Hong Kong and Macau, where such products are presumed to be more adequately regulated; numerous shops in Macau's tourist districts and integrated casino resorts stock cans of milk power, often stacked from floor to ceiling. Aside from such common-variety melamine ashtrays with their unfavorable allusions, more ornate ashtrays are often constructed of ordinary ceramic, and there are a number of factories in China that produce such products. However, among the most opulent ashtrays are those rendered from porcelain, an exquisitely refined ceramic material whose construction was perfected more than a millennium ago in the fiery kilns of the Chinese town of Jingdezhen, and which long served as one of China's most coveted luxury exports (Zhang et al. 2020).[7]

The Alchemy of Porcelain

Porcelain objects played a significant role in early trade between China and the West, including trade conducted via Macau (Jin and Wu 2006; Pierson 2013). Marco Polo reportedly first brought porcelain to Italy when he returned from his travels to the Middle Kingdom, and the obsessive desire that eventually grew among many wealthy Europeans for Chinese porcelain products, which came to be identified by the generic name of "China," was described by eighteenth-century essayist Samuel Johnson as "the contagion of China fancy" (Finlay 1998). This addictive acquisitiveness, which took the form of a discernible European "porcelain sickness" (*Porzellankrankheit),* would come to rival the obsessive attachments that others in the East and West alike would forge with opium, ambergris, tobacco, or gambling:[8]

> When the first steady trickle of Oriental porcelain began to reach Europe in the cargoes of Portuguese traders, kings and connoisseurs were instantly mesmerized by its translucent brilliance. As glossy as the richly coloured silks with which the ships were laden, as flawlessly white as the spray which broke over their bows on the long treacherous journeys, this magical substance was so eggshell

fine that you could hold it to the sun and see daylight through it, so perfect that if you tapped it a musical note would resound. Nothing made in Europe could compare. (Gleeson 1998, x)

Phillip II, the Spanish king, assembled a collection of more than three thousand pieces of porcelain that he housed in the New Tower of the Alcazar in Madrid. Augustus the Strong, elector of Saxony and king of Poland, eventually squandered his country's entire fortune in an effort to acquire Chinese porcelain treasures, as well as to derive the alchemical secrets necessary to create Europe's first porcelain manufacturer (Gleeson 1998; Krahe 2018).

Indeed, according to historian Robert Finlay (1998), "For over a thousand years, Chinese porcelain was the most universally admired and widely imitated product in the world." Finley argues that attention to porcelain in the historical record "yields the first and most extensive physical evidence for sustained cultural encounter on a worldwide scale, perhaps even for indications of genuinely global culture" (143), so it is no surprise to find porcelain objects in a transnational casino property in Macau today.[9] While the malady of porcelain sickness now appears as only an historical curiosity, porcelain's former role as a singularly ubiquitous, addictive, and even deleterious artifact in an emergent global consumer culture is perhaps taken up today by tobacco products. Indeed, in the sixteenth and seventeenth centuries, porcelain and tobacco moved along the same maritime trade routes that connected the Americas and the Far East, which made Macau an important conduit in the travels of both goods to Europe (Brook 2008).

THE PROBLEM OF VOLATILITY

The porcelain ashtray found in Macau's VIP rooms at the start of the twenty-first century is thus more than a mundane functional object. Understood as both archeological artifact and consumer fetish, the ashtray has a lengthy genealogy stretching back half a millennium. However, the pregnant propensity exhibited by an ashtray sitting on a VIP room baccarat table emanates not only from its strangely addictive materiality. The ashtray's somatic appeal also derives from its convenient hand-shaped size and heft, as well as the relationship it productively mediates between the gambler's accumulated stock of anatomical quality and the uncivilized cigarette he stubs out on its shiny surface. Perhaps most importantly, however, the ashtray's "thing power" is imbricated with the enticing yet ineffable affect of high-stakes gambling in Macau—a characteristic that emanates in large part from the peculiar nature of the game of baccarat.

When played for high stakes, such as the bets of $125,000 per hand that are common in Macau's VIP gambling rooms (not to mention those wagers that may sometimes total ten times that amount), baccarat is characterized by what is known in the gaming industry as volatility. That is, baccarat carries the possibility of extreme swings of profit and loss for both the individual gambler and the casino hosting the game. This volatility emanates from the recondite mathematics underlying the straightforward win-or-lose, up-or-down, all-or-nothing outcome of the baccarat game—at least when computed across a discrete temporal duration, such as a weekend gambling binge.[10]

The losing punter who grabs the nearest object on the table and throws it across the room in a fit of unbridled fury thereby embodies the evanescent and explosive volatility that imbues the game of baccarat with its very excitement. In fact, because the financial outcomes of the games are prone to such volatility, some Las Vegas casinos do not even offer high-stakes baccarat.[11] In a business where casino profits steadily accrue from the mathematical models that determine the inherent probabilities and statistical house advantages of each game, baccarat is an outlier, and at least in the short term, the game's financial outcomes are sometimes simply unpredictable.

To take just one example, the volatility of baccarat is exemplified by a February 2016 report from the Star casino in Sydney, Australia, which noted that a group of a mere six Asian gamblers, betting up to A$500,000 per hand at baccarat, won nearly A$80 million from the casino over a six-month period. The company CEO characterized this outcome as a "freakish result," commenting, "They were high rolling, big risk taking individuals who happened to have a lucky run here. They are all individuals who are well known to us—who have been coming here for many years—and normally we are ahead but this time they ended up ahead" (Williams 2016).[12] Given such "freakish" possibilities, one Australian casino executive, in an article published that same year in a gaming industry journal that explains the math underlying the game's unpredictable returns, notes, "Analysts and Senior Management need to have very strong stomachs if involved in Baccarat high end play" (MacDonald 2016, 77).

I should note here that volatility is the very attribute of the global economy that Strange (1998) identifies as both key ingredient and unnerving outcome of casino capitalism, which she believes is a degenerate quality of the post–Bretton Woods global economic system. For Strange, the post-1970 global economy has come to resemble a giant casino, characterized by extremely risky financial bets that contrast negatively with the more stable Fordist-Keynesian industrial production model of the 1950s and 1960s.[13]

However, to my mind, the word "volatility" describes not some aberrant aspect of contemporary financial capitalism but rather a quality indicative of what Braudel calls real capitalism. As I explain in chapter 6, real capitalism is exemplified by the profiteering in the junket credit system that finances Macau's VIP baccarat trade. Although it is a game of chance rather than a physical commodity, the city's baccarat trade shares affinities with the trade of silk, porcelain, tobacco, opium, and gold that was so important to Macau's maritime economy in earlier eras. Therefore, throughout this chapter, I will draw connections among volatility, baccarat play, and the specific market behaviors that are indicative of capitalism.

Volatility imbues high-stakes baccarat with its singular exhilaration. However, in the case of Macau, this characteristic of the card play resonates beyond the baccarat table and the exclusive confines of the VIP room. With the opening of the city's Sands Casino in 2004 (which, incidentally, was initially derided by some industry insiders as the "box of baccarat"), Macau's entire posthandover economy unexpectedly exploded with all of the volatility of a high-stakes baccarat game. This outcome not only produced Macau's record-setting casino revenues but also fundamentally altered the experiential qualities of city life itself. It appeared as if baccarat's potent affect was diffused throughout Macau's entire environs, transforming that once languid and sleepy enclave into something else altogether. For anyone who happened to live through it, the effects of Macau's rapid postretrocession metamorphosis were physically and psychically palpable. Indeed, given the significance of baccarat in Macau's gaming industry, we might understand the game's volatility as a vital element of the "animal spirits" of Macau's baccarat-based economy—to borrow the evocative idiom that Keynes used to describe the emotional and contagious qualities of the market.[14]

Challenging utilitarian assumptions about market behavior as well as the belief that individual economic action results from rational cost-benefit analyses, Keynes argues that investment decisions are often an expression of "animal spirits—of a spontaneous urge to action rather than inaction" instead of "an exact calculation of benefits to come" (quoted in Lears 2017).[15] This is certainly true of gambling on baccarat. As we will see, baccarat is purely a game of chance, so it is not possible for a gambler's bets to be motivated by rational calculations. This characteristic of baccarat distinguishes it from other casino games, such as poker or blackjack. "Keynes argued that when conditions for rational action are not present, people are driven by animal spirits" (Koppl 1991, 204). That is, such economic decisions are motivated by vitalist impulses, emotional urges, or innate dispositions rather than cognitive reason. The pure chance of baccarat, as well as the impossibility of making a rational wager on the cards, both produces the game's inherent excitement and activates the volatile animal spirits of Macau's entire baccarat-based economy.

BACCARAT'S ANIMAL SPIRITS

To appreciate the volatility of baccarat and its contribution to the animal spirits that animate Macau's economy, we must begin with the typical Chinese understanding of the game. In the Occidental imaginary, baccarat connotes luxury and sophistication, evoking images of well-heeled aristocrats and jet-setting celebrities sipping champagne around the gaming tables of Monte Carlo. This elite image is a product of the game's European historical development. Baccarat was invented in Italy, then introduced into France sometime in the late seventeenth or early eighteenth century, during the reign of Louis XIV. It became a popular pastime of the country's nobility and a bulwark of the nascent French gambling industry (Schwartz 2006). It is worth noting, however, that at least one games historian has suggested that the precursor to European baccarat was an even simpler game called Macao, which most likely originated in its namesake city, and which was transported to Europe in the seventeenth century by sailors returning from Asia (Parlett 1990).

Baccarat's elite image in the West was no doubt cemented in the twentieth century by its status as the favorite casino game of James Bond, and it appears in many of the books and films based on the character.[16] Clad in a tuxedo and sitting at a baccarat table, martini glass and cigarette in hand, Bond epitomized postwar cinematic cool and helped publicize the game for a new generation. However, in contrast to Bond's blue-blooded pretensions, baccarat in Macau is an egalitarian endeavor, taking its place alongside the popular Chinese game of mah-jongg as a gambling pastime of the people. Baccarat is played not only by the high-rolling denizens of Macau's VIP rooms but also by the ordinary tourists who populate the mass gaming floors. The rules of Macau baccarat reflect this communal characteristic. Bond played baccarat chemin de fer, an early version of the game that not only requires players (rather than the house) to stake the bets but also involves some player card-drawing discretion, which introduces an element of skill. However, the *punto banco* (player–banker) version of baccarat that is played in Macau, and that is the most common variation of the game in casinos around the world today, is purely a game of chance.[17]

Baccarat as a Simple Game of Chance

The objective of *punto banco* baccarat is for a player to accumulate a favorable sum of points in a two- or three-card hand, with the best hand being equal to 9. To quantify a hand of baccarat, each card is assigned a value: an ace is 1 point, cards 2 through 9 have their respective numerical face values, and 10 and the face cards each equal 0. Play ostensibly occurs between two positions at the table, which are designated as Banker and Player.[18] Each position is dealt two cards. Before any cards are revealed, punters wager simply on whether they believe that the Banker or Player position will have the best hand, or whether the two hands will result in a tie.[19] After the bets are made, the card values for Banker and Player are revealed. Depending on the respective point values of those first two cards, a third card may follow, but this is determined solely by the internal rules of the game, not player decision.[20] Ultimately, the cards in each hand are summed; if the total exceeds 10, then 10 is subtracted from that number to determine the final point value of the hand. That is, a hand that involves a 5 card and a 3 card equals a total of 8, while a hand that involves an 8 card and a

7 card equals a total of 5 (or 15 minus 10). Therefore, the final scores of each hand will always fall between 0 and 9, and the winning hand is the one in which the card total is closest or equal to 9.

Punto banco baccarat involves no decisions by the player, and the game likewise involves no skill on the part of the gambler, who simply guesses whether Player or Banker will prevail. Thus, baccarat is a simple game of chance, not unlike betting on the flip of a coin. At the same time, however, crucial to the appeal of baccarat for gamblers in Macau is that the game offers the best odds of any table game in the casino, and the lowest win percentage for the house.

Herein lies the fundamental paradox of baccarat. Because the game has the best casino odds, if an individual is determined to gamble, then it is entirely rational to choose to gamble on baccarat over the other options. However, because baccarat is a game of pure chance, there is no way for the gambler to calculate a rational outcome or to make a reasonable wager on the game. As Keynes notes, when conditions for rational action are not present, people's decisions toward action rather than inaction are necessarily driven by their innate animal spirits. Decisions that derive from an individual's animal spirits are not irrational per se; rather, they emerge outside the frame of the rational/irrational dualism.

This random up/down outcome of baccarat is the characteristic that generates the game's volatility—its extreme swings of profit and loss. This volatility is exacerbated with each significant increase in the scale of the stakes. Ultimately, the volatility of each individual hand of *punto banco* baccarat generates the volatile animal spirits of Macau's entire baccarat-based economy.

Macau's Lamborghini Metric of Volatility

The city's ephemeral volatility is physically manifested today in such visible phenomena as the sudden preponderance of brightly hued high-end sports cars, which have appeared in significant numbers on Macau's diminutive streets in the posthandover era. Before 1999, as far as I know, there was only one Lamborghini in Macau. That particular automobile was a handsome deep purple model owned by notorious gangster Wan "Broken Tooth" Kuok-Koi. The car sometimes appeared in photographs that accompanied Broken Tooth's interviews with international media; it also featured prominently in the autobiographical film he financed about his ascension through the ranks of Macau's underworld, which I discuss in chapter 4.

By 2011, more than a decade after Broken Tooth's 1999 prehandover imprisonment, there were a total of five Lamborghinis in Macau. But three short years later, in 2014, the number of Lamborghinis jumped nearly twentyfold, to 106 (Lee 2017). In addition to this impressive array of Lambos, Macau's transportation authorities reported that in 2014, there were 131 Ferraris and 158 Maseratis registered in the city. Automobili Lamborghini was so impressed by the Macau market that in 2017, the company spent US$1.24 million to open a local showroom. If one includes Macau's 523 Bentleys and 250 Rolls-Royces, then by 2014, there were approximately two such superlative cars for every kilometer of road in the city.[21]

The presence of such high-octane automobiles in Macau is often colloquially attributed to "junket money"—that is, the easy-come, easy-go wealth available to certain risk-taking young men with the financial wherewithal, sufficient muscle, and necessary strong stomachs to loan (and eventually recoup, with significant interest if they are

Figure 30. Lamborghini promotion in the MGM Resort. Between 2011 and 2014, the number of Lamborghinis registered in Macau jumped twentyfold. Automobili Lamborghini opened a local showroom in 2017. *Photograph by Adam Lampton.*

lucky) the cash that the high-rolling Chinese tourists gamble away in high-stakes baccarat games.

Of course, flashy cars are a normal consequence of quick money. But Macau's powerful coupes stand out as a brazen aberration in a tiny city whose streets are constrained by a maximum speed limit of only sixty kilometers per hour (thirty-seven miles per hour), which exceptionally reaches a modest eighty kilometers per hour only on the two longest bridges that connect the Macau peninsula across the narrow sea channel to the island of Taipa. The serpentine streets of the central city are more Byzantine medieval labyrinth than modern roadway system—certainly no place to drive a Lamborghini. The company's Huracán Spyder convertible, which debuted in 2017 at Macau's new Lamborghini showroom, accelerates from zero to a hundred kilometers per hour in 3.6 seconds, which means it would take a little over one second for the car to surpass the city's maximum speed limit. But legal limits aside, the fact is that the city streets are so full of ambling, distracted, selfie-snapping Chinese tourists that daredevil driving is virtually impossible. Lambo drivers have little to actually do in their cars other than noisily rev the idle engines in a way that contributes to the overall ambient volatility of the city.

THE POTENTIAL OF MACHINE GAMING TO TAME VOLATILITY

The very volatility that makes high-stakes baccarat so exciting—and so profitable—is also the source of the particular constellation of macroeconomic constraints and petty corruption concerns of the Chinese government. When the central government urges Macau to be more like Las Vegas, the underlying message is that the city should seek to tame the volatility of baccarat.[22] High-stakes baccarat in Macau is entirely dependent on the constant cross-border flow of financial liquidity from the mainland; these capital flows are a predominant target of China's crackdown on corruption. The singular pursuit of the potential profit that may be earned from baccarat high-roller play undercuts the state's desire to attract a more diverse tourist market (whose middle-class members might produce a more predictable profit margin) and create a more sustainable mode of economic development—that is, one that does not require credit from China.

Although motivated by an entirely different set of concerns, the international gaming industry actually shares this goal of the state. Although the VIP trade produces exceptional revenues, casino profits earned from high-stakes baccarat are problematic for several reasons. For one thing, the local concessionaire must share baccarat profits with the junket operator who manages a particular VIP room in the property. The operator's profits are in turn undercut by the commissions he must pay to junket agents who bring gamblers to the room, and those agents may share those fees with their own subcontracted workers. The profits and commissions therefore cascade throughout the VIP system.

In addition to these reductions to casino margins that are inherent in Macau's unique gambling model is the problem of baccarat volatility, which further renders casino profit projections unpredictable. In fact, most casino revenues in North America and Australia are generated not from table games such as baccarat, blackjack, or poker but from ordinary slot machines. For many years, the international gambling industry has searched, with limited success, for ways to make gaming machines attractive to Chinese gamblers. Gaming machines produce more modest returns than table games, but these machines have other inherent advantages.

First, slot machines are not labor intensive because they require no croupier to manage the play. A single, relatively low-skilled attendant can service a large group of machines on the casino floor. This labor-saving function enables the casino to dramatically lower the cost of a minimum bet on an electronic game. In the case of a baccarat table, even one on a Macau mass casino floor, a minimum bet averages around HK$1000 (US$125) per hand, which makes the cost of baccarat play prohibitive for many potential gamblers. In contrast, the minimum bet on a slot machine could be as little as a few cents. Lower minimum bets open games to a much larger potential market of gamblers. In addition, given the limited population of local workers to fill croupier positions, which are only open to local citizens holding a Macau ID, the possibility of reducing the role of such workers, or even removing them entirely from the gaming equation, is eminently attractive to the casino companies.

Second, electronic casino games are more easily accessible to novice gamblers than table games. It is not just that the financial bar for entry is lower for slots or poker machines; these games also put less pressure on inexperienced players who may not have the confidence to join a table game where they must gamble with strangers. In the case of the game of blackjack, for example, an individual's decision to accept or reject an additional card from the dealer may have actual financial consequences for other players at the table. The inexperienced gambler who is not familiar with blackjack's "basic strategy" (a style of play that minimizes the casino's odds), and who draws a card during a round in which the other players have each chosen to decline an additional card with the expectation that the dealer's hand will bust, may induce the ire of the other punters at the table. I have made this mistake playing (low-stakes) blackjack in Las Vegas, and the palpable annoyance of the other players was certainly discomforting. However, playing a solitary game of blackjack on a video machine at the casino bar provides low-key gambling entertainment without the added embarrassment.

Third, although slot machines produce more modest profits than table games, these profit margins have the benefit of being entirely predictable because the casino win rate percentage is actually pro-grammed into the algorithm of the gaming system. Las Vegas regula-tions mandate that slot machines must have a minimum payout return of 75 percent, although the actual returns vary from casino to casino and are typically higher than that number, ranging from 82 to 98 per-cent (Schwartz 2012). Therefore, the profit stability of slot machines is diametrically opposed to baccarat's volatility.

Fourth, in the specific case of Macau, electronic gambling does not require credit extended to the gambler by a junket in the form of a gambling loan. The "mass market" player of a slot machine or other electronic game therefore conforms to the expectations of China's crackdown on corruption. In fact, Macau's casino companies have designated a particular population of "premium mass market" gam-blers, who are defined as premium players who gamble for relatively high stakes, but who do so outside of VIP rooms and without the need for junket loans. This premium mass market has emerged today as the most coveted segment of Macau's tourist population.

Fifth, and again in the specific case of Macau, electronic games pro-vide a way to skirt a maximum cap on table games that the Macau government imposed on local casinos in an initial effort to tame the city's volatility. In an attempt to control the explosive growth of the industry, in 2011, the Macau government introduced a citywide cap on the expansion of table games, which remained in effect through 2022, limiting annual expansion of such games to 3 percent. Concessionaires opening new properties must be allocated a quantity of new tables by government regulators. This cap means that very few tables may be allocated to an individual property, especially in a year when multiple new resorts open and monopolize the quota.

The table cap is unpopular with concessionaires, who see it as an arbitrary and unreasonable imposition that constrains their ability to generate sufficient revenue to cover the loss-leading costs of the non-gaming attractions, like Ferris wheels and magic shows, that the government increasingly desires. In an infamous and candid 2015 investor conference call, which was extensively covered in the international business media and which prompted a direct rebuke from Macau government officials, Steve Wynn declared himself a "tremendous critic" of the table cap policy, calling it (with perhaps slight overstatement) "the single most counterintuitive and illogical decision that was ever made" (Wong 2015). However, one interesting feature of the table cap policy for our purposes here is that under Macau's regulatory regime, slot machines and other electronic games are not counted as equivalent to table games, so they are therefore not constrained in the same way by the cap. For example, for one type of stadium-style electronic game (which I describe in chapter 8), where a single live dealer can serve dozens of gamblers who place their bets at individual gaming terminals, one hundred such terminals are counted collectively as equivalent to one conventional table game.

In short, with the exception of the junket companies that make their money solely from granting loans to finance baccarat play, there is more or less unanimous agreement among industry executives and government officials alike that it would be ideal if Macau attracted a more diverse population of gamblers, and if a significant portion of those visitors gambled on machines. For the most part, however, Chinese gamblers prefer to play at a baccarat table, and slot machines have generated relatively little interest. This makes the Macau market qualitatively distinct from North American and Australian casino jurisdictions.

New York University anthropologist Natasha Dow Schüll (2014), in a definitive account of slot machine gambling in the United States, characterizes the peculiar American attachment to slots as a sort of programmed "addiction by design." For many tourists in Las Vegas, the slot machine provides an accessible, inviting, and relatively low cost form of play, and slot machines produce from 50 to 88 percent of the city's annual casino revenues.[23] For the so-called problem gamblers who are the specific subjects of Schüll's study, however, slot machine play involves an uncanny experience of immersive and affective distraction. Problem gamblers consistently describe their tendency to "zone out" in front of slot machines in a semiconscious state of "equilibrated affect" and "affective continuity" (Schüll 2014, 308) as awareness of their physical surroundings and the passing of time slips from their immediate consciousness. The experience is partly an effect of the efforts of machine programmers, who deploy innovative algorithms designed to capture the players through specific temporal gaming cadences.

Interestingly, Schüll (2013) demonstrates that most American slot machine addicts are not chasing the promise of big wins. Instead, these gamblers primarily desire to indefinitely extend their "time on device" (95), immersed within the confines of the cognitive zone created by the gaming experience. Some subjects even report annoyance at machine payouts for wins, which only serve to interrupt play and delay the experiential gratification that they seek. The individual and atomistic style of slot machine play in the United States therefore appears to be imbricated with some characteristics that are specific to the broader contemporary American society, which may in part explain why such games are so popular among gamblers in that particular context. Schüll describes the largely unsuccessful attempts by the international gaming industry to "attune" (98) the Chinese gambling market to slot machine play. However, for the most part, Chinese gamblers in Macau have displayed relatively little interest in slot machines.

ANIMAL SPIRITS AND THE APPEAL OF BACCARAT

If the solitary individuality of slot machine gaming is attractive to American gamblers, then the failure of machine gaming to capture Chinese gamblers in Macau in the same manner as their American counterparts may be attributed in part to a general set of dispositions toward risk and speculation that are characteristic of the animal spirits of Macau's casino economy. These dispositions correspond to the specific contours of the game of baccarat but are not well served by electronic gaming machines. There are a number of academic and industry theories, some supported by empirical data, that seek to explain why Chinese gamblers in Macau tend to eschew slot machines in favor of table games (Lam

2013; Liu and Wan 2011; Lam and Eadington 2009). While the gaming industry, as well as many researchers working in the field of social psychology, tend to attribute these traits to the construct of the "Chinese gambler," we may analyze these characteristics without resorting to such ethnocultural generalizations by instead referencing the animal spirits of Macau's casino economy. I will later demonstrate that attitudes about risk typical of Chinese gamblers in Macau's casinos are also evident in general market behavior outside the confines of the casino.

First and foremost, as architect Paul Steelman discovered when he conducted his initial fieldwork in preparation for his design of the Sands Casino, Chinese gamblers in Macau tend to prefer to play head to head against a live opponent rather than to engage with a machine. This agonistic play with another human allows the gambler to deploy strategies of luck or divination that he thinks may channel fate and ultimately benefit his odds (Festa 2007). In addition, sociability is an important component of Chinese gambling in Macau; crowding around a gaming table generates a form of "social heat" that attracts other gamblers (Steinmüller 2011). The Macau gambler's desire for this social atmosphere, combined with his belief that it contributes to luck, starkly contrasts with the lone American slot machine player's pursuit of a self-contained, solitary gaming experience, suspended within an individual zone of play.

Second, there is a lingering suspicion among many gamblers in Macau that slot machines are rigged to the disadvantage of the player (Liu and Wan 2011). Actually, as we have seen already, it is true that these machines are programmed to randomly allow a certain percentage of wins, at a certain rate, over a certain quantity of discrete games. The algorithms governing these processes are continually tweaked to appeal to different types of gamblers or the expectations of players in different gaming markets. Some are programmed to award large payouts that occur relatively infrequently to satisfy gamblers seeking the potential of a big jackpot; others are designed to dispense small winnings more regularly to sustain player interest in the game. The result of each program is the same (that is, the extraction of player money according to a programmed win percentage), but the gaming experience that each creates is unique. In any event, these programmed outcomes contradict the preference among many Macau gamblers to play with the unmediated fortunes of fate.

Third, Chinese gamblers in Macau tend to approach gambling as an entrepreneurial profit-generating activity rather than as a discrete form of play. Gambling constitutes a means to earn quick money, so gamblers are attracted to table games, which generally offer more substantial payouts than slot machines. Consider the advice of Cham Pui-ching, stockbroker, onetime Hong Kong legislator, and avid Macau gambler: "People should not take gambling as entertainment, because they will lose a lot of money if they go to the casino for pleasure. I take gambling as a serious investment and I measure how much I can lose" (quoted in Yiu 2008).

Indeed, the fact that baccarat offers the best odds of any table game in the casino makes baccarat particularly attractive as a gambling "investment" activity. Although presumably the lure of easy profits is a primary motivation for all gamblers, we may recall that the American slot machine addicts in Schüll's (2012) study are motivated not by profit but by maximizing their time on the machine. While the American slot machine gambler's disinterest in profit from gambling tends to be interpreted as evidence of a psychological malady, Cham's corresponding dismissal of play as a gaming attraction is characteristic of many gamblers in Macau's casinos.

The capacity for large payouts on table games not only motivates the specific forms of gambling in Macau but also plays well with the particular propensity for risk typical of gamblers in the city, which is the fourth relevant factor for understanding the disposition of Macau's animal spirits. Psychologists of risk have differentiated among two types of risk-taking behavior. In situations involving excitatory value (for example, gambling), people exhibit stimulating risk taking (SRT), whereas in situations involving instrumental economic activity (for example, investments, mortgages, or education), people exhibit instrumental risk taking (IRT). In one study of European subjects, risk taking was found to be situation specific (Zaleskiewicz 2001). High-risk activity in one domain (gambling) was not correlated with the other domain (investment). That is, subjects who were likely to make risky bets were not likely to engage in risky investment schemes. Studies conducted on mainland Chinese gamblers in Macau, however, find that high-risk SRT and IRT are significantly related in the city's casinos (Ozorio and Fong 2004; Vong 2007). Hong Kong gambler Cham's corresponding advice reflects an opinion shared by many of his fellow gamblers in Macau: "If you want to gamble, be more serious and have a strategy like making an investment," he advises. "I find gambling and investing have some similarities" (Yiu 2008).

Given the foregoing sketch of attitudes about gambling that are typical of Chinese gamblers in Macau's casinos, it is not surprising that during Macau's prehandover monopoly era, slot machines were an afterthought. The few such machines scattered across Macau's casinos were primarily decorative items; their function was to contribute to the casino's ambiance, not to act as actual games that the casinos expected gamblers to play. In 2002, there were only 808 slot machines in all of Macau. However, by 2009, the number of slot machines had climbed to more than 14,300 (Liu and Wan 2011). Given the tens of millions of Chinese gamblers who visit Macau each year, it is clear that there is tremendous room for growth of electronic games in Macau—that is, if gamblers in the city's casinos can be persuaded to play them.

However, the bottom line is that gamblers in Macau prefer table games over slot machines, and there is no doubt that baccarat is the table game of choice. Why baccarat? The answer, in a nutshell, is that *punto banco* baccarat is a perfect medium for expressing the gambling disposition that I have described above. As we have seen, the basic rules of *punto banco* baccarat are simple. Player and Banker are each dealt two cards, and gamblers at the table place their bets on the basis of what is essentially a random guess that one or the other will have the winning hand. Despite these simple rules, however, the experience of playing baccarat can be dramatic.[24] Indeed, its dramatic disposition is exactly the characteristic that many Macau gamblers consider to be missing from the automated slot machines that are so popular in casinos in the United States. In Macau, this drama is heightened in several ways that I describe below—most notably by integrating an element of player engagement into the game through an animated process known colloquially as card squeezing. This process aims to harness the vibrant "thing power" of the cards themselves.[25]

Squeezing Cards

In a hand of baccarat, cards are initially dealt to a position face down. The player at the table who wagers the largest bet on that particular hand is allowed to reveal the cards. Rather than simply flipping over the cards, the player methodically folds over the corners and the sides of the card in order to peek at its face, allowing the card's point value to be gradually and dramatically revealed. Squeezing the cards slows down the rate of play but increases player excitement; it also provides the gambler with the feeling that he is exercising some control over the game's outcome.

Card squeezing has an inherent aesthetic. The collective fate of the gamblers gathered around the table ultimately rides on the competence of the person conducting the squeeze; they hope his talent (or luck) will ensure a favorable outcome. In addition, there is a widely shared belief, readily evident when observing baccarat players in Macau, that dramatic intervention may alter the face value of a squeezed card before its face is revealed, in order to ensure that the final summed total of the cards is close to 9 (Lam 2008). Such intervention may take the form of ritual chanting, blowing on the cards, or banging on the table. For example, when players are hoping to uncover a 6 card (to accompany an already exposed 3 card), and they glimpse three hearts visible across the top of the folded card's edge, those players may lean over the table and collectively blow on the card's surface. In doing so, they hope to blow away a not yet visible, and undesirable, seventh heart, which may possibly be positioned in the center of the card's face.

The art of squeezing aside, there is actually no skill involved in *punto banco* baccarat. Bets are made before any cards are revealed, and Banker and Player make no decisions about whether or not they receive cards. Therefore, betting on baccarat is not unlike betting on flipping a coin. However, the simplicity and clarity of *punto banco* baccarat comprise the fundamental appeal of the game for gamblers in Macau, who envision the complex machinations of karmic fate demonstrated in the unveiling of cards. For this reason, many gamblers carefully record the succession of Player and Banker wins and losses in an effort to discern patterns of card play that may provide a window to understanding fate's opaque designs. Recording such results has been a common practice throughout the history of baccarat play in Macau's casinos, and the popularity of this practice in Macau has actually led to its normalization in casinos around the world where Chinese people gamble.

Reading Card Patterns with the Big Road

Macau gamblers originally recorded those outcomes in one of two ways. Some used colored pens to document Banker or Player wins, drawing red or blue circles, respectively, on a simple table printed on a paper card distributed by the casino. This diagram has become colloquially known as the Big Road. The specific details are not important, but the key idea here is that the chart displays the pattern of card play, such that the gambler may easily see if either Banker or Player is engaging a lucky streak. For example, if Player wins four hands in a row, this outcome will be clearly visible on the card in the form of a vertical column composed of four blue circles. If Player wins more than six consecutive hands, the six-row column on the table will be filled completely with blue circles, and the subsequent blue circles the gambler inscribes on the table will make a right-hand turn that continues across the bottom row, creating what is known in Macau as a Dragon Tail. Given this scenario in a baccarat game, and given what would appear to be a clear pattern of Player wins, every gambler at the table would most likely enthusiastically bet on Player to win the next hand, collectively seeking to ride Player's luck, or fate's control of the cards, before it ran out. This style of betting is called "chasing the dragon."[26] Aside from such pen-and-ink records, the other original method for tracking baccarat wins involved the use of a prefashioned "bead plate," which gamblers carried around the casino floor and on which they recorded the outcome of each hand by arranging colored tiles on the plate's surface. This account was known as the Bead Plate Road.

Although some gamblers still use pen and paper to track the Big Road, today these outcomes are also conveniently displayed on digital LED screens located on each baccarat table in the casino, making it possible for all bystanders to easily follow the sequence and distribution of winning hands. Though the displays may vary somewhat from one casino to another, they typically include no fewer than five specific types of graphical representations, each of which records the same basic information of Player and Banker wins, but presented in a different visual manner or via a distinct "road."

The primary digital graph is still called the Big Road, and it depicts the outcomes of play much as they would appear on the traditional paper card. There is also a digital Bead Plate Road, which is essentially an animation of the traditional bead plate and tiles. Aside from these graphs, however, there are three other digital tables of representation that are derived from these two main roads: Big Eye Boy Road, Small Road, and Cockroach Road. Each of these approaches entails a distinct

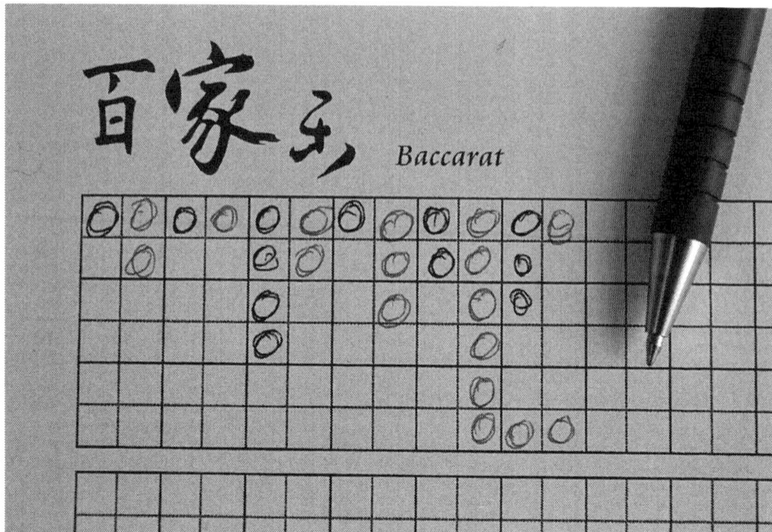

Figure 31. A baccarat gambler's card, with red and blue circles depicting the Big Road diagram of Player and Banker wins. The Big Road is one of five distinct divinatory charts that visually represent the dynamics of game play. Gamblers consult such charts of past play in an effort to predict the outcome of future games. *Photograph by author.*

method for recording the basic data of Player and Banker wins, but with the expectation that the visual presentation of each derived road demonstrates certain nuances of card patterns that are not immediately visible on the Big Road. Gamblers generally consult one or more of their favored roads during each hand of play in order to make decisions about betting.

Baccarat and Financial Chartism

One may dismiss as simple superstition the belief that card play follows discernible and repetitive patterns, but there is no doubt that it is a motivating factor in baccarat gambling in Macau. A minor publishing industry exists of Chinese-language books, such as *Baccarat Winning Formula* or *Winner Takes It All—Roadmap to Baccarat Fortune*, which instruct gamblers on how to interpret and (potentially) profit from such information (Huang 2015). However, given my eventual interest in demonstrating links among Macau gambling practices and more general economic behavior (which I explore in chapter 8), it is worth noting that the practice of charting predictive patterns is not limited to card play. Charting such patterns is also a common practice of a certain segment of the finance industry and has been an object of study among scholars involved in the academic discipline known as the social studies of finance. (Readers may recall that I drew on the social studies of finance literature in chapter 1 in my analysis of the Venetian Macau integrated resort as a "market device," which functions to cultivate a market-socialist subject. I return to this literature in chapter 8.)

Just as baccarat players hope to predict the movement of cards that will determine the next winning hand, financial analysts seek to foretell future price movements of stocks, indexes, and securities. There are two competing methods for accomplishing this task, fundamental analysis and technical analysis (also known as chartism), each of which takes a different approach to prognostication. Fundamental analysts attempt to discover cause–effect relationships among securities and prices by considering available economic fundamentals, such as a company's assets, liabilities, and annual revenue. Technical analysts, on the other hand, are not interested in explaining the cause of price movements; instead, they try to detect patterns of past movements in pricing histories, which they believe will reliably indicate future prices. They do this by examining financial charts that graphically depict those patterns, not unlike the baccarat player who charts the Big Road in hopes of spotting predictive trends. Financial chartism has a specialized vocabulary of "breaking gaps, flat bottoms, sauce bottoms, falling flags, head and shoulders, or symmetrical coils," which is not so far removed from the Big Eye Boy Roads and Dragon Tails of baccarat charts (Preda 2007, 42).

While one might assume that my gambling/finance analogy is entirely specious, fundamental analysts actually look on the practice of technical analysis much like mathematicians would look on the Macau gambler's belief that baccarat card play follows predictable patterns. As Alex Preda (2007) observes, "The tenets of financial chartism run counter to academic financial economics, which maintains that price movements are random; therefore future movements cannot be inferred from past ones" (42). The belief that such pricing follows a "random walk" allows those functional analysts to deploy random number tables in their financial instruments. But technical analysts completely reject such economic fundamentals, instead preferring to rely solely on chart analysis. These financial charts "are in reality no different from the charts of astrologers, psychics, tarot card operators, and other diagrammatic formats for prognostication" (Appadurai 2015, 25). Thus, this faith in the divinatory magic of charts as a tool to hedge against uncertainty is shared by both the Macau gambler and the technical financier. In the case of Macau, this faith may be understood as a component of the animal spirits of the city's volatile baccarat economy.

Card squeezing and chartism enhance the feeling that players may intervene in the outcome of the hand, to ride the luck of the cards or to temporarily stave off the eventual inevitability of a losing hand. Regardless of the drama derived from these practices, however, baccarat is essentially a simple game of chance. Although money is gambled, won, and lost, and although casino profits are ultimately accrued, *punto banco* baccarat decision-making, such as it exists, requires no actual calculation on the part of the gambler. Therefore, although baccarat play involves some of the same dispositions toward risk and speculation that are found in economic behavior, such as investing, and although the typical Macau gambler approaches the baccarat game as a potential profit-generating activity, the lack of genuine decision-making in baccarat means that the game remains embedded within the circumscribed social realm of play. Thus, baccarat play is distinct from the disembedded economic behavior indicative of market activity (Callon 1998).

I return to this observation in chapter 8 in an effort to demonstrate how an innovative gaming machine may be designed to attract Chinese gamblers to Macau's casinos while also potentially converting the casino into a kind of "social factory," in which baccarat gambling (with all of the ancillary "work" it entails) may be transformed into actual market behavior.[27] That is, a properly configured baccarat machine can translate the simple game of *punto banco* baccarat into a form of capitalist activity that is consistent with China's reform regime—and consistent with the central government's desire to foster "the emergence of more calculating, self-governing, 'market-socialist' subjects" (Greenhalgh 2010, 51). I understand this phenomenon as a literal expression of casino capitalism. We may thus understand the Macau casino itself as a site of Geertzian sentimental education in which gamblers are inadvertently schooled in the economic skills, habits, and animal spirits of the market.

CIGARETTES, BACCARAT, AND BIOPOLITICS

I began this chapter by recounting the volatile biosocial concoction of cigarette smoking, ashtray throwing, and high-stakes gambling in Macau. I suggested that this volatility is characteristic of the animal spirits of the game of baccarat as well as of Macau's entire baccarat-based economy. In addition, and in a manner consistent with the assemblage approach I have pursued throughout this project, I have also demonstrated that a diverse group of actors, operating at several different scales, have sought for different reasons to modify or recalibrate Macau's volatile gaming economy through strategies of biogovernance that modulate the behavior of Chinese tourists. These measures include attempts to regulate citizen smoking in casinos as well as to alter their choice of casino game and concomitant mode of gaming finance.

Local Macau officials, China's central government, and the international gaming industry each have reason to seek to tame the intense socioeconomic effects, and affects, that are indicative of high-stakes *punto banco* baccarat; each seek to convince Chinese tourists to gamble on machines rather than baccarat tables. Macau officials hope to enhance the health of local workers and prevent potential labor unrest among the city's crucial faction of croupiers. The central government wants to stem the cross-border flow of capital that funds high-stakes gaming. And the casino concessionaires seek both a more predictable source of revenue and a larger piece of the gaming pie.

Although they may not see it in exactly these terms, these state and nonstate actors each share a similar desire to comport a new kind of Chinese gambling subject in Macau, whose motivation for gambling and style of play will conform to their own specific goals. There is thus a collective desire to cultivate a Chinese gambler who requires no scarce or costly croupier; who does not need the services of a junket host or the advance of a credit loan; and who engages in gaming behavior that is defined by civility and stability rather than volatility. With this in mind, in chapter 8, I turn once again to the Macau SAR's function as a laboratory of consumption in which these various actors cooperate in a biopolitical experiment with global ramifications. The goal is to design a baccarat machine that might produce a new type of gambler in the city—one whose gaming preferences and general economic behavior are conducive to both China's reform era and the growth of global capitalism.

8

Baccarat Machines

ENGINEERING THE POST-MAO SUBJECT

> When we look at a piece of art, read a piece of literature, watch a
> film, or listen to a piece of music, it is commonplace to think of
> them as cultural expressions of the society and historical context
> in which they are created. Art, literature, film, and music are
> readily recognized as mediums of the Zeitgeist. Poker and other
> gambling games are rarely thought of in the same fashion.
>
> —Ole Bjerg, *Poker: The Parody of Capitalism*

In 2007, LifeTec Group, a Hong Kong biopharmaceutical company
dedicated to research and development of drug innovations to treat
hepatitis B infections and liver fibrosis, diversified into the design and
manufacture of gaming machines for Macau's burgeoning casino industry. The company's stock value subsequently tripled, and the name
was eventually changed to Paradise Entertainment Ltd. LifeTec's initial gaming product was a patented machine called LIVE Baccarat that
combines a live dealer with an electronic game. While positioned in
front of a video camera and a group of networked gaming terminals,
the croupier deals a hand of baccarat; the cards are displayed on a large
video screen overhead as well as on small screens at each individual
terminal, where players monitor the action and place electronic bets.

LifeTec's inaugural contract was with the tawdry casino located inside the New Century Hotel. That is, the company installed its first
baccarat machine system inside the very hotel in which Wan "Broken Tooth" Kuok-Koi battled Ng "Street Market" Wai during the city's
late 1990s casino wars, and which was the setting for the dramatic
drive-by shooting depicted in the opening scene of Broken Tooth's

Figure 32. Gamblers in Kampek Casino play the LIVE Baccarat game. The actions of the human croupier (who is not visible in the photograph) are displayed on the screens protruding from the ceiling of the venue, as well as on the small screen inset on the left side of each gaming terminal. *Photograph courtesy of Andrew W. Scott; originally appeared in* Inside Asian Gaming *and* World Gaming Magazine.

autobiographical gangland film. That notorious and déclassé locale enabled the unlikely genesis of a visionary machine era in Macau's casino economy. LifeTec soon reached agreements with several other local casinos to use the gaming system, and in December 2007, the company opened its own Kampek Paradise Casino next door to the Lisboa Hotel, featuring 280 LIVE Baccarat machines.[1]

The LIVE Baccarat gaming machine is specifically designed to appeal to Chinese gamblers in Macau. As I describe in chapter 7, slot machines and other electronic casino games have historically generated little interest among Chinese gamblers in the city, in part because of their preference to play against a live dealer in order to deploy rituals of divination and intervention that they believe might reveal predestined results or manipulate outcomes (Lam 2006, 2008). Therefore, the integration of a human dealer into the LIVE Baccarat device makes this particular electronic game more enticing than a conventional slot machine.

For the casino, the LIVE Baccarat machine's appeal is its ability to accelerate play and increase the casino "win" while reducing operating costs. A typical baccarat croupier can theoretically deal five hundred hands in twenty-four hours to a table with a maximum of nine players; in contrast, the LIVE Baccarat dealer, working in tandem with the electronic machine, can deal a thousand hands in twenty-four hours to seventy-five players simultaneously. This means that a casino using the LIVE Baccarat system in place of conventional gaming tables could service up to twenty times more gamblers per day, all without employing additional labor. One crucial advantage of this feature of the game is that the lower labor costs make it feasible for the casino to significantly reduce the minimum bet on a gaming unit without destroying profit margins. LIVE Baccarat offers minimum bets of HK$20 (US$2.50), compared to an average minimum bet of more than HK$1,000 for traditional baccarat in Macau's public gaming halls—and much higher amounts in the private VIP rooms that produce much of Macau's gaming revenues (O'Keeffe 2014a).[2]

For Chinese authorities, LIVE Baccarat's appeal is the way this lower minimum bet facilitates play by a certain type of aspirational "mass market" Chinese tourist. These tourist masses contrast sharply with the VIP gamblers, who have historically produced the majority of Macau's casino revenues but who have also induced a state of volatility in the city's gaming industry, economy, and everyday life. The influx of these mass market gamblers answers calls by the central government to diversify Macau's gaming industry and to help reduce the city's role as a conduit for capital flight from the mainland. In addition, the modest expenditures of these tourist masses may eventually contribute to the incremental growth of China's own consumer economy.

The benefit of the LIVE Baccarat machine is thus its ability to attract ordinary gamblers, tame casino volatility, and bolster China's efforts to comport quality citizens for the reform era. The precise articulation of the LIVE Baccarat device and the production of this post-Mao subject is the focus of this chapter. We will see that LIVE Baccarat has the potential to shape China's burgeoning urban masses into a coherent consumer mass market composed of calculating individuals seeking to maximize their own self-interest, but do so in a cooperative effort to advance the collectivist goals of the state. Just as Mao once exhorted China's rural masses to learn from Dazhai, the country's exemplary model of socialist agricultural production, today, the urban masses may learn from Macau to become consumer cadres for the country's market-socialist economy.[3]

GAMBLING ON CAPITALISM'S NEW FRONTIER

We may better understand LIVE Baccarat's significance in Macau today, on the coastal perimeter of the PRC, if we analyze the baccarat machine alongside the game of poker and if we explore poker's own historical relation to the growth and expansion of capitalism in the United States. Poker originated in the early nineteenth century around the U.S. city of New Orleans, Louisiana. It was played by the trappers and cowboys who settled the North American frontier. For Bjerg (2011), poker became a popular leisure pastime precisely because it entails fundamental tenets of capitalism. Inspired by postmodern sociologist Jean Baudrillard, Bjerg characterizes poker as a "parodic simulation" of capitalism. That is, gamblers making bets at the poker table metaphorically play with the mutating relationships among use value (embodied in the particular cards they hold) and exchange value (expressed through their wagers on those cards) that animated capitalism's historical development. Bjerg suggests that common varieties of poker have provided opportunities for gamblers to playfully embody the overarching spirit of capitalism endemic to different economic eras.

For example, in the primitive form of the game known as Flat Poker, players were dealt five cards from a twenty-card deck and simply bet on who had the strongest hand. This game mimicked the simple appropriation of natural resources typical of early American capitalism. The rules of the subsequent game of Draw Poker, in which players may improve their hand by drawing cards, then raise the game's financial stakes with additional bets, encouraged the sort of speculative risk that was typical of the capitalist entrepreneurs who powered nineteenth-century industrialism.

The more cerebral game of Seven-Card Stud reflects the disciplined managerial mind of mid-twentieth-century corporate capitalism. The skilled Stud player grinds out small but steady profits over a number of hands, much like a corporation's steady revenue stream in a competitive marketplace. In its heyday, Seven-Card Stud games typically took place after hours in the office or in the basement of a suburban home;

that is, the game was played not on the frontier of capitalist expansion but at the center of a mature capitalist society.

The most popular form of poker today is the raucous game of No Limit Texas Hold 'Em, which is widely promoted in televised competitions such as the World Series of Poker. The unlimited betting structure of this game simulates our own freewheeling era of post-Fordist financialization, "where financial markets tend to constitute a reality of their own decoupled from the sphere of the productive economy" (Bjerg 2011, 222). In these ways, contends Bjerg, poker play both simulates and parodies the changing contours of capitalist enterprise.

The role of poker in the historical development of capitalism is a useful model for my own analysis of the LIVE Baccarat machine's function in China's market reforms. However, although I embrace Bjerg's basic intuition about gambling and capitalism, I advance a different argument about Macau's own indigenous game and its role in the expansion of capitalism in China. LIVE Baccarat is more than a playful medium through which Chinese gamblers may engage with simulated characteristics of the contemporary economy. LIVE Baccarat is a literal biopolitical machine of subjection that functions, in tandem with the integrated resort machine I discuss in chapter 5, to cultivate Chinese capitalists. The LIVE Baccarat machine curates a Chinese *homo economicus,* or Foucault's (2004) "entrepreneur of himself": a nascent capitalist subject who embodies the kinesthetic comportment, calculative capacities, and speculative dispositions that are practical components of the country's market-socialist economy. Therefore, the baccarat machine is more than a playful distraction that mimics the characteristics of capitalism. Rather, LIVE Baccarat engineers a novel post-Mao citizen on the edge of capitalism's final planetary frontier in the PRC.

THE KEY COMMODITY OF MARKET-SOCIALISM

My analysis of LIVE Baccarat is informed by the pragmatic turn in economic sociology, which seeks to describe the material-semiotic networks that enable economic life. This scholarship is consistent with the Foucauldian focus on governmentality and biopolitics that I explore throughout this book. In this chapter, I draw specifically on Michel Callon's sociology of economic action to analyze capitalist pedagogy in

Macau's casinos. Callon's particular articulation of economic sociology with science and technology studies is expressly apposite to exploring the capitalist operations of the LIVE Baccarat apparatus. What is particularly useful about this approach is that it enables me to describe precisely what it means to say that Chinese economic subjects are produced, comported, and cultivated in Macau's casinos.

Psychoanalyst and philosopher Félix Guattari (1989, 1995) has provocatively claimed that the primary commodity produced in contemporary capitalism is subjectivity itself. Today subjectivity is manufactured much like a smartphone; it is assembled by piecing together semiotic components that are culled from everyday media environments (Genosko 2009; Lazzarato 2014). Guattari calls subjectivity the "key commodity" of capitalism because it is the prerequisite for the maintenance of the market system. That is, the precondition of a consumer society is the creation of consuming subjects, each with novel desires that promise to be satisfied only through the constant purchase of new commodities and experiences.

Throughout this book, I have explored attempts by China's central government to produce and mold post-Mao consumers whose spending behaviors are consistent with the country's macroeconomic goals. I have traced the spatial development of this process from the unique design of the GBA metropolis, which functions like a massive megamachine of subjectivity, through the architecture and activities of Macau's integrated casino resorts. However, in order to understand the role of gambling in the production of postsocialist subjects in Macau, Callon's sociology of economic action and "preoccupation with pragmatics offers an unparalleled prospect into how particular sorts of economic objects and persons, or particular versions of being economic are summoned into being" (McFall 2009, 268–69). It is this summoning into being of the Chinese *homo economicus,* and by extension the country's calculating consumer masses, that is enabled by Macau's LIVE Baccarat machine.

BIOPOLITICAL GAMES

To understand the pedagogical function of the otherwise banal gambling machine, we must first recognize that LIVE Baccarat is not merely a conventional baccarat game, but with bets automated and play mediated by digital technologies. Although baccarat is the basic building block of the game, LIVE Baccarat has distinguishing features that make it qualitatively distinct. As I outlined in chapter 7, baccarat—or at least the variety common in Macau and Las Vegas—is a simple game of chance played with cards that permits a limited set of possible wagers and a few potential outcomes. The LIVE Baccarat machine, by contrast, is a sociotechnical apparatus that translates the game of baccarat into an intricate "epistemic consumption object" (Zwick and Dholakhia 2006), a dynamic type of future-oriented economic activity that grows increasingly complex the longer the duration of the player's engagement with the game.

This prospective temporality of LIVE Baccarat is crucial to understanding its biopolitical function; this fact is illuminated if we foreground LIVE Baccarat's status as a video game. In an analysis of the kinesthetic economy of contemporary video games, Pasi Väliaho (2014) contends that "the key logics of biopolitics today" are "logics based on the management of future possibilities" (24). For Väliaho, popular first-person shooter or action-adventure games such as *Call of Duty* and *Grand Theft Auto* constitute a sort of Geertzian sentimental education that provides players with the cognitive and corporeal equipment necessary for navigating social life. Through such play, the gamer inadvertently trains his brain, body, and sensory apparatus to respond preemptively to threats that materialize on the gaming screen. Therefore, this play should not be dismissed as a frivolous pastime; video games comprise a dynamic window through which the contours of the contemporary sociopolitical order become visible. "The ostensibly inconsequential but viscerally compelling and rhythmically immersive activity of beating up a virtual adversary, killing virtual aliens, or stealing virtual cars may tell us something significant about what kinds of beings our society needs us to be," says Väliaho. "Crucial here is the way in which video games facilitate affectively intensive play with contingency and crisis, detached from real-world consequences" (31).

We may similarly understand LIVE Baccarat as a casino game that both entertains and educates players by equipping them with kinesthetic and cognitive skills that have a relevance beyond the confines of play. *Homo economicus* must learn to adapt productively to a contemporary regime of anticipation, an emergent episteme that enjoins subjects to think and live toward the future (Adams, Murphy, and Clark

2009). This regime is characterized by an overarching atmosphere of uncertainty that permeates contemporary life, marked as it is by imminent threats posed by financial crises, environmental disasters, terrorist attacks, and communicable diseases. We may recall that LifeTec Group initially engineered biopharmaceutical solutions for hepatitis B, one such looming threat to public health in the PRC, before focusing attention on gaming machine design.[4] Perpetual vulnerability to such risks means individuals today are increasingly cautioned to engage in speculative forecasting, actuarial calculations, and other such preemptive protections that might prepare them for the "routinized likelihoods, hedged bets and probable outcomes" that the future has in store (Adams, Murphy, and Clark 2009, 247).

"Anticipation is not just betting on the future" (although, as we will see in the case of LIVE Baccarat, it is exactly that); "it is a moral economy in which the future sets the conditions of possibility for action in the present, in which the future is inhabited in the present" (Adams, Murphy, and Clark 2009, 249). LIVE Baccarat is both an entertaining gambling machine and an educational device offering economic tutelage for a contemporary regime of anticipation. Much like Väliaho's video games, the LIVE Baccarat device enjoins habitual acts of calculation, projection, and speculation appropriate to everyday life under the pressures imposed by contemporary capitalism.

In chapter 5, I draw on Foucault's work to discuss the integrated resort in Macau as a governmental machine of subjection, a form of materialist pedagogy that normalizes the tenets of market-socialism for Chinese tourists who circulate through the resort environment. To understand this function, it is necessary to locate Macau's new integrated resorts within the broader sociohistorical context of the PRC. Viewing the design and operation of the integrated resort against the socialist *danwei* provides insight into how the integrated resort functions in Macau. The socialist *danwei* provided Chinese workers with jobs, residence, food, education, health care, community affiliation, and the other necessary components of daily life. In so doing, the *danwei* operated as a spatial machine of subjection that produced the collectivist workers necessary for China's socialist economy. The integrated resort similarly produces subjects for the country's market-socialist economic regime. Chinese tourists visiting the resort embody the "lesson" that the state has withdrawn from its role as guarantor of the communist social contract, so it is now the responsibility of the individual to manage everyday necessities under a market logic. The integrated resort is not a factory for production of goods but a factory for production of the self—a self that is understood as a so-called ability machine of remunerative characteristics that maximize competitive advantage. Travel enhances a citizen's urbanity and cosmopolitanism; spas, clinics, and medications tone individual bodies; and cosmetics, jewelry, and designer fashion serve to perfect appearances.

If the integrated resort is understood as a complex machine for living, then the LIVE Baccarat apparatus plays a complementary but distinct role in this process. Using Guattari's vocabulary, we can say that the integrated resort is a machine of molar subjection, while the gaming apparatus operates at the molecular register of subjectification. That is, the resort helps to fashion an individual identity, which it does by shaping the body and normalizing an ethos of individual responsibility. In contrast, the baccarat machine assembles the immaterial, affective, and cybernetic components of subjectivity. In this way, the gaming machine develops player skills in economic speculation and calculation that are necessary for navigating a market economy.

For the Chinese tourists who visit the casinos, Macau's gaming machines converge with an imminent mode of power that Foucault calls environmental intervention. This form of power "seeks to modulate and regulate the conduct of individuals," not through bodily discipline or mental subjugation but by calibrating and attuning the subject's own adaptive and self-governing competencies (Väliaho 2014, 46). In Foucault's (2004) words, *homo economicus* becomes "the correlative of a governmentality which will act on the environment and systematically modify its variables" (270–71).[5] In this way, the baccarat game entails a sentimental education that equips players to react to the unique challenges of contemporary capitalism.

PERFORMATIVE ECONOMICS

My analysis of the LIVE Baccarat machine draws generally on Callon's pragmatic sociology of economic action and more specifically on his contention that economics is performative. The performativity program explores relationships among the disciplines of economics and finance on the one hand, and the operations of markets, economies, and financialization on the other. This program presumes that the "economy is an achievement rather than a starting point or pre-existing reality," and it seeks to describe the processes of economization that constitute economic phenomena (Çaliskan and Callon 2009, 370).

Callon conceives of economic subjects, and market behavior, without recourse to such conceptual abstractions as a Weberian spirit of capitalism, overarching modes of production such as post-Fordism, or even the construct of a singular ahistorical and self-regulating market. Instead, he advances a novel approach to economic sociology in which he seeks to establish the existence of *homo economicus*—not by theorizing what an economic subject is but rather by describing what an economic subject does. To do so, Callon forges a middle path between two competing accounts of economic behavior. On one side is neoclassical economics, with its conception of rational, efficient, and calculating subjects who engage in market competition in efforts to maximize individual benefit. The neoclassical subject is a naturalized economic agent, a personification of the neoliberal supposition that people will endeavor to advance individual interests in a competitive marketplace. Of course the reliability of this conception of the economic subject is contentious. Do real people actually approach everyday life in the rationalist manner that is presumed in economics textbooks, as an agonistic arena of sober cost–benefit calculations and maximization of individual utility?

Scholars working in the fields of economic sociology and anthropology have mounted a vigorous critique of the neoclassical subject. These scholars reject the assumption of the autonomous calculating agent, focusing instead on what they call the embeddedness of economic activity in complex social networks.[6] They contend that economic calculations, if they occur at all, are influenced by a variety of factors other than rational deliberation.[7] For example, one chooses to purchase a particular automobile not only by deliberating fuel efficiency or calculating discretionary monthly income against annual interest rates on the loan, but also by seeking to impress a certain acquaintance or fulfill a teenage dream—or because the smell of the interior evokes a childhood memory. From this perspective, the one-dimensional conception of *homo economicus* as a calculating actor only obscures the complexity of actually existing social behavior.

Callon's originality (and his relevance for my purpose in this chapter) lies in his attempt to demonstrate the existence of *homo economicus* in a manner that rejects both the assumptions of neoclassical economists and the critique posed by the new economic sociology. Not only does Callon dismiss the notion of an essentialized actor who is, by virtue of some ahistorical human nature, a calculating economic agent, but he also rejects the metaphysical construct of "society" or "the social world," understood as an overarching entity that might serve as a pre-existing cause of economic decisions. Rather, he conceives of society as a collective achievement of social practices, including those exercised in market transactions. Therefore, the attempt by sociologists to embed the actor in layers of social or cultural networks that may inform individual economic decision-making is a tautology. Rather than conceiving of the economy as embedded within a social environment that determines economic behavior, the aim of Callon's performativity program is to understand how economic action becomes disembedded from the social world—autonomous from, say, religious traditions or community affiliations that might otherwise constrain market behavior (Dumez and Jeunemaitre 2010).

Therefore, instead of beginning with "society" and working his way down to economic action, Callon describes the economic subject from the ground up. Callon's pragmatic approach to performative economics provides a useful means by which to analyze the performativity of the LIVE Baccarat machine in Macau; further, it allows me to demonstrate how the game participates in the construction of the very economic subject it sets out to address: the Chinese mass market gambler. To do so, I must first illustrate that playing a game on the LIVE Baccarat machine constitutes a form of economic action, for which I will rely on several of Callon's key assumptions.

First, we must uncouple agency from human actors. Callon adopts a useful "agnosticism as to the nature of actors," who may certainly be human beings but who may also be nonhuman or inanimate entities (Hardie and MacKenzie 2007, 57). Subjectivity is a dynamic product of a person's engagement with material, technical, and spatial environments that afford particular outlooks and behaviors. From this perspective, Chinese tourists are not born with a propensity for economic calculation; nor is consumer desire simply the result of external psychosocial manipulations imposed by the ideology of a consumer society. Instead, a calculating subject emerges in the casino when a person engages with the cognitive and technical equipment necessary to be an economic actor. Agency is not an expression of an individual's internal consciousness. It is rather "distributed" across complex "hybrid collectives" that include not only human bodies but also their "prosthesis, tools, equipment, technical devices, algorithms," and the like (Callon 2005). Thus, one particular mode of economic agency emerges in the moment when a gambler sits at the LIVE Baccarat terminal and places a bet on the game. Callon refers to this cyborg assemblage of a human actor and his equipment as a sociotechnical *agencement.*

"The performativity program starts with an ethnography of sociotechnical *agencements,*" contends Callon (2005). Indeed, this assumption is the basis of my analysis of the LIVE Baccarat gaming device. I derived my data for this chapter from twenty-three patent applications that Paradise Entertainment filed to protect the intellectual property of the game, which detail the specific design innovations of the company's baccarat machines. I also analyzed the company's press releases and financial reports (from 2000 to 2017), as well as investor information generated by financial analysts who assess Paradise Entertainment's prospects in the market (Li and Xu 2013). These data form the basis of my understanding of the role this unique gaming machine plays in Macau's casino economy.

MACHINE GAMBLING IN MACAU

While LIVE Baccarat was specifically developed for the Macau gaming industry, the game has some common features that may be found, in different iterations or combinations, on gaming machines around the world. LIVE Baccarat belongs to the genus of electronic table games, including electronic versions of poker, blackjack, and roulette; because it involves a human dealer, it is known as a hybrid electronic table game. However, the Macau baccarat machine belongs generally to the family of electronic games best typified by the ordinary and ubiquitous slot machine.

In chapter 7, I discuss Natasha Dow Schüll's (2012) study of slot machine gaming in the United States; she understands the American attachment to slot machines as a programmed "addiction by design." Schüll's specific focus is on slot machine addicts, and she describes the problem gambler as a specific node or effect of an "exterior assemblage of technologies, design practices, regulatory policies, and political-economic values that configure the human–machine relationship in which players become caught" (308). Schüll highlights the tendency of slot machine addicts to zone out in front of the machines, entering a semiconscious state as awareness of the external world slips away. Although she does not use the term, this is an apt description of a Foucauldian apparatus, and her complementary theoretical focus on the relations among the Deleuzian assemblage and the machinic sub-jectivity it produces is generally consistent with my own approach to understanding electronic gaming in Macau. However, I attend to a dimension of this phenomenon that is qualitatively distinct from the object of Schüll's study.

Schüll (2012) describes the zone as a site of the individual's total cap-ture by the machine; the gambling addict whose subjectivity has been segmented into a set of programmed and mechanistic responses to coded prompts and algorithmic enticements is the epitome of Deleuze's (1992) "dividual" operating in a society of control. However, my focus is not on the gambler as mindless automaton, caught in a liminal zone of suspended cognition and unable to resist the lure of the machine. Quite the opposite. I analyze the heightened attention and acute cog-nition demanded by the LIVE Baccarat device, as well as the modes of instrumental rationality that are enabled by the game.[8]

Economizing Baccarat

When I explained the rules of *punto banco* baccarat in chapter 7, I de-scribed it as a simple game of chance. In a game of *punto banco* bac-carat, the croupier deals a hand of two cards each to the Banker and Player positions on the table, and punters gamble simply on whether they believe Banker or Player will have the better hand. Once the gam-blers place their bets, the card faces are exposed and the point value of each hand summed, revealing whether Banker or Player has the win-ning hand. In an effort to predict that winning hand, Chinese players often consult charts such as the Big Road that provide a visual record of the results of previous games at the table, or they may methodically "squeeze" the cards in an attempt to influence the outcome of a particular hand.[9] However, regardless of the gambler's supplementary work, when all is said and done, the decision to bet on either Player or Banker basically comes down to a 50/50 guess. There is no rational way to determine which one is likely to prevail.

Baccarat is therefore a simple game of chance. Although money is won and lost, and although casino profits are accrued, baccarat decision-making, such as it exists, requires no calculation on the part of the gambler. Therefore, baccarat remains embedded within the circumscribed social realm of play, distinct from the disembedded economic activity Callon contends is indicative of a market—and characteristic of *homo economicus.*

Foucault (2004) draws on the work of economist Gary Becker to characterize *homo economicus* as an "entrepreneur of himself, being for himself his own capital, being for himself his own producer, being for himself the source of [his] earnings" (226). I contend that the LIVE Baccarat machine produces a Chinese "entrepreneur of himself" by economizing baccarat, and translating this simple game into a complex form of market activity. For a phenomenon to become disembedded and differentiated market activity requires the use of a specific type of economic *agencement,* "one that renders things, behaviors, and processes economic" (Callon, Millo, and Muniesa 2007, 3). Callon refers to this economic *agencement* as a market device; to use Callon's terminology, the LIVE Baccarat machine is a market device that economizes the otherwise simple game of baccarat.

The LIVE Baccarat device translates baccarat from a simple game of chance with a limited set of possible outcomes into a complex, diversified, and open-ended economic activity. Indeed, *punto banco* baccarat's inherent simplicity was one motivation for the invention of the LIVE Baccarat machine; this point is repeated verbatim in several of Paradise Entertainment's patent applications for the game: "A feature of conventional baccarat games is that they have relatively simple rules. However, the simplicity of the rules has led to a corresponding simplicity in the relatively few types of wagers which may be placed during the play of the game, which may limit interest on the part of the player(s) and thus further limit the casino in terms of profit and payout" (Chun 2011). To address the game's simplicity, the LIVE Baccarat device uses several betting modifications that multiply the types and quantity of potential wagers that the gambler may make. These new wagering options translate baccarat into a form of economic activity that enables, even requires, modes of calculation on the part of the player. These forms of calculation that are necessary to play the LIVE Baccarat machine do not exist in the conventional baccarat game, and engaging in this novel calculative activity turns the gambler into an economic agent.

LIVE BACCARAT CALCULATIONS

By definition, *homo economicus* is a calculating actor. Max Weber (1930) identified calculation as fundamental to the capitalist ethos,[10] while his contemporary, Georg Simmel (1903), noted the "rationally calculated economic egoism" endemic to the metropolitan "mental life" that is produced by the money form (12). For Callon, however, calculation is not simply a mathematical operation that occurs in the mind of an individual shopper, investor, or gambler. Calculative activity, like other forms of cognition, is distributed throughout that person's relationship with specific equipment or devices that enable calculative processes, such as accounting ledgers, computer terminals, shopping carts—or baccarat machines.[11]

Macau's LIVE Baccarat apparatus enables several innovative wagers that each involve prospective or anticipatory calculations on the part of the gambler: the maximum bet, the Paradise Jackpot, and the betting portfolio. These new wagers orient the temporality of gambling on baccarat away from the Chinese gambler's "chartist" focus on compiling win–loss records of previous hands (which I explain in chapter 7) and toward anticipating emergent outcomes appropriate to the demands of contemporary capitalism. This feature of the baccarat machine is similar to the sentimental education of the video games described earlier by Väliaho, which train the gamer's brain and body in preemptive actions. I turn now to an analysis of these new forms of calculation that are enabled by the LIVE Baccarat device.

Calqulating Value with the Maximum Bet

One unique feature of LIVE Baccarat is that the game system introduces a collective maximum bet that may be wagered per hand of baccarat.

In and of itself, a maximum bet is not unique. All conventional casino table games set both minimum and maximum possible bets, but on table games, these limits refer to bets placed by individual gamblers. The amount that one gambler chooses to wager on a hand has no necessary relation to the amounts that other gamblers at the same table may wager, as long as each individual wager falls somewhere between the minimum requirement and the maximum limit.

However, the LIVE Baccarat game uniquely sets maximum bet limits that are shared collectively by a group of gamblers who are randomly assembled by the game. The gaming terminals are networked into groups of twenty machines, and the maximum bet per hand is shared across one bank of twenty machines. That is, assuming that the maximum bet is HK$10,000, if one player on that bank of machines initially places a single bet of HK$5,000, then the other nineteen players can collectively wager only HK$5,000 on that hand. From the perspective of the game designer, the aim of this feature is to produce artificial competition among a group of gamblers in order to produce a sense of urgency that may drive an individual gambler to place a wager quickly, before the betting limit is exhausted. A gambler who thinks that he is on a lucky streak may be driven to place bets rapidly in order to ensure that he may claim his share of the maximum bet before his luck runs out. In addition, the way the maximum bet functions to virtually connect individual players (even though they are sitting at different gaming terminals) also serves to generate the sort of social heat that Chinese gamblers desire from conventional table games. This feature makes LIVE Baccarat qualitatively distinct from a typical slot machine.

What is interesting about this maximum bet feature for my purposes here is how it manages to position the gamblers in an agonistic relationship of the sort imagined by neoclassical economists while at the same time requiring cooperative intersubjective responsibility among gamblers for the collective wager. This novel form of competitive–cooperative calculation afforded by the machine is characteristic of what scholars in the social studies of finance call "calqulation" (Cochoy 2008). This odd term is derived from the French word *calquer,* which refers to the act of adjusting one's standpoint to conform with the standpoint of another person. So a calqulation is an anticipatory or preemptive form of calculation in which one person models his behavior on another's. The concept of calqulation actually emerged in a study of shopping carts, but it illuminates the operations of the baccarat machine as well. Much as a parent pushing a child in a shopping cart past supermarket shelves must anticipate the child's product preferences and adjust his own behavior accordingly in order to navigate a satisfactory shopping experience, the successful LIVE Baccarat gambler must anticipate the actions of the other players in the game and adapt his own conduct to their behavior.

Calqulation "designates the building of a shared project" (Cochoy 2008, 30). The LIVE Baccarat maximum bet is just such a shared project, one that requires an intersubjective calqulation among the gamblers playing on the set of networked machines, regardless of whether or not they actually know one another. When placing bets, each gambler must anticipate the quantity and pace of betting by other players in order to "calqulate" the optimal amount and timing of his own wager. Therefore, the maximum bet constraint on the gaming machine necessitates a collective calculation among a group of gamblers, which makes this betting distinct from that of an individual gambler placing solitary wagers on the simple baccarat game.

Arbitrage and the Life-Changing Jackpot

Another LIVE Baccarat innovation is the so-called Paradise Jackpot wager. This jackpot is actually the most popular feature of the game among players, and it combines several different forms of calculation. The Paradise Jackpot is a side bet that the gambler may choose to make at the start of any hand. This bet is not directly related to the individual baccarat game unfolding between Player and Banker, where gamblers bet on which position will have the card total closest to 9. Rather, the jackpot bet locates the gambler in a distinct parallel activity that involves betting on the same cards but for a different desired outcome. The object of the jackpot game is that the croupier deal a certain group of cards in the hand, such as three of a kind, four of a kind, straight, full house, or royal flush.[12] If such a card combination should occur, it pays out a certain percentage of the total jackpot, and this jackpot payout is shared equally among each player who wagered that particular jackpot bet during the winning hand.

For a gambler to wager simultaneously on the same cards for both the baccarat game and the side jackpot is to engage in a simple version of the form of financial speculation known as arbitrage. In a nutshell, arbitrage involves "speculation that takes advantage of similar assets being priced differently in different markets at the same time" (Bjerg 2011, 267). That is, by simultaneously wagering both the baccarat bet and the jackpot bet, the player places two distinct bets on the same asset of cards—cards that have one value in the baccarat game and a completely different value in the jackpot game. If no jackpot win occurs on a particular hand, then the bets that were placed but not recouped will simply be added to the cumulative jackpot so that it accrues value over time. The Paradise Jackpot thus regularly accumulates over long periods before someone eventually wins it; as a result, the jackpot sum may ultimately become so large that it constitutes what is known in the industry as a life-changing jackpot.

We may recall from our discussion in chapter 7 of typical gambling dispositions in Macau that many Chinese players in the city approach gambling with the same risk-taking capacity and goals that they would use to approach an ordinary financial investment. Indeed, the accumulation of individual wagers in the Paradise Jackpot actually transforms the jackpot bet into an investment.[13] This is to say that the value of the Paradise Jackpot is not a random amount, like a flat sum of $100,000; nor is it is calculated according to simple probabilities, as are most casino win payouts on conventional table games.[14] Rather, the value of the Paradise Jackpot is the direct result of the wagers that all of the participating gamblers have collectively contributed to the pot. With each bet an individual gambler places in the jackpot, the size of the eventual payout is increased; the larger the jackpot becomes, the more likely gamblers are to wager the bet in an effort to win the jackpot. However, in order to have a chance to eventually recoup his original investment in the jackpot, the gambler must return to the same set of games in the same casino.[15]

As a collective financial project that depends entirely on individual contributions, the side jackpot itself is an expression of the mass market of gamblers. The jackpot only exists because individual gamblers have wagered money on it, and the value of the jackpot accrues with each wager. The total value of the jackpot is evidence of an existing mass market of individual gamblers who collectively "invest" in this pool of money. Therefore, this jackpot is a unique type of casino bet. It is not a case of individual gamblers competing against the house for a payout based on the odds of the game, but rather a case of those gamblers regularly depositing money in a joint account that will eventually be awarded to one, or even all, of them. Thus, the jackpot is an expression of this mass market—the sum total of all funds that gamblers place in the gaming machine.

The Paradise Box Portfolio

Paradise Entertainment followed the successful introduction of LIVE Baccarat with a subsequent innovation called the Paradise Box, a sort of second-generation version of the game that comprises a self-contained total gaming environment. The Paradise Box includes the LIVE Baccarat game and each corresponding type of wager offered in the system, but it features an additional slot machine that is integrated into each gaming terminal. This slot machine interface provides a menu of additional games that the gambler may choose to activate alongside LIVE Baccarat.

The Paradise Box also has a special ergonomic seat that the company contends was inspired by the film *The Matrix.* In the film, the hero Neo and his fellow revolutionary fighters use a special chair to "headjack" their brains into a computer, then upload their own consciousnesses into the artificial Matrix world. Despite the obvious cinematic excess, as well as the explicit allusions to Baudrillard's (1983, 1994) theory of simulation, this cyborg cognition is a suggestive analogy for the calculative networks among gamblers playing the LIVE Baccarat machine.

The slot machine function that is integrated into the Paradise Box introduces further complexity into the economic enterprise of LIVE Baccarat by allowing the gambler to play a variety of different slot machine games in the time between each individual hand of baccarat. As is explained in the patent application for the Paradise Box Gaming System, "In casino games, such as the baccarat game, there is generally a count-down time during which a player of the game will need to wait for the count-down result. This waiting period results in frustration of the player . . . waste of the resource of the gambling establishment,

Figure 33. The Paradise Box gaming terminal. The left-hand screen displays the LIVE Baccarat game; the right-hand screen features a slot machine interface with a menu of games that may be chosen by the gambler. *Photograph courtesy Andrew W. Scott; originally appeared in* Inside Asian Gaming *and* World Gaming Magazine.

and, as a result, reduced revenue by the gambling establishment" (Chun 2012). This description is illustrated in the patent application by a series of simple drawings depicting a gambler growing increasingly bored as he peers at the gaming screen, waiting passively for the croupier to deal the next hand of cards. In order to capture and monetize this downtime, the Paradise Box facilitates additional gambling opportunities.

However, playing multiple games simultaneously is not only a means to maximize opportunities for entertainment and profit during the downtime between hands of play; it also allows the discerning gambler to diversify his economic activity across a portfolio of different types of financial opportunities, each with different odds, payout schedules, and mathematically programmed volatility. A player using the machine can place a bet on the baccarat table game for Banker to win, and while waiting for the croupier to deal the cards, he can place another bet on a slot machine game that is programmed with an entirely different set of odds than is available in the baccarat game. He can also arbitrage a side wager in the Paradise Jackpot in an effort to hedge against his potential losses in the ongoing baccarat game, always with a mind to how many jackpot bets he has made, and therefore how much he has personally "invested" in the account. To be clear, all of this activity is still gambling, but it is a qualitatively distinct—and much more complex—form of gambling than is typical of conventional baccarat. This intricate economic activity approaches the calculative and speculative activities that comprise a market.

Ultimately, wagers on the Paradise Box constitute a financial portfolio of speculative economic decisions. The point of a financial portfolio is that an investor should diversify investments across a range of different equities and assets, with differing degrees of risk exposure such that the distinct risk profiles will help balance each other out (Haivan 2014).[16] When this general idea is applied to gamblers in Macau, it suggests that rather than wager regularly on the same game, hoping for eventual margins of return over the long term, as one might do with conventional baccarat, the LIVE Baccarat device enables the gambler to hedge bets across a variety of options. "Portfolio theory moves us out of the linear logic of finance," suggests Haivan (2014), "which implies the steady accumulation of profit from long-term investment in certain concerns, toward a more chaotic and scattered pattern" where profit is derived from a diverse variety "of even contradictory short term investments." With its diverse portfolio of options, the key to the LIVE Baccarat device is the manner in which it produces "a more dynamic financialized subjectivity" by which the gambler may "move through markets with fluidity, juggle commitments that are multiple and contingent, ephemeral and disposable, and partake in a culture of creative arbitrage" (126). Ultimately, this reflects the pedagogical dimension of LIVE Baccarat, which enables and facilitates a complex set of calculations that might be said to summon a *homo economicus* into being.

Betting on the Future

This innovation means that gambling on the baccarat machine no longer involves solitary and self-contained wagers but rather is part of an undetermined project that is connected to the future activity of the individual gambler as well as to other players on the network. Much like online investing or other forms of personal finance, the Paradise Box constitutes an epistemic consumption object that draws gamblers into a project of dynamic and continuous knowledge activity (Zwick and Dholakia 2006). This type of epistemic consumption object is distinct from more mundane commodities that are used up in the act of consumption. While typical consumption objects decrease in complexity over time, the epistemic object becomes increasingly complex as it is consumed. Financial software is such an epistemic object; with each mastery of a new digital technique, investment decision, interest payment, or redistribution of funds across accounts, the consumption object becomes more complex and engaging. The LIVE Baccarat machine likewise increases in complexity the longer the player engages with the device.

The epistemic consumption object features "material elusiveness" or lacks "ontological stability" such that the commodity is not simply used up in its entirety but is transformed into a "continuous knowledge project" for the consumer (Zwick and Dholakia 2006, 21).[17] In the case of LIVE Baccarat, this ontological uncertainty about the game enjoins the gambler to constantly calculate options and make wagers on the future. These behaviors are consistent with the contemporary regime of anticipation that entails a moral imperative, or injunction, for the subject to be aware of future risks, "engendering alertness and vigilance as normative affective states" (Adams, Murphy, and Clark 2009, 254). The LIVE Baccarat machine therefore cultivates the player's cognitive and corporeal market behavior, thus honing the characteristics of an economic actor.

CASINO CAPITALISM

I have demonstrated that Callon's economic sociology enlightens the economization of baccarat that is exemplified by the LIVE Baccarat device. However, the limitation of Callon's approach—and his distinction from Foucault and Guattari (as well as Simmel and Weber)—is his apolitical orientation and elision of normative claims (Butler 2010). Beyond simply describing the market device and the process of economization through which an economic actor is fashioned, we should also "ask political questions about who controls the assemblage, and what sociotechnical arrangements facilitate the exercise of that control." The fact is, scholars engaged in the social studies of finance "[too] often . . . miss that which is precisely capitalist about capitalism: namely that the aim of private enterprise is to generate profit, not construct a market" (Erturk et al. 2013, 339).[18]

Crucially, however, the aim of LIVE Baccarat is both: it seeks to generate profit by constructing a market of Chinese gambling subjects. Indeed, the mass market gamblers who play LIVE Baccarat are a metonym for the new consumer masses produced by China's National New-Type Urbanization Plan. No doubt this colossal consumer population is global capitalism's elusive holy grail: a billion bodies of remunerative human capital.

As a form of human capital, the baccarat machinist operates simultaneously as financier, producer, and consumer in an economic market. As an entrepreneur of himself, the gambler has no need for junket loans to finance his gambling, or even for a skilled croupier to manage the game. The casino need not demand from him large stakes; in fact, the imposition of a collective maximum bet constraint ironically ensures sufficient wagers to cover casino costs and guarantee returns. This system ultimately eliminates the volatility that characterizes VIP baccarat in Macau, with its huge scale of fluctuating wins and losses for the casino resulting from the low house margin and the stark up-or-down outcome of games. The baccarat machine replaces this volatility with modest yet systematic, predictable, and steady profits.

LIVE Baccarat is thus fundamentally different from the game of poker—and from that game's playful relation to capitalist enterprise. Bjerg (2011) demonstrates that such games do not develop in a vacuum; they may exhibit "structural homologies" (203) with their specific political-economic context. In charting those relations, however, Bjerg's treatment of the economic dimension of poker never moves beyond the first register of semiotics. In his narrative, each variation of poker is a simulation or representation of the mutating form of capitalism, a parody of labor and exchange value under different production regimes.[19] However, to understand LIVE Baccarat's relationship to capitalism in China today, we must attend to the asignifying and nonrepresentational register of semiotics theorized by Guattari, as well as the manner in which the logic of capital is immanent within the game itself. These asignifying semiotics are crucial to Guattari's theory of the contemporary subject—the key commodity of postindustrial capitalism.

Asignifying signs operate at the prepersonal and transpersonal level of affect and algorithm, the cybernetic intensities of which ensure the autopoetic functioning of the capitalist machine. For Guattari, what is distinct about such asignifying signs is that they do not represent an object; rather, "they participate directly in the process of generating their object" (Lazzarato 2010, 65). As such, the baccarat machine's distinction from poker is that it does not merely represent capitalism by parodying its characteristics in the form of an entertaining game. Rather, the baccarat machine comprises a mode of environmental intervention through which capital seizes hold of the ontological instability of Chinese gamblers in order to mold and produce adaptive and self-governing subjects; the subjects so produced are calculating economic actors equipped to effectively navigate the anticipatory regime. The goal is not to discipline their actions but to diversify their freedoms and modulate their environments in order that they may develop their own adaptive and self-governing capabilities.

This pedagogic dimension of Macau's gaming machines exemplifies my conception of casino capitalism; the Macau casino with the LIVE Baccarat device is a scholastic site of economic subjectivation that provides a sentimental education in the everyday habits of capitalist enterprise. Whereas poker turns capitalism into a game, the LIVE Baccarat machine turns the game of baccarat into capitalism. In so doing, it cultivates a Chinese *homo economicus* from the ground up by comporting a calculating postsocialist consumer.

Producing Capitalist Subjects

Much as I have argued of integrated resorts and other such market devices in Macau, LIVE Baccarat's relation to subjectivity is pedagogical rather than representational. Therefore, my exploration of the biopolitical function of LIVE Baccarat is indebted less to Bjerg's argument about poker and more to Donald MacKenzie's (2008, 2009) analysis, inspired by Callon, of the performativity of financial markets. For MacKenzie (2009), the economic models created in the second half of the twentieth century to measure risk in order to describe market movements functioned to actually create the very markets that were the ostensible object of analysis. Such theories were "prescriptive, not descriptive"; the theories "told rational investors what to do, rather than seeking to portray what they actually did" (87). Such sociotechnical models function in the manner evocatively captured by the title of MacKenzie's (2008) book, *An Engine, Not a Camera.*

LIVE Baccarat is one such engine of economization. The game does not simply attract a preexisting group of prospective Chinese gamblers, latent subjects awaiting the appearance in Macau of an affordable form of gambling in which they may participate. Rather, the baccarat machine constitutes the very market that is the object of its design. This is the game's performative dimension. We could presume that LifeTec's biopharmaceutical engineers devised a game that accurately targets the mass market gamblers the company hoped to attract, "but it is preferable to say that the world it supposes has become actual" (Callon 2007, 320).

The crux of the LIVE Baccarat machine is not that it allows gamblers to play with capitalism in the same way Bjerg describes poker. Rather, LIVE Baccarat produces capitalists through play. Therefore, LIVE Baccarat is not simply a metaphor for capitalism. The baccarat machine is a game of economization that exhorts, elicits, and engenders market behaviors. Rather than poker's playful parodic simulation of capitalism,

LIVE Baccarat functions for Chinese tourists in Macau as a pedagogic stimulation of economic action: it is an entertaining and educational market device. LIVE Baccarat is an apparatus of anticipation, a machine of post-Mao subjection, and an engine of the mass market that drives China's reform economy.

9
Geophilosophy in Macau

> You look at these hundreds of thousands, these millions
> of people humbly streaming here from all over the face
> of the earth—people who come with a single thought,
> peacefully, persistently, and silently crowding into this
> colossal palace—and you feel that here something has finally
> been accomplished, accomplished and brought to an end.
>
> —Fyodor Dostoyevsky, "Baal"

I began this book by proposing that Adelson's Venetian Macao resort is a contemporary successor to London's Crystal Palace, the building that Paxton designed in the nineteenth century to house the Great Exhibition and that Sloterdijk (2013) deemed an early architectural expression of the world interior of capital. By ingeniously conflating the immemorial Italian city-state and the enclosed shopping arcade, on the edge of the largest "state container" in global history, the Venetian exemplifies the spatial logic of capitalism's development over four long centuries of historical expansion, testifying to the ongoing relevance of the work of Braudel and Arrighi that I have explored herein.

However, as we saw in chapter 8, capital's most insidious operation is the somatic seduction of the interior life of the solitary human subject. This carnal domain is fertile terrain for the fundamental wagers of risk and return so integral to both capitalism and gambling. This elusive inner life of the individual is ultimately illuminated not by the tedious tomes of economists and historians but by the elegiac insights of novelists and playwrights, philosophers and psychiatrists, loan sharks and racketeers. Therefore, in this final chapter, I will revisit Dostoyevsky's critique of the Crystal Palace and explore its relevance for understanding both his rejection of the calculating *homo economicus* and his own destructive addiction to casino gambling.

In the final pages of the book, I will return one last time to the affinities among the capitalist city-states of Venice and Macau with which I started. I will trace the consanguineous relations linking Shylock's infamous debt of a pound of flesh in *The Merchant of Venice,* Shakespeare's tale of usury in the birthplace of capitalism, and the fantastical twenty-first-century pecuniary exploits of Macau's most infamous moneylender, Wan "Broken Tooth" Kuok-Koi. We will see that this unlikely troika of Dostoyevsky, Shylock, and Broken Tooth collectively enlighten what we might call the *geophilosophical* production of Macau's Crystal Palace project—as well as the geopolitical implications of the Venetian world interior of capitalism.

DOSTOYEVSKY, THE CRYSTAL PALACE, AND CONSUMER CULTURE

When Dostoyevsky visited the Crystal Palace in 1856, he was appalled by what appeared to him to be a monument to a soulless modern society, one enamored of the myth of progress and mired in the worship of an empty materialism. For Dostoyevsky, the glass walls that enclosed the palace structure posed not the transparent transcendence of the technological innovation and instrumental reason that were celebrated in the exhibition, but the sterile disposition of secular science and the fragility of the individual human spirit in an increasingly regimented world. The tourist "zombies" Dostoyevsky saw in London were also a cause for his concern (Dostoyevsky [1863] 1997, 38). Dostoyevsky, a proponent of Russia's native soil movement and dedicated to a belief in the inseparability of culture and geography, found the massive crowds moving through the palace structure—the "well-fed dilettantes out strolling for their own pleasure" (37)—to signal the cultural homogenization he feared would inevitably result from the global spread of European consumer capitalism.[1] The traditional Russian values that had been forged for centuries in the country's rural villages surely would not survive the onslaught of modernization from the West.

Dostoyevsky was therefore incredulous when, only a few months after the release of his Crystal Palace ruminations in *Winter Notes on Summer Impressions,* his countryman Nikolai Cherneshevsky published the novel *What Is To Be Done?*, in which he proffered the Crystal Palace as a symbol of socialist utopia. In the novel, the Crystal Palace is presented as the birthplace of a new social order, conceived by the scientific mind and structured entirely by reason, in which the young members of Russia's new generation could cooperate in egalitarian labor and free love (Guagnon and Aho 2009). In fact, Cherneshevsky's didactic book would influence a generation of both leftist and rightist Russian radical reformers. These included Vladimir Lenin, who led the Bolshevik Revolution that established the socialist Soviet state, and Ayn Rand, who fled Bolshevism for the United States in 1926 to seek fame as a Hollywood scriptwriter, and whose philosophy of objectivism influenced numerous American denizens of libertarian laissez-faire economics.

In the twentieth century, the once predominantly agrarian lifestyle of the United States was supplanted by the faux garden estates of a predominantly suburban society, with a domestic economy driven by the twin engines of industrial production and mass consumption. This Fordist-Keynesian regime eventually enabled one of the most stable and sustained programs of economic growth the world has ever seen, making the United States the largest consumer market on the planet. The suburban lifestyle was organized around the individual mobility of the automobile and the residential innovation of the mortgage-financed single-family home, overflowing with plush furniture and equipped with televisions and labor-saving kitchen appliances.

The realization of this American consumer transformation required the concerted efforts of a diverse variety of actors, including economists and investment bankers, commercial artists and department store window designers, museum curators and modeling agencies, advertising copywriters and credit specialists. American consumerism was neither inevitable nor happenstance. It was the result of a massive didactic project that aimed to mold individuals and the social order to conform to the expectations of commercial capitalism. Even Rand's novels *Atlas Shrugged* and *The Fountainhead* (as well as the 1949 film adaptation of the latter starring Gary Cooper and Patricia Neal), along with her unrepentant apologia for uncharitable selfishness, contributed to the realization of the country's consumer republic.

In fact, Rand acolyte Alan Greenspan would chair the U.S. Federal Reserve and practice his own radical social reform by helming the wave of neoliberal deregulation that enabled the post-1970 financial economy (Weiner 2016). Strange (1986) decried this risky and volatile financialization as casino capitalism, and the 2002 implosion of the dot-com bubble and 2007 subprime mortgage crisis were both tragic outcomes of this philosophical legacy. Greenspan even contributed to the Keynesian lexicon of animal spirits when he coined the phrase "irrational exuberance" to characterize the overconfident disposition of those unfortunate dot-com financiers.

At the turn of the twenty-first century, the PRC is engaged in a market transformation that in many ways aims to replicate the American mass consumption model, albeit with Chinese characteristics. One key distinction of the Chinese case was the immediate necessity, with Deng's implementation of economic reforms in 1978, to overcome the overtly anticonsumerist stance that was advanced by the former Maoist state. Indeed, the rejection of American-style consumerism had been a hallmark of twentieth-century state communism in both China and the Soviet Union.

Much like Dostoyevsky, Mao had his own vision of the importance of native soil to Chinese culture.[2] Mao, who was from rural origins himself, exalted the countryside's role in agricultural production; he elevated the rural peasant to the personification of the permanent socialist revolution. An antiurban bias was a hallmark of Mao's party leadership, differentiating Chinese communism from its Soviet counterpart. Mao aimed to transform China's cities from what he believed were wasteful environments of bourgeois consumption to centers of industrial production (Chung et al. 2001). Cosmopolitan cities such as Shanghai, which in the early twentieth century was a global hub of intellectual, cultural, and economic activity, "were to relinquish their existing roles as centers of commerce and trade, to become, instead, heavily industrialized to serve agriculture by manufacturing products that were unavailable in the countryside" (53).

The socialist government mobilized urban citizens for nationalist production in the new SOEs and refashioned the morphology of China's cities to reflect the logic of the *danwei*. Chinese planners designed each work unit much like a self-contained village within a city, whose residents would live and labor in close proximity and reproduce in quotidian life the egalitarian values of the new regime. The familial camaraderie and constant scrutiny that derived from residents' close cohabitation within a relatively small community produced an urban lifestyle characterized neither by the anomie and anonymity typical of capitalist cities in the West, nor by the heterogeneity, differentiation, and stimulation that made those cities so exciting (Wu 2009).

Therefore, the priority of China's reform-era technocrats was to reverse the Maoist logic of urban production for the countryside and instead to promote urban consumption as the key to modernization and development. As I have detailed throughout this book, the central government's National New-Type Urbanization Plan is currently relocating hundreds of millions of rural residents to the country's expanding cities in hopes that their residential and lifestyle purchases will sustain the country's economic development, much as the newly affluent suburbanites did in the United States. China's promotion of tourism as an inexpensive form of itinerant education has inverted Mao's Down to the Countryside Movement to cultivate a contemporary Chinese population comprising cosmopolitan quality citizens. Their patriotism may be measured in part by canny acts of consumption that enhance both personal development and the national economy. As a favored destination for cross-border mainland tourists, Macau is a model city for this program; it is also a vibrant microcosm of the socioeconomic changes that have swept across China over the past several decades. In Macau, we may trace the trajectory of those modern projects of rationalist social reform that animated the distinct twentieth-century imaginaries of the United States and the PRC. It is in the Venetian Palace that we can most clearly comprehend the underlying logic of postsocialism.

COGNAC AND THE QUALITY SUBJECT

During the annual Golden Week holiday that commemorates China's October 1 National Day, and which in 2019 marked the seventieth anniversary of the foundation of the PRC, French luxury brand Jas Hennessy and Co. organized Hennessy Declassified, a pop-up cognac promotion held at Macau's Galaxy Resort. In the first six days of October 2019, more than 744,000 tourists entered Macau from the mainland; the Galaxy was swarming with Chinese visitors throughout the holiday period (Newsdesk 2019a). The Hennessy promotion, which lasted for three weeks, was open to any curious passerby.

Cognac is a useful metric of China's consumer transformation. Cognac sales in China grew 146 percent in the first decade of the twenty-first century, reflecting the country's increasing wealth and embrace of luxury products (Gerth 2011). China is the now the world's largest market for cognac by value, matched only by the United States, which is the largest market by volume (Song, Wei, and Bergiel 2018). That is, while Americans may drink more cognac, their Chinese counterparts actually spend more of their hard-earned money on cognac purchases.

Hennessy Declassified was located in the Galaxy's Crystal Lobby, which is sandwiched between a Starbucks and an Apple Store, and the promotion apparently aimed to reach the same middle-class tourists who might frequent such venues. The immersive event aspired to demystify the Hennessy product as well as to develop in those tourists an appreciation of Hennessy's storied history and a taste for the distinct pleasures of cognac brandy. A large cinema screen looped a film made by British director Ridley Scott with a "sensorial narrative" that provided a simulated walk through the Cognac region of France across the four seasons of the year. With a depiction of an agricultural tradition clearly calculated to resonate with post-Mao mainland visitors, the film documented the cyclical process of planting, tending, and harvesting the ugni blanc grapes that are the sole ingredient of cognac brandy.

Directly adjacent to the film attraction was a small room that featured an interactive display melding touch, lights, and sounds, which was designed to provide a short course in the process of creating cognac. A tourist could touch an icon on the wall, such as a bunch of grapes, to illuminate various elements of the display with instructional information explaining the distillation of grapes into wine, or contextual details such as the fact that Cognac's grape-producing regions are actually six times larger than the entire city of Macau. Interactive audio components provided both the Chinese definitions and the French pronunciations of the winemaking vocabulary terms *terrier, eau-de-vie,* and *savoir faire.*

However, the main attraction of Hennessy Declassified was a mock-up of Hennessy's Grand Tasting Room, located on Rue de la Richonne in Cognac, France, where the company's most experienced vintners select the distilled eau-de-vie that will be blended into different grades of cognac. Interested guests could gather around a wooden table for a tasting demonstration. There they learned to first visibly in-

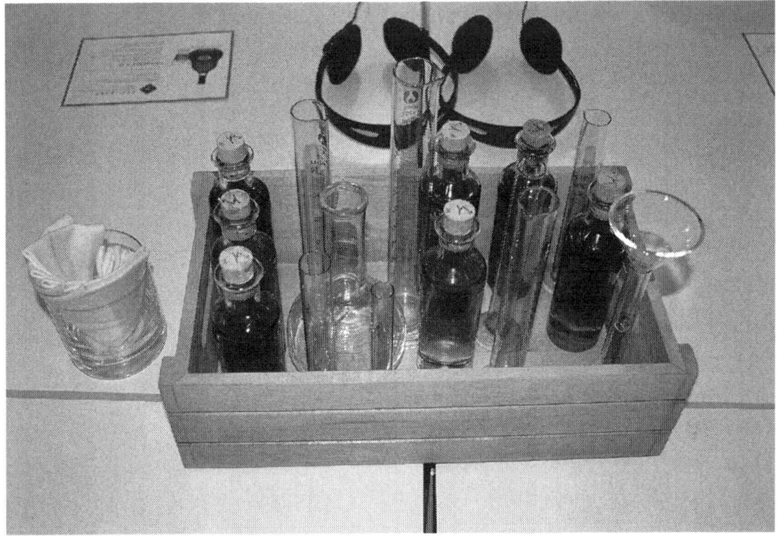

Figure 34. Bottles of eaux-de-vie from a cognac tasting demonstration in the Galaxy Resort in October 2019, held during the Golden Week holiday commemorating the seventieth anniversary of the PRC's founding. *Photograph by author.*

spect two different samples of eau-de-vie, presented in small snifter glasses that were passed around the room; to smell the distinct odors emanating from each glass; and finally to taste the way these elements could be properly blended to achieve a rarified glass of Hennessy XO.

Timed to the rhythms of the Golden Week holiday, and with its convivial mix of communication, theater, and commerce, the traveling cognac show is a contemporary iteration of the medieval Champagne fairs and other early periodic "mechanisms of trade" (Braudel 1979, 2:134) that both Braudel (1979, vol. 2) and Arrighi (2010) contend were crucial to the origins of capitalism. The Galaxy's Hennessy Declassified promotion was strategically positioned on the perimeter of what may well be consumer capitalism's final frontier in the PRC.

Of course, Macau is merely one of innumerable sites across China dedicated to the cultivation and distillation of the consumer quality, or savoir faire, that is the goal of the central government's macroeconomic urbanization plan. In fact, the traveling Hennessy Declassified show also stopped in the cities of Guangzhou, Xiamen, and Shanghai, each of which played a formative role in China's earlier engagements with global capitalism, and which a company representative told me are to-day among Hennessy's strongest markets in China.[3] However, a convergence of several factors in Macau—including the city's historical role as the original conduit of trade between Europe and the Middle Kingdom, the nationalistic Golden Week holiday, the playful ambiance of the Galaxy Resort, and the huge tourist crowds—contributed to the pedagogical resonance of the Macau Hennessy promotion.

When I purchased a bottle of Hennessy XO from the assortment of the branded products on offer at the Duty Free Americas counter on site at the event, I learned from the staff that product sales at the promotion were brisk. One saleswoman informed me that they had entirely sold out of an allotment of XO bottles specially created for the China promotion that were packaged in a translucent plastic display case that doubled as a reusable ice bucket. She also happily informed me that she had just sold the two most expensive cognac bottles on offer, combinations of superlative brandy and luxury packaging that together cost in excess of US$7,000. Finally, she helpfully noted that my receipt was good for a 12 percent discount on any purchase of perfume or cosmetics at the company's nearby outlet inside the Venetian Resort, in what would be an ornamental denouement for the comportment of a quality subject.

With the lingering memory of a Chinese tourist's purchase of $7,000 worth of cognac, we might pause to reflect on the relative recency of such consumer behavior. While it has been some forty years since Deng launched China's economic reforms, only two decades ago, there were no Golden Week holidays in the PRC, nor was there a significant population of mainland international travelers. Before the relaxation of visa controls in 2002, there were limited opportunities for cross-border travel among ordinary citizens. Although cognac was reaching China in increasingly significant amounts in the 1990s via reexportation from other Asian markets, in the last decades of the twentieth century, such widespread acts of conspicuous luxury consumption in China were still relatively rare.[4] Looking back further to the tumultuous years of the Cultural Revolution (coinciding with the apogee of American consumerism), the only state-sanctioned travel afforded to most young people in China was to be sent to the countryside to labor in a factory or farm, and the only pleasure-oriented consumption object most workers could dream about was an ordinary cigarette. However, today, China draws directly on the mass population mobilizations and agitprop campaigns of the country's socialist legacy in order to construct a postsocialist patria that is now the world's largest market for luxury goods (Joy, Sherry, and Wang 2018).

CITY OF THE NAME OF GOD IN CHINA

Macau has been crucial to this process. The city-state, established five hundred years ago at the onset of terrestrial globalization, was integral to the mode of enterprise that Weber (1930) calls "adventurers' capitalism" (76) but that Braudel calls "real capitalism," a freewheeling form of long-distance profiteering tied to piracy, usury, arbitrage, and trade.[5] The seminal Portuguese navigations not only founded Macau but also assimilated European, African, and Asian locales, once separated by vast distances of time and space, into a genuine world-economy. This adventurer's spirit has persisted in Macau for half a millennium, from the seaward labor of those early Portuguese explorers all the way to Stanley Ho's tacit confederations with Broken Tooth and the Chinese Triads operating out of VIP rooms in the Lisboa Hotel.

This adventurism survived so long in Macau in large part because of the city-state's endemic marginality. As a Catholic "City of the Name of God in China," Macau was an apotheosis of alterity, not quite Chinese or Portuguese but something entirely other. As the longest-occupied foreign territory in China, positioned on the porous edge of the vast Middle Kingdom, Macau managed China's tentative relations with global capital during both the Ming and Mao eras. As a nonsignatory of the postwar Bretton Woods Agreement that fixed the price of gold on the international market and unified most of the planet under the sign of the U.S. dollar, Macau was one of the last remaining "outsides" of the capitalist system, an overlooked enclave effectively detached from Sloterdijk's (2013) overarching "world interior." The city's disparate identity was only exacerbated by U.S. president Richard Nixon's fateful decision in 1971 to fight both rising inflation and the dollar's devaluation by dismantling the gold standard, thus ending Macau's monopoly on the illicit gold trade and engendering a new groundless and free-floating global economic regime.

The feeling of inhabiting an outside, a locale somehow forgotten by the global machine, was still palpable when I arrived in Macau in 2001. As a postcolonial Chinese SAR, a spatial exception to the PRC through which western capital could access Chinese consumers via the open door of Deng's reforms, Macau entered the twenty-first century as an unlikely node in an expanding, cross-border GBA megacity. Today this megacity is the world's largest and most populated urban space, and this disjunctive constellation of cities, districts, zones, factory towns, ports, and coastal enclaves manages movements of foreign capital and cultivates many of the country's postsocialist subjects.

The changes to Macau in the two intervening decades since the retrocession to China have been nothing short of remarkable. This tiny erstwhile elsewhere, the last remaining European colony in Asia and long enduring outside the global system, is now on the verge of becoming the world's wealthiest territory. Macau's newfound riches are produced not by the sweat and toil of plebian labor in the PRC but by the leisure play of the Chinese citizens who now comprise the city's primary tourist population. Today Macau's phantasmagoric cityscape features fantastical buildings designed by I. M. Pei and Zaha Hadid, entire Versace- and Lagerfield-branded hotel towers, and simulacra of Venice and Paris on a scale the world has never seen. These new structures are nestled among a sea of baroque cathedrals and pastel colonial buildings that have endured in the city since the early days of Portuguese rule.

By casting our gaze backward to the preceding four long centuries of capitalist history, we may better understand Macau's role in China's contemporary market reforms. The world's largest ships once plied the maritime routes that linked Macau to Malacca, Goa, Nagasaki, and Antwerp, laden with lucrative cargoes of fine silks, gold and silver bullion, tobacco leaf, porcelain china, and even the occasional Bengal tiger. Today, the Great Ship from Amacon has been replaced by two of the world's largest buildings, which facilitate a contemporary trade of Hermès bags, Shiseido cosmetics, Rolex watches, exfoliating spa treatments, and baccarat games. These fanciful new contraptions float atop fabricated terrain that was nothing but a swampy backwater when Sheldon Adelson first set eyes on it and dreamed of building Venice in China.

A LOGIC OF ASSEMBLAGE

By adopting an assemblage approach, I have endeavored in this book to make visible the operations of a massive Chinese megamachine that incorporates Macau, the various components of which are intertwined in a serial concatenation of descending scales. Like a collection of nestled Russian dolls, this interlocking apparatus integrates the GBA megacity, the Macau SAR, the city's enclosed and interiorized integrated casino resorts, and the solitary gambling machines where individual tourists labor at the game of baccarat.[6] To explore this assemblage, I have also attended to a variety of consonant devices that contribute to the function of this system, such as the particular constellation of VIP rooms, dead chips, pawnshops, credit card machines, cigarettes, and ashtrays that enable the city's high-stakes baccarat trade.

Each component of this assemblage apparatus is relatively autonomous from the other gradations such that we may analyze each appendage alone, as I have done in each preceding part (and individual chapter) of the book. However, by attending to the emergent relation of each systemic component with the corresponding operations at the scales above and below, we may contemplate a comprehensive program of consumer subjectification. I call this pedagogical program casino capitalism. I analyzed how it functions alongside numerous other sites in China to cultivate urbane consumer subjects appropriate to the market-socialist economy.

As a unique form of economic enterprise, market-socialism may also be understood as a sort of assemblage pieced together in part from recombinant elements of the country's earlier protocapitalist and socialist eras. With the introduction of economic reforms in the SEZs of southern China, the country's leaders chose not to simply replace the socialist system with a market economy. Instead, they sought to merge various exogenous markets with China's existing socialist substratum to create a sui generis composite regime. I have dedicated several chapters of this book to analyses of the various elements of this market-socialist assemblage. I explored how Macau and the other European concessions inspired the exceptional coastal economic zones that enabled the initial market reforms. These zones, along with the postcolonial administrative regions of Hong Kong and Macau, today exemplify the "one country, two systems" regime. By deploying a Maoist-inspired governmental guerrilla policy to test reform initiatives in the zones, then to replicate them "from point to surface," the central government gradually expanded those tentative, self-contained market experiments across the country.

I also explored how the Ming-era Macau formula for managing the country's original European interlopers eventually served as a model policy for the postcolonial Macau government's casino concession arrangement, through which Adelson became China's biggest foreign investor and constructed the Cotai resorts that comprise the Venetian Palace. A burgeoning population of new Chinese tourists was necessary to make Macau's posthandover casino liberalization experiment successful. To that end, Mao's Down to the Countryside Movement, with its rustication and reeducation of urban youth, became an exemplary model for China's reform-era tourism program. Today's popular grand tours to Hong Kong and Macau are a fundamental mode of travel for hundreds of millions of the country's postsocialist citizens.

The Macau formula, the Maoist guerrilla policy initiatives, and China's program of tourist reeducation are each central components of market-socialism. However, perhaps the clearest expression in Macau of this innovative socioeconomic hybrid is evident in the remunerative amalgamation of the socialist work unit and the integrated casino resort best exemplified by the Venetian Resort. For residents of China's Maoist cities, the *danwei* was the architectonic expression of socialist utopia. With its innovative combination of work, residence, and community life, organized under the umbrella of cradle-to-grave security provided by the socialist state, the *danwei* was the model of China's own Cherneshevsky-style communist Crystal Palace. Much like the American suburban home, the *danwei* served as a spatial machine by which to produce the proletarian citizens necessary for the regime. Today the integrated resort in Macau adopts the antecedent form of the socialist *danwei,* recasting it into an innovative apparatus of consumer subjectivation.

As Sloterdijk (2013) suggests, once we accept the Crystal Palace as a metaphor for capitalist modernity, we may observe that "the communist-socialist project was simply the second building of the palace project," an egalitarian and aesthetic complement to its American consumer counterpart (176). Market-socialism is therefore the ultimate assemblage of these dual dizygotic palace projects. Adelson's colossal Venetian property is the Crystal Palace of our own age, seamlessly merging communism and capitalism under the logic of the "one country, two systems" regime. As China's longest-enduring foreign territory, and with a colonial history coterminous with the entire trajectory of terrestrial globalization, the postcolonial Macau SAR perseverates the city-state's ancient gateway function to conjoin these two distinct palace projects into an overarching world interior. Once ensconced safely inside the vast, climate-controlled environment of the Venetian Palace, surrounded by every imaginable retail enticement and beneath an expansive bright blue sky complete with white clouds painted on the ceiling, it is impossible to escape the realization that there is no more *outside* to consumer capitalism.[7]

However, this world interior extends beyond the diminutive confines of Macau. In fact, in an inadvertent expression of the guerrilla logic of China's reform-era economic expansion, even the Venetian Palace has been replicated "from point to surface" on the mainland. Today there are multiple Venetians in the PRC, including the Venetian component of Dongguan's South China Mall, one of the world's largest indoor shopping environments; a Venice Garden residential estate in Beijing; and a Venice Water Town in Hangzhou, complete with functioning canals (Bosker 2013; Jewell 2015). It is possible to imagine that the golden globe the Venetian Resort management gifted to that hapless Chinese tourist to commemorate his US$75 million baccarat loss in Macau now decorates an ornate residence in one of these Venice-style Chinese gated communities.

THE FINAL FRONTIER AND THE POSTSOCIALIST SUBJECT

LIVE Baccarat, the electronic gaming machine I analyze in chapter 8, has emerged in Macau at the precise moment at which the city-state finds itself positioned on the final frontier of global economic expansion. The frontier has long played a formative role in global capitalism. Sloterdijk (2013) suggests that the "pure outside" of the planet's vast waterworld provided the initial frontier, a "terrestrial 'yonder'" (77) that propelled the early Iberian maritime explorations. The landed frontier of the Americas was likewise a defining element of European expansion in the New World. As Braudel (1979) says, "The 'frontier,' the open space to be conquered by human settlement, was forever on the horizon of American industry, whether in eastern Peru or southern Chile, whether looking across the Venezuelan *Ilnos* or the wastes of Canada, in the Far West of the United States, the rolling plains of Argentina in the nineteenth century, or even the Brazilian interior north-west of Sao Paulo in the twentieth century" (3:388). Whether waterworld or rolling plains, this frontier was not merely a physical space but also a profound psychosocial condition. The frontier prompted the "nautical ecstasies" of those Catholic Portuguese mariners who sought "transcendence to a horizontal plane" on the planet's oceans, as well as the more earthly devotional sentiments of America's Puritan pioneers. In nineteenth-century North America, where the game of poker originated, the frontier was an unexploited geophysical territory that not only provided the raw materials of enterprise but also provoked the opportunistic imaginary that would enable American industry and eventually propel the United States to global economic hegemony.

Frederick Jackson Turner's frontier thesis locates the frontier in the liminal border between savagery and civilization, symbolically separating our innate animal spirits from the cold calculus of cognitive reason. To conquer the frontier, then, is also to tame those vitalist animal urges. Therefore, in ways that Braudel (or even Arrighi) could not have foreseen, the Chinese frontier is not merely geospatial but biopolitical. It merges the goals of transnational marketplaces and the technocratic state with the molecular comportment of urbane citizen-consumers. Indeed, Braudel's (1979) own description of the maritime era economy of the Far East as a "world in itself" (386) is now an apt characterization of this solitary twenty-first century subject.[8]

As Guattari reminds us, subjectivity is the key commodity of contemporary capitalism. Today capital eagerly seeks access to the potential presented in the protean post-Mao subject. As such, the Macau SAR serves as a laboratory of consumption. The LIVE Baccarat machine is a cybernetic petri dish of accumulation, a sociotechnical apparatus designed by scientists at a biopharmaceutical company and explicitly engineered to engender a Chinese *homo economicus.* This entrepreneur of himself emerges as a calculating citizen-consumer whose discerning conduct, within a circumscribed context of enhanced individual autonomy, is increasingly consistent with the macroeconomic goals of the central government. In this way, an analysis of China's political economy is simultaneously a study of the country's subjective economy.

DOSTOYEVSKY'S CRITIQUE OF *HOMO ECONOMICUS*

With its playful cultivation of a calculating economic egoism, LIVE Baccarat is the embodiment of everything that Dostoyevsky despised about the intellectual and technological forces that constructed the Crystal Palace. His novel *Notes from the Underground* is a rejection of the rationalist assumptions underlying the utilitarian social philosophy of Jeremy Bentham, which informed the utopian reform movements of the nineteenth century; the novel is also a rejection of Bentham's conception of a calculating individual whose behavior is motivated by simple utility—a desire to maximize pleasure and minimize pain.[9] This mechanistic model of motivation is based on a naturalistic utility calculus by which every decision may be quantified and calculated; for modern citizens, the universal metric of this calculus is money. Therefore, the economic actor who maximizes his self-interest in the marketplace personifies Bentham's utopian, utilitarian social order.

At the heart of Dostoyevsky's rejection of both utilitarianism and the Crystal Palace is his critique of what we know today as the *homo economicus;* the rational market actor and calculating entrepreneur of the self. In the prophetic words of Dostoyevsky's Underground Man as he contemplated the bleak future of liberal rationalism, "New economic relations will be established, all ready-made, also calculated with mathematical precision, so that all possible questions will disappear in a single instant, precisely because all possible answers will have been provided." When this rational society is finally achieved, "then the crystal palace will be built" (18).

In his last novel, *The Brothers Karamazov,* Dostoyevsky takes particular aim at the scholarship of Claude Bernard and his nascent neuropsychological conception of individual motivation. The French physiologist, who in 1865 published *An Introduction to the Study of Experimental Medicine,* had proposed the possibility of subjecting the inner environment of the individual, what he calls the *milieu interieur,* to empirical study that he believed would reveal the specific neurochemical mechanisms that determine behavior (Carroll [1974] 2010).

In Bernard's pioneering science of the interior subject we can observe the origin of the same impulse that animates contemporary biopolitical efforts to delineate a corporeal construct such as individual human quality, to calibrate a science of moral behavior, or even to produce a sixty-four-page compendium of guidelines for civilized travel.

The Underground Man feared that when humans are subjected to the graphs, timetables, and test tubes typical of a utilitarian social order, the ultimate consequence would be the loss of free will and the taming of the individual's innate impulses, or man's ultimate reduction by science to a mere machine. Dostoyevsky would have no doubt rejected my own conception in this book of the GBA megamachine, along with the implicit assumption that human subjects are somehow the product of a massive clockwork mechanism. While the megamachine construct may be consistent with Guattari's assemblage ontology, this conflation of man and machine could also be construed as yet another unfortunate projection of the assumptions of nineteenth-century utilitarian social science.

Vital Gambling

Dostoyevsky desired to preserve a vitalist individual impulse that was not amenable to prediction, calculation, or control. One practical way he embraced this mystical vitalism was by gambling on the game of roulette, which he played religiously for a decade in the German spa-casinos in Wiesbaden, Homburg, and Baden-Baden.[10] For Dostoyevsky, gambling on roulette was one potent "socio-economic form of irrationalist rebellion against order" that was available in nineteenth-century industrial society (Carroll [1974] 2010, 132). Much like Chinese baccarat players in Macau, Dostoyevsky deployed his own betting system based in a form of predictive chartism that was in fashion in his day. Gambling is therefore a key to understanding Dostoyevsky's own creative efforts, as well as his protestations against the utopian thinkers who conceived the Crystal Palace.

The American Psychiatric Association's DSM-III provides a metric for assessing gambling addiction, within which at least four of nine possible indicators must be present to confirm the diagnosis. A careful reading of Dostoyevsky's letters and his wife's diary suggests that he actually experienced all nine factors; indeed, Dostoyevsky's severe gambling addiction had a profound effect on his personal life and literary productivity. "During the eight years when he was addicted to roulette, Dostoyevsky wrote *Notes from the Underground* (1864), *Crime and Punishment* (1866), *The Gambler* (1866), *The Idiot* (1868), and *Demons* (1871–2)," notes psychoanalyst Richard J. Rosenthal (2016). "He thus appears to have been simultaneously at his most creative and self-destructive" during this formative period of his life (148).

This addiction was apparently not confined to the roulette table. Dostoyevsky's contract to produce his novella *The Gambler* was itself a high-stakes wager, requiring him to complete a manuscript of a certain minimum length in thirty days or else forfeit the publication rights and the profits of his entire oeuvre for nine years. True to the self-destructive habits of an inveterate gambler, Dostoyevsky submitted the manuscript with just hours to spare in order to collect the publisher's payment and retain ownership of his books.

In his roulette games, Dostoyevsky embraced his innate animal spirits, those vitalist urges that were not reducible to rational calculations or to the logic of simple self-aggrandizement expressed in the utilitarian drive to pursue pleasure and avoid pain. Dostoyevsky's own gambling addiction and his fascination with roulette embodied his critique of both Bernard's science of the interior subject and Bentham's quantifiable, calculating man. Dostoyevsky's embrace of the mystical art of risk on pure chance was an affinity he shared with those seafaring Catholic entrepreneurs who were willing to risk everything for the transcendence of exploration; this affinity is also shared by the high-stakes baccarat players in Macau who wager millions on the random cards dealt to Banker or Player. The electronic baccarat machine is an innovative technological affront to those impulsive animal spirits. The utilitarian gaming machine attempts to discover a rationalist resolution to the vital volatility of baccarat; it seeks to dissolve the game's disruptive potential while simultaneously creating a knowable and predictable economic subject.

A POUND OF FLESH

We may better understand this new economic subject in Macau, as well as the role of the city's Venetian Palace project in China's consumer revolution, if we situate that subject within the historical context of capitalism's origins in the medieval city-state of Venice. I thus return one last time to the transhistorical articulations among Venice and the Venetian Resort.

In Shakespeare's play *The Merchant of Venice,* the titular merchant, Antonio, agrees to loan 3,000 ducats to finance the plan of a friend, Bassanio, to court the wealthy heiress Portia. But as would be typical of the city's budding capitalists, Antonio's cash is tied up in various long-distance ventures in Tripoli, the Indies, and South America. So Antonio seeks a cash advance from a local moneylender, Shylock, who requires an unusual form of corporeal security for the loan:

> Go with me to a notary, seal me there
> Your single bond; and, in a merry sport,
> If you repay me not on such a day,
> In such a place, such sum or sums as are
> Express'd in the condition, let the forfeit
> Be nominated for an equal pound
> Of your fair flesh, to be cut off and taken
> In what part of your body pleaseth me.

The "pound of flesh" that the moneylender demands from Antonio in the event of his failure to repay the loan is a vivid idiomatic synecdoche for the phantasm of embodied debt.[11] The "positivization" of such debt, which was formerly seen as a personal moral failing, is for Sloterdijk the key condition of capitalism; indeed, it enabled the creation of the figure of the entrepreneur (or "debtor-producer") on which the system depends.[12] Sloterdijk suggests that it is the entrepreneur's need to pay off future debts that created the modern business cycle, which is exemplified in the maritime circumnavigation of the globe. "It was the debtor-producers who began to turn the wheel of permanent monetary circulation in the 'age of the bourgeoisie,'" he notes. "The primary fact of the Modern Age was not that the earth goes around the sun, but that money goes around the earth" (46).

The pending threat of bodily harm as a means to lubricate the wheels of commerce is a recurring feature of "adventurer's capitalism" (Weber 1930, 76). Indeed, in a specific religious or politicojuridical context in which there is no actual theological or legal recourse to compel repayment of a loan, such as the junket credit extended to Chinese gamblers to fund wagers on high-stakes baccarat, the implicit threat of potential physical retribution ensures that such debts will be repaid.[13]

The resolution of Shylock's volatile demand for a pound of flesh drives the plot of *The Merchant of Venice* and ultimately prompts Portia's innovative courtroom technicality:

> This bond doth give thee here no jot of blood;
> The words expressly say "a pound of flesh."
> Take then thy bond, take thou thy pound of flesh,
> But in the cutting it if thou dost shed
> One drop of Christian blood, thy lands and goods
> Are by the laws of Venice confiscate
> Unto the state of Venice.

It was a search for the same sort of technical resolution that prompted the hybrid technosomatic innovation exemplified by the LIVE Baccarat gaming device. True to its origins in Catholic Macau, the baccarat machine manages to transubstantiate that wanton pound of flesh, once vulnerable to violent Triad retribution, into a remunerative and renewable form of human capital. Indeed, the machine requires neither "jot of blood" nor "pound of flesh," only the kinesthetic calculations of a discerning entrepreneur of the self. Therefore, the baccarat machine is a scientistic utilitarian triumph over both the ineffable animal spirits of the inveterate gambler and the vital *milieu interieur* of the quality citizen.

THE ONTOLOGY OF CAPITAL

According to Braudel, the ancient Italian city-states of Venice, Florence, and Genoa pioneered the use of the market device of the accounting ledger, financial instruments such as the *colleganza,* and a type of mercantilist trade that produced the planet's protocapitalists and enabled the first genuine world-economy. In 1557, Portuguese navigators participating in this long-distance profiteering founded the city-state of Macau. At the dawn of the twenty-first century, Macau's simulated Venetian Palace is a sort of interiorized and enclosed city-state constructed on the edge of the PRC in a post–Bretton Woods age of financialization that both Braudel and Arrighi suggest is indicative of the "autumn" of American hegemony. Whether China's particular brand of authoritarian capitalism will eventually reach planetary predominance is anyone's guess, but there can be no doubt about the resiliency of capital and its capacity for continual reinvention in the opaque zone in which it operates.

In 2012, Wan "Broken Tooth" Kuok-Koi emerged from a fourteen-year sentence in Macau's Coloane prison to become the chairman of a fraternal Chinese order called the World Hongmen History and Culture Association, which boasts several hundred thousand members around the world. Each individual inductee into the Heaven and Earth Society, or Tiandihui, the precursor to the modern Chinese Triads, concludes a ritual covenant of commitment under the watchful eye of both heaven and earth; each symbolically adopts the shared surname Hong to denote his membership in the group (Haar 2000). The World Hongmen History and Culture Association is therefore a striking public affirmation of the ongoing relevance of the global Triad brotherhood.

In 2018, Broken Tooth participated in the launch, by a company called World Hong Men Investment ("Hung Mun" in Cantonese), of the world's largest cryptocurrency initial coin offering (ICO). The stated goal of the Dragon Coin ICO was to leverage blockchain tech-

Figure 35. Wan "Broken Tooth" Kuok-Koi is released from Coloane prison on December 2, 2012. *Courtesy of Getty Images.*

nology to build a Chinese cultural town in Cambodia, which has its own burgeoning casino industry, and to organize chess and poker tournaments in the coastal Chinese SEZ of Hainan. In what might be the final act of convergence among European maritime enterprise and casino capitalism, the money earned from the ICO would also allegedly fund the construction of an eco-friendly floating casino in Norway, which would be transported to Macau upon its completion (Fraser 2017, 2018a, 2018b; Popper and Confessore 2018; Zhang 2018). The company, which employed infamous data broker firm Cambridge Analytica for promotional assistance, claimed that when trading began, the ICO venture raised an astounding US$750 million in less than five minutes. If the ICO goals are fully realized (which of course remains to be seen), the venture's planned issue of one billion Dragon Coin crypto tokens will comprise 1 percent of the entire planetary supply of bitcoin.

This observation brings us to the close of this book in which we have implicitly traced capital's autopoietic emergence and transmutation from armillary spheres to ashtrays, Portuguese carracks to integrated casino resorts, translucent porcelain to plastic dead chips, junket loans to baccarat machines, a usurious "pound of flesh" to remunerative human capital, glittering gold bullion to computational bitcoin. Capital embodies myriad forms of such vibrant matter. But no matter the specific guise, each monetary mutation demonstrates Braudel's crucial insight that *real* capitalism hovers somewhere in the opaque and shadowy zone above the material life of the marketplace.

Epilogue

> Let us not forget that today's so-called consumer society was invented in a greenhouse—in the very same glass-canopied, nineteenth-century arcades in which the first generation of "experience customers" learned to breathe the intoxicating scent of an enclosed, interior-world full of commodities.
>
> —Peter Sloterdijk, *Terror from the Air*

Stephen Soderbergh's 2011 film *Contagion* presents a nail-biting narrative of a fictional viral pandemic that originates in China, and a Macau casino plays a crucial role in the initial global outbreak. In a montage of scenes in the final two minutes of the film, the viewer discovers the origins of the cinematic virus, dubbed MEV-1, and its implicit links to the Chinese urbanization and tourism projects that I have explored in this book. Gwyneth Paltrow plays the part of a Minneapolis businesswoman visiting Hong Kong for the groundbreaking ceremony of a new factory, presumably located in the adjacent SEZ of Shenzhen. Paltrow's character becomes MEV-1 patient zero after she is infected with a recombinant paramyxovirus of pig and bat RNA genomes when she greets a chef during a celebratory meal in a Hong Kong restaurant. The chef's unwashed hands are still bloody from his kitchen prep work on a small pig that he earlier purchased from a Chinese hog farm. The pig, in turn, had eaten an ill-fated piece of banana dropped in his pen by a bat, whose respite was disturbed when a tractor operator clearing land at a China construction site felled a grove of banana trees.

As researchers in the film investigate the provenance of the virus, they study surveillance camera footage from a Macau casino that shows Paltrow playfully placing bets on the Chinese game of Fish–Prawn–Crab, inadvertently infecting several other patrons who handle the same gaming chips. (Incidentally, the film's connections to Macau extend beyond the fictional narrative. Josie Ho, the actress daughter of Macau casino tycoon Stanley Ho, plays the sister of a hapless waiter who collects Paltrow's empty cocktail glass from a table and later becomes the film's first MEV-1 fatality.)

Contagion of course proved eerily prophetic. Less than a decade after the film's premiere (and just as I was completing this book), Macau's tourist industry was devastated by the onset of the Covid-19 pandemic, which may have spread from a wet market in the Chinese city of Wuhan to Macau during the 2020 Lunar New Year celebration. Unlike the filmic portrayal of MEV-1, however, Macau played no substantive role in the global dissemination of Covid-19. Rather, the Macau government reacted quickly to the virus, canceling the city's New Year festivities; systematically locating, quarantining, and repatriating at-risk tourists; closing the city's borders and locking down the local population; and even, in an unprecedented move, shuttering the city's casinos for a two-week period. As a result of these aggressive measures, Macau has arguably been among the safest places in the world in which to endure the Covid crisis, with only a handful of local infections and an admirable portfolio of medical, social, and financial response measures. However, the effects of the virus have ravaged Macau's casino economy, raising lingering concerns about the future viability of the mass tourist movements on which the city relies.

Tourist visits to Macau during the October 2020 National Day Golden Week holiday, a year after the pop-up Hennessey cognac promotion I describe in chapter 9, were 87 percent lower than the same period in 2019. Although many of these visitors continued to gamble in the city, casino profits (and gambling tax revenues) were a mere shadow of their prepandemic numbers. Macau's casinos ended 2020 with a year-on-year 79 percent reduction in gambling revenues (LUSA 2021). In a city almost entirely dependent on casino tourism-related jobs and taxes on gaming receipts, the lack of visitors is simply unsustainable. The Covid pandemic has therefore bared the Achilles' heel of a once-robust economy based almost entirely on the annual foot traffic of tens of millions of Chinese tourists.

CROSSROADS FOR THE CASINO INDUSTRY

Covid-19 coincidentally arrived in Macau at what was already an important historical crossroads for the local casino industry. In December 2022, around the time of this book's publication, each of Macau's six original twenty-year casino operator concessions and subconcessions will expire. The licenses that allow Sands China, Wynn Resorts, MGM, Galaxy Entertainment Group, Melco, and SJM to operate casinos in the city will lapse, and the local government must decide to renew, terminate, or replace each of the gaming licenses, or to even expand the size of the market by soliciting applications for additional concessions. The renewal exercise is also an opportunity for officials to engage in a comprehensive review of the framework of the agreement and to impose new conditions on operators. The stakes became clear when the Macau government's first official statement about the gaming tender in September 2021, to announce a public consultation concerning several proposed changes, prompted a one-day sell-off frenzy of Macau gaming company stocks that resulted in the loss of more than US$18 billion in value in a single twenty-four-hour period (Master and Kwok 2021).

This is therefore a unique moment of reckoning for Macau's entire gaming industry, and the outcome is far from certain. It is indeed impossible to identify another gaming jurisdiction, much less another comparable multibillion-dollar industry, in which an entire oligarchy of operators could simultaneously lose their legal authorization to conduct the primary profit-making component of their business.

It is of course unlikely that the entire set of casino concessions would be canceled. The massive contribution made by the current gaming companies to Macau's posthandover economy is undeniable. Since the original concession agreement was put in place in 2002, Macau's casino concessionaires have invested a combined US$45 billion to construct resort attractions in the city, including adding 26,000 hotel rooms to the city's tourism infrastructure (Moura 2020a). They have generated cumulative casino revenues of more than US$430 billion and contributed tax receipts to Macau totaling US$160 billion, making the city-state one of the world's wealthiest territories. Aside from their economic consequences, however, the concession renewal decisions also have delicate legal and political ramifications for reasons that I will briefly discuss here. The stakes are therefore exceedingly high for all concerned.

In addition, as if to add insult to injury, two Macau gaming visionaries who each played a crucial role in the events I have described in this book have died during the Covid era in relatively rapid succession (although not as a result of the virus). Stanley Ho, the creator of Macau's modern gaming industry, died in May 2020 at the age of ninety-eight after a decade spent mostly bedridden after a fall in his home. American entrepreneur and Venetian Resort owner Sheldon Adelson likewise died in January 2021 of complications stemming from treatment of non-Hodgkin's lymphoma. The Forbes 400 list of world billionaires for 2020 ranked Adelson twenty-eighth; his US$26.8 billion fortune is a stunning recognition of the success of Macau's postcolonial economic experiment (Cohen 2021).

THREE CRISES, AND THE CONCESSION RENEWAL

With the billion-dollar casino concessions in the balance, it would seem that Covid-19 could not have struck Macau at a worse time. However, the sudden spread of Covid only two short years before Macau's concession renewal decision is not a novel phenomenon but rather a remarkable repetition of the actual biopolitical context surrounding the original 2002 licensing agreement. Though the plot of *Contagion* may appear to be a prescient account of the coming Covid era, the film was actually inspired by an antecedent viral event: the 2003 severe acute respiratory syndrome outbreak that originated in China—and that profoundly affected both Macau and Hong Kong—soon after each city's respective reunification with the PRC. I argue in this book that this 2003 virus outbreak was a key factor in the rapid development of Macau's casino industry. It was China's desire to stimulate the postepidemic economies of Hong Kong and Macau that prompted the central government to implement the IVS, which for the first time enabled many mainland citizens to travel to the country's new SARs. It is therefore possible that Covid will prompt other such bold population measures to aid Macau's economic recovery.

However, the context surrounding the 2022 gaming license renewals resembles the original 2002 industry liberalization decisions for more reasons than the unexpected return of the coronavirus. I argue in chapter 4 that it was actually the unanticipated convergence of three distinct crises—those of public health, public order, and public finance—at the turn of the twenty-first century that created the "conditions of possibility" for Macau's postcolonial transformation. That is, the collapse of public order caused by the city's casino wars of the 1990s, the regional reverberations of the 1997 Asian financial crisis, and the fallout from the 2003 public health epidemic each inadvertently helped lay the groundwork for the liberalization of Macau's gaming industry and the rapid ascendance of the city's baccarat-based economy.[1] The 2022 concession decision therefore feels like déjà vu all over again. The prospective renewal of the casino concessions only two decades after their inauguration will similarly take place within a context of converging contingencies that collectively complicate the licensing process. These include not only the Covid-19 pandemic but also increased political tensions between the planet's two remaining superpowers, as well as the ambiguous legal climate created by new Chinese antigambling legislation that targets cross-border gambling by the country's citizens.

U.S.–China Relations

Increasingly strained relations between the United States and the PRC create potential complications for the American-based companies in Macau who are hoping to renew their casino licenses; instead, they may perhaps find themselves unwitting pawns on a larger political chessboard. This is especially true for Sands China, whose late chairman, Sheldon Adelson, was a prominent Republican Party activist and the largest donor to Donald Trump's reelection campaign. However, although Adelson donated $25 million to Trump's failed efforts, this amount pales in comparison to the $2 billion that Sands China committed in 2020 to create a new Londoner theme for the company's Cotai Central property (Moura 2020b).

Perhaps in recognition of this political climate and the emerging contours of a post-Covid global economy, in early 2021, Las Vegas Sands, the parent company of Sands China, threw its full weight behind its businesses in Macau and Singapore. The company announced the historic sale of the original Venetian Resort property in Las Vegas as well as the sale of the adjoining Sands Expo Convention Center for $6.25 billion (Sebastian 2021). Beyond the symbolic importance of becoming an ostensibly Asian company in the lead-up to the concession renewal decision, the move makes sound business sense. In 2019 alone, before the onset of Covid, Sands China's profits in Macau and Singapore totaled US$3.2 billion and $1.2 billion, respectively, while the Las Vegas properties produced company revenues that year of a relatively meager $487 million (Blaschke 2020).

Criminalizing Overseas Gambling

Of additional concern to Macau's gaming industry is the PRC's introduction on March 1, 2021, of new antigambling legislation (Moura 2021a). The new law was prompted by reports from the country's ministry of public security that each year, an astounding RMB 1 trillion (US$157 billion) flows out of mainland China and into cross-border gambling activities (Meneses 2020). The central government has therefore sought to criminalize attempts by foreign operators to lure Chinese citizens abroad to gamble; they also seek to potentially blacklist citizen travel to select gambling-oriented tourist locales such as the Philippines, Cambodia, Vietnam, and Australia. The ambiguous scope of the law, which denotes problematic gambling that occurs "outside the country (borders)," initially made it difficult to comprehend its relevance for the semiautonomous Macau SAR, which is paradoxically positioned both inside and outside of the geographic boundaries of China. It was initially unclear whether the new law might benefit Macau by eliminating regional competition, or whether Macau itself was actually an intended target.

However, Macau's VIP industry suffered a prominent setback with the shocking arrest on November 28, 2021, of Alvin Chau, the founder and CEO of Suncity, Macau's largest junket operator. In recent years, the company has controlled nearly 50 percent of Macau's VIP gaming business. However, the Chinese city of Wenzhou issued a surprise arrest warrant for Chau for alleged links to illegal cross-border casino operations and money-laundering activities in China; Macau authorities arrested Chau and ten accomplices (Baptista 2021). Within a week, Suncity closed all of its VIP rooms in Macau. (The fate of Suncity's resorts and VIP rooms in the Philippines and Vietnam is unclear.) In addition, several Macau casino concessionaires indicated plans to indefinitely shutter VIP rooms managed by other junkets (Moura 2021b). The die was cast with the subsequent arrest in January 2022 of Levo

Chan Weng Lin, the boss of Tak Chun, the city's second-largest junket company. As this book goes to press, it appears to be the unceremonious end of a monumental era in Macau gaming, and the future viability of the city's immensely lucrative VIP industry and innovative dead chip currency hangs in the balance.

Although many of the eighty-five junkets registered in Macau in 2021 may soon go out of business, with numerous employees of those companies facing termination of their jobs, Macau's government probably has the most to lose. Over the past fifteen years, the VIP gambling industry generated US$89 billion in local tax revenues; although the significance of VIP gambling in the local economy has declined in recent years, it still produced one third of the total tax contribution to city coffers in 2019 (Blaschke 2021a). In a postpandemic environment, it will be difficult for authorities to compensate for the disappearance of this massive pool of public money.

Viral Threats and Consumer Atmospheres

As for Covid-19, the virus not only poses a direct threat to Macau's casino economy but also exposes another fundamental contradiction of the population displacement at the root of China's National New-Type Urbanization Plan. In chapter 5, I contend that one potential danger of urbanization for China's central government is the way it inevitably assembles large numbers of citizens in cities in a manner that is conducive to political organization, assembly, and protest. If Macau's massive Venetian Palace structure may be understood as an architectonic resolution to this challenge that urbanization poses to central government authority, then the Covid pandemic exposes an additional viral vulnerability to the government's biopolitical planning.

As China's urbanization initiative crowds hundreds of millions of rural citizens into the country's myriad expanding megacities, the possibility for the incubation and proliferation of further epidemics appears even more pronounced. Aside from the human toll, the coronavirus threatens to contaminate China's carefully crafted consumer atmospherics. In this way, the Covid-era management of Macau's own transient tourist population serves as an experimental micromodel of the government of China's emerging megacity environments.

Perhaps the innovative Individual Visit Scheme, retail velvet ropes, and exclusive VIP gaming rooms that so productively managed Macau's itinerant tourist population during the initial twenty-year concession agreement will eventually be replaced by Covid passports, regulatory travel bubbles, N95 face masks, and other bespoke biopolitical strategies for governing tourist movements in the coming era. In any event, Macau will continue to serve as a unique urban petri dish for those consumer-tourist experiments that originated 150 years ago in the intoxicating atmosphere of Paxton's Crystal Palace. Given the vital importance of the Venetian Palace to both Macau's mass tourism economy and China's consumption regime, it is appropriate that the revamped Londoner property in this world interior of capital features a signature Crystal Palace lobby, whose thirty-three-meter Victorian-style glass-and-iron atrium actually rivals the copious size and greenhouse function of its namesake structure. For now, the Crystal Palace lobby is largely fallow, waiting to be seeded with millions of selfie-snapping tourists.

Acknowledgments

This book has been many years in the making, but it benefited significantly from a 2017 sabbatical that I spent as a visiting research fellow in the School of Design Strategies, Parsons School of Design, New York, as well as from a 2018 Resident Eadington Fellowship granted by the Center for Gaming Research, University of Nevada, Las Vegas. The research for some individual chapters was funded by grants from the University of Macau Research Committee. I am grateful to these institutions for their generous support.

I owe a special thanks to my friend Cathryn Clayton, whose excellent book about Macau has been a major influence on my own thinking, and who carefully reviewed multiple drafts of the book. This research also benefited from the feedback of a number of other scholars who read, reacted, or simply engaged in productive conversations about the subject matter. To that end, I would like to thank the following people, in no particular order: Chua Beng Huat, Michael Feener, Kevin Hannam, Engseng Ho, Benjamin Hodges, Agnes Lam Iok Fong, Kah-Wee Lee, Miodrag Mitrašinović, Martin Montgomery, Andrew Moody, Fiona Nicoll, Philippe Peycam, João de Pina-Cabral, José Luís de Salas Marques, Tony Schirato, Natasha Dow Schüll, and Grahame Shane.

My understanding of the gaming industry in both Macau and Las Vegas has similarly benefited from friendships with many people working in that profession. I am indebted to Nicholas Niglio, who taught me more than anyone about the casino business; he also introduced me to dozens of interesting people over the years who contributed to my analysis. In addition, I would like to acknowledge the insights and assistance of Robert Drake, Buddy Lam, Ralph Lewis, Reggie Martin, Charles Meredith, and Danny Tang. I would also like to thank Paul

Steelman for granting me an interview about Macau's casino archi-tecture, and Andrew Scott for providing permission to reprint photo-graphs from his publications *Inside Asian Gaming* and *World Gaming Magazine.* Finally, Adam Lampton's photographs always somehow de-pict Macau in the same way that I see the city, and I am grateful that he contributed images to my book.

Notes

1. See Dostoyevsky ([1863] 1997). In *Notes from the Underground,* Dostoyevsky was also reacting to Nikolai Chernyshevsky's idealistic invocation of the Crystal Palace as a symbol of socialist utopia in his influential novel, *What Is to Be Done?,* which was published in 1863, soon after the publication of the travel memoir. Dostoyevsky visited the Crystal Palace after the structure was relocated from its original Hyde Park location to the London suburb of Sydenham. On the Crystal Palace, see Katz (2002).
2. Sloterdijk (2013) borrows the phrase "world interior," or "global inner space" (*Weltinnenraum*), from a poem by Rainer Maria Rilke.
3. Ho was originally the semireluctant third partner for the concession bid in a team led by Yip Hon and Teddy Yip, who recruited Ho because of his local connections and business acumen. (Ho was Teddy Yip's brother-in-law.) However, after the successful bid, Ho soon emerged as the company leader and eventually bought out the other partners (Lintner 2003).
4. These include wife number four, Angela Leong, as well as Daisy and Lawrence Ho, two of the five children from Ho's marriage with his second wife, Lucina Ho. On Ho's life, see Cohen (2020).
5. "Indeed, Chinese idioms of neoliberalism specify micro-freedoms for citizens to experiment with—taking care of the self in the domains of livelihood, commerce, consumption, and lifestyles. In the 1990s citizens were urged to 'free up' (*jiefang*) their individual capacities to confront dynamic conditions in all areas of life without seeking guidance from the state, society, or family. There were calls for people to shift from 'relying on the state' (*kao guojia*) to 'relying on yourself' (*kao ziji*). . . . Increasingly individuals are obliged to exercise diligence, cunning, talents, and social skills to navigate ever-shifting networks of goods, relationships, knowledge, and institutions in the competition for wealth and personal advantage" (Ong and Zhang 2008, 8–9).
6. Foucault calls this governmentality, merging the top-down aims of state government with the emergent mentalities of individuals. Sigley (2006) says of governmentality in the PRC, "We have witnessed . . . the emergence of a

hybrid socialist-neoliberal (or perhaps 'neoleninist') form of political rationality that is at once authoritarian in a familiar political and technocratic sense yet, at the same time, seeks to govern certain subjects . . . through their own autonomy" (489).

7. On the percentage of casino revenue in government expenditures, see Tao and Li (2018); on Macau's GDP ranking, see Fraser (2018c).

8. A simple Google search locates numerous academic and popular articles with titles that identify Macau variously as "Las Vegas in Asia" (Loi and Kim 2009), the "Asian Las Vegas" (Wong and Fong 2010), the "Vegas of China" (Dumelo 2016), "Asia's Vegas" (Erheriene 2018), "the orient's Las Vegas" (Yu 2008), and the "Las Vegas of the East" (Sinha 2008). However, a few scholars still refer to Macau as the "Monte Carlo of the Orient" (Kwan 2004; Shi, Liu, and Li 2018).

9. In 1960, "62 percent of Americans could claim they owned their own homes in contrast to only 44 percent as recently as 1940—the biggest jump in home-ownership rates ever recorded. . . . Between 1947 and 1953 alone, the suburban population increased by 43 percent, in contrast to a general population increase of only 11 percent. . . . Over the course of the 1950s, in the twenty largest metropolitan areas, cities would grow by only 0.1 percent, their suburbs by an explosive 45 percent" (Cohen 2006, 49–50).

10. Schwartz (2003) suggests that the gambling regulatory regime that developed in the United States was an expression of a suburban ethos that sought to locate casinos outside of urban areas where they were more difficult to control, and he claims that Las Vegas casino resorts are therefore characterized by a "fundamental incompatibility with urban space" (6).

11. Jewell (2015) makes a similar distinction among suburban shopping malls in the United States and their predominantly urban counterparts in China.

12. Harvey (2012) claims that China today provides a giant reservoir for the global investment of excess capital: "The effects of China's urbanization in recent decades have been simply phenomenal and world-shaking in their implications. The absorption of surplus liquidity and overaccumulated capital in urbanization at a time when profitable opportunities are otherwise hard to come by has certainly sustained capital accumulation not only in China but around much of the rest of the globe over the last few crisis years" (65).

13. Specifically, from 1900 to 1999, the United States' cement consumption totaled approximately 4.4 gigatons (or about 4.4 billion metric tons), while China's consumption for just that recent three-year period was 6.4 gigatons, or 140 percent of America's collective century's worth of cement consumption (Swanson 2015).

14. On England, see McKendrick, Brewer, and Plumb (2018); on France, see Harvey (2006), Miller (1994), and Williams (1982); on the United States, see Cohen (2003) and Leach (1994); on Japan, see Nishimura (2006) and Yoshimi (2006).

15. On China's household savings rate, see Zhang et al. (2018).

16. According to brokerage firm Sanford C. Bernstein, the typical "mass market" gambler in Macau loses 1.2 times more money than an average Las Vegas visitor; a "premium mass" customer loses 14 times more than his counterpart in Vegas; and a VIP gambler loses 54 times more than a Vegas VIP (Moura 2019a).

17. While table games produce the large bulk of Macau's gambling revenues, it is also important to note that Macau's biggest market is VIP gambling, the activities of which are financed and managed by local junket operators and conducted in private rooms. VIP gambling in Macau generates anywhere from 50 to 70 percent of the casino take each year, which makes the local industry fundamentally different from Las Vegas.

18. "It is not absurd to try diagnosing a civilization in terms of the games that are especially popular there. In fact, if games are cultural factors and images, it follows that to a certain degree a civilization and its content may be characterized by its games" (Caillois [1958] 2001, 83).

19. "Gambling, like any social practice, most clearly yields its meaning when it is historicized," says Thomas Kavanaugh (1993, 1) in his study of the culture of gambling in eighteenth-century France.

20. Geertz borrowed this term from philosopher Jeremy Bentham, who coined it in reference to a gambling game with stakes so high it was irrational to play because of the diminishing marginal utility of an individual bet.

21. On the relationship among gambling and Chinese economic behavior, see Basu (1991); on Macau gambling as "deep play," see Chan (2016).

22. The "principal qualities" that Virno (2006) claims comprise the typical "job description" of contemporary capitalism are indicative of casino gambling in Macau: "habituation to uninterrupted and nonteleological change, reflexes tested by a chain of perceptive shocks, a strong sense of the contingent and the aleatory, a nondeterministic mentality, urban training in traversing the crossroads of differing opportunities" (15).

23. My approach is distinct from Geertz's; he interprets play as an activity that has no real consequence, meaningful but ultimately unproductive (Malaby 2009). Geertz suggests that the cockfight "makes nothing happen" and therefore does not change Balinese life itself. In a description of the unproductivity of play remarkably similar to Geertz's, game theorist Caillois ([1958] 2001) claims that play produces "neither goods, nor wealth, nor new elements of any kind." When the game is over, players find themselves "ending in a situation identical to that prevailing at the beginning of the game" (128). In contrast to these approaches, I focus on the efficacy and productivity of play.

24. On the informal educational qualities of train travel, tourism, and other mundane elements of modern society, see Löfgren (1999, 2008). On the city as a site of informal learning, see McFarlane (2011). On leisure as a form of emotional and intellectual labor, see Rojek (2009).

25. The conventional definition of the word *comport* is "to behave" in accordance

with a set of rules or expectations, but I also use it throughout this book to refer to external efforts "to fashion" or "to produce" a certain kind of actor or behavior. That is, *comport* refers to both the effort to mold a subject according to a plan and the subject's complementary attempt to act in accordance with that plan. My use of *comportment* is inspired by Bordieu's (1990) concept of "bodily hexis," which he defines as "a political mythology realized, embodied, turned into a permanent disposition, a durable way of standing, speaking, and walking, and thereby of feeling and thinking" (69–70). My play on this dual meaning of *comport* also mimics Foucault's definition of governmentality as the "conduct of conduct." It denotes both state efforts to direct a mode of behavior with certain ethicoeconomic characteristics and individual attempts to act in accordance with that desired mode of behavior. Thus, with the microphysics of comportment, a political economy of the state merges with a political anatomy of the body to produce a certain sort of citizen-consumer.

26. On the subjective economy, see Lazzarato (2014).

27. The concept of spatial history is derived from Elden (2002).

28. "The history of this 'micro-physics' of punitive power would then be a genealogy . . . of the modern 'soul.' Rather than seeing this soul as the reactivated remnants of an ideology, one would see it as the present correlative of a certain technology of power over the body" (Foucault 1979, 29).

29. My goal in this book is to understand contemporary Macau, so I have not written a history of Macau, although I draw on historical sources in later chapters. For readers interested in Macau's history, Ptak (1998) provides an excellent review of the field before 1998, with helpful English summaries of numerous studies published in Chinese and Portuguese. English-language sources about Macau history, trade, and foreign relations include the following: Alves and Barreto (2009), Boxer (1968), Chang (1934), Cheng (1999), Coates (2009), Gunn (1996), Hao (2020), He (2015), Jesus ([1902] 1984), Mendes (2013), Puga (2013), Tang (2015), and Van Dyke (2011).

30. Although Arrighi and Braudel share much in common, there are important differences in their respective accounts that emanate from their different goals. Braudel provides an empirical description of capitalism's geohistorical expansion, whereas Arrighi develops a theoretical model of accumulation and state hegemony to explain the patterns that are observable in Braudel's narrative. Although these technical distinctions are less important for my own analysis of Macau, interested readers will find a discussion of these differences in chapter 2 and an exploration of Arrighi's theoretical model in chapter 6, where it illuminates my discussion of a type of financial transaction that is unique to Macau's VIP junket industry.

31. With the construction of the Hoover Dam on the nearby Colorado River in 1931, as well as Nevada's legalization of gambling around the same time, the city began a process of rapid growth and reached a population of one million

by 2000. On the history of Las Vegas, see Denton and Morris (2002), Moehring and Green (2005), Rothman (2002), and Schumacher (2015).

32. "So we are now switching to a new pattern," he says. "Instead of going from one container to another, spatially larger, one, we are going from a container with a low population density to containers with high population densities" (Arrighi 2009b, 93).

33. Transnational capital flows into China, as well as into the construction of Macau's Cotai Strip resorts, may be understood as a classic example of the way investment in the built environment provides the material solution to periodic problems of financial overaccumulation that are endemic to capitalism. Lefebvre (2003) referred to such investment in the urban fabric as constituting the "secondary circuit of capital," differentiating it from the "primary circuit" of industrial production. When a particular industrial project has run its course, if the producer is left with excess capital but no profitable means to invest it in further production, he then turns to investment in the production of space itself. This investment in the built environment provides a temporary solution to stave off the inflationary devaluation of those profits.

1. VENICE AND THE VENETIAN

1. In addition, the Cotai Central property's innovative solar thermal-heat pump, powered by 222 solar panels installed on the roof of the Sheraton Hotel Sky Tower, makes it a literal Crystal Palace–style environmental "hothouse." The hybrid plant, the largest of its kind in Southeast Asia, generates 500 megawatt-hours of thermal energy each year—enough to produce sufficient hot water for two thousand hotel rooms (Newsdesk 2020).

2. See Barthes (1957), Baudrillard (1994), and Eco (1986). For a sample of postmodern criticism of Las Vegas–themed environments, see Bégout (2004), Cass (2004), Franci and Zignani (2005), Minca (2005), Raento and Flusty (2006), and Waldrep (2002).

3. On material semiotics, see Law (2008); for a geological perspective, see DeLanda, Protevi, and Thanem (2005). My approach is consistent with the typical assumptions of Chinese tourists who visit Macau, who tend to be less concerned with the authenticity of sites than their western "post-tourist" counterparts (Nyiri 2006).

4. On Venice, see Braudel (1979, 3:116–78).

5. Braudel explains that capitalism actually emerged in synchronous fashion across Venice, Florence, and Genoa, but he selects Venice as the point of origin for several reasons, which are also indicative of Macau. One primary indicator is the fact that Venice's per capita income was much higher than any other European state of the period. Macau's current rank as the world's second-highest per capita GDP likewise positions the city-state as

the figurative birthplace of twenty-first-century Chinese capitalism. In addition, Braudel (1979) says that medieval Venice, much like Macau, was a "town reduced to bare essentials, stripped of everything not strictly urban, and condemned, in order to survive, to obtain everything from trade" (3:108). Finally, he highlights the fact that Venice's entire population lived outside the "primary" economic sector, and all of their activities fell within the secondary or tertiary sectors, much like Macau's tourist economy today.

6. Marxist scholars who remain committed to the labor theory of value, including assemblage theorists such as Deleuze and Guattari (1987), tend to disagree with the claim that Venice is the birthplace of capitalism because trade and financial exchange do not produce value in a Marxian sense (DeLanda 2006).

7. According to this schema, Macau was founded in the world economy in which Antwerp was the core city. We will see that Arrighi ([1994] 2010) defines the entire Venice–Antwerp–Genoa span of domination as what he terms the Genoese–Iberian era of capitalism, in which Italian merchant-bankers cooperated profitably with Spanish and Portuguese navigators.

8. Braudel (1979) draws direct connections among capitalism and gambling. "In the course of this book, the reader will have noticed that reference is often made to the underlying notion of gambling, risk-taking, cheating; the rule of the game was to invent a counter-game, to oppose the regular mechanisms and instruments of the market, in order to make it work *differently*—if not in the opposite direction." These connections involve "a multitude of different and contradictory realities—forward gambling, playing by the rules, legitimate gambling, reverse gambling, playing with loaded dice" (2:578).

9. This accounting technique was a testament to Venice's status as a site of cultural mediation, a role which emerged naturally from its centrality to exchange networks stretching from Christian Europe to the Muslim world; for example, the use of Arabic numbers and algebra were central to this practice.

10. The rhetorical aspects of double-entry bookkeeping included "a series of concise, clear, orderly, and painstakingly correct entries," which led to a "conclusion proving that profits and capital of the business are justly earned" (Aho 1985, 42).

11. Here I borrow the title of an essay on usury in the medieval imagination that was penned by Braudel's Annales School colleague Jacques Le Goff (1990).

12. As one Jesuit father commented, "The merchants have so many tricks for inventing ingenious practices that we can hardly see what is going on at the bottom of it" (quoted in Braudel 1979, 2:565)

13. Setting aside a circumscribed exceptional zone such as the Macau SAR, with a distinct legal and administrative system, and cooperating in governmental projects with nonstate actors such as Macau's casino concessionaires, exemplifies what Ong (2008) calls a state-transnational network. With this type of governmental strategy, the state cooperates with foreign agents in special

programs of population governance that are designed to articulate select segments of the population with global capital.

14. "The whole of the great scheme now working to completion, known as the Crystal Palace, might be properly described as one vast and combined experiment of visual education; and I think it would be easy to show that its educational powers and design constitute its legitimate claims to the support of all civilized Europe" (Hawkins 1854, 444).

15. "With the erosion of basic education in the rural areas as a consequence of the dismantling of rural collectives, migration is celebrated as a substitute to fill the void" (Yan 2008, 124).

16. McFarlane (2011) argues that learning is not simply a cognitive process of knowledge acquisition but rather should be understood "as a distributed assemblage of people, materiality, and space that is often neither formal nor simply individual" (3).

17. Indeed, if we were to make normative assessments of such environments solely in regards to their historical or cultural authenticity, we would be obliged to note that the city-state of Venice today is a sort of simulation or second-order version of itself. By the late eighteenth century, Venice was already something like "Europe's first theme park," which came to be "perhaps the first postmodern city, selling no product other than itself and its multiple images to the tens or even hundreds of thousands of free-spending foreigners who came there annually" (Davis and Marvin 2004, 3). As for the Venetian Resort, Daniel (2018) notes that there is actually something entirely authentic about its relationship to Cotai. While the Venetian is certainly unrelated to Macau's Portuguese or Chinese history or culture, in the context of the two-decade-old tabula rasa Cotai land reclamation, the contrived nature of the Venetian is consistent with the ahistorical context of the immediate environment.

18. The goal of producing "civilized" tourist subjects through cross-border travel is consistent with countrywide campaigns in the PRC to "civilize" the population. In 1997, the Communist Party established a Central Guidance Commission for Building Spiritual Civilisation, which promoted and assessed provincial-level projects to create civilized cities in the PRC that, among other things, involves ensuring healthy and hygienic environments. Cities regulate "uncivilized conduct" (e.g., spitting and smoking); they also encourage positive civic behaviors such as donating blood or organs "by dictating that such noble deeds will be recorded in the person's 'civilised behavior archives', entitling them to benefits including cash rewards and priority in receiving blood transfusions" (Cartier 2013a, 277).

19. "Theories about China's present must more consciously engage how it is built on the past" (Buckingham 2017, 310).

20. In a neoliberal regime, "everything becomes an enterprise: work, but also consumption, not to mention leisure," because the goal is to derive maximum self-benefit from each activity (Dardot and Laval 2013, 267).

2. TERRESTRIAL GLOBALIZATION

1. "It was almost accidental that at the climax of Portuguese pioneering enterprise, the most crucial of all discoveries was made by a Genoese in the service of Spain" (Ralph Davis quoted in Braudel 1979, 3:139).
2. This recounting of Portugal's navigational innovations and long-distance control of global territories is derived from the pioneering work of Law (1984, 1987, 2012). The members of the scientific commission included Master Rodrigo, the royal physician; Diego Ortiz, a former professor of astrology at the University of Salamanca; Martin Behaim, a geographer from Nuremberg who used Portuguese cartographic data to construct the Erdapfel (earth apple), the oldest such globe that survives today; and José Vizinho, a Jewish doctor who studied with a noted Spanish astronomer.
3. "All of a sudden, the Europeans of the early 16th century were expected to understand that in the face of the predominance of water, the planet earth had been named rather inappropriately. What they called the earth was revealed as a waterworld; three quarters of its surface belonged to the damp element" (Sloterdijk 2013, 40).
4. Sloterdijk (2013) contends that the very idea of discovery motivated the Portuguese explorers. He notes that "the central epistemological and political word of the Modern Age" actually "referred not to an autonomous theoretical category, but rather to a special case of the investment phenomenon; and investment is in turn a case of risk-taking" (46).
5. "This importation of a medieval Iberian city to south China represents the incursion of a city model from one tradition into the territory of another," says Lee (2017). "The city that grew out of this incursive settlement made no attempt to be contextual or to integrate with its surroundings. It is by being absolute that the city as a settlement exerted its presence, identity, and autonomy in an unwelcoming foreign land" (110).
6. On the Portuguese and Chinese design influence, see Pinheiro, Yagi, and Korenaga (2005a, 2005b).
7. Evidence of this remarkable trade survives today in the form of Japanese *nanban byōbu* (literally "southern barbarian screens"), colorful paintings that were produced at the time by Japanese artists and that were devoted to the subject matter of the arrival of these Portuguese ships in Japan (Boxer 1968, 20).
8. According to Clayton (2009), the PRC also did not want Macau to be declared a colony because to do so would imply that the city-state's natural telos should be sovereign independence from the colonial power, and the PRC's goal was not an independent Macau but rather Macau's reunification with the mainland.
9. An account by the Tsinghua News Agency captured the moment: "The Chinese residents in Macao are determined to continue to hold high the great red banner of the invincible thought of Mao Tse-tung and pull tighter and

tighter the noose Portuguese imperialism has put around its neck" (quoted in Dicks 1984, 124).

10. Officials followed by handing over seven Nationalist agents to the PRC, prompting Taiwan to complain to the United Nations that Portugal's actions violated the international Convention on the Status of Refugees (Dicks 1984, 118).

11. Amaral's own statue, which was made by the same Portuguese artist, and which depicted him on a horse with a riding crop raised to ward off attacking Chinese villagers, stood near the Lisboa Hotel for many years before it was also removed and eventually repatriated to Portugal (Pina-Cabral 2002). Today Macau's central bus terminal is located in the vicinity of the site where the statue stood and bears Amaral's name.

12. Sloterdijk (2013) notes the following "symbolically laden scenes" denoting the end of terrestrial globalization: "During the Nuremberg Rally of 1937 Hitler had the Behaim Globe brought to his hotel . . . to draw motivation for his imperial plans from the sight of the venerable object. At the Bretton Woods conference in July 1944, the agreement on the gold exchange standard of the dollar and the pound sterling established the first binding world currency of the Global Age; in 1969, American astronauts brought back photographs of the rising earth from the moon voyage" (158). He also cites "1974, the year in which the last Portuguese colonies separated from the motherland in the wake of the Carnation Revolution" (163). However, Sloterdijk apparently overlooks the fact that Macau's actual separation from Portugal occurred only in 1999.

13. The trade enriched both Pedro Lobo, the longtime Malay-Chinese head of Macau's economic affairs department, who lunched with Ian Fleming; and merchant Ho Yin, the father of Macau's first posthandover chief executive, who managed the trade from his Tai Fung exchange post on San Malo, which would later become the Tai Fung Bank.

14. Economists have identified a number of such cycles of varying links: Kitchin cycles of three to four years; Jugler cycles of six to eight years; Labrousse cycles of ten to twelve years; Kuznets cycles of twenty years; and Kondratieff waves of fifty or more years. Braudel (1979) focuses on Kondratieff waves, which are supposed to identify regular and recurring boom-and-bust cycles of capitalism, as well as longer-term "secular" cycles that are theorized to persist for a hundred years or more (3:72).

15. "At all events, these prices that rise and fall in unison provide us with the most convincing evidence of the coherence of a world-economy penetrated by monetary exchange and developing under the already directive hand of capitalism" (Braudel 1979, 3:75).

16. Arrighi ([1994] 2000) identifies four "long centuries" of capitalist hegemony, which more or less correspond with Braudel's model. Arrighi ultimately rejects Braudel's reliance on Kondratieff waves and secular cycles, calling them

"empirical constructs of uncertain theoretical standing" (7), arguing instead for the superior explanatory value of what he calls "systemic cycles," which he derives from Marx's general formula of capital. Because systemic cycles each last more than a hundred years, he poetically identifies them as "long centuries" of capitalist hegemony. While there are differences between Braudel's and Arrighi's arguments, the specific details need not concern us here. It is sufficient to note that both Braudel and Arrighi identify four primary cycles, or eras, which define capitalism's historical development (although they indicate different cyclical logics and time frames for their respective emergence and decline). And both scholars arrive at exactly the same moment, in the early 1970s, as indicative of a profound transformation of global capitalism. Although I will address Arrighi's four "long centuries" in chapter 6, for the moment I will follow Braudel's argument simply to provide narrative coherence to this discussion in Part I.

17. Such crises "mark the beginning of a process of destructuration: one coherent world system which has developed at a leisurely pace is going into or completing its decline, while another system is being born amid much hesitation and delay" (Braudel 1979, 3:85).

18. Indeed, 1975 was the year of New York's technical bankruptcy (Harvey 1991).

19. "We do not know the end of the story, nor consequently the exact meaning of these long cycles which seem to obey certain rules or trends which remain hidden from us" (Braudel 1979, 3:82).

3. GREATER BAY AREA

1. On the National New-Type Urbanization Plan, see Casey and Koleski (2011), Chan (2014), Griffiths and Schiavone (2016), and Looney and Rithmire (2016).

2. Some of this rocky debris is mined from former mountains in the adjacent mainland city of Zhuhai, which were dynamited to make way for the construction of golf courses and other landscaped resort attractions (Chung et al. 2001).

3. Cox (1959), like Braudel, also locates the origins of capitalism in Venice. Although Braudel (1979, vol. 3) rejects Cox's particular rationale for this claim, a close reading of Cox's book finds a number of elements in his account that are central to Braudel's narrative, including the crucial role of core cities to capitalist development, the monopoly characteristic of capitalism, and the role of the state in supporting capitalist enterprise. However, what I take from Cox is his conception of Venice, Florence, and Genoa, as well as the Hanseatic League cities, Amsterdam, and London, as "urban experiments" in capitalist organization (3:139). As this section of the book should make clear, I conceive of both premodern and contemporary Macau as comprising similar urban experiments, with crucial respective roles in the formation and expansion of capitalism.

4. The Greater Bay Area includes eleven cities within the PRD, with a population of sixty-eight million and a combined GDP of $1.3 trillion (Heaver 2018).

5. Of the twenty-five million mainland Chinese tourists who visited Macau in 2018 alone (out of thirty-six million tourists), 41 percent were residents of Guangdong province (Newsdesk 2019b).

6. The centrally organized GBA region is composed of a number of integrated but relatively autonomous elements. The GBA "is a model of multi-tiered urbanism because it is made up of diverse regulatory regimes, physically linked but acting almost like micro-states" (Bie, de Jong, and Derudder 2015, 105).

7. "Following the precedent of establishing Hong Kong and Macao as concessions for trade with foreigners, the Party chose to adopt the enclave model for these new socialist market experiments, designating select regions in the Pearl River Delta as Special Economic Zones" (Chung et al. 2001, 85).

8. In the PRD, "a new ideology was founded, based on parallel regimes of identities. The ensuing dialectic between an inside (perceived as real and Chinese) and an outside (perceived as virtual, or western) pervades the history of modern China. The enclaves, where modernization has been defined in terms of coexistence rather than overall transformation, harbor the juxtaposition between tradition and Western influence. . . . Over time, the Pearl River Delta became the paradigm of Chinese modernization and entrepreneurial spirit, an area where Western interference became assimilated as know-how" (Chung et al. 2001, 83).

9. We will see later that this condition of "no outside," which is also explored in Hardt and Negri's (2000) conception of a contemporary society under the condition of the "real subsumption of capital," is important to my own analysis of Macau's interiorized urbanism. On planetary urbanization, see Lefebvre (2003).

10. My account of the post-Fordist and postcolonial logics of the megalopolis and megacity is indebted to McGrath and Shane (2012), and Haar and Marshall (2012).

11. In its later "Tokyo–Yokohama" iteration, the megalopolis also exemplifies a parallel transformation of Japan's American-influenced postwar economy.

12. The megacity that Castells ([1966] 2000) describes is not a coherent "cultural form" resembling traditional capitalist cities such as Brussels, Amsterdam, or London (368). Rather, Castells contends, "Mega-cities are discontinuous constellations of spatial fragments, functional pieces, and social segments" that do not comprise a coherent cultural whole (436).

13. "The difficulty of trying to force China's development experience into a procrustean bed of conventional categories is not accidental: the dynamics and capacities of China's political system are driven by particular patterns that are ill-suited to such a taxonomic exercise" (Heilmann and Perry 2011, 23).

14. Castells ([1996] 2000) says that the PRD "is not the traditional megalopolis as identified by Gottman in the 1960s on the northeastern seaboard of the United

States. Unlike this classical case, the Hong Kong–Guangdong metropolitan region is not made up of the physical conurbation of successive urban/suburban units with relative functional autonomy in each one of them" (439).

15. According to Campanella (2008), Wu modeled the Guangzhou–Shenzhen Expressway on the North American New Jersey Turnpike, part of the very Interstate 95 defining the Boston-to-Washington corridor at the heart of Gottman's (1964) megalopolis model. In addition, Wu based his 1982 proposal for the construction of the PRD Guangzhou–Yueyang Expressway on the logic of the integrative economic geography provided by New York's Erie Canal. Wu's original inspiration for the Hong Kong–Zhuhai–Macau Bridge was prompted by two American infrastructure landmarks: Virginia's Chesapeake Bay Bridge-Tunnel and Louisiana's Lake Pontchartrain Causeway.

16. In addition, this Chinese internal migration to cities is shaped by such central planning measures as the administration of the *hukou,* or household residency registration; *hukou* closely manages population movements by tying Chinese citizens to particular locales through their acquisition of government services, such as education, and therefore determining where migrating peasants may relocate.

17. Rather than conducting policy analysis and formulating legislation before implementing new measures, the Chinese state often innovates via "implementation first, drafting universal laws and regulations later" (Heilmann 2008, 4). On "guerilla policy," see Heilmann and Perry (2011).

18. According to Heilmann (2008), the PRC practices three main forms of experimentation: "(1) experimental regulation (provisional rules made for trial implementation), (2) 'experimental points' (model demonstrations and pilot projects in a specific policy domain), and (3) 'experimental zones' (local jurisdictions with broad discretionary powers)" (5).

19. Castells ([1996] 2000) claims that "the Information Age is ushering in a new urban form, the informational city" (429); see also Castells (2002).

20. The key to Castells's ([1996] 2000) theory of globalization is the information network, which he contends has transformed terrestrial space into a "space of flows." Globalization has caused the mass or volume of physical space to be subsumed by what he calls nodes, nodal points, and hubs. But Sloterdijk (2016) cautions that using such "textile metaphors" common to network theory "encourages a tendency toward despatialization or disregarding space," by understanding it through analogies of "nets," "weaves," or "tiny nodes." "In network thinking there are only interfaces and points derived from the model of two or more intersecting planes or curves," he says (155). In his "sphereology," Sloterdijk proposes not points or nodes but rather the Leibnizian monad, represented by the bubble, cell, or capsule, and which comprises a "micro-world" (156). I adopt this "worlding" approach in my attention to the importance of environments such as the Venetian's interiorized city

(see also Roy and Ong 2011). As Sloterdijk says, an entire world may be encompassed within a point.

21. With this interest in the persistence of former spatial forms in the region, I take issue with the Harvard Design School's characterization of the socialist-era PRD as a tabula rasa (see also Buckingham 2017). This recombination of prior spatial forms exemplifies a Chinese case of what David Stark has called (in the context of socialist Eastern Europe) "playing capitalism with non-capitalist pieces" (Stark and Bruszt 2001, 1129).

22. "The kind of mind that designed the pyramid was a new human type, capable of abstraction of a high order, using astronomical observations for the siting of the structure, so that each side was oriented exactly in line with true points of the compass. . . . But the workers who carried out the design also had minds of a new order: trained in obedience to the letter, limited in response to the word of command descending from the king through a bureaucratic hierarchy, forfeiting during the period of service any trace of autonomy or initiative; slavishly undeviating in performance" (Mumford 1971, 318).

23. As Gary Genosko (2016) says of what Guattari calls the subjective city: "Given that Guattari relies on the concept of the megamachine borrowed from Lewis Mumford in order to describe large machinic assemblages at the scale of urban agglomerations, he has a specific usage in mind: to discover the ways that cities produce subjectivities" (242).

24. "The material infrastructure, communications and services of cities cannot be separated from functions that may be described as existential. Megamachines model sensibility, intelligence, inter-relational styles, and even unconscious phantasms" (Guattari quoted in Genosko 2016, 242). As such, Guattari was cognizant of the need to transcend methodological cityism: "If there is only one machine in the future, it is a planetary city whose 'diverse components are scattered over every surface of a multipolar urban rhizome encircling the planet'" (243).

25. Castells's ([1996] 2000) example is the unlikely but complementary development of the Mayo Clinic in Rochester, Minnesota, and the French health administration's cancer treatment facility in the Paris suburb of Villejuif.

26. Shenzhen was the site of what Heilmann (2011) calls practice-based epistemology, and a wide variety of innovations were pilot tested in the SEZ.

27. "In fact, the Special Economic Zones share many characteristics with the old colonies. Both were created to serve a particularly elite group of people that brings in foreign capital, expertise, and other social or cultural conventions. Both draw on the immense, disadvantaged pool of cheap labor from the hinterland to fuel the growth of the exclusive territories. Both enjoy preferential treatment, with policies and tax incentives to accelerate development. Both, without reservation or hesitation, exacerbate the differences between the protected territory and surrounding regions" (Chung et al. 2001, 440).

THE CRYSTAL TOWER

1. This account of the attack is culled from Boxer (1949), Garrett (2010), and Pinheiro, Yagi, and Korenaga (2005a).
2. The architect claimed to have been inspired by the Vegas showgirl, whereas Ho indicated that the building is meant to resemble a lotus, the symbol of Macau's posthandover government. On "profane illumination," see Cohen (1995).

4. MACAU SAR

1. My account of the casino wars is drawn primarily from Clayton (2009), Lintner (2003), and Pina-Cabral (2002, 2005); see also Simpson (2011).
2. Street Market is known as both Ng Wai and Ng Man-Sun. Although Ng is the surname, he is commonly called Wai or Market Wai. Broken Tooth's surname is Wan, but he is routinely referred to as Broken Tooth Koi.
3. "The newspapers kept a running toll of annual homicide rates, 21 murders in 1996; 29 in 1997; 30 in 1998; 42 in 1999" (Clayton 2009, 70).
4. In her analysis of contemporary Asian architecture and urbanism, Ong (2011) highlights Foucault's concept of the urban milieu: "Foucault counsels us to consider the city as a milieu, or 'field of intervention' in which individuals, populations, and groups put into conjunction of elements and events that circulate beyond the site itself," and Macau today is such a "field of intervention." Ong instructs attention to "the array of problem-solving and spatializing practices that are in play in shaping an urban world" (10).
5. This understanding of Chinese planning is consistent with a more general tendency in traditional Chinese thought to understand present conditions not in terms of cause and effect but in terms of situational disposition or propensity (Easterling 2013; Jullien 1995; Keith et al. 2014). Disposition is captured in Foucault's notion of the *dispositif,* or apparatus, which locates a nascent positivity or potential in a configuration of diverse factors (Hillier and Cao 2011; Pløger 2008).
6. Two decades later, that Macau businessman, Ng Lap Seng, would be jailed in the United States for bribing U.N. officials in an effort to persuade the United Nations to build a conference facility in Macau (Associated Press and Reuters 2018).
7. This account of Adelson's meeting in China is from Bruck (2008).
8. This was revealed during testimony from a government official during one of the three Suen trials (Las Vegas Sands Corp. 2016; Sanders and Stanley 2006; Stutz 2008). The concept of the subconcession, which under Portuguese law is normally applied to subcontractors who are appointed by a monopoly concession, such as an electric or gas company, is attributed to Portuguese civil law practitioner Marcelo Caetano, who incidentally also served as Portugal's

prime minister after Salazar's death. Caetano's regime was overthrown in the country's 1974 Carnation Revolution (Ascensção 2017).

9. When the New Jersey Gaming Commission conducted an investigation of Pansy Ho's suitability as an MGM partner (given that MGM operated Atlantic City's Borgata Casino within the commission's jurisdiction), investigators discovered that of Pansy Ho's $80 million equity contribution to the Macau joint venture, $72 million (or 90 percent) was a gift from her father, Stanley Ho (Milgram and Lichtblau 2009).

10. Readers will note the similarity to the 2020 coronavirus pandemic, which occurred while this book was being completed.

11. These formative integrated resort experiments include Kerkorian's MGM Grand, which was the world's largest resort when it opened; Wynn's opulent Mirage, Treasure Island, Bellagio, and Wynn properties, which attracted a new tourist clientele, one willing to pay expensive hotel rates and patronize fine restaurants and art galleries; and Adelson's Venetian and Palazzo properties, which are linked to the adjacent Sands Expo Convention Center, whose regular tourist traffic helps ensure hotel occupancy during otherwise slow weekdays.

12. One observer of the Lisboa VIP rooms in the early 2000s remarked in a blog post: "I think they should pool their money together to chip in for a remodel, because the parts I saw were straight out of a *Remington Steele* episode. There's terrible carpet on the floor and the wood panel on the walls looks like it came from the side of an 80's station wagon. Most of the rooms are done up in gold but the designs are so dated that the intended effect of projecting prestige or power just backfires completely" (https://wizardofmacau.com/en/casinos/lisboa).

13. These include the Mirage, Desert Inn, Tropicana, and Genting's Resorts World in Las Vegas; Australia's Gold Coast Resort; Caesar's Atlantic City; Nagaworld in Phnom Penh, Cambodia; and Grand Ho Tram Strip in Vietnam. After completing the Sands, Steelman participated in the design of a number of other Macau projects for several different concessionaires, including the Four Seasons Resort, which is part of Adelson's Venetian complex; SJM's Oceanus; and both Galaxy Resort in Cotai and a redesign of the casino inside of the company's StarWorld Resort on the Macau peninsula.

14. My analysis of the Sands design is drawn primarily from an interview I conducted with Steelman in July 2018, but it is also informed by two podcast interviews in the UNLV Special Collections (Steelman 2011a, 2011b).

15. See also the 2007 Forbes 400 list (http://www.forbes.com/lists/2007/SA/richlist07 Sheldon-Adelson-ER90.html).

16. I agree with Rebecca Cassidy's (2009) suggestion that in regards to financial markets, "the expression 'casino capitalism' is a conflation of a particularly unhelpful kind" (10). Whereas contemporary finance is characterized by the radical uncertainty that underpins the enterprise, casinos deal not in

uncertainty but in risk, where the outcomes are clearly known. "The uncertainty of international finance is not reproduced in the casino, where returns are a direct reflection of the game and the stake, and the probabilities are fixed and calculable," she says, which makes the analogy misguided (13).

5. INTEGRATED RESORT

1. These new structures are far too numerous to catalog, but examples include UNStudio's Hanjie Wanda Square luxury mall in Wuhan; the angular Aedas-designed Starlight Place shopping center in Chongqing; and Beijing's Sanlitun Village, a sprawling shopping complex designed by Japanese architect Kengo Kuma and modeled after *hutong* and *siheyuan,* traditional Chinese alleys and courtyard homes. Some of these shopping environments have a distinct didactic quality. For example, the unique "Play Stack" kid's themed mall in Shenyang is specifically designed to appeal to children and to serve as a community "third place" for family gatherings, while the 123+ Kindergarten in Shanghai is a Montessori method educational facility integrated with a shopping center.

2. On reclamation sites as enclaves within Macau, see Daniel (2018).

3. As Haldrup and Larsen (2006) argue, "Cultural studies in tourist studies have been dominated by a visual or representational paradigm that has examined material culture in relation to 'symbolic value' through semiotic analysis with the result that the 'use-value' of things have been trivialized" (276).

4. Steelman designed the Sands Casino in Macau, undertook the original planning for the Venetian Las Vegas and master planning for some components of the Venetian Macau, and designed Macau's Four Seasons Resort.

5. Jewell (2015) describes a similar stratification in Shanghai's Plaza 66 shopping mall, where the general public may engage the mall at street level while affluent customers are escorted to private underground rooms, where they browse products assisted by a personal attendant.

6. *Suzhi* is a significant component of Chinese educational theory. Understood as both a set of anatomical characteristics and an innate potentiality that is subject to enhancement, *suzhi* comprises a human developmental theory. In a case where an individual's *suzhi* appears defective or an impediment to development, it "may be corrected through pedagogical means" (Lin 2017, 6).

7. In late 2017, the Macau government suspended the Malo Clinic operations for allegedly providing unauthorized services in oncology and assisted reproduction technology, as well as trafficking illegal anticancer medicines from China (*Macau Post Daily* 2017).

8. Key to Callon's conception of the market device is that "the subject is not external to the device," as in the case of an autonomous actor who mobilizes a piece of inanimate equipment to complete a task; rather, "subjectivity is enacted in the device" (Muniesa, Millo, and Callon 2007, 2).

9. An instructive model for the integrated resort in this literature (especially when we take into account the VIP rooms and gaming machines I discuss later) may be found in Beunza and Stark's (2004) analysis of arbitrage techniques in a stock trading room. They argue that these techniques are enabled by the specific sociospatial and sociotechnical configurations of the trading room design, including the arrangement of desks and spatial atmospherics, as well as the distributed calculations that emerge across the arbitrageurs' shared computational metrics, formulas, cognitive frames, and Bloomberg terminals.

10. Marx contends that the way in which the urban industrial factory collected together otherwise isolated rural workers and created the means for their affective associations meant that the factory was not only a site of labor production but also of potential working-class enlightenment and organization. Hardt and Negri (2009) argue that under contemporary conditions of biopolitical production and planetary urbanism "without an outside," the city itself takes on this potential revolutionary function: "The metropolis is to the multitude what the factory was to the industrial working class" (250).

11. "Bigness no longer needs the city: it competes with the city; it represents the city; it preempts the city; or better still, it is the city" (Koolhaas 1997, 505).

12. "Spectacle is not primarily concerned with looking at images but rather with the construction of conditions that individuate, immobilize, and separate subjects, even within a world in which mobility and circulation are ubiquitous" (Crary 2001, 74).

6. VIP ROOM

1. "Without being imprisoned by geographical determinism or rigidly sequential history, one can make a pertinent use of Braudel's interpretations of the Mediterranean in the Asian context for several reasons. The Mediterranean may be viewed simultaneously as maritime space, a trading crossroads and a link between different civilizations; but it may also be seen as a transnational space, within which several autonomous cities and urban regions, jointly controlling the flows of goods and money, make up together a matrix of economic supremacy" (Gipouloux 2011, 9)

2. "If Venice was the prototype of all subsequent capitalist states," contends Arrighi (2010), "the Genoese diaspora of merchant bankers was the prototype of all subsequent nonterritorial systems of capital accumulation on a world scale" (83). Braudel (1979) likewise says, "To me Genoa seems to have been, in every age, the capitalist city par excellence" (3:157).

3. Shadow banking essentially means any financial lending that happens outside of conventional banks (Collier 2017).

4. For Schoon (2014), the key to China's "experimental urban governance" in the PRD is a strategy of "conceded informality," whereby the authoritarian state

allows local governments "creative freedom for trying out new measures" (195), such as this engagement with Chinese diasporic capital. This conceded informality is not an occasional anomaly of governance but rather may be understood as a strategic component of the "practice-based epistemology" that undergirds Chinese policy innovation (Heilmann 2008, 5). Such informality has long been conceded to Macau by both China and Portugal, and we will see that such creative informal approaches to local problem solving are also an important element of Macau's gaming industry.

5. The Kimren Group agent who disappeared with $1.3 billion is from the Chinese city of Guizhou.

6. East Asia developed indigenous business platforms like South Korea's family-owned chaebol, which have not been fully integrated into the international corporate-capitalist system.

7. On the PRC's practice-based policies, see Heilmann (2011).

8. For discussion of Macau's junkets, see Lam (2013), Lam and Eadington (2009), Leong (2002), Lo and Kwok (2017), Siu (2007), Wang and Eadington (2008), and Wang and Zabielskis (2010).

9. Dead chips are also used in some regional gambling locales, such as Cambodia, that Macau has inspired, and in which the same junkets operate.

10. The Portuguese presence in Macau must be understood within the context of the Sinocentric tribute-trade system that prevailed in the region before their arrival. According to Takeshi Hamashita (2008), "Westerners newly arrived in Asia during and after the sixteenth century, particularly the Portuguese and Spanish, had to participate in an intra-Asian trade network that already existed in order to obtain the goods they wanted" (13).

11. Braudel ([1949] 1995) observes in the context of the Mediterranean that city-states are "much lighter machines than the cumbersome territorial states" (117).

12. Indeed, while visiting the city in 2019, Xi Jinping announced plans to make Macau a financial hub, including the creation of a yuan-denomination stock exchange in the city, and allegedly sought to implement the Macau model in Hong Kong (https://www.cnbc.com/2019/12/12/china-set-to-award-protest -free-macau-with-financial-policy-rewards.html).

13. "At the time of the rise and full expansion of the Genoese regime, the Republic of Genoa was a city-state small in size and simple in organization, which contained very little power indeed. Deeply divided socially, and rather defenseless militarily it was by most criteria a weak state in comparison with and in relation to all the great powers of the time, among which its old rival Venice still ranked fairly high. Yet, thanks to its far-flung commercial and financial networks the Genoese capitalist class, organized in a cosmopolitan diaspora, could deal on a par with the most powerful territorialist rulers of Europe, and turn the relentless competition for mobile capital among these

rulers into a powerful engine for the self-expansion of its own capital" (Arrighi and Silver 2001, 264–65).

14. Braudel (1979, vol. 1) cites the example of gold in the Middle Ages as a monopoly currency held by select capitalists, while ordinary people had only copper.

15. While Adelson's beneficence has raised such questions concerning the role of Chinese casino revenues in domestic U.S. politics, an investigative report commissioned by Adelson's own company claimed that Chinese central government authorities have symmetrical concerns that American intelligence agents working for the CIA or FBI may have potentially used Adelson's casinos to monitor Chinese government officials who gamble in Macau (McGreal 2015).

16. According to one study, between 2000 and 2011, illicit financial flows from China abroad, not including the country's trade with Hong Kong and Macau, totaled US$3.79 trillion (Kar and Freitas 2012). The *New York Times* reported that in 2015 alone, China lost US$1 trillion to gray-market cross-border transfers as citizens used a quasi-legal method colloquially known as smurfing to move cash out of the country to offset the falling value of the RMB (Bradsher 2016).

17. Although we cannot know the exact number of mainland officials who were regularly visiting Macau before the corruption crackdown, one empirical analysis of the effects of corruption arrests in Shanxi province demonstrates a correlation among the crackdown and declining number of visits by officials from that province to Macau (Tao and Li 2018).

18. The Macau Monetary Authority requested that the city's banks provide lists of high-risk local businesses that use the UnionPay banking system, particularly specifying transactions involving "watches and jewelry, wine, pharmaceutical products, dried seafood and telecommunications businesses," thereby identifying the typical facilitators of such gambling-oriented movements of cash (Fraser and Ap 2014). In addition to controls on spending, the central government also prohibited Chinese officials from gambling in Macau, and it required the installation of "Know Your Customer" facial recognition technology on all Macau bank machines that process UnionPay transactions.

19. We may understand this tripartite confluence in the PRC of Hong Kong's Umbrella Movement, China's corruption crackdown, and Macau's smoking regulations, respectively, as a reprise of the "three crises" of public order, public finance, and public health that I discuss in chapter 5.

20. Both Adelson and Wynn served on Trump's inaugural committee.

21. Arrighi (2010) argues in the postscript to the updated edition of *The Long Twentieth Century,* "To use Braudel's imagery, each and every financial expansion is simultaneously the 'autumn' of a capitalist development of world-historical significance that has reached its limits in one place and the 'spring' of a development of even greater significance that is beginning in another place" (374).

22. On the resurgence of "medieval modernity," see Alsayyad and Roy (2006).
23. Braudel actually alternates between references to "real" and "true" capitalism.
24. In China, "Shadow banking has been the glue that has tied the capitalist and non-capitalist economy together in one untidy bundle," constituting what one Chinese political scientist calls a "parallel political economy" (Collier 2017, 8).

7. PORCELAIN ASHTRAYS

1. A 2012 Gallup poll indicated that there were 320 million adult smokers in China, and nearly two thirds of China's male population smoked at least occasionally (McCartney 2016). On the relations among smoking and gambling, see McGrath and Barrett (2009).
2. Cigarettes are a crucial component of everyday acts of camaraderie among mainland Chinese men, who exchange them in a common ritual of social interaction (*fayan*). The authors of one study of tobacco sharing in China contend, "It is difficult to overestimate how important this trading of individual cigarettes can be for men in Chinese society" (Rich and Xiao 2011, 259).
3. In 2014, frontline casino workers formed an association and organized upward of a dozen public demonstrations to voice their demands for better pay packages, promotion opportunities, and working conditions. On Macau casino workers' complaints about smoking, see Bloomberg (2014), Wan and Pilkington (2009), and Wong (2016).
4. Macau's health bureau reported that by the end of April 2019, thirty-one of Macau's thirty-five casinos had a combined total of 546 government-authorized smoking rooms (Moura 2019b).
5. For discussions of Macau gamblers throwing ashtrays, see Lam (2015) and Woodhouse (2015).
6. I learned this figure from an executive working in one of Macau's largest junkets; the cost was mentioned in relation to a specific VIP room constructed within a Wynn property in Macau, circa 2018. Wynn also constructed an adjacent VIP room for another large junket operator for a comparable cost.
7. Incidentally, Jingdezhen today exemplifies the importance the central government ascribes to national tourist sites. Not only is Jingdezhen listed as a UNESCO Creative City of Crafts and Folklore, but China has also bestowed on the city the titles of National Excellent Tourism City, with nineteen designated A-level scenic spots; National Famous Historical and Cultural City in China; and National Forest City, with 66.66 percent forest coverage (Zhang et al. 2020).
8. For a clever discussion of the formative role of ambergris and opium in the very existence of Macau, see Wu (2002).
9. The addictive attraction of Chinese porcelain has apparently not entirely abated. In 2006, casino concessionaire and art collector Steve Wynn purchased an early Ming-era porcelain vase at an auction in Hong Kong for a

record-setting US$10.2 million and donated it to the city of Macau (Pierson 2013). In 2011, Wynn set another record when he acquired a set of four ormolu-mounted porcelain vases for $12.7 million—more than double the previous record price for that specific type of porcelain object.

10. Over the long term, and assuming a high volume of play, the house theoretical-win average for baccarat is 2.85 percent (Oliver 2009).

11. "In Las Vegas, Harrah's got out of the high roller baccarat market after losing money in that segment. CEO Gary Loveman was quoted as saying 'it didn't make sense' to have 10,000 to 12,000 people enjoying themselves in your property but be nervous that one 'whale' in the high limit room could undo it all" (Newsdesk 2009).

12. In a similar case, Las Vegas Sands recorded a net loss of US$48.5 million in Q3 of 2007, which was attributed in part to baccarat volatility in VIP gaming in the company's Macau properties. The company's president and CEO said about the loss at the time, "We got shellacked. It is what it is" (Newsdesk 2009).

13. As Strange (1998) says in her follow-up to *Casino Capitalism,* "The dominant theme of the book to which this is some sort of sequel was—in a word— volatility. That word seemed to sum up how the international monetary and financial system had changed in the twelve years between 1972/3 and 1984/5, when the book was written" (4).

14. The term "animal spirits" refers to "contagious spirits like confidence, fear, 'irrational' exuberance, bad faith, corruption, confidence, a sense of fairness, and the very stories we tell ourselves about our economic fortunes, with all the push that they encapsulate" (Thrift 2008, 84). Thrift's discussion links disposition, animal spirits, and the history of smoking in China.

15. On animal spirits, see also Dow and Dow (2011), Koppl (1991), and Thrift (2008).

16. The plot of the first Bond novel, *Casino Royale,* revolves around a competition between Bond and his criminal nemesis at the baccarat table, although in the 2006 version of the film by the same name, baccarat has been replaced with No Limit Texas Hold 'Em poker.

17. For a discussion of the historical evolution of baccarat and the nature of probabilities related to different versions of the game, see Ethier and Lee (2015).

18. The names are merely symbolic in this version of the game, although these positions are significant in other versions.

19. In Macau casinos, players may also bet on whether the first two cards dealt to either the Player or the Banker position will be a pair—for example, a pair of 4s.

20. The rules for drawing the third card benefit the Banker position, which makes the odds of Banker win slightly higher; therefore, the casino generally takes a 5 percent commission from Banker wins (although there are also no-commission baccarat games with slightly different payout rules).

21. On the number of superlative cars in Macau, see Lee (2017) and Newsdesk (2015). In addition, in 2014, the company constructing The 13, a Versailles-inspired Macau resort property billed as the world's most luxurious hotel, placed an order for thirty bright red Rolls-Royce sedans that were to serve as the hotel's limousine fleet. The order—the largest ever commission in the history of Rolls-Royce motor cars—included two flagship models whose solid gold accoutrements and diamond-studded company logos made them the most expensive Rolls-Royce vehicles ever produced (Keegan 2016).

22. In the words of one *Wall Street Journal* headline, "China Prods Macau to Be More Like Las Vegas" (https://www.wsj.com/articles/china-presses-macau -revamp-as-gambling-revenue-plunges-1441101284).

23. The variation includes on-Strip and off-Strip casinos (Schwartz 2018).

24. Although Hughes (1976) initially dismisses baccarat as "a tedious and boring game, as insubstantial as a morning mist cleared by the rising sun," he rightly acknowledges that for truly devoted players, when the stakes are sufficiently high, "the game probably provides the only situation in which they feel vicariously alive" (77).

25. This thing power may be understood as a sort of ontological animism that is inherent in the cards. See Melitopolous and Lazzarato (2012).

26. In support of this observation, one study of Chinese gamblers in a Macau casino who were wagering on the game Big–Small found that in situations where successive outcomes occur in random fashion, those gamblers tended to endorse the psychological fallacy of "positive recency," or the belief that the next outcome will be the same as the last outcome. Previous studies conducted among gamblers betting on roulette in Reno, Nevada, as well as lottery players in the U.S. state of Maryland, found those gamblers more likely to exhibit the fallacy of "negative recency," or the belief that the next outcome will differ from the previous one (Fong, Law, and Lam 2014).

27. The term "social factory" was developed in Italian Marxism in the 1960s to reference the way in which the entire contemporary social fabric was becoming increasingly subsumed by the capital relation (or what theorists of Italian autonomism or *operaismo* refer to today as the "real subsumption" of society to capital). Even those sites outside of the specific production regime may take on factory characteristics, such that we may understand the leisure space of the casino today to be homologous with the overarching logic of contemporary labor.

8. BACCARAT MACHINES

1. Both New Century and Kampek Paradise are so-called satellite casinos—privately owned properties licensed under SJM's gaming concession in a profit-sharing agreement with the host company.

2. Typically the lowest minimum bet allowed on conventional baccarat in the main casino area is HK300 per hand, and the highest is typically HK3000 per hand.

3. Here I am drawing on Mao's concept of the "mass line," which may be the most important "Chinese characteristic" that the PRC contributed to European Marxism. Mass line development refers to the idea that socialist governmental policies are ideally not centralized, top-down commands but rather are diffused throughout the entire society and embodied by citizen-producers at the basic social level. Mao believed that the socialist transition should involve a widening scale of increasingly enlightened and self-motivated communities of producers who would contribute to material social development. The members of these communities would come to recognize their own individual interests as congruent with the interests of the state and society. "'Self-reliance,' for which Dazhai brigade became noted, would come to have a political and rational component, as well as economic significance at mass levels" (Meisner 1978, 29). We will see a similar confluence of political, rational, and economic components in the baccarat apparatus, as well as the development of a mass line of responsible and self-reliant consumers necessary to market-socialism.

4. As LifeTec (2005) notes in a press release, "The world has never been free from the imminent threat of an epidemic where the moment of the possibility of a major outbreak is a concern of the public." In the same release, the company for the first time announces the subsidiary LT Capital Limited and its use for "non-biopharmaceutical investments" in the LIVE Baccarat gaming system.

5. "*Homo economicus* is someone who accepts reality," says Foucault (2004, 269). "Rational conduct is any conduct which is sensitive to modifications in the variables of the environment and which responds to this in a non-random way" (269). The manner in which *homo economicus* has been mobilized to respond to environmental modifications in a rational—that is, nonrandom—manner, makes the subject "eminently governable" (270).

6. That is, to understand how individuals shop, invest, or otherwise engage in daily economic activities, their actions must be considered "alongside other cultural, social, or affective elements which combine to determine choice" (McFall 2009, 269).

7. Although I have conflated these positions for the sake of convenience, we can actually differentiate the so-called new economic sociology of embeddeness (Granovetter 1985; Polanyi 2001; Zelizer 2013) and the economic anthropology of consumption (Miller 2002). For Callon's reaction to each of these approaches, see Çaliskan and Callon (2009).

8. According to Väliaho (2014), under neoliberal processes of economization, "the market rationality of investment-cost-profit is seen as something that

needs to be developed and disseminated across all dimensions of life," and with LIVE Baccarat, this rationality characterizes the casino game (19). Väliaho focuses specifically on the game's modification of the brain to serve as a locus of capture under the neoliberal regime. However, in my study of the economic calculation endemic to electronic baccarat, to focus so specifically on the brain, neuroscience, and the "cerebral subject" (20) risks conflating the study with the assumptions of neoclassical economics. For this reason, I focus on embodied calculation.

9. Interestingly, squeezing also crumples and creases the edges of the cards; the cards are destroyed in the process and discarded after each hand. This emphasizes another way in which Macau's *punto banco* baccarat is differentiated from poker, which is played with a single deck of cards that may conceivably be reshuffled and reused. Macau baccarat is therefore not merely a simulation of production, like poker, but is a genuine form of consumption, where the gaming materials are actually used up in the process of gambling.

10. "Where capitalistic acquisition is rationally pursued, the corresponding action is adjusted to calculations in terms of capital. The important fact is always that a calculation of capital in terms of money is made, whether by modern book-keeping methods or in any other way, however primitive and crude. Everything is done in terms of balances" (Weber 1930, 18).

11. Callon conceives of calculation broadly as a process of recognizing distinctions. "Calculation starts by establishing distinctions between things or states of the world, and by imagining and estimating courses of action associated with those things or with those states and their consequences" (Callon and Muniesa 2005, 1231).

12. These card combinations are recognizable as meaningful hands in poker, but they have no meaning in baccarat.

13. For an account of Chinese gambling as a form of investment, see Bosco, Liu, and West (2009).

14. For example, given the 9.5156 percent probability that the cards dealt to Banker and Player hands will result in a tie, the payout for the successful wager is 8 to 1.

15. The jackpot also complicates the game's temporality. Conventional baccarat is a game of pure chance with simple betting rules, and with each hand of play, the game begins anew. Although many Chinese gamblers in Macau study charts of the Big Road in an effort to delineate a pattern of play, the game actually has no memory; the cards played and bets made in a previous hand are irrelevant to the outcome on subsequent hands. However, the LIVE Baccarat side jackpot transforms this feature of baccarat by making the bet on one hand of cards directly relevant to the winnings and payout that might occur as a result of a hand dealt at some point in the future.

16. Markowitz's portfolio theory was one of the first mathematical innovations

that transformed finance into a quantitative field of economics, enabling the performative dimension of the economics discipline explored by Callon and others (MacKenzie 2008).

17. "Material elusiveness points to the fact that epistemic consumption objects are morphing and changing on the ontological level, and not just the semiotic and functional levels; and that this uncertainty about 'what the object might become' motivates the consumer to persistently engage with the object" (Zwick and Dholakia 2006, 21).

18. Their point is that scholars in this field often become so concerned with describing how a market device articulates the individual with market activities typical of capitalism that they lose sight of the exploitative nature of capitalism itself.

19. Bjerg (2011) argues that the game of Texas Hold 'Em is a wild parody of postindustrial, post–Bretton Woods capitalism. He notes that under the current postindustrial regime, "production, consumption, and financing are dispersed" across the globe, and each moment of the commodity may occur in a different time and place, inhabiting distinct currency regions and monetary systems. "This dispersion installs a particular vulnerability in the capitalist system for accumulation of surplus value" (229). This spatial and temporal dispersion of the commodity chain has created the need for financial derivatives, the function of which is to hedge against the insecurities produced by the inherent inefficiencies of this system. One thing that makes LIVE Baccarat interesting, however, is the way it articulates these abstracted and dispersed moments of production, consumption, and finance together in the activity of the player sitting at the gambling machine.

9. GEOPHILOSOPHY IN MACAU

1. Dostoyevsky's commitment to native soil was embodied in his philosophy of *pochvennichestvo* and his work with the literary journal *Vremia* (Time); see Chapman (2014) and Jones (2008).

2. Writing during the socialist revolution, Chinese sociologist Fei Xiaotong ([1947] 1992) characterized the Chinese people as characteristically rural, derived physically and culturally "from the soil." Noting that the predominant deity represented in China's countryside shrines was Tudi, the god of the earth, Fei contends that "the Chinese are really inseparable from the soil" (38), arguing that the fecund earth serves as both the foundation of Chinese society and the progenitor of what he views as its problematic parochialism.

3. Guangzhou and Xiamen were formerly known, respectively, as Canton and Amoy.

4. In 1992, 5.9 million bottles of cognac were reexported from Hong Kong to China (van Westering 1994).

5. Weber (1930) differentiates adventurers' capitalism, which he says is "oriented to the exploitation of political opportunities and irrational speculation," from "an individualistic capitalistic economy that is rationalized on the basis of rigorous calculation," which for him is exemplified by the Protestant ethic (76).

6. Though for the sake of narrative convenience I have thus organized my analysis, we need not stop at the GBA megacity or gaming machine, but could trace further such scales of upward or downward emergence.

7. While this account understands capital and instrumental reason as the motive forces of modern history, we may also see in this merging of the two palace projects a convergence of two great global ecumenes: the western ecumene, which emerged in the Mediterranean with the Homeric origins of Greek civilization, and the concurrent Chinese ecumenic empire of *t'ien-hsia,* or "everything below heaven" (Voegelin 2000). Sloterdijk (2013) conceives of the contemporary "synchronous world" (139) that emerged after the end of terrestrial globalization as the "second ecumene" (143), a global age to replace the ancient era (or first ecumene).

8. My claim is consistent with Sloterdijk's contention in his spherology—and his focus on globes, bubbles, cells, and capsules—that an entire world is encompassed within a single point. My approach is also consistent with Deleuze and Guattari's (1987) assemblage approach to the subject, which they conceive as "a multiplicity of 'agents' by showing that the distribution of agents in a population of subjects is itself amenable to analysis on the level of social systems, thereby attacking the implicit methodological individualism of much cognitive science" (Bonta and Protevi 2004, 33).

9. This utilitarian assumption is the basis of Bentham's design of the panopticon, where the individual prisoner's rational response to the organization of punishment would lead him to bear the burden of his own surveillance.

10. This account of Dostoyevsky's gambling addiction is drawn from George (2012) and Rosenthal (1997, 2016).

11. "Man is a 'calculating animal.' But the origin of calculation, measure, evaluation, comparison, and accounting (all of which are also functions of money) must not be sought in economic exchange or in labor but in debt" (Lazzarato 2014, 43).

12. "Debt therefore implies subjectivation, what Nietzsche calls the 'labor of man on himself,' a 'self-torture.' This labor produces the individual subject, a subject answerable and indebted to his creditor. Debt as economic relation, for it to take effect, has thus the peculiarity of demanding ethico-political labor constitutive of the subject" (Lazzarato 2011, 42).

13. "The performative of the promise implies and presupposes a 'mnemotechnics' of cruelty and a mnemotechnics of pain, which, like the machine of Kafka's penal colony, inscribe the promise of debt repayment on the body itself" (Lazzarato 2011, 40–41).

EPILOGUE

1. In chapter 6, I similarly argue that the tripartite influence of Hong Kong's Umbrella Movement of 2014, China's anticorruption campaign of 2012, and Macau's antismoking regulations implemented between 2012 and 2019 constitute a reprise of these three crises of public order, public finance, and public health, and profoundly threatened the industry's profitability.

Bibliography

Adams, Vincanne, Michelle Murphy, and Adele E. Clarke. 2009. "Anticipation: Technoscience, Life, Affect, Temporality." *Subjectivity* 28: 246–65.

Aho, James A. 1985. "Rhetoric and the Invention of Double Entry Bookkeeping." *Rhetorica* 3 (1): 21–43.

Alsayyad, Nezar, and Ananya Roy. 2006. "Medieval Modernity: On Citizenship and Urbanism in a Global Era." *Space and Polity* 10: 1–20.

Alves, Jorge Manuel dos Santos, and Luís Filipe Barreto, eds. 2009. *Macau during the Ming Dynasty.* Lisbon: Centro Scientifico e Cultural de Macau.

Anagnost, Ann. 2004. "The Corporeal Politics of Quality (*Suzhi*)." *Public Culture* 16 (2): 189–208.

Angelo, Hilary, and David Wachsmuth. 2014. "Urbanizing Urban Political Ecology: A Critique of Methodological Cityism." In *Implosions/Explosions: Towards a Study of Planetary Urbanization,* edited by Neil Brenner, 372–85. Berlin: Jovis.

Appadurai, Arjun. 2015. *Banking on Words: The Failure of Language in the Age of Derivative Finance.* Chicago: University of Chicago Press.

Armental, Maria. 2019. "Las Vegas Sands Settles Macau Dispute." *Wall Street Journal,* March 14, 2019. https://www.wsj.com/articles/las-vegas-sands -settles-macau-dispute-11552608443.

Arrighi, Giovanni. (1994) 2010. *The Long Twentieth Century: Money, Power, and the Origins of Our Time.* London: Verso.

Arrighi, Giovanni. 2003. "The Rise of East Asia and the Withering Away of the Interstate System." In *State/Space: A Reader,* edited by Neil Brenner, Bob Jessop, and Gavin MacLeod, 131–46. Oxford: Blackwell.

Arrighi, Giovanni. 2004. "Spatial and Other 'Fixes' of Historical Capitalism." *Journal of World Systems Research* 10 (2): 527–39.

Arrighi, Giovanni. 2009a. *Adam Smith in Beijing: Lineages of the Twenty-First Century.* London: Verso.

Arrighi, Giovanni. 2009b. "The Winding Paths of Capital: Interview by David Harvey." *New Left Review* 56: 61–94.

Arrighi, Giovanni, and Beverly J. Silver. 2001. "Capitalism and World Disorder." *Review of International Studies* 27: 257–79.

Ascensção, Bruno Beato. 2017. "Macau Gaming Concessions: A Brief Insight into Their Term and Renewal." *Asian Gaming Lawyer,* May 2017, 9–11. https://www.imgl.org/sites/default/files/media/publications/macau gamingconcessions_beatoascencao_agl_spring2017.pdf.

Asome, John. 2014. "The Indentured Coolie Trade from Macao." *Journal of the Royal Asiatic Society Hong Kong Branch* 54: 157–79.

Associated Press and Reuters. 2018. "Chinese Billionaire Ng Lap-Seng Gets Four Years in U.S. Prison for Bribing U.N. Officials US$1.7 Million to Support Plans for Macau Conference Center." *South China Morning Post,* May 12, 2018. https://www.scmp.com/news/china/article/2145819/ chinese-billionaire-ng-lap-seng-gets-four-years-prison-bribing-un.

Baehr, William Peter. 2008. "City Under Siege: Authoritarian Toleration, Mask Culture, and the SARS Crisis in Hong Kong." In *Networked Disease: Emerging Infections in the Global City,* edited by S. Harris Ali and Roger Keil, 138–51. Oxford: Blackwell.

Bakken, Borge. 2000. *The Exemplary Society: Human Improvement, Social Control, and the Dangers of Modernity.* Oxford University Press.

Baptista, Eduardo. 2021. "Arrest of Macau's 'Junket Mogul' Rattles the World's Largest Gambling Hub." *Reuters,* November 30, 2021. https://www.reuters .com/world/asia-pacific/macau-gambling-group-suncitys-shares-hit-record -low-after-chairman-arrested-2021-11-30/.

Barthes, Roland. 1957. *Mythologies.* New York: Farrar, Straus and Giroux.

Basu, Ellen Oxfeld. 1991. "Profit, Loss, and Fate: The Entrepreneurial Ethic and the Practice of Gambling in an Overseas Chinese Community." *Modern China* 17: 227–59.

Butler, Judith. 2010. "Performative Agency." *Journal of Cultural Economy* 3 (2): 147–61.

Baudrillard, Jean. 1983. *Simulations.* Los Angeles: Semiotext(e).

Baudrillard, Jean. 1994. *Simulacra and Simulation.* Ann Arbor: University of Michigan Press.

Bégout, Bruce. 2004. *Zeropolis: The Experience of Las Vegas.* London: Reaktion.

Benjamin, Walter. 1969. "Paris, Capital of the Nineteenth Century." *Perspecta* 12: 163–72.

Bennett, Jane. 2010. *Vibrant Matter: A Political Ecology of Things.* Durham, N.C.: Duke University Press.

Benson, Susan. 1987. *Counter Cultures: Saleswomen, Managers, and Customers in American Department Stores, 1890–1940.* Urbana: University of Illinois Press.

Benston, Liz. 2008. "Las Vegas Sands Warns of Potential Bankruptcy." *Las Vegas Sun,* November 6, 2008. https://lasvegassun.com/news/2008/nov/06/ las-vegas-sands-may-miss-covenant-requirements/.

Beunza, Daniel, and David Stark. 2004. "Tools of the Trade: The Socio-technology of Arbitrage in a Wall Street Trading Room." *Industrial and Corporate Change* 13 (2): 369–400.

Bie, Jiangbo, Martin de Jong, and Ben Derudder. 2015. "Greater Pearl River Delta: Historical Evolution towards a Global City-Region." *Journal of Urban Technology* 22 (2): 103–23.

Bjerg, Ole. 2011. *Poker: The Parody of Capitalism.* Ann Arbor: University of Michigan Press.

Blaschke, Ben. 2020. "Move to Become Purely Asian Operator Seen as 'Beneficial' to Las Vegas Sands with REIT Deal on Vegas Assets Most Likely." *Inside Asian Gaming,* October 28, 2020. https://www.asgam.com/index .php/2020/10/28/move-to-become-purely-asian-operators-seen-as -beneficial-to-las-vegas-sands-reit-deal-on-vegas-assets-most-likely/.

Blaschke, Ben. 2021a. "Macau Government to Take Biggest Financial Hit from Junket Decline." *Inside Asian Gaming,* December 9, 2021. https://www .asgam.com/index.php/2021/12/09/macau-government-to-take-biggest -financial-hit-from-junket-decline/.

Blaschke, Ben. 2021b. "Sands China 'No Chance' of Being Overlooked for New Macau Casino Concession: Goldstein." *Inside Asian Gaming,* October 21, 2021. https://www.asgam.com/index.php/2021/10/21/sands-china-no -chance-of-being-overlooked-for-new-macau-casino-concession-goldstein.

Bloomberg. 2014. "Macau Casino Workers Join Protests for Higher Wages as Labour Unrest Sweeps Territory." *South China Morning Post,* September 3, 2014. https://www.scmp.com/news/china/article/1584558/macau-casino -workers-join-protests-higher-wages-labour-unrest-sweeps.

Bonta, Mark, and John Protevi. 2004. *Deleuze and Geophilosophy: A Guide and Glossary.* Edinburgh: Edinburgh University Press.

Bosker, Bianca. 2013. *Original Copies: Architectural Mimicry in Contemporary China.* Honolulu: University of Hawaiʻi Press.

Bosco, Joseph, Lucia Huwy-min Liu, and Matthew West. 2009. "Underground Lotteries in China: The Occult Economy and Capitalist Culture." *Research in Economic Anthropology* 29: 31–62.

Bourdieu, Pierre. 1990. *The Logic of Practice.* Stanford, Calif.: Stanford University Press.

Boxer, Charles. 1968. *Fidalgos in the Far East, 1550–1770.* Oxford: Oxford University Press.

Boxer, Charles. 1991. "Jesuits at the Court of Peking." *History Today* 41 (5): 41–47.

Bradsher, Keith. 2003. "Hundreds of Thousands in Hong Kong Protest Security Laws." *New York Times,* July 1, 2003. https://www.nytimes.com/2003/07/01/ international/asia/hundreds-of-thousands-in-hong-kong-protest-security -laws.html.

Bradsher, Keith. 2016. "Chinese Start to Lose Confidence in their Currency." *New York Times,* February 13, 2016. https://www.nytimes.com/2016/02/ 14/business/dealbook/chinese-start-to-lose-confidence-in-their-currency .html.

Branigan, Tania. 2008. "Chinese Figures Show Fivefold Rise in Babies Sick from

Contaminated Milk." *Guardian,* December 2, 2008. https://www.theguardian
.com/world/2008/dec/02/china.

Braudel, Fernand. (1949) 1995. *The Mediterranean and the Mediterranean World in
the Age of Phillip II.* Berkeley: University of California Press.

Braudel, Fernand. 1979. *Civilization and Capitalism: 15th–18th Century.* 3 vols.
New York: Harper & Row.

Bray, David. 2005. *Social Space and Urban Governance in China: The Danwei System from Origins to Reform.* Stanford, Calif.: Stanford University Press.

Breitung, Werner. 2007. *Overcoming Borders, Living with Borders: Macao and the
Integration with China.* Macau: Instituto Cultural do Governo da R.A.E. de
Macau.

Brenner, Neil. 2014. "Introduction: Urban Theory without an Outside." In
Implosions/Explosions: Towards a Study of Planetary Urbanization, edited by
Neil Brenner, 14–35. Berlin: Jovis.

Brook, Timothy. 2008. *Vermeer's Hat: The Seventeenth Century and the Dawn of
the Global World.* New York: Bloomsbury.

Bruck, Connie. 2008. "The Brass Ring." *New Yorker,* June 30, 2008. https://www
.newyorker.com/magazine/2008/06/30/the-brass-ring.

Buck, Daniel, and Richard Walker. 2007. "The Chinese Road: Cities in the Transition to Capitlaism." *New Left Review* 46: 39–66.

Buckingham, Will. 2017. "Uncorking the Neoliberal Bottle: Neoliberal Critique
and Urban Change in China." *Eurasian Geography and Economics* 58 (3):
297–315.

Buckley, Sarah. 2015. "What Are China's Shenzhen Shoppers Buying in Hong
Kong?" *BBC News,* April 13, 2015. https://www.bbc.com/news/world-asia
-china-32283440.

Bush, George W. 2007. "The President's News Conference with Prime Minister John W. Howard of Australia in Sydney, Australia." *American Presidency
Project,* September 5, 2007. http://www.presidency.ucsb.edu/ws/index
.php?pid=75734.

Caillois, Roger. (1958) 2001. *Man, Play, and Games.* Urbana: University of Illinois
Press.

Çaliskan, Koray, and Michel Callon. 2009. "Economization, Part 1: Shifting Attention from the Economy towards Processes of Economization." *Economy
and Society* 38 (3): 369–98.

Callon, Michel. 1998. "Introduction: The Embeddedness of Economic Markets
in Economics." *Sociological Review Monograph Series* 46 (suppl. 1): 1–57.

Callon, Michel. 2005. "Why Virtualism Paves the Way to Political Impotence:
A Reply to Daniel Miller's Critique of *The Laws of the Markets.*" *Economic
Sociology: European Electronic Newsletter.* http://econsoc.mpifg.de/archive/
esfeb05.pdf.

Callon, Michel. 2007. "What Does It Mean to Say Economics Is Performative?"
In *Do Economists Make Markets? On the Performativity of Economics,* edited

by Donald MacKenzie, Fabio Muniesa, and Lucia Sui, 311–57. Princeton, N.J.: Princeton University Press.

Callon, Michel, and Fabian Muniesa. 2005. "Economic Markets as Calculative Collective Devices." *Organization Studies* 26 (8): 1229–50.

Callon, Michel, Yuval Millo, and Fabian Muniesa. 2007. *Market Devices.* Oxford: Wiley-Blackwell.

Campanella, Thomas. 2008. *The Concrete Dragon.* Princeton, N.J.: Princeton University Press.

Cano, Regina Garcia. 2019. "Nevada Casinos Win $11.9 Rillion in 2018, Up from 2017 Revenue." *AP News,* February 1, 2019. https://apnews.com/article/3b3fc8f7066049b2b3ea82ee342ecc81.

Carroll, John. (1974) 2010. *Break-out from the Crystal Palace: The Anarcho-psychological Critique: Stirner, Nietzsche, Dostoyevsky.* New York: Routledge.

Carruthers, Bruce G., and Wendy Nelson Espeland. 1991. "Accounting for Rationality: Double-Entry Bookkeeping and the Rhetoric of Economic Rationality." *American Journal of Sociology* 97 (1): 31–69.

Cartier, Carolyn. 2013a. "Building Civilised Cities." In *Civilising China: China Story Yearbook 2013,* edited by Geremie R. Barme and Jeremy Goldkorn, 258–85. Canberra: Australian National University.

Cartier, Carolyn. 2013b. "Production/Consumption and the Chinese City-Region: Cultural Political Economy and the Feminist Diamond Ring." *Urban Geography* 30 (4): 368–90.

Carvalho, Raquel. 2016. "Macau Police Investigate HK$99.7 Million Theft from VIP Gaming Room." *South China Morning Post,* January 9, 2016. https://www.scmp.com/news/hong-kong/law-crime/article/1899650/macau-police-investigate-hk997-million-theft-vip-gaming.

Carvalho, Raquel. 2017. "How Macau Became North Korea's Window to the World." *South China Morning Post,* May 6, 2017. https://www.scmp.com/week-asia/geopolitics/article/2093189/how-macau-became-north-koreas-window-world-and-its-nexus.

Casey, Joseph, and Katherine Koleski. 2011. "Backgrounder: China's 12th Five-Year Plan." U.S.–China Economic & Security Review Commission.

Cass, Jeffrey. 2004. "Egypt on Steroids: Luxor Las Vegas and Postmodern Orientalism." In *Architecture and Tourism: Perception, Performance, and Place,* edited by D. Medina Lasansky and Brian McLaren, 241–63. Oxford: Berg.

Cassidy, Rebecca. 2009. "Casino Capitalism and the Financial Crisis." *Anthropology Today* 25 (4): 10–13.

Castells, Manuel. (1996) 2000. *The Rise of the Network Society, Vol. 1.* 2nd ed. Cambridge: Blackwell.

Castells, Manuel. 2002. "The Culture of Cities in the Information Age." In *The Castells Reader on Cities and Social Theory,* edited by Ida Susser, 367–89. Oxford: Blackwell.

Chan, Kam Wing. 2014. "China's Urbanization 2020: A New Blueprint and Direction." *Eurasian Geography and Economics* 55 (1): 1–9.

Chan, Vincy, and Billy Chan. 2013. "Macau to Strengthen Junket Licensing System." http://www.bloomberg.com/news/2013-02-07/macau-to-strengthen-casino-junket-licensing-system.html.

Chan, Yuk Wah. 2016. "A Tale of Two Borderlands: Material Lucidity and Deep Play in the Transborder Tourism Space in Hong Kong and Macao." *Asian Anthropology* 15 (2): 186–206.

Chang, Tien Tse. 1934. *Sino-Portuguese Trade from 1514–1644: A Synthesis of Portuguese and Chinese Sources.* Leyden: Brill.

Chapman, Roger. 2014. "Fyodor Dostoyevsky, Eastern Orthodoxy, and the Crystal Palace." In *Historic Engagements with Occidental Cultures, Religions, Powers,* edited by Anne R. Richards and Iraj Omidvar, 35–55. New York: Palgrave.

Chen, Teng. 2017. *A State Beyond the State: Shenzhen and the Transformation of China.* Rotterdam: Nai010 Publishers.

Cheng, Christina Miu Bing. 1999. *Macau: A Cultural Janus.* Hong Kong: Hong Kong University Press.

Cheng, Yinghong. 2008. *Creating the New Man: From Enlightenment Ideals to Socialist Reality.* Honolulu: University of Hawai'i Press.

Chun Wu Ho Development Holdings Limited. n.d. "Project Fact Sheet: Piling Works of Venetian Macau Exhibition and Conference Center." http://chunwo.com/chunwoimages/files/Piling%20Works%20of%20Venetian%20Macau%20Conference%20and%20Exhibition%20Centre.pdf.

Chun, Jay. 2011. "Methods and Systems for Playing Baccarat Jackpot with an Option for Insurance Betting." United States Patent 7,914,368B2.

Chun, Jay. 2012. "Paradise Box Gaming System." United States Patent 8,308,559B2.

Chung, Judy Chuihua, Jeffrey Inanba, Rem Koolhaas, and Tsung Leong Sze. 2001. *Great Leap Forward.* Cambridge, Mass.: Harvard Design School.

Clayton, Cathryn H. 2009. *Sovereignty at the Edge: Macau and the Question of Chineseness.* Cambridge, Mass.: Harvard University Press.

Coates, Austin. 2009. *A Macao Narrative.* Hong Kong: Hong Kong University Press.

Cochoy, Frank. 2008. "Calculation, Qualculation, Calqulation: Shopping Cart Arithmetic, Equipped Cognition and the Clustered Consumer." *Marketing Theory* 8 (1): 15–44.

Cohen, Lizabeth. 2003. "A Consumer's Republic: The Politics of Mass Consumption in Postwar America." *Journal of Consumer Research* 31 (1): 236–39.

Cohen, Lizabeth. 2006. "The Consumer's Republic: An American Model for the World?" In *The Ambivalent Consumer: Questioning Consumption in East Asia and the West,* edited by Sheldon Garon and Patricia L. Maclaclan, 45–62. Ithaca, N.Y.: Cornell University Press.

Cohen, Margaret. 1995. *Profane Illumination: Walter Benjamin and the Paris of Surrealist Revolution.* Berkeley: University of California Press.

Cohen, Muhammed. 2014. "Sands Macao: The House that Built Sheldon Adelson." *Forbes,* May 15, 2014. https://www.forbes.com/sites/muhammad cohen/2014/05/15/sands-macao-the-house-that-built-sheldon-adelson/ #1eee07025d1c.

Cohen, Muhammed. 2016. "Behind VIP Headlines, Macau Turnaround Takes New Directions." *Forbes,* December 1, 2016. https://www.forbes.com/sites/ muhammadcohen/2016/12/01/behind-vip-headlines-macau-turnaround -takes-new-directions/.

Cohen, Muhammed. 2017a. "How the Venetian made Macau Great Again." *South China Morning Post,* August 28, 2017. https://www.scmp.com/week -asia/society/article/2107790/how-venetian-made-macau-great-again.

Cohen, Muhammed. 2017b. "Macau Megacasino Born of a Broken Marriage." *Asia Times,* August 29, 2017. http://www.atimes.com/article/macau-mega -casino-born-broken-marriage/.

Cohen, Muhammed. 2018. "Design for Profit." *Inside Asian Gaming,* January 29, 2018. https://www.asgam.com/index.php/2018/01/29/design-for-profit/.

Cohen, Muhammed. 2020. "Stanley Ho: Father of Modern Macau." *Inside Asian Gaming,* May 26, 2020. https://www.asgam.com/index.php/2020/05/26/ stanley-ho-father-of-modern-macau/.

Cohen, Muhammed. 2021. "Sheldon Adelson: Supercharged by Asia." *Inside Asian Gaming,* January 12, 2021. https://www.asgam.com/index.php/ 2021/01/12/sheldon-adelson-supercharged-by-asia/.

Collier, Andrew. 2017. *Shadow Banking and the Rise of Capitalism in China.* London: Palgrave MacMillan.

Cormier, Claudia K., and Robert D. Faiss. 1986. "The International Effect of the Nevada Gaming Control Act." *Southwestern Law Review* 16: 437–60.

Cox, Oliver. 1959. *The Foundations of Capitalism.* New York: Philosophical Library.

Crary, Jonathon. 2001. *Suspensions of Perception: Attention, Spectacle and Modern Culture.* Cambridge, Mass.: MIT Press.

Daly, Andrew, and Chris L. Smith. 2011. "Architecture, Cigarettes, and the *Dispositif.*" *Architectural Theory Review* 16 (1): 22–37.

Daniel, Thomas. 2018. "Uncommon Ground." In *Macau and the Casino Complex,* edited by Stefan Al, 25–48. Reno: University of Nevada Press.

Dardot, Pierre, and Christian Laval. 2013. *The Way of the World: On Neoliberal Society.* London: Verso.

Davis, Mike. 1998. "Las Vegas Versus Nature." In *Reopening the American West,* edited by Hal Rothman, 53–74. Tucson: University of Arizona Press.

Davis, Robert C., and Garry R. Marvin. 2004. *Venice, the Tourist Maze: A Cultural Critique of the World's Most Touristed City.* Berkeley: University of California Press.

Debord, Guy. 2011. *Comments on the Society of Spectacle.* London: Verso.

DeLanda, Manuel. 2006. *A New Philosophy of Society: Assemblage Theory and Social Complexity.* London: Continuum.

DeLanda, Manuel, John Protevi, and Torkild Thanem. 2005. "Deleuzian Interrogations: A Conversation with Manuel DeLanda and John Protevi." *Tamara: Journal of Critical Postmodern Organization Science* 3 (4): 65–88.

Deleuze, Gilles. 1992. "Postscript on the Societies of Control." *October* 59:3–7.

Deleuze, Gilles, and Félix Guattari. 1987. *A Thousand Plateaus.* Minneapolis: University of Minnesota Press.

Denton, Sally, and Roger Morris. 2002. *The Money and the Power: The Making of Las Vegas and Its Hold on America, 1947–2000.* New York: Vintage.

Dicks, Anthony R. 1984. "Macao: Legal Fiction and Gunboat Diplomacy." In *Leadership on the China Coast,* edited by Göran Aijmer, 90–127. London: Curzon.

Dostoyevsky, Fyodor. (1863) 1997. "Baal." In *Winter Notes on Summer Impressions,* 35–42. Chicago: Northwestern University Press.

Dostoyevsky, Fyodor. (1864) 2001. *Notes from the Underground.* Translated by Michael R. Katz. New York: Norton.

Dow, Alistair, and Sheila C. Dow. 2011. "Animal Spirits Revisited." *Capitalism and Society,* 6 (2): 1–23.

Dumelo, Juno. 2016. "48 Hours in Macau: The Vegas of China." *Vogue,* August 16, 2016. https://www.vogue.com/article/two-days-in-macau-vegas-of -china.

Dumez, Hervé, and Alain Jeunemaitre. 2010. "Michel Callon, Michel Foucault and the 'Dispositif'—When Economics Fails to be Performative: A Case Study." *Le Libellio a Aegis* 6 (4): 27–37.

Eadington, William R., and Ricardo C. S. Siu. 2007. "Between Law and Custom—Examining the Interaction between Legislative Change and the Evolution of Macao's Casino Gaming Industry." *International Gambling Studies* 7 (1): 1–28.

Easterling, Keller. 2013. "Disposition." In *Cognitive Architecture: From Bio-politics to Noo-politics,* edited by Deborah Hauptmann and Warren Neidich, 251–65. Delft School of Design.

Eco, Umberto. 1986. *Travels in Hyperreality.* New York: Harcourt Brace.

Elden, Stuart. 2002. *Mapping the Present: Heidegger, Foucault, and the Project of a Spatial History.* London: Continuum.

Erheriene, Ese. 2018. "Macau, Asia's Vegas, Can't Beat the Real McCoy for Fun." *Wall Street Journal,* August 1, 2018. https://www.wsj.com/articles/ macau-asias-vegas-cant-beat-the-real-mccoy-for-fun-1533115803.

Erturk, Ismail, Juile Froud, Sukhdev Johal, Adam Leaver, and Karel Williams. 2013. "(How) Do Devices Matter in Finance?" *Journal of Cultural Economy* 6 (3): 336–52.

Ethier, Stewart N., and Jiyeon Lee. 2015. "The Evolution of the Game of Baccarat." *Journal of Gambling Business and Economics* 9 (2): 1–13.

Evans, Harriet, and Stephanie Donald. 1999. *Picturing Power in the People's Republic of China: Posters of the Cultural Revolution.* Lanham, Md.: Rowman & Littlefield.

Fei Xiaotong (1947) 1992. *From the Soil: The Foundations of Chinese Society.* Translated by Gary G. Hamilton and Wang Zheng. Berkeley: University of California Press.

Festa, Paul E. 2007. "Mahjong Agonistics and the Political Public in Taiwan: Mate, Mimesis, and the Martial Imaginary." *Anthropological Quarterly* 80 (1): 93–125.

Finlay, Robert. 1998. "The Pilgrim Art: The Culture of Porcelain in World History." *Journal of World History* 9 (2): 141–87.

Fjellman, Stephen. 1992. *Vinyl Leaves: Walt Disney World and America.* New York: Routledge.

Fleming, Ian. (1963) 2013. *Thrilling Cities.* Las Vegas: Thomas and Mercer.

Fok, Kai-cheong. 1999. "Portuguese Macao's Impact on the Pearl River Delta during the Ming and Ch'ing Periods." *Portuguese Studies Review* 7 (2): 36–53.

Fong, Lawrence Hoc Nang, Rob Law, and Desmond Lam. 2014. "An Examination of Factors Driving Chinese Gamblers' Fallacy Bias." *Journal of Gambling Studies* 30: 757–70.

Foucault, Michel. 1972. *The Archaeology of Knowledge.* New York: Pantheon.

Foucault, Michel. 1977a. "The Confession of the Flesh." In *Power/Knowledge: Selected Interviews and Other Writings, 1972–1977,* edited by Colin Gordon, 194–228. New York: Vintage.

Foucault, Michel. 1977b. "Nietzsche, Genealogy, History." In *Language, Counter-memory, Practice,* edited by Donald F. Bouchard, 76–99. Oxford: Basil Blackwell.

Foucault, Michel. 1979. *Discipline and Punish: The Birth of the Prison.* New York: Vintage.

Foucault, Michel. 1986. "The Eye of Power." In *The Impossible Prison: A Foucault Reader,* edited by Alex Farquharson, 8–15. Nottingham: Nottingham Contemporary.

Foucault, Michel. 1994. "The Subject and Power." In *The Essential Foucault,* edited by Paul Rabinow and Nicolas Rose, 126–44. New York: The New Press.

Foucault, Michel. 2004. *The Birth of Biopolitics: Lectures at the College de France, 1978–1979.* New York: Picador.

Franci, Giovanna, and Federico Zignani. 2005. *Dreaming of Italy: Las Vegas and the Virtual Grand Tour.* Reno: University of Nevada Press.

Fraser, Niall. 1997. "Colonel Gets Safety Gear." *South China Morning Press,* February 16, 1997. https://www.scmp.com/article/185048/colonel-gets-safety-gear.

Fraser, Niall. 2014. "Casino Junket Operator Leaves US$1.3b in Debts." *South China Morning Post,* May 3, 2014.

Fraser, Niall. 2017. "A Cryptocurrency Deal and a Triad Boss Called Broken Tooth—What Can Possibly Go Wrong?" *South China Morning Post,* October 8, 2017. https://www.scmp.com/week-asia/society/article/2114310/cryptocurrency-deal-and-triad-boss-called-broken-tooth-what-can.

Fraser, Niall. 2018a. "The Cryptocurrency Linking Cambridge Analytica and Macau's Most Notorious Gangster." *South China Morning Post,* April 19, 2018. https://www.scmp.com/news/hong-kong/economy/article/2142342/cryptocurrency-linking-cambridge-analytica-and-macaus-most.

Fraser, Niall. 2018b. "Former Macau Triad Boss 'Broken Tooth' Wan Kuok-koi to Use Blockchain and Overseas Chinese Links in Cambodia Venture." *South China Morning Post,* June 7, 2018. https://www.scmp.com/news/hong-kong/hong-kong-economy/article/2149679/former-macau-triad-boss-broken-tooth-wan-kuok-koi.

Fraser, Niall. 2018c. "Macau 'Set to be Richest Place on Planet.'" *South China Morning Post,* August 8, 2018.

Friedman, Bill. 2000. *Designing Casinos to Dominate the Competition.* Reno: Institute for the Study of Gambling and Commercial Gaming.

Garreau, Joel. 1992. *Edge City: Life on the New Frontier.* New York: Anchor.

Gaylord, Mark S. 2008. "The Banco Delta Asia Affair: The USA Patriot Act and Allegations of Money Laundering in Macau." *Crime, Law, and Social Change* 50 (4–5): 293–305.

Garrett, Richard J. 2010. *The Defences of Macau.* Hong Kong: Hong Kong University Press.

Geertz, Clifford. (1972) 1973. "Deep Play: Notes on the Balinese Cockfight." In *The Interpretation of Cultures.* New York: Basic Books.

Genosko, Gary. 2016. "Postscript: For an Urban Machinic Ecology." In *Deleuze and the City,* edited by Hélène Frichot, Catharina Gabrielsson, and Jonathon Metzger, 241–45. Manchester: Manchester University Press.

George, Sanju. 2012. "From the Gambler Within: Dostoyevsky's *The Gambler.*" *Advances in Psychiatric Treatment* 18: 226–31.

Gerth, Karl. 2011. "Lifestyles of the Rich and Infamous: The Creation and Implications of China's New Aristocracy." *Comparative Sociology* 10: 488–507.

Gipouloux, François. 2011. *The Asian Mediterranean: Port Cities and Trading Networks in China, Japan, and Southeast Asia, 13th–21st Century.* Northampton: Edward Elgar.

Gleeson, Janet. 1998. *The Arcanum.* London: Bantam.

Gleeson-White, Jane. 2013. *Double Entry: How the Merchants of Venice Created Modern Finance.* New York: Norton.

Gottman, Jean. 1964. *Megalopolis: The Urbanized Northeastern Seaboard of the United States.* Cambridge, Mass.: MIT Press.

Gough, Neil. 2007. "Macau Losing Billions from Betting Scam." *South China Morning Post.* http://www.scmp.com/article/619001/macau-losing-billions-betting-scam.

Granovetter, Mark. 1985. "Economic Action and Social Structure: The Problem of Embeddedness." *American Journal of Sociology* 91 (3): 481–510.

Greenhalgh, Susan. 2008. *Just One Child: Science and Policy in Deng's China.* Berkeley: University of California Press.

Greenhalgh, Susan. 2009. "The Chinese Biopolitical: Facing the Twenty-First Century." *New Genetics and Society* 28 (3): 205–22.

Greenhalgh, Susan. 2010. *Cultivating Global Citizens: Population in the Rise of China.* Harvard University Press.

Greenhalgh, Susan, and Edwin A. Winckler. 2005. *Governing China's Population: From Leninist to Neoliberal Biopolitics.* Stanford, Calif.: Stanford University Press.

Griffiths, Martin, and Michael Schiavone. 2016. "China's New Urbanization Plan, 2014–20." *China Report* 52 (2): 73–91.

Guattari, Félix. 1989. *Schizoanalytic Cartographies.* London: Bloomsbury.

Guattari, Félix. 1995. *Chaosmosis: An Ethico-aesthetic Paradigm.* Bloomington: Indiana University Press.

Guattari, Félix. 2015. *Machinic Eros: Writings on Japan.* Minneapolis: University of Minnesota Press.

Guignon, Charles, and Kevin Aho. 2009. Introduction to *Notes from the Underground,* by Fyodor Dostoyevsky. Cambridge: Hackett.

Gunn, Geoffrey C. 1996. *Encountering Macau: A Portuguese City-state on the Periphery of China, 1557–1999.* Boulder, Colo.: Westview.

Haar, Barend J. 2000. *Ritual and Mythology of the Chinese Triads: Creating an Identity.* Leiden: Brill.

Haar, Sharon, and Victoria Marshall. 2012. "Mega Urban Ecologies." In *Urban Design Ecologies,* edited by Brian McGrath, 146–61. Oxford: Wiley.

Haivan, Max. 2014. "The Creative and the Derivative: Historicizing Creativity under Post–Bretton Woods Financialization." *Radical History Review* 118: 113–38.

Haldrup, Michael, and Jonas Larsen. 2006. "Material Cultures of Tourism." *Leisure Studies* 25 (3): 275–89.

Hamashita, Takeshi. 2008. "The Tribute Trade System and Modern Asia." In *China, East Asia and the Global Economy: Regional and Historical Perspectives,* edited by Takeshi Hamashita, Mark Selden, and Linda Grove, 12–26. New York: Routledge.

Hamlin, Katrina. 2019. "Breaking Views—China Sends Two Messages with One Macau Invitation." *Reuters,* October 31, 2019. https://www.reuters.com/article/us-macau-trade-breakingviews/breakingviews-china-sends-two-messages-with-one-macau-invitation-idUSKBN1XA0IM.

Hanna, Willard A. 1969a. "A Trial of Two Colonies, Part 1: Precarious Balance in Portuguese Macao." *American Universities Field Staff East Asia Series* 26 (1): 1–14.

Hanna, Willard A. 1969b. "A Trial of Two Colonies, Part 2: The City of the Name of God Hails a New Messiah." *American Universities Field Staff East Asia Series* 26 (2): 1–16.

Hao, Zhidong. 2020. *Macau: History and Society.* 2nd ed. Hong Kong: Hong Kong University Press.

Hardie, Iain, and Donald MacKenzie. 2007. "Assembling an Economic Actor: The *Agencement* of a Hedge Fund." *Sociological Review* 55 (1): 57–80.

Hardt, Michael. 2005. "Into the Factory: Negri's Lenin and the Subjective Caesura (1968–1973)." In *The Philosophy of Antonio Negri: Resistance in Practice,* edited by Timothy Murphy and Abdul-Karim Mustapha, 7–37. London: Pluto Press.

Hardt, Michael, and Antonio Negri. 2000. *Empire.* Cambridge, Mass.: Harvard University Press.

Hardt, Michael, and Antonio Negri. 2009. *Commonwealth.* Cambridge, Mass.: Harvard University Press.

Hartzell, Freyja. 2009. "The Velvet Touch: Fashion, Furniture, and the Fabric of the Interior." *Fashion Theory* 13 (1): 51–81.

Harvey, David. 1989. "From Managerialism to Entrepreneurialism: The Transformation in Urban Governance in Late Capitalism." *Geografiska Annaler, Series B* 71 (1): 3–16.

Harvey, David. 1991. *The Condition of Postmodernity: An Inquiry into the Origins of Cultural Change.* Oxford: Wiley-Blackwell.

Harvey, David. 2005. *The New Imperialism.* Oxford: Oxford University Press.

Harvey, David. 2006. *Paris, Capital of Modernity.* New York: Routledge.

Harvey, David. 2007. *A Brief History of Neoliberalism.* Oxford: Oxford University Press.

Harvey, David. 2008. "The Right to the City." *New Left Review* 53: 23–40. https://newleftreview.org/issues/ii53/articles/david-harvey-the-right-to-the-city.

Harvey, David. 2012. *Rebel Cities: From the Right to the City to the Urban Revolution.* London: Verso.

Hawkins, B. Waterhouse. 1854. "On Visual Education as Applied to Geology, Illustrated by Diagrams and Models of the Geological Restorations at the Crystal Palace." *Journal of the Society of Arts* 2: 444–49.

He, Sibing. 2015. *Macao and the Making of Early Sino-American Relations, 1744–1844.* Macau: Cultural Affairs Bureau of Macau SAR.

Heaver, Stuart. 2018. "Knowing Our Place." *South China Morning Post,* October 18, 2018.

Heilmann, Sebastian. 2008. "Policy Experimentation in China's Economic Rise." *Studies in Comparative International Development* 43: 1–26.

Heilmann, Sebastian. 2011. "Policy-Making through Experimentation: The Formation of a Distinctive Policy Process." In *Mao's Invisible Hand: The Political Foundations of Adaptive Governance in China,* edited by Sebastian Heilmann and Elizabeth Perry, 62–101. Cambridge, Mass.: Harvard University Press.

Heilmann, Sebastian, and Elizabeth Perry. 2011. *Mao's Invisible Hand: The Political Foundations of Adaptive Governance in China.* Cambridge, Mass.: Harvard University Press.

Henders, Susan J. 2001. "So What If It's Not a Gamble? Post-Westphalian Politics in Macau." *Pacific Affairs* 74 (3): 342–60.

Herwig, Oliver. 2006. *Dream Worlds: Architecture and Entertainment.* Photographs by Florian Holzherr. Munich: Prestel Verlag.

Hillier, Jean and Kang Cao. 2011. "Enabling Chinese Strategic Spatial Planners to Paint Green Dragons." *Planning Theory* 10 (4): 366–78.

Howard, M. C. 1985. "Fernand Braudel on Capitalism: A Theoretical Analysis." *Historical Reflections* 12 (3): 469–83.

Huang, Guihai. 2015. "Erroneous Perceptions of Chinese Baccarat Players: Evidence from Guidebooks." *Journal of Gambling and Commercial Gaming Research* 1 (1): 1–11.

Hughes, Barrie. 1976. *The Educated Gambler: A Guide to Casino Games.* London: Stanley Paul.

Huxley, Margo. 2007. "Geographies of Governmentality." In *Space, Knowledge and Power: Foucault and Geography,* edited by Jeremy W. Crampton and Stuart Elden, 185–204. Aldershot: Ashgate.

Jacka, Tamara. 2009. "Cultivating Citizens: *Suzhi* (Quality) Discourse in the PRC." *positions* 17 (3): 523–35.

Jesus, C. A. Montaldo. (1902) 1984. *Historic Macao.* Oxford: Oxford University Press.

Jewell, Nicholas. 2015. *Shopping Malls and Public Space in Modern China.* New York: Routledge.

Jim, Clare. 2014. "China's Xi Preaches Diversification in China's Gambling Hub Macau." Reuters, December 20, 2014. https://www.reuters.com/article/us-macau-china-xi-idUSKBN0JY02J20141220.

Jin, Guoping, and Zhilian Wu. 2006. "Ming and Qing Dynasty Chinese Porcelain in Portugal." *Palace Museum Journal* 3: 98–112.

Jones, Malcolm. 2008. Introduction to *Notes from the Underground* and *The Gambler,* by Fyodor Dostoyevsky, 9–23. Oxford: Oxford University Press.

Joy, Annamma, John F. Sherry, and Jeff Jianfeng Wang. 2018. "Tasting, Savouring, Signalling: Articulating the Luxury Brand Experience in Chinese Cities." In *Chinese Urbanism: Critical Perspectives,* edited by Mark Jayne, 109–20. New York: Routledge.

Jullien, François. 1995. *The Propensity of Things: Towards a History of Efficacy in China.* New York: Zone Books.

Kahn, Joseph. 2003. "Beijing Hurries to Build Hospital Complex for Increasing Number of SARS Patients." *New York Times,* April 27, 2003. https://www

.nytimes.com/2003/04/27/world/sars-epidemic-treatment-beijing-hurries
-build-hospital-complex-for-increasing.html.

Kar, Dev, and Sarah Freitas. 2012. "Illicit Financial Flows from China and the
Role of Trade Misinvoicing." Global Financial Integrity Report, October
2012.

Katz, Michael R. 2002. "But This Building: What on Earth Is It?" *New England
Review* 23 (10): 65–76.

Kavanaugh, Thomas M. 1993. *Enlightenment and the Shadows of Chance: The
Novel and the Culture of Gambling in Eighteenth-Century France.* Baltimore,
Md.: Johns Hopkins University Press.

Kayden, Jerold S. 2000. *Privately Owned Public Space: The New York City Experience.* Oxford: Wiley.

Keegan, Matthew. 2016. "Rolls Royce Deliver 30 Phantoms to Ultra-Luxury The
13 Hotel in Macau." *South China Morning Post,* September 28, 2016. https://
www.scmp.com/destination-macau/article/2023243/rolls-royce-deliver
-30-phantoms-ultra-luxury-13-hotel-macau.

Keith, Michael, Scott Lash, Jakob Arnoldi, and Typer Rooker. 2014. *China Constructing Capitalism: Economic Life and Urban Change.* London: Routledge.

Keynes, John Maynard. (1934) 2016. *The General Theory of Employment, Interest,
and Money.* Boston: Houghton Mifflin Harcourt.

Kong, Qingjiang. 2003. "Closer Economic Partnership Agreement between
China and Hong Kong." *China: An International Journal* 1 (1): 133–43.

Koolhaas, Rem. 1997. "Bigness, or The Problem of Large." In *S, M, L, XL,* 495–516.
Cologne: Taschen.

Koolhaas, Rem. 2000. "Harvard Project on the City." In *Mutations,* 280–337.
New York: ACTAR.

Koppl, Roger. 1991. "Retrospectives: Animal Spirits." *Journal of Economic Perspectives* 5 (3): 203–10.

Krahe, Cinta. 2018. "The Reception and Value of Chinese Porcelain in Habsburg
Spain." In *EurAsian Matters: China, Europe, and the Transcultural Object,
1600–1800,* edited by Anna Grasskamp and Monica Juneja, 221–35. Cham,
Switzerland: Springer.

Kwan, Fanny Vong Chuk. 2004. "Gambling Attitudes and Gambling Behavior
of Residents of Macao: The Monte Carlo of the Orient." *Journal of Travel
Research* 42 (3): 271–78.

Lai, Tung-Yiu Stan. 2016. "The Rise of Tall Podia and Vertical Malls." In *Mall
City: Hong Kong's Dreamworlds of Consumption,* edited by Stefan Al, 53–64.
Honolulu: University of Hawai'i Press.

Lam, Agnes Iok Fong, and Cathryn Clayton. 2016. "One, Two, Three: Evaluating
Macau's Cultural Revolution." *Modern China Studies* 23 (2): 163–86.

Lam, Carlos Siu. 2013. "Changes in the Junket Business in Macao after Gaming
Liberalization." *International Gambling Studies* 13 (3): 319–37.

Lam, Carlos Siu. 2015. *On the Frontline in Macao: Casino Employees, Informal Learning, and Customer Service.* Las Vegas: UNLV Gaming Press.

Lam, Carlos Siu, and William R. Eadington. 2009. "Lessons from the Nevada Model on Macao's Junket Operations." *Gaming Law Review and Economics* 13 (1): 6–22.

Lam, Desmond. 2006. "Slot or Table? A Chinese Perspective." *UNLV Gaming Research and Review Journal* 9 (2): 69–72.

Lam, Desmond. 2008. "An Observation Study of Chinese Baccarat Players." *UNLV Gaming Research and Review Journal* 11 (2): 63–73.

Landsberger, Stephen R. 2001. "Learning by What Example? Educational Propaganda in Twenty-First Century China." *Critical Asian Studies* 33 (4): 541–71.

Las Vegas Sands Corp., Appellant, vs. Richard Suen, and Round Square Company Limited, Repondents. 2016. *Gaming Law Review and Economics* 20 (9): 806–10.

Law, John. 1984. "On the Methods of Long-Distance Control: Vessels, Navigation and the Portuguese Route to India." *Sociological Review Monograph* 32 (1): 234–63.

Law, John. 1987. "On the Social Explanation of Technical Change: The Case of the Portuguese Maritime Expansion." *Technology and Culture* 28 (2): 227–52.

Law, John. 2008. "On Sociology and the STS." *Sociological Review* 56 (4): 623–49.

Law, John. 2012. "Technology and Heterogeneous Engineering: The Case of Portuguese Expansion." In *The Social Construction of Technological Systems: New Directions in the Sociology and History of Technology,* edited by Wiebe E. Bijker, Thomas Parke Hugues, Trevor Pinch, and Deborah G. Douglas, 105–27. Cambridge, Mass.: MIT Press.

Lazzarato, Maurizio. 2010. "'Exiting Language,' Semiotic Systems and the Production of Subjectivity in Félix Guattari." In *Cognitive Architecture: From Biopolitics to Noopolitics. Architecture and Mind in the Age of Communication and Information,* edited by Deborah Hauptmann and Warren Neidich, 503–20. Rotterdam: 010 Publishers.

Lazzarato, Maurizio. 2011. *The Making of Indebted Man.* Los Angeles: Semiotext(e).

Lazzarato, Maurizio. 2014. *Signs and Machines: Capitalism and the Production of Subjectivity.* Los Angeles: Semiotext(e).

Leach, William. 1994. *Land of Desire: Merchants, Power, and the Rise of a New American Culture.* New York: Vintage.

Lears, Jackson. 2017. "Animal Spirits and the Vitalist Currents in Modernity." *Hedgehog Review* 19 (2). https://hedgehogreview.com/issues/the-meaning -of-cities/articles/animal-spirits-and-the-vitalist-currents-in-modernity.

Lee, Wing-Sze. 2017. "Lamborghini Expands in Macau with Opening of 10,000 sq ft Showroom." *South China Morning Post,* June 11, 2017. https://www.scmp.com/magazines/style/peopleevents/article/2102189/ lamborghini-expands-macau-opening-4s-showroom.

Lefebvre, Henri. 1976. *The Survival of Capitalism: Reproduction of the Relations of Production.* New York: St. Martin's Press.

Lefebvre, Henri. 1992. *The Production of Space.* Cambridge: Wiley-Blackwell.

Lefebvre, Henri. 2003. *The Urban Revolution.* Minneapolis: University of Minnesota Press.

Le Goff, Jacques. 1990. *Your Money or Your Life: Economy and Religion in the Middle Ages.* New York: Zone.

Leong, Angela Veng Mei. 2002. "The 'Bate-ficha' Business and Triads in Macau's Casinos." *QUT Law and Justice Journal* 2 (1): 83–97.

Letter from Macau. 1997. "Of Greyhounds and Gangsters." *Economist,* April 3, 1997. https://www.economist.com/moreover/1997/04/03/of-greyhounds -and-gangsters.

Lilius, Aleko E. 1930. *I Sailed with Chinese Pirates.* Hong Kong: Earnshaw.

Li, Min, and Jose Xu. 2013. "Paradise Entertainment (1180 HK)." *Oriental Patron,* December 2, 2013. http://pg.jrj.com.cn/acc/Res/HK_RES/STOCK/2013/12/ 23/1b2f85f5-4c3f-414a-9774-9ab54f6925a6.pdf.

Li, Peilin. 2019. "Urbanization and the New Phase of Growth in China." In *Urbanization and its Impact in Contemporary China,* edited by Peilin Li, 1–20. New York: Springer.

Li, Tao and Li Sheng. 2018. "Corruption and Travel: Effects of China's Anti-Graft Campaign on Macao." *Die Erde* 149 (1): 44–51.

LifeTec. 2005. "LifeTec Group Limited Announces Annual Results Ended 31 December 2005." http://www.hkexnews.hk/listedco/listconews/ sehk/2006/0428/ltn20060428061.pdf.

Lin, Delia. 2017. *Civilising Citizens in Post-Mao China: Understanding the Rhetoric of Suzhi.* New York. Routledge.

Lintner, Bertil. 2003. *Blood Brothers: The Criminal Underworld of Asia.* London: Palgrave.

Linter, Bertil. 2007. "Stanley Ho's Luck Turns Sour." *Far Eastern Economic Review,* May 2007. http://www.asiapacificms.com/articles/luck_turns_sour/.

LiPuma, Edward. 2017. *The Social Life of Financial Derivatives: Markets, Risk, and Time.* Durham: Duke University Press.

Liu, Xiaoming Rose, and Yim King Penny Wan. 2011. "An Examination of Factors that Discourage Slot Play in Macau Casinos." *International Journal of Hospitality Management* 30: 167–77.

Lo, Sonny H. 2005. "Casino Politics, Organized Crime and the Post-colonial State in Macau." *Journal of Contemporary China* 14 (43): 207–24.

Lo, Sonny H. 2007. "One Formula, Two Experiences: Political Divergence in Hong Kong and Macao." *Journal of Contemporary China* 16 (2): 359–83.

Lo, T. Wing, and Sharon Ingrid Kwok. 2017. "Triad Organized Crime in Macau Casinos: Extra-Legal Governance and Entrepreneurship." *British Journal of Criminology* 57 (3): 589–607.

Löfgren, Orvar. 1999. *On Holiday: A History of Vacationing.* Berkeley: University of California Press.

Löfgren, Orvar. 2008. "Motion and Emotion: Learning to be a Railway Traveler." *Mobilities* 3 (3): 331–51.

Loi, Kim-leng, and Woo Gon Kim. 2009. "Macao's Casino Industry: Reinventing Las Vegas in Asia." *Cornell Hospitality Quarterly* 55 (2): 268–83.

Lonsway, Brian. 2009. *Making Leisure Work: Architecture and the Experience Economy.* New York. Routledge.

Looney, Kristen, and Meg Rithmire. 2016. "Urbanization with Chinese Characteristics? China's Gamble for Modernization, 2016." Harvard Business Schools Working Papers Collection, Series 48, Fiscal Year 2016. https://hollisarchives.lib.harvard.edu/repositories/11/archival_objects/3078853.

Lopes, Rui. 2016. "'A Fabulous Speck on the Earth's Surface': Depictions of Colonial Macao in 1950s' Hollywood." *Portuguese Studies* 32 (1): 72–87.

Lu, Xiaoning. 2020. *Moulding the Socialist Subject: Cinema and Chinese Modernity.* Amsterdam: Amsterdam University Press.

LUSA. 2021. "Gov't Collected 73 pct y-on-y Less in Gaming Taxes in 2020." *Macau Business,* February 22, 2021. https://www.macaubusiness.com/govt-collected-73-pct-y-on-y-less-in-gaming-taxes-in-2020/.

Macau Daily Times. 2020. "Macau Sees Rise in Population Density in 2019." April 23, 2020. https://macaudailytimes.com.mo/macau-sees-rise-in-population-density-in-2019.html.

Macau Monetary Affairs Bureau. 2014. "News Release on the Inter-bureau Meeting Concerning the Prevention and Handling of Cross-Border Financial Crime." November 21, 2014.

Macau Post Daily. 2017. "Govt Shuts Malo Clinic for Illegal Services." November 27, 2017. https://www.macaupostdaily.com/article3762.html.

MacDonald, Andrew. 2016. "Game Volatility at Baccarat." *UNLV Gaming Research and Review Journal* 6 (1): 73–78.

MacKenzie, Donald. 2008. *An Engine, Not a Camera: How Financial Models Shape Markets.* Cambridge, Mass.: MIT Press.

MacKenzie, Donald. 2009. *Material Markets: How Economic Agents Are Constructed.* Oxford: Oxford University Press.

Malaby, Thomas M. 2009. "Anthropology and Play: The Contours of Playful Experience." *New Literary History* 40 (1): 205–18.

Mao Tse Tung. 1937. "On Practice." https://www.marxists.org/reference/archive/mao/selected-works/volume-1/mswv1_16.htm.

Mao, Sihui. 2006. "Desire for the (Hyper)real: New Challenges for Macao Tourism in the Age of Simulation." *Chinese Cross Currents* 3 (1): 67–82.

Mao, Sihui. 2016. "A Fabulous Speck: Oriental Imaginaries of Macao as the Veiled Other in Post-WWII Western Cinema." *Intercultural Communication Studies* 25 (1): 110–32.

Master, Farah. 2015. "Macau's House of Cards Topples as Investors Lose Big on Junkets." *Reuters,* November 24, 2015. https://www.reuters.com/article/macau-gambling/macaus-house-of-cards-topples-as-investors-lose-big-on-junkets-idUSL3N13E2OU20151124.

Master, Farah, and Donny Kwok. 2021. "Billions Blown as Macau Casino Investors Fold Amid Gambling Review." *Reuters,* September 16, 2021. https://www.reuters.com/business/macau-kicks-off-public-gaming-consultation-ahead-casino-rebidding-2021-09-15/.

Matos, Cátia. 2018. "How Portugal's Malo Clinic Is Conquering the World." *Essential Business,* March 22, 2018. https://www.essential-business.pt/2018/03/22/how-portugals-malo-clinic-is-conquering-the-world/.

McCartney, Glenn. 2015. "When the Eggs in One Basket All Cracked: Addressing the Downturn in Macao's Casino and VIP Junket System." *Gaming Law Review and Economics* 19 (7): 527–37.

McCartney, Glenn. 2016. "How Much to Puff? Macao's Casino Smoking Ban Debate and the Implication for Mainland Chinese Visitation." *Gaming Law Review and Economics* 20 (7): 571–79.

McFall, Liz. 2009. "Devices and Desires: How Useful Is the 'New' New Economic Sociology for Understanding Market Attachment?" *Sociology Compass* 3 (2): 267–82.

McFarlane, Colin. 2011. *Learning the City: Knowledge and Translocal Assemblage.* Cambridge: Wiley-Blackwell.

McGrath, Daniel S., and Sean P. Barrett. 2009. "The Comorbidity of Tobacco Smoking and Gambling: A Review of the Literature." *Drug and Alcohol Review* 28: 676–81.

McGrath, Brian, and David Grahame Shane. 2012. "Introduction: Metropolis, Megalopolis, and Metacity." In *The Sage Handbook of Architectural Theory,* edited by Greig Crysler, Stephen Cairns, and Hilde Heynen, 641–56. Thousand Oaks, Calif.: Sage.

McGreal, Chris. 2015. "China Feared CIA Worked with Sheldon Adelson's Macau Casinos to Snare Officials." *Guardian,* July 22, 2015. https://www.theguardian.com/world/2015/jul/22/china-cia-sheldon-adelson-macau-casinos.

McKendrick, Neil, John Brewer, and J. H. Plumb. 1982. *The Birth of a Consumer Society: The Commercialization of Eighteenth-Century England.* London: Europa. [[Added.]]

Meisner, Mitch. 1978. "Dazhai: The Mass Line in Practice." *Modern China* 4 (1): 27–62.

Melitopolous, Angela and Maurizio Lazzarato. 2012. "Machinic Animism." *Deleuze Studies* 6 (2): 240–49.

Mendes, Carmen Amado. 2013. *Portugal, China, and the Macau Negotiations, 1986–1999.* Hong Kong: Hong Kong University Press.

Meneses, João Paulo. 2020. "Special Report—Fighting the Opium of the 21st

Century." *Macau Business,* October 20, 2020. https://www.macaubusiness .com/special-report-fighting-the-opium-of-the-21st-century/.

Merrifield, Andy. 2012. "The Urban Question under Planetary Urbanization." *International Journal of Urban and Regional Research* 37 (3): 909–22.

Milgram, Anne, and Josh Lichtblau. 2009. Special report of the division of gaming enforcement to the casino control commission on its investigation of MGM Mirage's joint venture with Pansy Ho in Macau, Special Administrative Region, People's Republic of China. State of New Jersey Department of Law and Public Safety, May 18, 2008. https://www.njccc.gov/casinos/home/ info/docs/MGM/dge_%20report_redacted.pdf.

Miller, Daniel. 2002. "Turning Callon the Right Way Up." *Economy and Society* 31 (2): 218–33.

Miller, Michelle. 1994. *The Bon Marche: Bourgeois Culture and the Department Store, 1869–1920.* Princeton, N.J.: Princeton University Press.

Minca, Claudio. 2005. "Bellagio and Beyond." In *Seductions of Place: Geographical Perspectives on Globalization and Touristed Landscapes,* edited by Carolyn Cartier and Alan A. Lew, 103–20. New York: Routledge.

Mitrašinović, Miodrag. 2006. *Total Landscape, Theme Parks, Public Space.* New York: Routledge.

Moehring, Eugene P., and Michael S. Green. 2005. *Las Vegas: A Centennial History.* Reno: University of Nevada Press.

Morrison, Micah. 1998. "The Macau Connection." *Wall Street Journal,* February 26, 1998. https://www.wsj.com/articles/SB888439204883313500.

Moura, Nelson. 2019a. "546 Casino Smoking Lounges Approved as of April-End—Macau Business." *MNA Daily Newsletter,* April 10, 2019. https:// www.macaubusiness.com/546-casino-smoking-lounges-approved-as-of -april-end/.

Moura, Nelson. 2019b. "Weight of Gaming Sector in Local Economy Has Continued to Increase since 2016—Report." *Macau Business,* December 13, 2019. https://www.macaubusiness.com/weight-of-gaming-sector-in-local-economy -has-continued-to-increase-since-2016-report/.

Moura, Nelson. 2020a. "Gov't Likely to Extend Gaming Licenses until 2025—Brokerage." *Macau Business,* December 14, 2020. https://www.macau business.com/govt-likely-to-extend-gaming-licenses-until-2025-brokerage/.

Moura, Nelson. 2020b. "Sheldon Adelson Already Biggest Contributor to Trump's Re-election Campaign." *Macau Business,* October 16, 2020. https:// www.macaubusiness.com/sheldon-adelson-the-largest-contributor-to -trumps-re-election-campaign/.

Moura, Nelson. 2021a. "Chinese Gov't Considering Criminalizing Overseas Gambling Operations Luring Country's Nationals." *Macau Business,* January 1, 2021. https://www.macaubusiness.com/chinese-govt-considering-crimi- nalising-overseas-gambling-operations-luring-countrys-nationals/.

Moura, Nelson. 2021b. "Gaming and Labour Authorities Following Employment Situation of VIP Room Employees." *Macau Business,* December 9, 2021. https://www.macaubusiness.com/gaming-and-labour-authorities-following-employment-situation-of-vip-room-employees/.

Mumford, Lewis. (1967) 1971. *The Myth of the Machine: Technics and Human Development.* Vol. 1. New York: Mariner.

Mungello, D. E. 1999. *The Great Encounter of China and the West, 1500–1800.* Lanham, Md.: Rowman & Littlefield.

Muniesa, Fabian, Yuval Millo, and Michel Callon. 2007. Introduction to *Market Devices,* edited by Michel Callon, Yuval Millo, and Fabian Muniesa, 1–12. Oxford: Blackwell.

Newsdesk. 2009. "House on Edge." *Inside Asian Gaming,* January 15, 2009. https://www.asgam.com/index.php/2009/01/15/house-on-edge/.

Newsdesk. 2010. "Golden Rules." *Inside Asian Gaming,* November 1, 2010. https://www.asgam.com/index.php/2010/11/01/golden-rules/.

Newsdesk. 2014a. "Pansy Ho Says Chinese Visitors Becoming Choosier." *Macau Business,* July 3, 2014. https://www.macaubusiness.com/pansy-ho-says-chinese-visitors-becoming-choosier-2/.

Newsdesk. 2014b. "Steve Wynn 'Confused' by October Downturn in Macau." *GGRAsia,* October 29, 2014. https://www.ggrasia.com/steve-wynn-confused-by-october-downturn-in-macau/.

Newsdesk. 2014c. "Time of Sands." *Inside Asian Gaming,* May 13, 2014. https://www.asgam.com/index.php/2014/05/13/time-of-sands/.

Newsdesk. 2015. "Flash Cars Almost Bumper-to-Bumper in Macau." *Macau Business,* February 9, 2015. https://www.macaubusiness.com/flash-cars-almost-bumper-to-bumper-in-macau-2/.

Newsdesk. 2019a. "Macau Draws Nearly 36mln Visitors, Up 10pct in 2018: Govt." *GGRAsia,* January 23, 2019. https://www.ggrasia.com/macau-draws-nearly-36mln-visitors-up-10pct-in-2018-govt/.

Newsdesk. 2019b. "Macau Golden Week Visitor Tally Up 13pct in First Six Days, October." https://www.ggrasia.com/macau-golden-week-visitor-tally-up-13pct-in-first-6-days/.

Newsdesk. 2020. "Sands China Breaks New Ground for Macau IRs with Solar Energy Plant Installation at Sands Cotai Central." *Inside Asian Gaming,* April 29, 2020. https://www.asgam.com/index.php/2020/04/29/sands-china-breaks-new-ground-for-macau-irs-with-solar-energy-plant-installation-at-sands-cotai-central/.

Nisen, Max. 2012. "How Globalization Created and Destroyed the City of Venice." *Business Insider,* September 8, 2012. https://www.businessinsider.com/the-economic-history-of-venice-2012-8.

Nishimura, Takao. 2006. "Household Debt and Consumer Education in Postwar Japan." In *The Ambivalent Consumer: Questioning Consumption in*

East Asia and the West, edited by Sheldon Garon and Patricia L. Maclaclan, 260–80. Ithaca, N.Y.: Cornell University Press.

Ng, Mee Kam. 2008. "Globalization of SARS and Health Governance in Hong Kong under 'One Country, Two Systems.'" In *Networked Disease: Emerging Infections in the Global City,* edited by S. Harris Ali and Roger Keil, 70–85. Cambridge: Blackwell.

Ng, Mee Kam, and Wing-shing Tang. 1999. "Urban System Planning in China: A Case Study of the Pearl River Delta." *Urban Geography* 20 (7): 591–616.

Nyiri, Pal. 2006. *Scenic Spots: Chinese Tourism, the State, and Cultural Authority.* University of Washington Press.

Nyiri, Pal. 2009. "Between Encouragement and Control: Tourism, Modernity and Discipline in China." In *Asia on Tour: Exploring the Rise of Asian Tourism,* edited by Tim Winter, Peggy Teo, and T. C. Chang, 153–69. London: Routledge.

Nyiri, Pal. 2010. *Mobility and Cultural Authority in Contemporary China.* Seattle: University of Washington Press.

O'Donnell, Mary Ann, Winny Wong, and Jonathon Bach. 2017. *Learning from Shenzhen: China's Post-Mao Experiment from Special Zone to Model City.* Chicago: University of Chicago Press.

O'Keeffe, Kate. 2014a. "The Cheapest, Richest Casino in Macau." *Wall Street Journal,* February 5, 2014. https://www.wsj.com/articles/macau-casino -wins-big-catering-to-gamblers-others-shun-1391645959.

O'Keeffe, Kate. 2014b. "Junket Figure's Disappearance Shakes Macau's Gaming Industry." *Wall Street Journal,* May 2, 2014. https://www.wsj.com/articles/ junket-figures-disappearance-shakes-macaus-gambling-industry -1398972546.

Oliver, Chris. 2009. "Wynn Macau Defies the Odds in High-Roller Baccarat Mystery." *MarketWatch,* July 16, 2009. https://www.marketwatch.com/story/ wynns-abnormal-lucky-streak-baffles-analysts.

Ong, Aihwa. 2006. *Neoliberalism as Exception: Mutations in Citizenship and Sovereignty.* Durham, N.C.: Duke University Press.

Ong, Aihwa. 2011. "Worlding Cities, or the Art of Being Global." In *Worlding Cities: Asian Experiments in the Art of Being Global,* edited by Ananya Roy and Aihwa Ong, 1–26. Oxford: Wiley-Blackwell.

Ong, Aihwa, and Li Zhang. 2008. Introduction to *Privatizing China: Socialism from Afar,* edited by Li Zhang and Aihwa Ong, 1–20. Ithaca, N.Y.: Cornell University Press.

Ozorio, Bernadete, and Davis Ka-Chio Fong. 2004. "Chinese Casino Gambling Behaviors: Risk Taking in Casinos vs. Investments." *UNLV Gaming Research and Review Journal* 8 (2): 27–38.

Parlett, David. 1990. *The Oxford Guide to Card Games.* Oxford: Oxford University Press.

Perlman, Janice R. 1976. *The Myth of Marginality: Urban Poverty and Politics in Rio de Janeiro.* Berkeley: University of California Press.

Pessanha, Luís. 2008. "Gaming Taxation in Macau." *Gaming Law Review and Economics* 12 (4): 344–48.

Pierson, Stacey. 2013. *From Object to Concept: Global Consumption and the Transformation of Ming Porcelain.* Hong Kong: Hong Kong University Press.

Pina-Cabral, João. 2002. *Between China and Europe: Person, Culture and Emotion in Macao.* London: Continuum.

Pina-Cabral, João. 2005. "New Age Warriors: Negotiating the Handover on the Streets of Macao." *Journal of Romance Studies* 5 (1): 9–22.

Pinheiro, Francisco Vizeu, Koji Yagi, and Miki Korenaga. 2005a. "St. Paul College Historical Role and Influence in the Development of Macau." *Journal of Asian Architecture and Building Engineering* 4 (1): 43–50.

Pinheiro, Francisco Vizeu, Koji Yagi, and Miki Korenaga. 2005b. "The Role of Iberian Institutions in the Evolution of Macao." *Journal of Asian Architecture and Building Engineering* 4 (2): 285–92.

Pløger, John. 2008. "Foucault's Dispositif and the City." *Planning Theory* 7 (1): 51–70.

Polyani, Karl. 2001. *The Great Transformation: The Political and Economic Origins of Our Time.* Boston: Beacon Press.

Pomfret, James. 2014. "Special Report: How China's Official Bank Card Is Used to Smuggle Money." *Reuters,* March 11, 2014. https://www.reuters.com/article/us-china-unionpay-special-report-idUSBREA2B00820140312.

Popper, Nathaniel, and Nicolas Confessore. 2018. "Inside Cambridge Analytica's Virtual Currency Plans." *New York Times,* April 17, 2018. https://www.nytimes.com/2018/04/17/technology/cambridge-analytica-initial-coin-offering.html.

Porter, Jonathon. 1993. "The Transformation of Macau." *Pacific Affairs* 66 (1): 7–20.

Porter, Jonathon. 2009. "'The Past Is Present': The Construction of Macau's Historical Legacy." *History and Memory* 21 (1): 63–100.

Preda, Alex. 2007. "Where Do Analysts Come From? The Case of Financial Chartism." In *Market Devices,* edited by Callon, Michel, Yuval Millo, and Fabian Muniesa, 40–64. Oxford: Wiley-Blackwell.

Ptak, Roderick. 1998. "Macau and Sino-Portuguese Relations, ca. 1513/1514 to ca. 1900: A Bibliographical Essay." *Monumenta Serica,* 46: 343–96.

Puga, Diego, and Daniel Trefler. 2014. "International Trade and Institutional Change: Medieval Venice's Response to Globalization." *Quarterly Journal of Economics* 129 (2): 753–821.

Puga, Rogério Migel. 2013. *The British Presence in Macau, 1635–1793.* Hong Kong: Hong Kong University Press.

Pun Ngai. 2005. *Made in China: Women Factory Workers in a Global Marketplace.* Durham, N.C.: Duke University Press.

Raento, Pauliina, and Steven Flusty. 2006. "Three Trips to Italy: Deconstructing the New Las Vegas." In *Travels in Paradox: Mapping Tourism,* edited by Claudio Minca and Tim Oakes, 97–124. Lanham, Md.: Rowman & Littlefield.

Ren, Xuefei. 2011. *Building Globalization: Transnational Architecture Production in Urban China.* Chicago: University of Chicago Press.

Rich, Zachary C., and Shuiyuan Xiao. 2011. "Tobacco as a Social Currency: Cigarette Gifting and Sharing in China." *Nicotine and Tobacco Research* 14 (3): 258–63.

Righini-Bonelli, Maria Luisa. 1967. "The Armillary Sphere in the Library of El Escorial in Madrid." *Vistas in Astronomy* 9: 35–40.

Riley, Charles. 2014. "Macau Trumps Vegas with $270 Minimum Bet." *CNN,* October 22, 2014. https://money.cnn.com/2014/10/22/news/macau-casino -gambling/index.html.

Ritzer, George, and Todd Stillman. 2001. "The Modern Las Vegas Casino-Hotel: The Paradigmatic New Means of Consumption." *M@n@gement* 4 (3): 83–99.

Rojek, Chris. 2009. *The Labour of Leisure: The Culture of Free Time.* Thousand Oaks, Calif.: Sage.

Rosenthal, Richard J. 1997. "The Gambler as Case History and Literary Twin: Dostoevsky's False Beauty and the Poetics of Perversity." *Psychoanalytic Review* 84 (4): 593–616.

Rosenthal, Richard J. 2016. "Gambling." In *Dostoyevsky in Context,* edited by Deborah A. Martinsen and Olga Malorova, 148–56. Cambridge: Cambridge University Press.

Rothman, Hal. 2002. *Neon Metropolis: How Las Vegas Started the Twenty-First Century.* New York: Routledge.

Roy, Ananya, and Aihwa Ong. 2011. *Worlding Cities: Asian Experiments in the Art of Being Global.* Oxford: Wiley-Blackwell.

Rudoren, Jodi. 2013. "A Mogul Comes to Lunch, and He Doesn't Hold His Tongue." *New York Times,* May 28, 2013. http://www.nytimes.com/2013/ 05/29/world/middleeast/sheldon-adelson-is-honored-in-jerusalem.html.

Sanders, Peter, and Bruce Stanley. 2006. "Rolling the Dice: Casino Giants Take Their Vegas Battle to Tables of Macau." *Wall Street Journal,* September 7, 2006.

Schoon, Susan. 2014. "Chinese Strategies of Experimental Governance: The Underlying Forces Influencing Urban Restructuring in the Pearl River Delta." *Cities* 41:194–99.

Schüll, Natasha Dow. 2012. *Addiction by Design: Machine Gambling in Las Vegas.* Princeton, N.J.: Princeton University Press.

Schüll, Natasha Dow. 2013. "Turning the Tables: The Global Gambling Industry's Crusade to Sell Slots in Macau." In *Qualitative Research in Gambling: Exploring the Production and Consumption of Risk,* edited by Rebecca Cassidy, Andrea Pisac, and Claire Loussouarn, 92–106. London: Routledge.

Schumacher, Geoff. 2015. *Sun, Sin, and Suburbia: The History of Modern Las Vegas.* Reno: University of Nevada Press.

Schwartz, David G. 2003. *Suburban Xanadu: The Casino Resort on the Las Vegas Strip and Beyond.* New York: Routledge.

Schwartz, David G. 2006. *Roll the Bones: The History of Gambling.* Las Vegas: Winchester.

Schwartz, David G. 2012. "Penny Wise, Player Foolish? Slot-Hold Regulation and Consumer Preference." *Journal of Business Research* 66:1623–28.

Schwartz, David G. 2018. "How Casinos Use Math to Make Money When You Play the Slots." *Forbes,* June 4, 2018. https://www.forbes.com/sites/davidschwartz/2018/06/04/how-casinos-use-math-to-make-money-when-you-play-the-slots/#49f8c2a794d0.

SCMP Reporter. 2003. "Clinging to the Past Is a Gamble with the Future." *South China Morning Post,* September 21, 2003. https://www.scmp.com/article/428602/clinging-past-gamble-future.

Sebastian, Dave. 2021. "Sands to Sell Las Vegas Properties for $6.25 Billion to Apolo Global, REIT." *Wall Street Journal,* March 3, 2021. https://www.wsj.com/articles/sands-to-sell-las-vegas-properties-for-6-25-billion-as-it-focuses-on-asia-11614776358.

Sharr, Adam. 2015. "The Cultural Politics of Queuing Tape." *Cultural Politics* 10 (3): 389–403.

Shears, Jonathon. 2017. *The Great Exhibition, 1851: A Sourcebook.* Manchester: Manchester University Press.

Shell, Marc. 2014. *Islandology: Geography, Rhetoric, Politics.* Stanford, Calif.: Stanford University Press.

Shi, Tiantian Tiana, Xiaoming Rose Liu, and Jun Justin Li. 2018. "Market Segmentation by Travel Motivations under a Transforming Economy: Evidence from the Monte Carlo of the Orient." *Sustainability* 10: 3395.

Shields, Rob. 2013. "The Tourist Affect: Escape and Syncresis on the Las Vegas Strip." In *Ecologies of Affect: Placing Nostalgia, Desire, and Hope,* edited by Tonia K. Davidson, Ondine Park, and Rob Shields, 105–26. Waterloo, Ontario: Wilfrid Laurier University Press.

Sigley, Gary. 2006. "Chinese Governmentalities: Government, Governance, and the Socialist Market Economy." *Economy and Society* 35 (4): 487–508.

Sigley, Gary. 2009. "*Suzhi,* the Body, and the Fortunes of Technoscientific Reasoning in Contemporary China." *positions* 17 (3): 537–66.

Simmel, Georg. 1903. "The Metropolis and Mental Life." In *The Blackwell City Reader,* edited by Gary Bridge and Sophie Watson, 11–19. Oxford: Wiley-Blackwell.

Simpson, Tim. 2011. "Macao Noir: Criminal Brotherhoods, Casino Capitalism, and the Case of the Post-socialist Chinese Consumer." *Fast Capitalism* 8 (1). https://www.uta.edu/huma/agger/fastcapitalism/8_1/simpson8_1.html.

Simpson, Tim. 2014. "Macau Metropolis and Mental Life: Interior Urbanism and the Chinese Imaginary." *International Journal of Urban and Regional Research* 38 (3): 823–842.

Simpson, Tim. 2018. "Macau's Materialist Milieu: Portuguese Pavement Stones and the Political Economy of the Chinese Urban Imaginary." In *Companion to Urban Imaginaries,* edited by Christoph Linder and Miriam Meissner, 232–47. New York: Routledge.

Simpson, Tim, Thomas Chung, and Heinrich Tieben. 2009. "A Conversation on Casino Architecture in Las Vegas and Macau." *World Architecture* 12: 86–91.

Singleton, Sharon. 2018. "Are Slots Finally Gaining a Foothold in Macau?" *Asia Gaming Brief,* June 7, 2018. https://agbrief.com/headline/are-slots-finally-gaining-a-foothold-in-macau/.

Sinha, Meenakshi. 2008. "Marketing Macau: Las Vegas of the East." *Economic Times,* August 10, 2008. https://economictimes.indiatimes.com/industry/services/travel/marketing-macau-las-vegas-of-the-east/articleshow/3347989.cms?from=mdr.

Sink, Justin. 2012. "McCain Says Casino Mogul Is Putting 'Foreign Money' into 2012 Campaign." *Hill,* June 15, 2012. https://thehill.com/blogs/blog-briefing-room/news/232963-mccain-says-adelson-routing-foreign-money-to-romney-campaign.

Siu, Ricardo C. S. 2007. "Formal Rules, Informal Constraints, and Industrial Evolution—The Case of the Junket Operator Regulation and the Transition of Macao's Casino Business." *UNLV Gaming and Research Review Journal* 11 (2): 49–62.

Sklair, Leslie. 2000. *The Transnational Capitalist Class.* Oxford: Wiley-Blackwell.

Sloterdijk, Peter. 2013. *In the World Interior of Capital: Towards a Philosophical Theory of Globalization.* London: Polity.

Sloterdijk, Peter. 2016. *Selected Exaggerations: Conversations and Interviews, 1993–2012.* London: Polity.

Song, Lingfang, Yujie Wei, and Blaise J. Bergiel. 2018. "COGNAC Consumption: A Comparative Study on American and Chinese Consumers." *Wine Economics and Policy* 7: 24–34.

Stark, David, and László Bruszt. 2001. "One Way or Multiple Paths? For a Comparative Sociology of East European Capitalism." *American Journal of Sociology* 106 (4): 1129–37.

Steelman, Paul. 2011a. "The Future of Casino Architecture." Interview by David Schwartz. UNLV Gaming Podcast 49. https://digitalscholarship.unlv.edu/gaming_podcasts/49/.

Steelman, Paul. 2011b. "Thoughts on Atlantic City, Las Vegas, and Several Other Gaming Jurisdictions." Interview by David Schwartz. UNLV Gaming Podcast 35. https://www.library.unlv.edu/center-gaming-research/2011/11/unlv-gaming-podcast-35-paul-steelman.html.

Steinmüller, Hans. 2011. "The Moving Boundaries of Social Heat: Gambling in Rural China." *Journal of the Royal Anthropological Institute* 17: 263–80.

Strange, Susan. 1986. *Casino Capitalism.* Cambridge: Basil Blackwell.

Strange, Susan. 1998. *Mad Money: When Markets Outgrow Government.* Ann Arbor: University of Michigan Press.

Stutz, Howard. 2008. "Macau Official: Subconcession Necessary to Save Sands from Elimination." *Las Vegas Review-Journal,* May 3, 2008. https://www .reviewjournal.com/business/macau-official-subconcession-necessary-to -save-sands-from-elimination/.

Swanson, Ana. 2015. "How China Used More Cement in 3 Years than the U.S. Did in the Entire 20th Century." *Washington Post,* March 24, 2015. https:// www.washingtonpost.com/news/wonk/wp/2015/03/24/how-china-used -more-cement-in-3-years-than-the-u-s-did-in-the-entire-20th-century/.

Tang, Kaijian. 2015. *Setting Off from Macau: Essays on Jesuit History during the Ming and Qing Dynasties.* Leyden: Brill.

Thomas, Daniel. 2018. "Balenciaga Sorry Over Mistreatment of Chinese Shoppers in Paris." *BBC News,* April 27, 2008. https://www.bbc.com/news/ business-43925802.

Thrift, Nigel. 2008. "Pass It On: Towards a Political Economy of Propensity." *Emotion, Space and Society* 1: 83–96.

Trentmann, Frank. 2016. *Empire of Things: How We Became a World of Consumers, from the Fifteenth Century to the Twenty-First.* New York: Harpers.

Turner, Frederick Jackson. 1893. "The Significance of the Frontier in American History." http://nationalhumanitiescenter.org/pds/gilded/empire/text1/ turner.pdf.

Väliaho, Pasi. 2014. *Biopolitical Screens: Image, Power, and the Neoliberal Brain.* Cambridge, Mass.: MIT Press.

Van Dyke, Paul. 2011. *Merchants of Canton and Macao: Politics and Strategies in 18th Century Chinese Trade.* Hong Kong: Hong Kong University Press.

Van Westering, Jetske. 1994. "The Cognac Market: An Examination of the Cognac Market in the Far East." *International Journal of Wine Marketing* 6 (1): 5–19.

Velotta, Richard N. 2019. "Nongaming Revenue Continues to Grow in Nevada's Casino-Resorts." *Las Vegas Review-Journal,* October 18, 2019. https://www .reviewjournal.com/business/casinos-gaming/nongaming-revenue-continues -to-grow-in-nevadas-casino-resorts-1873383/.

Ventura, Patricia. 2012. *Neoliberal Culture: Living with American Neoliberalism.* London: Ashgate.

Virno, Paolo. 2006. "The Ambivalence of Disenchantment." In *Radical Thought in Italy: A Potential Politics,* edited by Paolo Virno and Michael Hardt, 13–36. Minneapolis: University of Minnesota Press.

Voegelin, Eric. 2000. *Order and History, Volume 4: The Ecumenic Age.* Columbia: University of Missouri Press.

Vong, Fanny. 2007. "The Psychology of Risk-Taking in Gambling among Chinese Visitors to Macau." *International Gambling Studies* 7 (1): 29–42.

Wallace, Jeremy. 2014. *Cities and Stability: Urbanization, Redistribution, and Regime Survival in China.* Oxford: Oxford University Press.

Waldrep, Shelton. 2002. "Postmodern Casinos." In *Productive Postmodernism: Consuming Histories and Cultural Studies,* edited by John N. Duvall and Linda Hutcheon, 137–66. Albany: SUNY Press.

Wan, Yim King Penny, and Paul A. Pilkington. 2009. "Knowledge, Attitudes and Experiences of Macao's Casino Workers with Regard to Second-Hand Smoke Exposure at Work." *International Gambling Studies* 9 (3): 207–24.

Wang, Jessica Ching-Sze. 2008. *John Dewey in China: To Teach and to Learn.* Albany: SUNY Press.

Wang, Wuyi, and William R. Eadington. 2008. "The VIP-Room Contractual System and Macao's Traditional Casino Industry." *China: An International Journal* 6 (2): 237–60.

Wang, Wuyi, and Peter Zabielskis. 2010. "Making Friends, Making Money: Macau's Traditional VIP Casino System" *Global Gambling: Cultural Perspectives on Gambling Organizations,* edited by Sytze F. Kingma, 114–33. London: Routledge.

Waters, D. W. 1976. *The Planispheric Astrolabe.* Greenwich, U.K.: Greenwich National Maritime Museum.

Weber, Max. 1930. *The Protestant Ethic and the Spirit of Capitalism.* London: Unwin Hyman.

Weiner, Adam. 2016. "The Most Politically Dangerous Book You've Never Heard Of." *Politico Magazine,* December 11, 2016. https://www.politico.com/ magazine/story/2016/12/russian-novel-chernyshevsky-financial-crisis -revolution-214516.

Williams, Perry. 2016. "VIP Gamblers Roll Sydney's The Star Casino in 'Freakish Result.'" *Sydney Morning Herald,* February 16, 2016. https://www.smh.com .au/business/vip-gamblers-roll-sydneys-the-star-casino-in-freakish-result -20160216-gmv6lo.html.

Williams, Rosalind. 1982. *Dreamworlds: Mass Consumption in Late Nineteenth-Century France.* Berkeley: University of California Press.

Wirth, Louis. 1938. "Urbanism as a Way of Life." *American Journal of Sociology* 44 (1): 1–24.

Wong, Hio Hei Albert. 2016. "The Summer 2014 Protests in Macau: Their Contexts and Continuities." *Asian Education and Development* 6 (1): 57–71.

Wong, Ipkin Anthony, and Veronica H. I. Fong. 2010. "Examining Casino Service Quality in the Asian Las Vegas: An Alternative Approach." *Journal of Hospitality Marketing and Management* 19 (8): 842–65.

Wong, Stephanie Hoi-Nga. 2015. "Steve Wynn's Most Candid Conference Call Ever: In His Own Words." *Bloomberg,* October 16, 2015. https://www .bloomberg.com/news/articles/2015-10-16/steve-wynn-s-most-candid -conference-call-ever-in-his-own-words.

Woodhouse, Alice. 2015. "Croupiers Anxious about Industry Reshuffle." *South China Morning Post,* January 18, 2015.

Wu, Fulong. 2003. "Transitional Cities." *Environment and Planning A* 35: 1331–38.

Wu, Fulong. 2005. "Rediscovering the 'Gate' under Market Transition: From Work-Unit Compounds to Commodity Housing Enclaves." *Housing Studies* 20 (2): 235–54.

Wu, Fulong. 2009. "Neo-urbanism in the Making under China's Market Transition." *City* 13 (4): 418–31.

Wu, Zhiliang. 2002. "Ambergris and Opium in Macau's History." *China Perspectives* 44: 4–17.

Yan, Hairong. 2008. *New Masters, New Servants: Migration, Development, and Women Workers in China.* Durham, N.C.: Duke University Press.

Yeung, Ruth M. W., and Wallace M. S. Yee. 2012. "A Profile of the Mainland China Cross-Border Shoppers: Cluster and Discriminant Analysis." *Tourism Management Perspectives* 4: 106–12.

Yiu, Enoch. 2008. "Lawmaker Takes the Sting Out of Chance." *South China Morning Post,* October 5, 2008. https://www.scmp.com/article/655062/lawmaker-takes-sting-out-chance.

Yoshimi, Shunya. 2006. "Consuming America, Producing Japan." In *The Ambivalent Consumer: Questioning Consumption in East Asia and the West,* edited by Sheldon Garon and Patricia L. Maclachlan, 63–84. Ithaca, N.Y.: Cornell University Press.

Young, Sarah J. 2015. "Crystal Palace." In *Dostoyevsky in Context,* edited by Deborah A. Martinsen and Olga Malorova, 176–86. Cambridge: Cambridge University Press.

Yu, Xiaojiang. 2008. "Growth and Degradation in the Orient's Las Vegas: Issues of Environment in Macau." *International Journal of Environmental Studies* 65 (5): 667–83.

Yuen, Samson. 2014. "Disciplining the Party." *China Perspectives* 3: 41–47.

Zaffuto, Grazia. 2013. "'Visual Education' as the Alternative Mode of Learning at the Crystal Palace, Sydenham." *Victorian Network* 5 (1): 9–27.

Zaleskiewicz, Tomasz. 2001. "Beyond Risk Seeking and Risk Aversion: Personality and the Dual Nature of Economic Risk Taking." *European Journal of Personality* 15: S105–22.

Zandonai, Sheyla and Vanessa Amaro. 2018. "The Portuguese *Calçada* in Macau: Paving Residual Colonialism with a New Cultural History of Place." *Cultural Anthropology* 59 (4): 378–96.

Zelizer, Viviana A. 2013. *Economic Lives: How Culture Shapes the Economy.* Princeton, N.J.: Princeton University Press.

Zhang, Karen. 2018. "Former Macau Gangster 'Broken Tooth' Signs Poker Deal with Secretive Chinese Firm after Raising US$750 Million in ICO." *South China Morning Post,* July 14, 2018. https://www.scmp.com/news/hong-kong/community/article/2155218/former-macau-gangster-broken-tooth-signs-poker-deal.

Zhang, Longmei, Ray Brooks, Ding Ding, Haiyan Ding, Hui He, Jing Lu, and

Rui Mano. 2018. "China's High Savers: Drivers, Prospects, and Policies." IMF Working Paper, WP/18/277.

Zhang, Xinmin, Hualin Xie, Caihua Zhou, and Bindan Zeng. 2020. "Jingdezhen: The Millennium Porcelain Capital." *Cities* 98: 1–9.

Zhu, Jianfei. 2008. *Architecture of Modern China: A Historical Critique.* New York: Routledge.

Zwick, Detlev, and N. Nikhilish Dholakia. 2006. "The Epistemic Consumption Object and Postsocial Consumption: Expanding Consumer-Object Theory in Consumer Research." *Consumption, Markets, and Culture* 9 (1): 17–4.

Index

(*continued from page ii*)

Tim Simpson is associate professor in the Department of Communication, University of Macau. He is coauthor of *Macao Macau* and editor of *Tourist Utopias: Offshore Islands, Enclave Spaces, and Mobile Imaginaries.*